American Fiction 1865–1940

Front cover picture:

MARIN, John.
Lower Manhattan. 1920.
Watercolour, $21\frac{7}{8} \times 26\frac{3}{4}''$ (55.4 × 68 cm).
Collection, The Museum of Modern Art, New York.
   The Phillip L. Goodwin Collection.
Photograph © 1987 The Museum of Modern Art, New York.

Longman Literature in English Series

General Editors: David Carroll and Michael Wheeler
University of Lancaster

For a complete list of titles see pages viii and ix

American Fiction
1865–1940

Brian Lee

Longman

London and New York

Longman Group UK Limited
Longman House, Burnt Mill, Harlow,
Essex CM20 2JE, England
Associated companies throughout the world

*Published in the United States of America
by Longman Inc., New York*

© Longman Group UK Limited 1987

First published 1987

BRITISH LIBRARY CATALOGUING IN PUBLICATION DATA
Lee, Brian, *1932–*
    American fiction 1865–1940.
    1. American fiction — History and criticism
    I. Title
    813'.4'09   PS371

ISBN 0-582-49317-X   CSD
ISBN 0-582-49316-1   PPR

LIBRARY OF CONGRESS CATALOGING IN PUBLICATION DATA
Lee, Brian
    American fiction, 1865–1940.

    (Longman literature in English series)
    Bibliography: p.
    Includes index.
    1. American fiction — 19th century — History and
criticism.   2. American fiction — 20th century — History
and criticism.   I. Title.   II. Series.
PS377.L44   1987   813'.4'09   86-27584
ISBN 0-582-49317-X
ISBN 0-582-49316-1 (pbk.)

Set in Linotron 202 9½/11 pt Bembo
Produced by Longman Singapore Publishers (Pte) Ltd.
Printed in Singapore

Contents

Editors' Preface

The multi-volume Longman Literature in English Series provides students of literature with a critical introduction to the major genres in their historical and cultural context. Each volume gives a coherent account of a clearly defined area, and the series, when complete, will offer a practical and comprehensive guide to literature written in English from Anglo-Saxon times to the present. The aim of the series as a whole is to show that the most valuable and stimulating approach to literature is that based upon an awareness of the relations between literary forms and their historical context. Thus the areas covered by most of the separate volumes are defined by period and genre. Each volume offers new informed ways of reading literary works, and provides guidance to further reading in an extensive reference section.

As well as studies on all periods of English and American literature, the series includes books on criticism and literary theory, and on the intellectual and cultural context. A comprehensive series of this kind must of course include other literature written in English, and therefore a group of volumes deals with Irish and Scottish literature, and the literatures of India, Africa, the Caribbean, Australia, and Canada. The forty-six volumes of the series cover the following areas: pre-Renaissance English Literature, English Poetry, English Drama, English Fiction, English Prose, Criticism and Literary Theory, Intellectual and Cultural Context, American Literature, Other Literatures in English.

David Carroll
Michael Wheeler

Longman Literature in English Series

General Editors: David Carroll and Michael Wheeler
University of Lancaster

Pre-Renaissance English Literature

★ English Literature before Chaucer *Michael Swanton*
English Literature in the Age of Chaucer
★ English Medieval Romance *W. R. J. Barron*

English Poetry

★ English Poetry of the Sixteenth Century *Gary Waller*
★ English Poetry of the Seventeenth Century *George Parfitt*
English Poetry of the Eighteenth Century 1700–1789
★ English Poetry of the Romantic Period 1789–1830 *J. R. Watson*
English Poetry of the Victorian Period 1830–1890
English Poetry of the Early Modern Period 1890–1940
English Poetry since 1940

English Drama

English Drama before Shakespeare
English Drama: Shakespeare to the Restoration, 1590–1660
English Drama: Restoration and the Eighteenth Century, 1660–1789
English Drama: Romantic and Victorian, 1789–1890
English Drama of the Early Modern Period, 1890–1940
English Drama since 1940

English Fiction

★ English Fiction of the Eighteenth Century 1700–1789 *Clive T. Probyn*
English Fiction of the Romantic Period 1789–1830
★ English Fiction of the Victorian Period 1830–1890 *Michael Wheeler*
English Fiction of the Early Modern Period 1890–1940

English Prose

English Prose of the Renaissance 1550–1700
English Prose of the Eighteenth Century
English Prose of the Nineteenth Century

Criticism and Literary Theory

Criticism and Literary Theory from Sidney to Johnson
Criticism and Literary Theory from Wordsworth to Arnold
Criticism and Literary Theory from 1890 to the Present

The Intellectual and Cultural Context

The Sixteenth Century
the Seventeenth Century
★ The Eighteenth Century, 1700–1789 *James Sambrook*
The Romantic Period, 1789–1830
The Victorian Period, 1830–1890
The Twentieth Century: 1890 to the Present

American Literature

American Literature before 1880
American Poetry of the Twentieth Century
American Drama of the Twentieth Century
★ American Fiction 1865–1940 *Brian Lee*
American Fiction since 1940
Twentieth-Century America

Other Literatures

Irish Literature since 1800
Scottish Literature since 1700

Australian Literature
Indian Literature in English
African Literature in English: East and West
Southern African Literature in English
Caribbean Literature in English
★ Canadian Literature in English *W. J. Keith*

★ *Already published*

Author's Preface

Writing literary histories has never been a simple, straightforward matter; but in the last twenty years the subject has come to seem so fraught with theoretical difficulties that scholars who might once have busied themselves with such tasks are now more likely to spend their energies convincing themselves and their readers that the whole project is impossible. For many, the status of the literary artefact itself has become problematical, and nearly everyone agrees that the task of relating works of art to the society that produced and consumed them involves operations of almost infinite complexity.

It is impossible, for example, to ignore such seemingly unresolvable dilemmas as the one posed by Frederic Jameson. In any effort to represent the past, he tells us, we are immediately faced with an inescapable choice between two assumptions: those of Identity or Difference. There is, he insists, no middle way. If we choose to affirm the identity of the alien object with ouselves – as many recent Feminist critics have done in their attempts to reinterpret earlier literatures – we shall be forced to admit that in projecting our world and its values onto the past we have "never left home at all", and will inevitably fail to touch the strangeness of a genuinely different reality. If, on the other hand, we assume the radical difference of the alien object, we shall be faced with the prospect of being shut off from its otherness by all the intervening accumulations of history that have made us what we are.

In the book that follows I have tried to take cognizance of such problems without being unduly inhibited by them. America at the end of the Civil War does constitute an alien reality and it takes an immense imaginative effort to enter that lost time and space. There are, however, continuities of consciousness that help to forge links between the past and present, and these are what I take to form the basis of an interpretive mastercode.

In tracing such lines of development as those of Realism or Modernism, I have been only too aware of the selections and exclusions forced upon me by such initial choices. I have tried to balance my attention between major and minor writers, individual texts and complete canons, and mainstream movements and fascinating counter-currents. In the last analysis, though, decisions about what to include and what to exclude are arbitrary and subjective; which is only to say that literary history is not, and cannot be, a science.

In the appendices to this volume, however, I have tried to attain a greater degree of objectivity. The individual and general bibliographies are as comprehensive as space permits and the Chronology offers a wider literary and social context to suggest alternative lines of development and interpretation. References within the appendices are generally to works published first in America, but in the text I have identified quoted passages wherever possible by chapter number in order to facilitate the book's use by British readers.

In the course of writing this book I have, I believe, learned a great deal more than I hitherto knew about American life and literature. I learned even more in hundreds of discussions both inside and outside classrooms and shall remain grateful to all those who took part in them. I have also incurred some more specific debts which I am pleased to acknowledge here: to my editor, Michael Wheeler, for his constant support and advice; to Freda Duckitt and Jenny Staniland for transforming my scrawl into a typescript; to my friend and colleague, Nicholas Luker, whose knowledge of European literature and sense of style saved me from a multitude of errors; and finally to my wife, Adrienne, who gave me what I needed most – space, time and unstinting encouragement.

BCL
February, 1987.

For my children,
Martin, Nick, Sarah-Jo,
Rebecca and Adam.

Part One:

Reconstruction
1865–1900

Chapter 1
Introduction

The dates chosen to limit the period studied in this volume are usually associated with wars: 1865 marked the end of the American Civil War and 1940 the year in which the United States began to prepare seriously for the Second World War by introducing conscription. For American social and economic historians, however, these dates have an additional significance. The year 1865 is normally taken to indicate the beginning of the aptly named Gilded Age – a period of unparalleled industrialization that involved the transformation of almost every aspect of American life. On the other hand, 1940 finally brought an end to the Great Depression – arguably the worst economic slump in history, certainly when it is contrasted with the degree of expansion that had preceded it.

Perhaps the most remarkable domestic factor in American life during this period was the growth of the country's population, from 31 million in 1860 to 131 million in 1940. Natural increase accounted for much of this growth, but the unique element in it was the largest movement of population in Western history, which saw nearly 40 million people succumb to 'American fever', uproot themselves and emigrate there from their homelands. This westward exodus reached its peak in the period 1870–1920, helped by the development of the steamship, which reduced the Atlantic voyage from eight weeks to eight days, and by the expansion of the railroads which made possible the immigrants' dispersal within the country. During this time, Europe was also invaded by numbers of American emigration agents who travelled the length and breadth of every country painting a rosy picture of life in 'Dollar land' and offering transportation to a new and better life for as little as thirty-five dollars. Among the inducements that tempted so many to uproot themselves were the promise of free land for the taking as a result of the Homestead Act of 1862, freedom from conscription, equality in government and religion, and not least, high wages and low taxes. What was not made apparent to prospective immigrants was that they would be moving to a country in the throes of an unprecedentedly rapid and massive urbanization with all the problems associated with that process. The quadrupling of America's urban population in the second half of the nineteenth century brought with it enormous problems of housing, employment, education, sanitation, and health care, so that it was not surprising that James Bryce was led to write in 1888 in *The American Commonwealth* that 'There is no denying that the government of cities is the one conspicuous failure of the United States.' When one considers the rapidity of their expansion – Saint Louis and Philadelphia, for example, added 100,000 each to their populations in the 1860s, and Chicago nearly 200,000! – it is not surprising that the conditions of life in them often verged on the chaotic. The difficulties were exacerbated by the huge numbers of foreign-born and often non-English-speaking people crammed into such centres. In eighteen of the twenty-eight cities over 100,000 in 1890, foreign-born adults preponderated, and New York at this time had twice as many Jews as Warsaw, twice as many Irish as Dublin, and as many Germans as Hamburg. It was the greatest emigrant centre in the world.[1] For the great majority of immigrants, the conditions of life in American cities were appalling. Some commentators believed that the fault lay with foreign governments who were actively assisting their criminal and pauper populations to migrate, but it was difficult to ignore the effects, too, of living conditions suffered by the newly arrived. In 1876 the *New York Times* reported:

> The truth is that in no city of the civilised world does this terrible evil and cause of disease and crime exist in nearly the same degree as in New York. . . . In the Eleventh Ward, where so large a German population lives, near East Houston Street . . . there are 196,510 [people] to the square mile, so each person has sixteen and one-tenth square yards for his . . . space of living. . . . Portions of particular yards are even worse.
> And this especially accounts for the mortality as of a pestilence which desolates the juvenile population of our crowded quarters every summer – children dying every July and August at the rate of 1,000 per week. . . . From the nearly 20,000 tenement houses come 93 per cent of the deaths and 90 per cent of the crimes of our population.

Statistics like these were soon to be brought vividly to life, first in such works as Richard Dugdale's *The Jukes* (1877), an influential study of a large, poor family, in which 17 out of 29 young males were criminals, and 84 out of 168 women had become prostitutes, and later in naturalistic novels like Stephen Crane's *Maggie* (1893). The story of the Jukes also showed that degeneration and vice were not restricted to immigrants in the cities; they were New Englanders whose American roots reached back to colonial times.

In so volatile an economy and so fluid a society, it is not surprising that the American Dream of individual success was able to take such firm root. Indeed, great individual fortunes were actually made at this time by such men as John Jacob Astor, Cornelius Vanderbilt, Jay Gould, J. P. Morgan, Henry Frick, John D. Rockefeller and Andrew Carnegie. It has been estimated that by 1883 there were approximately four thousand people in the United States worth at least one million dollars, enough certainly to inspire hope in every immigrant arriving at Ellis Island. In the same newspapers that reported on the living conditions in New York slums, one can also find accounts of the most lavish and ostentatious displays of wealth so characteristic of the Gilded Age. In 1883, for example, *The Times* enthusiastically described the Vanderbilts' Costume Ball as 'perhaps the most brilliant and pictur-esque entertainment of the kind ever given in the metropolis'. So it must have seemed to those attending it, but viewed in a wider social context it stands as a colossal vulgar monument to conspicuous consumption. The host, Alva Vanderbilt spent $250,000 on costumes, flowers, and food, and the city's élite vied with each other to exhibit their nonchalant spending power. Mrs Cornelius Vanderbilt epitom-ized the spirit of the affair by appearing as 'The Electric Light' in white satin trimmed all over with glittering diamonds.

Despite the number of vast private fortunes accumulated in manufacturing, communications, and real estate, it has been convinc-ingly argued that the American way of life in the latter part of the nineteenth century was determined more by the development of corporations than by the influence of heroic individuals, and that corporate life, affecting, as it did, every aspect of culture and individual psychology, was a reality starkly and wantonly opposed to the myth of freedom and individualism. According to this view, the corporate ideal reached a symbolic culmination in 1893 in its embodiment in the White City, the site of the world's Columbian Exposition in Chicago. It was here that the corporate mentality achieved its supremacy, and in doing so also settled the question of the force and real meaning of America itself. 'It seemed the victory of elites in business, politics and culture over dissident but divided voices of labor, farmers, immigrants, blacks and women.'[2] Of course, that supremacy has been continuously subject to challenge, and the ensuing conflicts form a fascinating dialectical strand in twentieth-century cultural history, but the fact that by 1974 no fewer than 51 of the world's 100 largest economic units were multinational corporations and only 49 were nations, may be taken as an indication of the extent to which Western industrial nations have been 'incorporated'.

The tensions and ironies created by conflicting social and political ideals throughout this period are clearly reflected in America's proliferating literature, and especially in the novel, dealing as it does with the interactions of individuals within society. It is even possible to maintain that the American novel itself is a product of this period, and that the form did not really exist before the Civil War. What is indisputable is that early American prose fiction, whatever its literary quality, generally sacrificed temporal or geographical actualities to the remote, the exotic, or the purely imaginary. American romanticism in the hands of Poe, Melville, and Hawthorne, created a body of literature unsurpassed in its exploration of moral, psychological, and metaphysical ideas. The *Narrative of Arthur Gordon Pym*, *Moby Dick*, and *The Scarlet Letter* are undisputed masterpieces of world literature, but they qualify rather as romances than as novels. The same is true of James Fenimore Cooper's best work, the 'Leatherstocking Saga', a brilliant evocation of the myth of the American West, but as one might expect from a writer who never visited western America, it is an inadequate account of the realities of frontier experience.

For all these writers, as for their contemporaries, Emerson and Thoreau, the major field of enquiry was spiritual rather than social, and personal rather than political. Their efforts to discover an ideal, if natural, self, led again and again to a rejection of social reality in favour of solitary communion with nature. Ishmael's impulses which drive him to sea at the beginning of *Moby Dick* and which he takes to be universal in appeal, would certainly have been shared by Emerson, Thoreau, Poe, and Hawthorne:

> Circumambulate the city of a dreamy Sabbath afternoon.
> Go from Corlears Hook to Coenties Slip, and from
> thence, by Whitehall, northward. What do you see? –
> Posted like silent sentinels all around the town, stand
> thousands upon thousands of mortal men fixed in ocean
> reveries. Some leaning against the spikes; some seated
> upon the pier-heads; some looking over the bulwarks of
> ships from China; some high aloft in the rigging, as if
> striving to get an even better sea-ward peep. But these are
> all landsmen; of week days pent up in lath and plaster –
> tied to counters, nailed to benches, chained to desks. How
> then is this? Are the green fields gone? What do they here?

In 1851 Melville's question about the green fields was rhetorical but the process that was to make it less so had already begun. Within forty years the frontier itself would be officially closed, bringing to an end the existence of free land in a 'wilderness', and within another forty, urban planners would be talking calmly of a megalopolis stretching from Washington, DC to Boston. The forests around Boston itself, to which Hawthorne's Hester Prynne and Arthur Dimmesdale retreated from the city, had already been cleared, and it would not be long before Melville's beloved whaling ships, crowding New England ports at this time, became things of the past.

The impact of these changes and related developments upon human consciousness is the major subject of this study, and will be traced in its evolution and mutations through American fiction. But the need to appreciate and understand something about the pre-industrial consciousness is equally important and requires an immense imaginative effort, if only because the reader has to come to terms as much with mental absences as presences. If, as has been claimed, the modern mind can be characterized by its need to assimilate an 'overpopulation of surfaces' – an environment that in its excessive detail saturates consciousness – then the opposite is true of men living in the larger spaces of the early nineteenth century, and, as one might expect, the forms of literature produced by them are radically different.

One of those major differences has already been alluded to in referring to the major works of Poe, Hawthorne, and Melville as romances – defined later by Henry James as those whose structures are not governed by our sense of the way things really happen. More specifically, romance sacrifices specificity and probability to the general and exemplary in an attempt to formulate truths which are not subject to empirical validation. It is concerned more with Fate than Character, Man rather than Men, Metaphysics not Manners. Its chief literary modes are those of myth, symbolism, and allegory, and stylistically it foregrounds language as an opaque rather than a transparent medium.

A related difference can be discerned at the more pervasive level of prose style. Richard Poirier in his book *A World Elsewhere* has illustrated the ways in which American writers have attempted to create in language environments radically different from those supported by economic, political, and social systems. In the most interesting American books, he argues, actual space, time, freedom and necessity are resisted or annihilated in favour of 'imaginary worlds'. These books are written, he says, as if history itself can give no life to 'freedom' and only language can provide the liberated place. He does not accept the above distinction between novel and romance stemming from a view that was often adduced by writers themselves in the nineteenth century: that America did not provide a sufficiently dense environment for novelists to work in, and that they were necessarily forced into imaginary worlds. He does, however, discriminate between those writers who succeed in producing alternative linguistic environments, and those whose imaginations are overpowered by the environment of the real world. It is my contention that throughout the latter part of the nineteenth century, the urge to portray things 'as they are' and as they 'really happen' is paramount, and that this accounts for the more important developments in American fictional structure and prose style. It reflects a preoccupation with the material world and with causality and perception in American culture generally, and even those writers temperamentally and artistically unsuited to realism and naturalism, such as Henry James and Stephen Crane, either allow their work to be occasionally distorted by the prevailing intellectual ethos, or devise strategies to combat it. Others, such as Dreiser and Howells, are much more closely attuned to the *Zeitgeist*, and this is reflected in the openness of their manner, their lack of irony, and their realism.

Needless to say, the writers under consideration do not neatly divide themselves into mutually exclusive categories. For one thing, many of them share a tendency to become disenchanted with realism in later life. Others develop more eccentrically as they are influenced by literary or non-literary events. And all of them combine to a greater or lesser degree elements of both realism and romance within their novels.

Indeed, in 1871, at the very beginning of the Gilded Age, Walt Whitman, looking into America's possible future in *Democratic Vistas*, called for a similar combination of elements to safeguard the essential values of civilization:

> the highly artificial and materialistic bases of modern
> civilisation, with the corresponding arrangements and
> methods of living, the force-infusion of intellect alone, the
> depraving influence of riches just as much as poverty, the
> absence of all high ideals in character – with the long
> series of tendencies shapings, which few are strong enough
> to resist, and which now seem, with steam-engine speed,
> to be everywhere turning out the generations of humanity
> like uniform iron casting . . . must either be confronted
> and met by at least an equally subtle and tremendous
> force-infusion for purposes of spiritualisation, for the pure
> conscience, for genuine aesthetics, and for absolute and
> primal manliness and womanliness – or else our modern
> civilisation, with all its improvements, is in vain, and we
> are on the road to a destiny, a status, equivalent, in its real
> world, to that of the fabled damned.[3]

It did not take any remarkable prescience on Whitman's part to foresee the likely sources of conflict. At the time he wrote this, England had already undergone more than half a century of industrialization and had experienced many of the social traumas to which he alludes. The ideas of Cobbett, Mill, Bentham, Carlyle, and Dickens were equally familiar on both sides of the Atlantic, and the arguments about the place of man in modern society had been thoroughly rehearsed in pre-industrial America. Even so, there remains in American thought a strain of buoyant optimism and expectation that after the experiences of the Luddites, the Chartists, and the 1840s, the decade of Revolution had been almost thoroughly extinguished in Europe. Similarly, the debates about Darwinism, science, religion, pragmatism, and socialism took interestingly different forms in America, and these differences were necessarily reflected in fiction. In 1865 American thinkers not unnaturally believed that it should be possible for the New World to avoid the errors of the Old, and for the most part they anticipated the future with equanimity or even eagerness. But by 1900 the general mood had darkened and disillusionment was widespread. Henry Adams, whose optimism in the immediate post-Civil War years almost matched that of Whitman and who had called for greater expenditure of energy and capital in all areas of American life, had come to feel very differently in 1904. He gives eloquent expression to the fears shared by many of his countrymen in the last chapter of his autobiography, *The Education of Henry Adams*:

> The outline of the city became frantic in its effort to
> explain something that defied meaning. Power seemed to
> have outgrown its servitude and to have asserted its
> freedom. The cylinder had exploded, and thrown great
> masses of stone and steam against the sky. The city had
> the air and movement of hysteria, and the citizens were
> crying, in every accent of anger and alarm, that the new
> forces must at any cost be brought under control.
> Prosperity never before imagined, power never yet
> wielded by man, speed never reached by anything but a
> meteor, had made the world irritable, nervous, querulous,
> unreasonable and afraid. All New York was demanding
> new men, and all the new forces, condensed into
> corporations, were demanding a new type of man – a man
> with ten times the endurance, energy, will and mind of
> the old type – for whom they were ready to pay millions
> at sight. As one jetted over the pavements or read the last
> week's newspapers, the new man seemed close at hand,
> for the old man had plainly reached the end of his

strength, and his failure had become catastrophic.
Everyone saw it, and every municipal election shrieked
chaos. A traveller in the highways of history looked out of
the club window on the turmoil of Fifth Avenue, and felt
himself in Rome, under Diocletian, witnessing the
anarchy, conscious of the compulsion, eager for the
solution, but unable to conceive whence the next impulse
was to come or how it was to act. The two-thousand-
years-failure of Christianity roared upward from Broadway
and no Constantine the Great was in sight.

At the beginning of this period, though, with the Civil War over,
most Americans looked forward to unlimited expansion in every
sphere. In his poem 'Passage to India', Whitman captures this mood
as he surveys the remainder of the nineteenth century:

After the seas are all cross'd (as they seem already cross'd)
After the great captains and engineers have accomplish'd
    their work,
After the noble inventors, after the scientists, the chemist,
    the geologist, ethnologist,
Finally shall come the poet worthy of that name.

Even Henry James, by nature far less sanguine than Whitman, felt
in 1867 the touch of this general buoyancy:

We are Americans born – *il faut en preudre son parti*. I look
upon it as a great blessing, and I think that to be an
American is an excellent preparation for culture. We have
exquisite qualities as a race, and it seems to me that we
are ahead of the European races in the fact that, more than
either of them, we can deal freely with forms of
civilization not our own, can pick and choose and
assimilate and in short (aesthetically, etc.) gain our
property wherever we find it. To have no national stamp
has hitherto been a regret and a drawback, but I think it
not unlikely that American writers may yet indicate that a
vast intellectual fusion and synthesis of the various national
tendencies of the world is the condition of more important
achievements than any we have yet seen. We must, of
course, have something of our own – something
distinctive and homogeneous – and I take it that we shall
find it in our moral consciousness, in our unprecedented
spiritual lightness and vigour.[4]

Some of these opinions would undoubtedly have been shared by Mark Twain who – though a few years older than Henry James – was still in 1867 barely at the threshold of his prodigious literary career, avidly collecting materials in Europe and the Middle East for his first great popular success, *The Innocents Abroad*. In some respects, the careers and works of these two major artists present fascinating, if widely spaced, parallels, though their responses to almost every aspect of life in America and Europe were so antithetical that one critic has been led to contrast them as prime members, if not actual founders, of divergent cultural streams, which he calls 'Redskin' and 'Paleface'. The distinctions made by Philip Rahv between James and writers like Emily Dickinson, on the one hand, and Twain and Whitman on the other, can be viewed as a more comprehensive version of my earlier discussion of Romance and Realism. Indeed, Rahv includes the tend-encies towards the 'distillations of symbolism' and 'a gross, riotous naturalism' in his list of opposing characteristics, but he sees these mainly as the means for expressing a much deeper divisiveness, the outward signs of a disabling split in the American personality, that has – he claims – prevented modern literature from achieving any real balance or maturity.

The Paleface, in this version of cultural history, is a 'high brow' though not quite an intellectual in the European sense of the term, while the Redskin, who may or may not be badly educated, is a 'low brow' in the sense that his reactions are primarily emotional, spon-taneous, and lacking in personal culture. In extending these traits, Rahv builds up portraits of men who exactly fit the popular image of James and Twain:

> The paleface continually hankers after religious norms,
> tending towards a refined estrangement from reality. The
> redskin, on the other hand, accepts his environment, at
> times to the degree of fusion with it, even when rebelling
> against one or other of its manifestations. At his highest
> level the paleface moves in an exquisite moral atmosphere;
> at his lowest, he is genteel, snobbish and pedantic. In
> giving expression to the vitality and to the aspirations of
> the people, the redskin is at his best; but at his worst he is
> a vulgar anti-intellectual, combining aggression with
> conformity and reverting to the crudest form of frontier
> psychology.[5]

If one accepts that the elements – good and bad – attributed to the Redskin here, were beginning to dominate American life in the latter part of the nineteenth century, it is hardly surprising that Ernest

Hemingway who, according to Rahv, was himself a late manifestation of the same trend – a perennial boy-man descendant of Natty Bumppo – should assert that 'all modern American literature comes from one book by Mark Twain called *Huckleberry Finn*'. Hemingway's unconcealed scorn for those of his countrymen who wrote like 'exiled English colonials' is well known and his appreciation of Twain has much to do with the earlier writer's ability to create art out of 'the words that people always have used in speech, the words that survive in language'.

But there are stronger bonds than just linguistic ones between the two of them, and if Mark Twain has a genuine claim to be the true precursor of the modern American spirit, it surely lies in his original exploration of a theme that was to influence and eventually dominate American literature far more thoroughly than did his brilliant manipulation of the vernacular.

It is the same theme hinted at by Henry James in his letter to T. S. Perry in which he contrasts the individual American's moral consciousness with the socially constructed persona of the European, and optimistically predicts a future fusion between the two. Twain, who was less enamoured of European society anyway, conceived the issue more simply as a dilemma that confronted the American in his native land as he strove to cope with the forces emerging in late-nineteenth-century America. For him, and by extension for his fictional characters, it presented itself as a choice between freedom and conformity. This, as Alan Trachtenberg has demonstrated,[6] is the central dilemma of Huck Finn himself as he pits his sound heart against a deformed conscience and consciously chooses 'to go to Hell' for his crimes against society. In one way or another, it is a choice that Americans of every generation have felt the need to confront. It lies behind and gives urgency to the nineteenth-century debates about Free Will and Determinism just as it remains the central issue in recent debates between Noam Chomsky and B. S. Skinner on the subject of Behaviourism. In fiction, it forms a strong connecting thread linking the Naturalists, the Realists, and the Modernists, who oscillate wildly between the claims of social necessity and individual identity. It is above all an inescapable theme in American social and political debate, occupying the very centre of the American psyche where the often antagonistic ideals of liberty and equality constantly struggle for supremacy.

If Mark Twain has a genuine claim to be the originator of modern American literature, it is because, more than any of his contemporaries, he identified the central issues of his own and our culture, and gave life to them in a story about a boy and a slave escaping to freedom down the Mississippi River.

Notes

1. A detailed account of urban expansion in the nineteenth century can be found in Blake McKelvey, *The City in American History* (London and New York, 1969). For a more general account of social and economic developments in the period, see Ray Ginger, *The Age of Excess: American Life from the End of Reconstruction to World War I* (New York, 1965).

2. Alan Trachtenberg, *The Incorporation of America: Culture and Society in the Gilded Age* (New York, 1982), p. 231.

3. *Complete Prose Works* (New York, 1909), p. 248.

4. Letter to T. S. Perry, 20 September 1867, in *Selected Letters of Henry James*, edited by Leon Edel (London, 1956).

5. Philip Rahv, *Image and Idea* (London, 1952), p. 2.

6. 'The Form of Freedom in *Adventures of Huckleberry Finn*', *The Southern Review*, no. 4 (October 1970), 954–71.

Chapter 2
Mark Twain

Mark Twain was 'born' in 1863 when his creator, Samuel Langhorne Clemens, was already twenty-eight years old. He first used his pseudonym as the author of a humorous travel letter he contributed to a Nevada newspaper, the *Territorial Enterprise*. In masking his true identity, he was following an established custom exemplified by a multitude of comic journalists including Artemus Ward and Josh Billings in America and even Charles Dickens in England, who, unlike Twain, abandoned 'Boz' when it began to restrict the scope of his literary ambitions. At this point in his life Mark Twain can hardly be said to have had any real ambition as a writer, having drifted into journalism after a varied career as a river-boat pilot, a soldier, and latterly, a prospector in the years following the California gold rush and the discovery of the Comstock silver lode in Nevada. It was only when his short story 'The Jumping Frog of Calaveras County' brought him recognition from a wider public that he began to appreciate the potential of his talent. Even after this, though, and indeed throughout his life, Twain was always liable to be tempted away from his vocation by the promise of easy money and exciting new ventures. He saw himself as an inventor and a patron of America's rapidly developing technology. He interested himself in every aspect of publishing, amassing a fortune by developing his own sales through a subscription scheme, only to lose it by his involvement with the Paige typesetting machine. In an age of professional public lecturers, William Dean Howells said that Twain was the finest performer he had ever seen. He had a great need to project himself to the public, and when he was not doing so in print, had to do so in person. It was said that at the height of his career he was probably the most famous man in the world, a role he relished and lived up to, both in his flamboyant style and in his ready pronouncements on almost any topical issue.

Many of these interests and characteristics eventually manifested themselves in his writing, making it virtually impossible for him in his later career to create self-contained, coherent fictions. Indeed, it can be argued with some justice that it is only when he is able to smuggle himself into his books as a character, and so find an outlet for his own powerful ego, that he is free to create an otherwise independent world. Failing this, his work is too often deformed by his need to insinuate himself and his emotions indiscriminately and deviously into his fictions.

This need did not present itself as a difficulty during his early career, however, as he restricted himself to short stories based on the Western 'tall tale' or travel books like *Innocents Abroad* (1869). Even when he did turn to a larger fictional work, *The Gilded Age* (1873), he took the precaution of working with a collaborator, Charles Dudley Warner, and so freed himself from the responsibility of sustained independent invention. In later years Twain always claimed that he contributed the facts to the book but left the fiction to Warner. And though 'facts' is perhaps not the most accurate word to describe the contents, Twain's share in the work is largely restricted to wide-ranging social criticism in which he draws upon his experience of business and politics in order to satirize the corruption of his age, and to ride one or two of his favourite hobby-horses, such as the wickedness and stupidity of universal suffrage, or the injustices of the contemporary legal system. To accomplish all this, he relied not so much on the sentimental, romantic plot of the novel as on the ability to embody his ideas in vividly created characters, and particularly in one that became so large that he outgrew the novel and was sporadically and variously resurrected by Twain throughout his career: Colonel Sellers.

Sellers was based upon his uncle, James Lampton, and Twain's ambivalent feelings – love for the original of his inspiration, mixed with reservations about the type to which he belongs – give the character an exuberant vitality worth everything else in the book. Sellers is not just a peculiarly American type, but also a typical feature of the Gilded Age itself: a man of social pretensions who, down on his luck, is determined to adjust to the new commercial culture that is being created all around him. He is first and foremost a Promoter, an entrepreneur who without any capital or specific skills of his own, contrives to prosper by using his talents to bring commercial projects, often of dubious legality or morality, into being. In addition to being a fast talker and publicist, he is acutely aware of which government officials and politicians to soften up with bribes. These activities give Twain the opportunity to turn his satiric attention to the institutions of democracy itself, and the strongest parts of the novel derive from his reaction to the corruption and greed of nineteenth-century American society.

Unfortunately, though, the authors had a further, more pressing aim in writing the book: to prove to their wives that they could write a popular, sentimental novel. The story of Laura's passage from childhood innocence, through an acquaintance with the sordid realities of money and sex, to a broken-hearted death, cannot be blamed on Warner. The idea of it, based on a recent murder case in San Francisco, was certainly Twain's, and it bears all the marks of his own sentimentality, a trait that always threatened to undermine the integrity of his fiction. Throughout his career this fault is compounded by a chronic inability to structure his novels consciously, and the resulting chaos can only occasionally be redeemed by his intuitive sense of organizational propriety, as in *The Adventures of Huckleberry Finn* (1884), or by the brilliance of individual fragments, as in *Pudd'nhead Wilson* (1894).[1]

Mark Twain's difficulties stemmed from what appears to have been a deeply traumatic dichotomy in his own nature. *The Gilded Age* is subtitled 'A Tale of Today', and Twain was passionately interested in exposing the flaws under the veneer of polite Eastern commercial society. As a Western outsider, he could find a fresh viewpoint for these criticisms, but as a man who was also determined to become a member of this élite and who was rapidly doing just that, he also experienced an alienation from himself and a suspicion that the fault he wished to expose was not local and social but psychological and, therefore, universal. The only escape possible from such knowledge was the one he found in his next major work, his first unaided attempt at sustained fiction, *The Adventures of Tom Sawyer* (1876), where he returned for the first time to the memories of his pre-Civil War boyhood.

He began to write it in the summer of 1874, cocooned from all noise in his little 'pilot house' of a study in a farmhouse near Elmira in upper New York State. His initial plan was to devote only a quarter of the novel to Tom's boyhood, the rest being divided between his early manhood, his travels, and the 'Battle of Life', and his return where he would 'meet grown babies and toothless old drivellers who were the grandees of his boyhood'. A year later, when he was almost at the end of the work, he still had no idea of its final shape, and told his friend Howells that 'Since there is no plot to the thing it is likely to follow its own drift.'[1]

Twain's uncertainty about the novel's shape was related to his deeper uncertainty about an audience for his story. At first he insisted that it was only written for adults, but later agreed under pressure that it should be seen as 'a book for boys, pure and simple'. Finally, in his Preface written in 1876 he attempted a compromise, claiming that though the book was intended mainly for the entertainment of boys and girls, it also attempted 'pleasantly to remind adults of what they once were themselves'.

In helping to liberate such memories in his readers, Twain transcends all the technical deficiencies of his art to re-create the timeless joys and terrors of childhood. The plot, involving body-snatching, robbery, and murder, is absurdly melodramatic, but as such it exactly matches the boyish imaginations of Huck and Tom. Reality is not a relevant criterion here, any more than it is in the idyllic picture of ante-bellum rural America. What matters, as Bernard DeVoto has truly said, is that 'something formed from America lives as it lives nowhere else'.[2] At a still more profound level, something from an even more general source is created, so that the descriptions of Tom's gang in their innocent sport on the beach at Jackson's Island reaches to the core of every reader's memory:

> After breakfast they went whooping and prancing out on
> the bar, and chased each other round and round, shedding
> clothes as they went, until they were naked, and then
> continued the frolic far away up the shoal water of the
> bar, against the stiff current, which latter tripped their legs
> from under them from time to time, and greatly increased
> the fun. And now and then they stood in a group and
> splashed water in each other's faces with their palms,
> gradually approaching each other with averted faces, to
> avoid the straggling sprays, and finally gripping and
> struggling till the best man ducked his neighbour and then
> they all went under in a tangle of white legs and arms,
> and came up blowing, spluttering, laughing, and gasping
> for breath at one and the same time. (16)

Equally evocative is the description of lonely terror as Huck waits for Tom to return from his exploration of Injun Joe's room:

> It seemed hours since Tom had disappeared. Surely he
> must have fainted; maybe he was dead; maybe his heart
> had burst under terror and excitement. In his uneasiness
> Huck found himself drawing closer and closer to the alley,
> fearing all sorts of dreadful things, and momentarily
> expecting some catastrophe to happen that would take
> away his breath. There was not much to take away, for he
> seemed only able to inhale it by thimblefuls, and his heart
> would soon wear itself out, the way it was beating.
> Suddenly there was a flash of light, and Tom came tearing
> by him:
>   'Run!' said he; 'run for your life!'
> He needn't have repeated it; once was enough; Huck was
> making thirty or forty miles an hour before the repetition

was uttered. The boys never stopped till they reached the
shed of a deserted slaughter-house at the lower end of the
village. Just as they got within its shelter the storm burst
and the rain poured down. (29)

In passages such as these Twain is beginning to experiment with
the problem of articulating the consciousness of innocent, uneducated
characters. Sometimes he can move in and out of Huck's perceptions
even within a single sentence, as when he writes: 'Huck was making
thirty or forty miles an hour before the repetition was uttered.'

For the most part, though, *Tom Sawyer* is addressed to the sophisticated reader, enabling him to enjoy his recollections of childhood
from the safe and sentimental viewpoint of age. Tom Sawyer's rebellion against society is temporary and superficial. The villain of the
novel, Injun Joe, is a social outcast anyway, who is easily disposed of,
enabling Tom to be reconciled to and even honoured by the citizens
of Saint Petersburg. Judge Thatcher invests Tom's new fortune for him
at six per cent, and plans his education at the best law school in the
country or even at the National Military Academy. Tom is restored
to the affections of Becky Thatcher, and we last see him trying to
convince Huck to embrace the life of respectability and regularity.

The great idyll is thus brought to an end by Tom's recuperation into
the adult world. But luckily, towards the end of the story Twain
apparently realised the possibilities – till then largely ignored – present
in his secondary character, Huck. As Tom fades out of the picture, so
Huck begins to come into the foreground, and the book ends with him
ready to occupy the vacated role at the centre. One of his last speeches,
protesting against the life he is now being forced to endure, brings the
story full circle, reminding us, even in its detailed imagery, of the
position Tom occupied so unwillingly before their adventures began:

> Don't talk about it, Tom. I've tried it, and it don't work;
> it don't work, Tom. It ain't for me; I ain't used to it. The
> widder's good to me, and friendly, but I can't stand them
> ways. She makes me git up just at the same time every
> morning; she makes me wash, they comb me all to
> thunder; she won't let me sleep in the woodshed; I got to
> wear them blamed clothes that just smothers me, Tom;
> they don't seem to let any air git through 'em, somehow;
> and they're so rotten nice that I can't set down, nor lay
> down, nor roll around anywheres; I hain't slid on a cellar-
> door for – well, it 'pears to be years; I got to go to
> church, and sweat and sweat – I hate them ornery

sermons! I can't ketch a fly in there, I can't chaw, I got to
wear shoes all Sunday. The widder eats by a bell; she goes
to bed by a bell; she gits up by a bell – everything's so
awful reg'lar a body can't stand it.'
'Well, everybody does that way, Huck.' (36)

The difference, and it is of the greatest significance, is that now we
are completely within Huck's consciousness. Twain's skill in creating
a vernacular literature, and his manifest enjoyment of it, become
increasingly evident towards the end of *Tom Sawyer*. His decision not
just to retain Huck as the hero of his next novel, but also to employ
him as its narrator, is one that allowed him to use his ambivalence
about innocence and experience, nature and culture, as a compositional
principle. The device of seeing American society through the eyes of
an innocent and reluctant rebel allowed him to polarize the dualism of
his own confused nature and work the oppositions for all the irony and
pathos inherent within them. In his famous description of his masterpiece as 'a book of mine where a sound heart and a deformed
conscience come into collision and conscience suffers defeat', he effectively pinpoints the difference between it and the earlier book, which
he quite accurately but damningly calls 'simply a hymn' to boyhood.[3]

Another important difference is that he hit upon an ideal situation
within which Huck's agonizing conflicts could be presented – that of
a runaway slave in the pre-Civil War South. There are other novels
such as *Tom Sawyer Abroad* (1894) and *Tom Sawyer, Detective* (1896),
in which Twain effectively uses Huck as a first-person narrator, but
these are both flawed by weak plots that produce little more than
random comedy. *Huckleberry Finn's* great strength come from the
shape given to it by the course of the raft's journey down the Mississippi as Huck and Jim seek their different kinds of freedom. Twain,
who knew the river intimately and wrote about it in detail in *Life on
the Mississippi* (1883), uses it here both realistically and symbolically,
often fusing two kinds of perception with the greatest subtlety, as in
Huck's lyrical reminiscences:

Two or three days and nights went by; I reckon I might
say they swum by; they slid along so quiet and smooth
and lovely. Here is the way we put in the time. It was a
monstrous big river down there – sometimes a mile and a
half wide; we run nights, and laid up and hid day-times;
soon as night was most gone, we stopped navigating and
tied up – nearly always in the dead water under a tow-
head; and then cut young cotton-woods and willows and

hid the raft with them. Then we set out the lines. Next
we slid into the river and had a swim, so as to freshen up
and cool off; then we set down on the sandy bottom
where the water was about knee-deep, and watched the
daylight come. Not a sound anywheres – perfectly still –
just like the whole world was asleep, only sometimes the
bull-frogs a-clattering maybe. The first thing to see,
looking away over the water, was a kind of dull line –
that was the woods on t'other side – you couldn't make
nothing else out; then a pale place in the sky; then more
paleness, spreading around; then the river softened up,
away off, and warn't black any more, but grey; you could
see little dark spots drifting along, ever so far away –
trading scows, and such things; and long black streaks –
rafts; sometimes you could hear a sweep screaking; or
jumbled up voices, it was so still, and sounds come so far;
and by and by you could see a streak on the water which
you know by the look of the streak that there's a snag
there in a swift current which breaks on it and makes that
streak look that way; and you see the mist curl up off the
water, and the east reddens up, and the river, and you
make out a log cabin in the edge of the woods, away on
the bank on t'other side of the river, being a wood-yard,
likely, and piled by them cheats so you can throw a dog
through it anywheres; then the nice breeze springs up, and
comes fanning you from over there, so cool and fresh, and
sweet to smell, on account of the woods and flowers; but
sometimes not that way, because they've left dead fish
laying around, gars, and such, and they do get pretty
rank; and next you've got the full day, and everything
smiling in the sun, and the song-birds just going it! (19)

The contrast lightly touched on here is one that determines the
entire framework of the novel, and it is that between nature and
society. The book begins with a description of how Widow Douglas
attempts to civilize Huck and ends with him deciding not to let it
happen again at the hands of Aunt Sally. In between we are given in
episode after episode a picture of so-called civilized life as it is practised
in the small settlements which the fugitives visit as they flee down
river.

Before he can even begin his main adventure, though, Huck has to
fake his own death in order to escape from his brutal, drunken father.
It is only as a 'dead' boy divested of all his background that he can start
to grow as a person. Similarly, his companion Jim, a slave, only begins

to own himself and discover his true worth by running away from his old owners. Together they head down river, making for Cairo where they plan to sell the raft and take a steamboat up the Ohio to the Free States. But the plan soon has to be abandoned when they sail right past Cairo and the confluence with the Ohio in a dense fog. At this point in the novel, with sixteen chapters written and no obvious solution to the impasse into which he had written himself, Twain engineered another climax by having a passing steamboat smash the raft to pieces and bring the pair's flight to a premature halt.

This was in 1876, and between that date and the summer of 1883 when Twain finished the novel in another of his great creative bursts, he produced only three or four chapters. These, however, pointed the way out of his difficulties. Instead of concentrating on Huck and Jim, he used their drift towards the deep South to explore the social conditions in frontier settlements along the banks of the river. In episodes such as those describing the feud between two families of aristocratic barbarians, or the murder of a town drunk, as well as in the creation of new comic characters such as the Duke and the King, he discovered a context in which he could resume his quarrel with the corruptions of the Gilded Age. Religious and political hypocrisy, brutality and sentimentality, greed and deception, are all exposed by Huck's innocent vision and contrasted with the loving bond that develops between boy and escaped slave. Here, for example, is part of Huck's description of Emmeline Grangerford's pictures:

> One was a woman in a slim black dress, belted small under the arm-pits, with bulges like a cabbage in the middle of the sleeves, and a large black scoop-shovel bonnet with a black veil, and white slim ankles crossed about with black tape, and very wee black slippers, like a chisel, and she was leaning pensive on a tombstone on her right elbow, under a weeping willow, and her other hand hanging down her side holding a white handkerchief and a reticule, and underneath the picture it said, 'Shall I Never See Thee More Alas?' Another one was a young lady with her hair all combed up straight to the top of her head, and knotted there in front of a comb like a chair-back, and she was crying into a handkerchief and had a dead bird laying on its back in her other hand with its heels up, and underneath the picture it said, 'I Shall Never Hear Thy Sweet Chirrup More Alas!' There was one where a young lady was at a window looking up at the moon, and tears running down her cheeks; and she had an open letter in one hand with a black sealing-wax showing on one edge

of it, and she was mashing a locket with a chain to it
against her mouth, and underneath the picture it said,
'And Art Thou Gone Yes Thou Art Gone Alas!' These
was all nice pictures, I reckon, but I didn't somehow seem
to take to them, because if ever I was down a little, they
always gave me the fan-tods. (17)

Before her early death, Emmeline had made a hobby of the subject,
and Twain creates, in his description of her effects, a rich satire of the
current preoccupation with the morbid. Good in itself, the passage
takes on an additional critical dimension, though, when read in the
context of her family's involvement in the pointless and bloody
butchery of their neighbours, the Shepherdsons.

Moreover, this section of the novel has a coherence lacking in
similar passages in *The Gilded Age*, in that it is firmly bound up with
the theme of Huck's development. It comes to an end with Huck
having to choose between his heart and his head. Having capitulated
to his conscience by deciding to write to Miss Watson to inform her
where Jim is, he falls into a reverie in which he sees Jim 'all the time,
in the day, and in the night-time, sometimes moonlight, sometimes
storms, and we a floating along, talking, and singing, and laughing'.
He finds that he cannot harden his heart sufficiently to go through with
this plan, so in fear and trembling he destroys the note and opts for
a life of wickedness and an eternity in hell.

For many readers this moment marks the true conclusion of the
novel, and the final chapters in which Huck allows Tom Sawyer to
manipulate him into playing a childish, cruel game of rescuing Jim,
are merely futher evidence of Twain's incomprehension of his own
genius which he so easily subordinated to a penchant for low comedy.
In choosing to dwell upon Tom's romantic charade at such tedious
length, Twain appears to lose sight of the elements that had held everything so far in focus, and he sacrifices much of the credibility in Huck's
character. No amount of critical ingenuity can reconcile most readers
to Huck's sad relapse after his magnificent development. Twain
appears to have been constitutionally incapable of sustaining the
fictional world which he created so effortlessly, even in this, his
masterpiece, and the flaw was to become more and not less marked
as his career progressed.

At an unconscious level, however, the unsatisfactory ending can be
explained in terms of the unresolved tensions that dominated Mark
Twain himself and prevented him from casting off the bourgeois
respectability of his Hartford circle and the New England literati. Seen
in this light, Huck's capitulation to Tom, Aunt Polly and the Phelpses,
mirrors Twain's own dilemma, and Huck's final defiant pledge to

'light out for the Territory' before Aunt Polly can get to work 'sivil-ising' him, is more a nostalgic reflection of Sam Clemens's past than a realistic promise for the future.

Twain's ambivalence about the conflicting claims made by nature and society or by innocence and experience pervades nearly everything he wrote. It lies behind his constant recourse to twins, claimants, or look-alikes in his fiction, figures who provide the means, by way of changing positions, to explore the effect of different environments upon the formation of character. In *The Prince and the Pauper* (1882), for example, he examines the link between luxury and morality, and in *Pudd'nhead Wilson* substitutes racial characteristics in working out a similar equation. He even toyed with the idea of trying out the same formula in a novel examining the importance of sexual roles.

What he appeared to be unable or unwilling to do, though, was to apply his ideas about Determinism in a realistic way to a novel of contemporary America. The nearest he came to it was in *A Connecticut Yankee in King Arthur's Court* (1889), where the hero, Hank Morgan, a 'Yankee of the Yankees' and a superintendent in an arms factory, receives a blow on the head at the start of the novel, and comes to in sixth-century Arthurian England. In transposing a version of indus-trialized America to the sixth century, Twain set out to defend his own society against the attacks mounted on it by visiting Europeans – the most recent and damning being that made in Matthew Arnold's *Discourses in America* (1885). Arnold's aristocratic gibes at American institutions and the 'glorification of the average man', stung Twain who saw an opportunity of turning the 'irreverent fun' he had been planning about the nobility into a penetrating satire on injustice and privilege.

In Twain's notebook containing the original idea for the novel there is no indication of any aim beyond fairly crude burlesque humour. He envisages a good deal of slapstick comedy in the antics of a knight errant with a bad cold or an itch, trapped inside a suit of armour, and the novel still retains much of this kind of farcical writing, often based on the simple idea of contrast. For example, Twain constantly juxta-poses Hank Morgan's vernacular speech with a parodied version of the language of Malory's *Morte d'Arthur*:

'And then they rode to the damsels and either saluted
other, and the eldest had a garland of gold about her head,
and she was threescore winter of age or more. . . .'
'The *damsel* was?'
'Even so, dear lord – and her hair was white under the
garland. . . .'
'Celluloid teeth, nine dollars a set, as like as not – the

loose-fit kind, that go up and down like a portcullis when
you eat, and fall out when you laugh.' (15)

In similar vein, Twain sets up a tournament between Hank and Sir
Sagramor in which the knight is defeated by Hank's cowboy skills
with the lasso. But by this stage in the novel (Ch. 39) Twain had
become deeply involved with his more serious cultural criticism, and
Hank sees the combat as one in which a whole way of life is at stake:

> I was a champion, it was true, but not the champion of
> the frivolous black arts. I was the champion of hard
> unsentimental common sense and reason, I was entering
> the lists to either destroy knight-errantry or be its victim.
> (39)

This is the pattern of the novel's plot: a contest between Yankee
practicality and medieval superstition. It allowed Twain to satirize
those aspects of European civilization he had come to despise, such as
the class system and the Established Church; and at the same time to
celebrate American democracy and progress in Hank's social revolution
that has been brought about by the introduction of modern
technology.

Many of Twain's 'inventions' are deployed humorously to allow
him to milk such ideas as knights on bicycles, but the novel reaches
its climax in an apocalyptic confrontation in which Hank unleashes the
destructive power of technology in a remorseless and quite excessive
carnage.

Hank's embryonic republic is attacked by 25,000 mailed knights
who are promptly electrocuted, shot, blown up, or drowned in an
orgy of bloodshed, leaving the fifty-four freedom fighters trapped and
dying in the poisonous odour emitted by the rotting corpses.

In these final images Twain makes explicit the ambivalences which
create a continuous submerged theme in the novel and surface more
and more in his later fiction. Beneath his overt celebration of industrial
democracy lurk growing doubts both about the value of the common
people he sets out to champion but ends up calling 'human muck', and
the scientific and mechanical marvels that can so easily bring blight
upon the world.

Another aspect of this ambivalence is the current of powerful, if
sentimental, nostalgia for the pastoral simplicity of the 'lost land' felt
by Hank throughout the novel. His description of rural England has
some of the qualities of unreality associated with Twain's re-creation
of his Missouri boyhood:

We crossed broad natural lawns sparkling with dew, and
we moved like spirits, the cushioned turf giving out no
sound of footfall; we dreamed along through glades in a
mist of green light that got its tint from the sun-drenched
roof of leaves overhead, and by our feet the clearest and
coldest of rivulets went frisking and gossiping over its
reefs and making a sort of whispering music, comfortable
to hear; and at times we left the world behind and entered
into the solemn great deeps and rich gloom of the forest.
(12)

The world that Twain himself sought imaginative escape from was
becoming increasingly uncomfortable for many sensitive Americans in
the 1880s, and too much has been made of the purely individual
psychological reasons for Twain's growing disillusionment as
expressed in late works such as *The Mysterious Stranger*, 'The Man that
Corrupted Hadleyburg', and his philosophical essay 'What is Man?'

While it is undoubtedly true that Twain's reading of Darwin,
Huxley, and Lecky helped to undermine his faith in a benevolent
universe and the goodness of man,[4] his scepticism and pessimism were
shared by many of his contemporaries who were not similarly overwhelmed by a naive, deterministic philosophy. The human and social
concomitants of unbridled industrialization were beginning to make
themselves felt in the 1880s in such incidents as the Haymarket riot of
1886, the agitation for legislation against business and the monopolies,
and the organization of labour unions.

Many other writers besides Twain were appalled by the impersonal-
ality, stupidity, and greed which appeared to be inseparable from
modern life, and like him, many yearned for the simplicity and goodness of an American past that seemed to have disappeared for ever. The
various attempts made to come to terms with the harsh realities of the
present and to relate them to older values, constitute major strands in
American fiction until well into the twentieth century.

Notes

1. The circumstances in which *Tom Sawyer* and Twain's other novels were
   composed are described very fully by Justice Kaplan in *Mr Clemens and Mark
   Twain* (Harmondsworth, 1970).

26   AMERICAN FICTION 1865–1940

2. Bernard DeVoto, *Mark Twain's America and Mark Twain at Work* (Boston, 1967), p. 307.

3. For a discussion of the way in which Twain uses different kinds of language to mediate the worlds of the vernacular and the official culture of his age see Jules Chametzky, 'Realism, Cultural Politics, and Language as Mediation in Mark Twain and Others', in *Prospects*, 8 (1983), 183–95.

4. A description of these influences can be found in H. H. Waggoner, 'Science in the Thought of Mark Twain', *American Literature*, 8 (1936), 357–70.

Chapter 3
Realism and Naturalism: Howells, Crane, Norris, Dreiser

Much of the confusion, as well as the controversy, surrounding discussions of nineteenth-century Realism, comes from the misguided attempts of critics and literary historians to produce a simple definition for what was, in fact, a broad and heterogeneous movement that can only be fully understood when its methods are seen in relation to wider social and philosophical contexts. It is particularly tempting for literary critics to concentrate their attention on method and technique, but even this narrow focus has produced a bewildering multiplicity of emphases and definitions. There are those, for example, who maintain that the documentary rendering of external detail is the primary characteristic of realism, and that the only justification for any statement in a realistic discourse must be its referent. Others reject the particularity inherent in this view in favour of the notion of a realistic 'norm', a statistical average which demands that the realist text should aim at representing the typical rather than the unique. Set against these views, or even alongside them, is another that identifies the essential technique of realism not so much in its style as in its narrative method. Objectivity can only be achieved by the elimination of the mediation and manipulation of the author or his *alter ego*, the narrator. Novels must seek the impersonality of drama and the impartiality of science before they can be called realistic.

If the concept of realism could be restricted in this way and used merely to describe characteristics of texts, the task of the literary historian would be much simpler. But this would be to fly in the face of actual usage which has always acknowledged certain 'extra-textual' elements in the description of realism. For those novelists who believe that realism stems from an account of the typical or normal, the question of the referent itself becomes problematical, the implication being that some subjects are in themselves more 'real' than others. Traditionally, this 'reality' has always been associated with 'low life' material, though as we shall see, writers have occasionally protested against what they regard as the elevation of proletarian subjects and have concentrated instead upon the blander aspects of middle-class existence.

On the other hand, for novelists whose interest lies primarily in the documentary representation of the world there are equally difficult problems relating to the 'realistic' priority of social, psychological, and physiological aspects of the subject. Every novelist must make assumptions or choices concerning the reality of his subject-matter, and many of the critical disputes about realism in the nineteenth century centred on this rather than on literary techniques.

The last decades of the nineteenth century were marked, as Eric Sundquist has noted[1] by 'an increasing discrepancy between the figurative life of the mind and the literal life of the material'. What Sundquist is describing here, as he discusses the fiction of Henry James and Stephen Crane, is a central characteristic of Modernism. The dichotomy he refers to between subject and object, and the way it manifests itself in twentieth-century literature, will be explored later, but it is also important to remember that subsequent developments in linguistics and philosophy have stretched this chasm much further to the point where the referent itself is often now posited as a mere myth or mirage by post-structuralist theorists. This partly accounts, not only for the absence of any major development in the theory of Realism in our own time, but also for the fact that the nineteenth-century Realist movement itself has for the most part been described only in negative terms by modern critics unsympathetic to its general aims.

Exceptions to this neglect or hostility can be found in Roland Barthes's studies of Balzac, and in the writing of Marxist theorists like Georg Lukacs who, in *The Meaning of Contemporary Realism*, mounts a sophisticated defence of Realism against what he calls the 'ahistorical inauthenticity of Modernism'. More recently this line of argument has been extended by the American theorist Fredric Jameson who quite properly insists on the importance of the bourgeois cultural revolution in changing our world view:

> In general, only the negative or destructive features of the
> bourgeois cultural revolution have been insisted on: most
> particularly the vast demolition efforts of the
> Enlightenment *philosophes*, as they seek to clear a space for
> what will become contemporary science. But the positive
> features of such a revolution are no less significant, and
> essentially include the whole new life world to which
> people are to be retrained: a new form of space, whose
> homogeneity abolishes the old heterogeneities of various
> forms of sacred space – transforming a whole world of
> qualities and libidinal intensities into the merely
> psychological experience of what Descartes called
> 'secondary sensations', and setting in their place the grey

world of quantity and extension, of the purely measurable
– together with the substitution of the older forms of
ritual, sacred or cyclical time by the new physical and
measurable temporality of the clock and the routine, of the
working day. In this sense, we may go even further in our
account of the ideological mission of the nineteenth-
century realistic novelists, and assert that their function is
not merely to produce new mental and existential habits,
but in a virtual or symbolic way to produce this whole
new spatial and temporal configuration itself: what will
come to be called 'daily life', the *Alltag*, or, in a different
terminology, the 'referent' – so many diverse
characterisations of the new configuration of public and
private spheres or space in classical or market capitalism.[2]

Jameson's achievement here, and in his book, *The Political Unconscious*, is to have identified and defined the importance of the 'Realist
moment', thus freeing realism from the charge of being merely passive
or representational. Alan Trachtenburg makes a similar effort in *The
Incorporation of America* where he argues that the most profound
changes in these decades of swift industrialization and urbanization lay
at the level of culture, manifesting themselves 'in the quality as well
as the substance of perceptions, in the style as well as the content of
responses'.[3] The way in which a novelist like Dreiser constructs his
subjects is a perfect illustration of what happens to an individual in
what has been aptly called an age of reification or commodification.[4]
   An effect related to that produced by the work of Marxist critics
can also be traced in recent writing by Feminist theorists who have
been re-examining the nineteenth-century literary canon. In seeking to
create new perspectives from which to study American writing, they
have inevitably called into question earlier normative assumptions
about that world and its representation. Whether one believes that the
gender-related restrictiveness of the traditional canon derives from
cultural realities suffered by contemporary women writers, or maintains that it has been imposed by modern critical theories, makes little
real difference. The attempt to expose the melodramatic core of so-
called 'realist' fiction produced by men, and to supplement this with
work that exhibits a different, complementary social and psychological
reality, has had the effect of creating new dimensions of historical
actuality – of alerting us to the inadequacy of our literary and critical
conventions.[5]
   The 'productive' nature of the Realist novel – the creation of new
worlds with radically different spatial or psychological outlines – has
been partly obscured by Realism's close association with Naturalism.

In an effort to resist earlier ideologies and to portray life as scientifically as possible, the nineteenth-century novelist was led inexorably towards a world-view that reflected the prevalent mechanistic philosophies whereby man was seen as a creature without freedom of will, and adrift in a meaningless universe, a helpless victim of the random operation of hereditary and environmental forces. While it may be true, as George J. Becker claims in an influential article,[6] that 'naturalism is no more than a philosophic position taken by some realists', it is equally true that the very fact of adopting a philosophical position and attempting to propound it in fiction militates against the ideals of objectivity and inclusiveness upon which realism imagines itself to be based. As we shall see in this chapter, American naturalists were just as likely to employ the techniques of romantic writers as of the early American realists. The dissimilarities of philosophy, subject-matter, technique, and style in the work of W. D. Howells, Stephen Crane, Frank Norris, and Theodore Dreiser are sufficient to show, if not the inadequacy, then at least the necessary elasticity of the term.

Some historians, such as Alfred Kazin, reject such eclecticism and accuse the movement of having 'no center, no unifying principle, no philosophy, no joy in its coming, no climate of experiment'.[7] What it did have, however, was a number of impassioned champions of whom the most influential was undoubtedly William Dean Howells.

Howells

Howells was a man who lacked both the artistic genius of Twain and the intellectual power of James, yet produced more fiction and criticism than either of them. His geniality and generosity enabled him to retain the friendship of both those dissimilar eccentrics as well as that of a multitude of younger writers who were helped and encouraged by the Dean of American Letters, as he was called, either directly or in his capacity as editor of the *Atlantic Monthly* and as a prolific essayist and reviewer.

Towards the end of his long and productive life, when in H. L. Mencken's words he had become 'almost the national ideal . . . enveloped in a web of superstitious reverence',[8] Howells became aware that despite all the honours heaped upon him, his 'beautiful time was past and his cult was dead'. The kind of realism in which he believed had been overtaken, if not overwhelmed, first by naturalism and then by modernism. His growing isolation and the reasons for it are clearly indicated in Mencken's critique which compares him unfavourably with Frank Norris and Theodore Dreiser. Unlike his younger contemporaries, he was unable to evoke the race spirit, the essential conflict of forces, or the peculiar drift and colour of American life. The world Howells continued to move in seemed to Mencken in 1917 to be suburban, caged, and flabby. It was, in fact, the world of the 1880s, and it was during that decade that Howells really came into his own as a daring, even shocking, chronicler of the realities of American urban life.

In order to understand this change of attitude towards a man who himself had changed very little, it is essential to start from the position which Howells himself occupied when he became assistant editor of the *Atlantic Monthly* in 1866. Like Twain, he had been reared in provincial journalism, and his respect for truthfulness and factual observation was offended by the false, idealized pictures of life contained in the majority of works on which he was obliged to comment. In his early reviews, and later in the regular feature he contributed to *Harper's Monthly* in the 1880s, he fought a simple and straightforward battle to rescue American literature from the artificiality that threatened to engulf it in a tide of historical romances and sentimental novels. The two sides in the 'Realism War' were so far apart that it was unnecessary for either of them to question or refine Howells's simple definition of fiction as being that which is 'true to the motives, the impulses, the principles that shape the life of actual men and women'. The more urgent question for those taking part in the controversy was whether it was morally justifiable to portray such things or whether, as Charles Dudley Warner and others maintained, it was more noble to create fiction that would 'lighten the burdens of life by taking us for a time out of our humdrum and perhaps sordid conditions, so that we can see familiar life somewhat idealized'.[9]

Later, of course, Howells's views on human motives and the principles that shape life would be rejected by a generation of writers who had similar aims but very different perceptions of reality. It is not so much Howells's literary technique that Mencken or Sinclair Lewis – who called him a 'pious old maid' – attack, as the subjects he chose to treat. Howells remained convinced that fiction must deal with the ordinary, the average, even the mundane aspects of existence. For him the 'profound dread and agony of life, the surge of passion and aspiration, the grand crash and glitter of things, the tragedy that runs eternally under the surface', were exactly what falsified the novels and romances of the decadent writers from which he recoiled, and as he saw it, Mencken's demand for such things seemed like a rejection of all he valued. And Lewis's remark to Mencken that Howells's novels had 'no more glow and gusto than so many tables of bond prices' would not have seemed as terrible to Howells himself.[10]

From the very beginning of his career, in his early travel books *Venetian Life* (1866) and *Italian Journeys* (1867), Howells was intent on avoiding sentimental or romantic responses to European culture. Unlike Twain, though, or his fellow-American realist, John de Forest, in his *European Acquaintance* (1858) and *Oriental Acquaintance* (1856) (who both responded to the conventional beauties of the Old World by describing them satirically), Howells chose to concentrate on the small domestic details of Italian life, writing about ordinary people in normal situations pursuing everyday pleasures, and he did so in the firm belief that 'whatever pleases is equal to any other thing there, no matter how low its origin'.

The same conviction inspired Howells's fiction, which aimed to illuminate as clearly as possible the conditions of existence in contemporary America, though to say this is not to deny that he also wrote from a firm and personal moral standpoint. Contemporary reviewers at the opposite extreme to Mencken and Lewis, who thought his work vulgar, unspiritual, and corrupting, were reacting to his objective manner and failed to perceive the moral scheme that always informs his plots. It has become a platitude of modern criticism to say of Howells that he had no perception of evil, and if by that term one means the quality shown by many characters in the fiction of Poe, Hawthorne, Melville, or Faulkner, the observation is just. Howells himself suggested when writing about Dostoevsky that spiritual extremism was an inappropriate, if not an impossible, response to the unruffled, smiling aspects of American life. Political events in the late 1880s, and particularly the execution of four randomly chosen anarchists involved in a violent incident in Chicago in 1886, led Howells to modify his views on man's propensity for evil, but even so he was always temperamentally incapable of creating such monsters of unconditioned wickedness as Melville's Claggart or Faulkner's Popeye.

What he does excel at, though, is showing how the real conditions of American capitalism erode the moral fabric of society and help to create such corrupt characters as Bartley Hubbard in *A Modern Instance* (1882), men whose professional and personal integrity are insidiously undermined by the nature of business and social life in the rapidly expanding American city. Lional Trilling calls Hubbard 'the quintessence of the average sensual man as the most sanguine of us have come to fear our culture breeds him',[11] and according to Edwin H. Cady, he is '*the* modern man, the "new man", a foregone failure'.[12]

Both critics rightly stress Hubbard's representative elements, for these are the qualities that are new in Howells's fiction of the 1880s, lifting the novel into the company of his two or three minor masterpieces and distinguishing it from his competent but unremarkable works of the 1870s such as *Their Wedding Journey* (1872), *A Chance Acquaintance* (1873), or *The Lady of the Aroostook* (1879).

Howells was well aware of the novel's significance for him at the time of writing. He had decided to give up his prestigious post as editor of the *Atlantic Monthly* in order to devote more energy to writing novels, and he cast around very carefully for a suitable subject that would do justice to his momentous decision. Like Henry James a couple of years later, who also wanted a socially significant theme for *The Bostonians* (1886), Howells was drawn to the position of women in American society, but being more committed to family life than James, the subject that appealed to him was divorce rather than the women's movement itself. By focusing on the break-up of Bartley and Marcia's marriage, he was able to describe the rich texture of modern life in depth and breadth. Unlike James who always bemoaned his inability to bring life to the material environment in which his characters move, Howells was never happier than when describing the essential trivia of existence, and he does so with a nice sense of the pressure which these things bring to bear on human life and of the way they can be used to indicate moral and spiritual positions. The Hallecks's house, its position and furnishings, are clear examples of the way Howells uses such description to place characters on a scale of values both moral and social:

> Rumford Street is one of those old-fashioned
> thoroughfares at the west end of Boston, which are now
> almost wholly abandoned to boarding-houses of the poorer
> class. Yet they are charming streets, quiet, clean and
> respectable, and worthy still to be the homes, as they once
> were, of solid citizens. The red brick houses, with their
> swell fronts, looking in perspective like a succession of
> round towers, are reached by broad granite steps, and
> their doors are deeply sunken within the wagon-roofs of
> white painted Roman arches. Over the door there is
> sometimes the bow of a fine transom, and the parlor
> windows on the first floor of the swell front have the
> same azure gleam as those of the beautiful old houses
> which front the common on Beacon Street. (19)

In such set pieces as this Howells can subtly suggest the family's old-fashioned fidelity to codes of behaviour that are fast disappearing among people of their class. Passages of this kind recur throughout the novel, illuminating a wide cross-section of minor characters. These range from the wealthy philanthropist, Clara Kingsbury, whose days 'were divided between the extremes of squalor and fashion', and her rigid lawyer, Eustace Atherton, the epitome of 'Proper Boston', to the cracker-barrel philosopher from the logging camp, Kinney, and a multitude of Maine villagers, doubtless imaginatively transported from Howells's remembered childhood in small Ohio towns. An unstrained realism guarantees the solidity of the created world and of the couple who stand at its centre, Bartley Hubbard and Marcia Gaylord.

Though Howells thought of the book as his 'Divorce Novel' and sometimes called it his 'new Medea', it could also claim to be a work about journalism. This was a profession he knew intimately and could write about with confidence. In addition, though, the slick, superficial aggressiveness of the New Journalism gave him the perfect tone with which to confront the old order and embody in his central character who finally brings about his own downfall by 'stealing' and refurbishing Kinney's article about life in the logging camp. This is the undramatic but climactic incident in a whole series of petty immoralities that serves to alienate Bartley from his wife, colleagues, and friends. It precipitates his flight westward to Indiana where he sues for divorce and is foiled by the last-minute intervention of Marcia's father, Squire Gaylord, who makes a final impassioned speech in his daughter's defence. This is a melodramatic episode that, to some extent, betrays the tenor of the novel, but Howells restores the realistic atmosphere in his account of Marcia's bleak existence with her dying father back in Equity, where she 'saw no one whom she was not forced to see'. Bartley's death in Whited Sepulchre, Arizona, where he has fled to indulge in a form of gutter journalism, comes ironically at the hands of someone whose domestic affairs have been exposed in the gossip sheet he writes. But the reported event cannot make any real difference to Marcia whose widowhood had actually begun long before this, her passionate heart finally shrivelled by the bitter experience of marriage. Ben Halleck, the crippled friend of Bartley's youth and now a Methodist minister, still pursues her, hoping somehow to atone for the secret love he felt for her during her marriage. But the end of the novel, true to its roots in Greek tragedy and to Howells's perception of the breakdown of secular society, holds out no hope of future happiness. The final images we are left with are those of uncertainty, disintegration, and futility. And even if we did not have the novel's title to confirm it, we are left in no doubt that the fate of Bartley and Marcia is a representative one. By refusing to create central characters of black, unmitigated wickedness, Howells increases their plausibility and typicality. The evils that he sees clearly enough are insidious, petty, and frighteningly real.

The temptations that undo Bartley also beset the hero of *The Rise of Silas Lapham* (1885), the novel widely regarded as Howells's masterpiece. Silas is a self-made businessman, a type that was to become more and more familiar in American realist and naturalist fiction in the next twenty years. Unlike the great majority of his successors, though, who are usually seen as corrupt, ruthless predators, Silas is a man of moral principle who resists the opportunity to enter into a shady deal which would save his flagging fortunes, and chooses instead the path of honourable bankruptcy. The 'rise' referred to in the novel's title is as much the moral one at the end of the story as it is the earlier economic and social one. Howells's critics have not always recognized the point, as he himself sadly indicates in his book *Literary Friends and Acquaintances* (1900), and the fault may not be entirely theirs. Howells's best writing certainly revolves around the comedy of manners involved in the awkward relationships between the *nouveau riche* Laphams and the aristocratic Bostonians, the Coreys. Tom, the son of this family, works in Lapham's paint factory and is in love with his daughter, Penelope. He is generally thought, however, to be pursuing the other daughter, Irene, and this comedy of errors provides the novel with its sub-plot which is resolved by the application of common sense. When the mistake is discovered, the lovers are dissuaded from renouncing each other in futile self-sacrifice by the utilitarian argument that it is better for one person, Irene, to suffer than for all three to lose their happiness. Howells uses this story to introduce a good deal of criticism aimed at the influence of romantic fiction, as well as to create the social comedy involved in the juxtaposition of older members of the families.

Silas is introduced through the device of an interview which Bartley Hubbard is conducting for his newspaper series 'Solid Men of Boston'. Like Faulkner, Howells constantly transfers characters from one novel to another, giving the knowledgeable reader added pleasure in the recognition of a familiar world. In this instance our awareness of Bartley's habitual contempt for provincial virtue helps to emphasize the rough character of Lapham as we learn, first in his own words then in Hubbard's interpretation of them, about his meteoric business career based on the discovery of a mineral paint substance on his father's Vermont farm. We also learn that there is something in Lapham's background that he does not want to discuss, but whether this is sufficient cause for Hubbard's cynical dismissal of him as 'one of nature's noblemen' is not revealed at this point.

Later, however, we discover that in order to finance his expansion, Lapham had taken on a partner, Rogers, only to get rid of him ruthlessly, if not dishonestly, when he had served his purpose. Lapham's behaviour is not unlike that of other great robber barons, both fictional and actual, and he attempts to rationalize it as sound business practice. His conscience, stirred from time to time by his wife Persis, is not easy, though, and the episode has an 'inextinguishable vitality' that continues to haunt him.

Eventually it is Rogers who fittingly offers Silas the opportunity to save himself by proposing the crooked land deal. Howells again shows how well he understands the subtle pressures that push a man into an inescapable web of compromising entanglements. But the scheme itself does not shock Lapham:

> It addressed itself in him to that easy-going, not evilly intentioned, potential unmorality which regards common property as common prey, and gives us the most corrupt municipal governments under the sun – which makes the poorest voter, when he has tricked into place, as unscrupulous in regard to others' money as an hereditary prince. (25)

There is an additional, external pressure exerted by Rogers himself, who paints a picture of his own and his family's destitution if Lapham does not go through with the plan. So that, when Silas finally does stand firm for right and justice, and brings financial destruction upon himself, his reward is 'to feel like a thief and a murderer'. He ends where he began, back on the farm in Vermont, unpretentious and shabby, but as Howells says, 'more the Colonel in these hills than he could ever have been on the Back Bay', where he had been building a fine mansion to symbolize his entry into the world of the Coreys.

The aristocratic Coreys represent the dominance of the aesthetic sensibility in late-nineteenth-century Boston society, and Howells, like Henry James, maintains a continuous debate on the subject of art and morality that runs throughout his fiction. This debate is brought to the forefront of the novel at the dinner party given for the Laphams by the Coreys. Even taken out of context, the episode constitutes a brilliant piece of sustained comic writing, ranging over such topics as architecture, fiction, philanthropy, and military heroism, each of which is dimly reflected through Lapham's progressively more drunken consciousness. Seen in relation to the larger stories of Irene's abortive romance and Lapham's moral struggles, though, the inadequacies of the Brahmin culture are given sharper focus, anticipating the direction taken by Howells's thought in the years following the traumatic experience of the Haymarket riot in 1886, and brought to its fullest expression in his next major novel, *A Hazard of New Fortunes* (1890).

It was in 1886, too, that Howells began reading Tolstoy in earnest. The impact of the great Russian's Christian socialism and Howells's own developing awareness of new and ugly forces in society, led him to reassess his social philosophy and with it his theory of fiction.

Without renouncing realism, he began to insist on its critical function in an art whose main purpose must be to 'make men know each other better, that they may be all humbled and strengthened by a sense of their fraternity'. He is quite clear about the need for art to teach those principles, and came to believe that an art which 'disdains the office of teacher is one of the last refuges of the aristocratic spirit'.[13] This spiritual crisis is the immediate background to the economic novels which he began writing at this time, among them *Annie Kilburn* (1888) and *The World of Chance* (1893), and also to his decision to forsake the cosy environment of Boston for the more turbulent world of New York.

Howells actually uses this momentous migration autobiographically at the beginning of *A Hazard of New Fortunes*. Basil March, another of his favourite recurring characters, is persuaded to give up his comfortable profession in Boston in order to become editor of a new magazine, *Every Other Week*. As in his earlier novel, *Their Wedding Journal*, Basil and Isabel March are used as observers and commentators, and their extended house-hunting in New York which takes up nearly a fifth of the whole book, helps to delineate the larger and less homogeneous environment commensurate with the novel's more ambitious scope.

Centring upon the publication of the magazine, Howells creates a broad spectrum of characters to reflect a wide variety of political and economic views. More than any of his previous works, this is a novel of ideas, and the conflicts brought about by their juxtapositions and confrontations are presented with an urgency and dedication new to him. Similarly, the climactic scene of the novel which describes a riot during a transport strike and culminates in the violent deaths of two of the central characters, is far removed from the minor domestic disorders found in his earlier works. The events Howells describes, based as always on his own meticulous observation, confirm his privately expressed fears that the direction taken by industrial society was wrong and that the fabric of civilized life was becoming dangerously threadbare.

The two victims of violence are, appropriately, two idealists: Conrad Dryfus, the Tolstoyan son of an egotistical capitalist, and' Lindau, an old German socialist. Their deaths were the only plausible outcome Howells could envisage, given the current state of contemporary society. In their portrayal Howells suggests certain Old and New Testament parallels which point to the possibility of spirituality redeeming the world of the Social Darwinians whose only gospel was the Gospel of Wealth. To have pursued this theme more energetically, though, would have taken Howells into unfamiliar and even irrelevant areas, given his preference for social and economic themes. Instead, he opted for the popular alternative of writing Utopian novels, and his two Altrurian romances, which constitute an important contribution to the genre, will be discussed in chapter 5.

By the end of the century Howells had exhausted his major themes and had seen the triumph of realism taken to extreme limits by his younger protégés. Though he continued to produce novels until 1920 with indomitable professionalism, for the most part they are largely devoid of literary or political inspiration, being mainly elaborations of the romantic sub-plots of his earlier fiction.

Crane

One of the most gifted of Howells's younger contemporaries, whose brief career began much later than his and ended much earlier, was Stephen Crane. Though he died at the age of only twenty-eight in 1900, Crane's achievements in fiction and the long reach of his influence since are such that it is awesome to speculate on his possible career had he lived a fuller life into the twentieth century. As it is, one might note that at the same age – twenty-eight – Crane's great contemporary Joseph Conrad, had not even begun to write fiction, and that his compatriot, Henry James – one of the most prolific of novelists – had published a mere handful of mediocre stories that would surely have been forgotten by now had they not been followed by so much distinguished work.

Crane, befriended by Howells and inspired by Hamlin Garland, not unnaturally described himself as a realist. The novel that brought him to their critical attention, *Maggie: A Girl of the Streets* (1893), owes much to Howells's suggestion that the Bowery offered a promising fictional field to a young writer, and also to Garland's praise of *A Hazard of New Fortunes* as the greatest study of a city in fiction. Yet Crane's own description of his aim to come closer to nature and truth in his work provides no indication at all of the form his realism actually took. For Crane, truth is habitually reflected obliquely in the angles of his ironic vision, and nature is presented in a style that is selectively impressionistic. When contrasted with the painstaking delineation of surface detail in the fiction of his fellow realists, Crane's art only serves to prove the inadequacy of the term 'realism' as a decription of a manner, or even a mode of perception. The most he shares with Howells and Dreiser is a preference for urban subjects, and even this only accounts for a fraction of his writing. He also thought of himself as a naturalist and claimed that *Maggie* aims to show that environment is a 'tremendous thing' in the world and 'frequently shapes lives regardless'. But Crane's notion of 'environment' was so much more fluid and subtle than Dreiser's, and his description of its shaping effects so less mechanical, that the differences between the two authors are more apparent than the similarities. Maggie herself, for example, seems somehow to have escaped the effects of the filth and poverty of the New York slums in which she grows up. Her parents, brothers, and neighbours are vividly presented as subhuman denizens of a foul-smelling and dangerous urban jungle who are constantly warring with each other for survival, while she, we are told, 'blossomed in a mud puddle'. Maggie's frail prettiness and purity, preserved amid the squalor and vice of crowded tenements, puzzles not only the neighbourhood 'philosophers' but also many literary critics who see it as a flaw in the novel's design. For Crane, though, the pressures of the material environment must be balanced against the more subtle though equally powerful effects of a society's manipulative value-system and its coded beliefs. Maggie and, to a lesser extent, those around her, are shown as victims of an ideology which is utterly inappropriate to the real nature of their existence, and it is this yawning gap between appearance and reality that both accounts for the work's multiple ironies and causes Maggie's tragic self-destruction.

The opening sentence of the story points out this discrepancy:

> A very little boy stood upon a heap of gravel for the honor of
> Rum Alley. (1)

Throughout the novel Crane insistently contrasts notions of chivalry and descriptions of barbaric behaviour or, in the case of Maggie's mother, those of middle-class morality and respectability with her brutal and animalistic behaviour towards her family. The same dichotomies characterize the entire urban society and are embodied, for example, in the inability or unwillingness of the Church to relate its Christian teachings to the real lives and needs of those around it.

In Maggie's own case these idealistic concepts are reinforced by the propaganda of popular culture. She is conditioned by sentimental ballads and plays to believe in the fulfilment of romantic and domestic love, just as the unmistakably evil people who watch these plays are led to hiss at vice and applaud virtue. For all of them the pictured drama becomes 'transcendental reality', only serving to set in stark contrast their very different and inescapable destinies. For Maggie this means prostitution. Having forfeited the respectability of her home life and her job when she takes up with Pete, a flashy, small-time womanizer of the Bowery, she has no alternative from the inevitable moment when he deserts her. From then on she is no longer able to maintain even the tenuous threads that have linked her dreams to her life, and she begins the slow drift down through the lower depths of her world to inevitable suicide.

Rather than document Maggie's decline in detail, however, as some of his fellow naturalists would have done, Crane compresses this period of her life into a single brief chapter in which she traverses the various social strata of her professional territory, moving down from the rich young man protected by evening dress and ennui through the ranks of the cheerfully uncaring middle classes, to the ultimate spectre of 'a ragged being with shifting, bloodshot eyes and grimy hands'. Beyond these human encounters she comes face to face with the hostility of the very buildings:

> She went into the blackness of the final block. The
> shutters of the tall buildings were closed like grim lips.
> The structures seemed to have eyes that looked over them,
> beyond them, at other things. Afar off the lights of the
> avenues glittered as if from an impossible distance. Street-
> car bells jingled with a sound of merriment.
>
> At the feet of the tall buildings appeared the deathly
> black hue of the river. Some hidden factory sent up a
> yellow glare, that lit for a moment the waters lapping
> oilily against timbers. The varied sounds of life, made
> joyous by distance and seeming unapproachableness, came
> faintly and died away to a silence. (27)

But Crane will not allow this silence to bring his novel to an end. Had he done so, emphasis would have remained on Maggie's tragic fate, and the reader's abiding emotion would have been one of pity. Instead, he offers a coda of social satire in which he first shows Pete deserted by the woman for whom he left Maggie. She takes his money and, brushing aside his incoherent adorations, contemptuously leaves him in a drunken stupor. Finally, Maggie's death is announced to her mother who racks herself into spasms of sentimental grief – after first finishing her meal – then, true to an unshakeable belief in her own virtue, offers her dead child a mother's forgiveness. The picture of this gross and maudlin figure who is obsessed with the grotesque idea of forcing Maggie's baby boots on to the dead whore's feet, brilliantly recapitulates both the theme of the novel and its bitter, sardonic tone.

Crane's ironies are etched so deeply in his fiction that it would seem difficult for any reader to miss them, but this has certainly been the case with his masterpiece *The Red Badge of Courage* (1895). A great many critics have interpreted Crane's Civil War novel as though its

values were exactly those of its confused, misguided hero, Henry
Fleming, thus redefining it as one of those classic rites of initiation
which, as Harry Levin points out, often use war as the subject of a
realist text to show man confronted and sometimes subjugated – even
reified – by matter.[14] In this case, of course, the hero, in his own mind,
finally triumphs over the mechanistic forces that threaten his individuality, and asserts his maturity by the strength of his conscience and
will. He triumphs over the sickness of battle that has come close to
robbing him of his humanity, and so can wear with pride his famous
red badge of courage. Nature herself confirms his victory by beaming
out a ray of golden sunshine through the leaden rain-clouds. Such a
reading of the novel, however, seems determinedly perverse. It contra-
dicts not only the pattern of action so carefully established in the story
but also the book's entire texture and tone.

Throughout his life, Henry Fleming has nurtured his imagination
on dreams of epic battle, and though the Civil War does not appear
to possess any distinctly Homeric qualities, he enlists in the Union
Army in the hope that he will discover something of glory there. To
his dismay, his mother does not share his dream of returning home
in triumph, either with a shield or on one, and can only talk of keeping
himself out of trouble and making sure that he has clean socks to wear.

Before Henry can put himself to the actual test, though, he is faced
with a long period of inactivity during which he listens to a variety
of rumours and the conflicting opinions of his regimental companions
on the nature of warfare and the effect it has upon particular men. He
is tortured by doubts about himself, and decides they can only be
resolved by the actual experience of 'blood, blaze and danger'. In the
event, his actions and reactions during the first battle produce a variety
of conflicting rationalizations for his instinctive or unconditioned
behaviour. Whether he remains in the firing line, trapped by the
inability to move, or flees in terror like a rabbit when the opportunity
comes, he finds it easy to produce specious justifications for what he
does. In rapid sequence he congratulates himself on his unyielding
courage and then on his superior strategic wisdom when he runs. He
convinces himself that he is an organic part of nature, or that nature,
at least, extends sympathy towards him:

> This landscape gave him assurance. A fair field holding
> life. It was the religion of peace. It would die if its timid
> eyes were compelled to see blood. He conceived Nature to
> be a woman with a deep aversion to tragedy. (7)

This assurance, like all his others, is immediately undercut when he
enters a chapel-like clearing in the forest. Seeking solace in the ecclesi-

astical half-light under the trees, he is confronted by a hideous spectacle:

> He was being looked at by a dead man, who was seated
> with his back against a column-like tree. The corpse was
> dressed in a uniform that once had been blue, but was
> now faded to a melancholy shade of green. The eyes,
> staring at the youth, had changed to a dull hue to be seen
> on the side of a dead fish. The mouth was open. Its red
> had changed to an appalling yellow. Over the gray skin of
> the face ran little ants. One was trundling some sort of
> bundle along the upper lip. (7)

Here, as elsewhere in his work, Crane shows profoundly ironic contempt for romantic applications of the pathetic fallacy, and for those who delude themselves that nature reinforces their arguments with 'proofs that lived where the sun shone'. Characters throughout Crane's fiction are prey to this kind of specious complacency and are invariably subjected to ironic mockery. Failure to recognize this fact has led to innumerable misinterpretations of *The Red Badge of Courage*, the most notorious of which purports to discover in the image of the sun pasted 'like a wafer' in the sky, a clue to the religious significance of the entire novel. Such a view is so much at odds with Crane's temper that it hardly seems worth considering, and in any case, it has been thoroughly discredited by a number of other critics.[15]

Nature remains obstinately aloof from and indifferent to man in Crane's work. One only has to read his short story 'The Open Boat' to discover that truth. The 'inevitable' sun, as Crane describes it, shines down on our triumphs and failures alike, and it is manifestly futile to attribute to it our own philosophical predilections.

This is, of course, exactly what Crane's hero does after his last battle. This time he has not run away, and though still occasionally conscience-stricken by his behaviour during his absence from the regiment, he has little difficulty first in manufacturing excuses for himself, then in discovering a spiritual lesson to bolster his self-esteem:

> He was emerged from his struggles with a large sympathy
> for the machinery of the universe. With his new eyes, he
> could see that the secret and open blows which were being
> dealt about the world with such heavenly lavishness were
> in truth blessings. It was a deity laying about him with
> the bludgeon of correction.
> His loud mouth against these things had been lost as
> the storm ceased. He could no more stand upon places

high and false, and denounce the distant planets. He
beheld that he was tiny but not inconsequent to the sun.
In the spacewide whirl of events no grain like him would
be lost. (24)

This last quotation is taken from the text of the novel edited by John
T. Winterich, which includes manuscript material not included in the
first edition.[16] The additional passages in the final chapter make Crane's
ironic intent much clearer, it is true, consisting as they do largely of
sardonic commentary and Henry Fleming's final interior monologues.
The very existence of these two texts, emphasizing different aspects
of Fleming's character, lends weight to John Berryman's view of Crane
as being 'simultaneously at war with the people he creates and on their
side'.[17] According to Berryman, Crane continually vacillates between
two views of his character. In the first, he shows the *Alazon* (impostor)
after vaunting and posturing, being routed by the *Eiron* who affects
to be a fool. In the second, he comes closer to the form of Greek
tragedy in which the characters, swollen with Hubris are seen as
victims of Heaven's jealousy. The existence of this duality in *Maggie*
and *The Red Badge of Courage* helps to account, not only for the variety
of interpretations they have provoked, but also for the complexity they
share with stories such as 'The Open Boat' (1898) and 'The Blue
Hotel', and the better parts of novels such as *George's Mother* (1896)
and *The Monster* (1897).

Stephen Crane also produced work – notably his poems – in which
his complexity of ironic attitude is sometimes compressed into a
teasing obscurity that defies interpretation. Nevertheless, he wrote
enough 'pills' as he called them to make up the most important body
of poetic work in the 1890s. He also wrote potboilers when in need
of cash, among them *The Third Violet* (1897) and the unfinished
O'Ruddy (1903), written when he was dying in his rented medieval hall
in Sussex – that should not be held against him. That he created the
masterpieces we do possess is an astonishing achievement.

Norris

Frank Norris's life occupied almost exactly the same short span as
Stephen Crane's. Like Crane, he learned his craft as a journalist,
though he sought to perfect his art by studying creative writing at

Harvard. Also like Crane, he reported the Spanish-American War in Cuba. Indeed, the two young prodigies of American literature actually met in the Caribbean in 1899, but failed to strike up any kind of friendship and their acquaintance was not renewed. Despite the regularity with which their names are linked in histories of American naturalism, they were temperamentally, socially, and philosophically poles apart, and their fiction mirrors those differences rather than any similarities.

Their fiction also reflects their geographical separation. Norris's California was, in some respects, as remote from New York as both were from the rural heartland of America that separated them. Norris is primarily a Westerner in outlook and style, and when he does forsake his own region in *The Pit* (1903), it is because the subject of that novel, finance capitalism, requires a different setting from the one in which he is most at home. Not surprisingly, then, *The Pit* lacks the energy and force that make his three other main works, *Vandover and the Brute* (1914) *McTeague* (1899), and *The Octopus* (1901), so remarkable.

Vandover, mainly written while Norris was at Harvard in 1894, was not actually published until 1914, after the manuscript, believed lost in the great San Francisco fire of 1906, had been completed by his brother, Charles. The additions only amount to about five thousand words, and according to Warren French, are probably confined to the beginning.[18] *Vandover* belongs to the same period as *McTeague*, and has gradually come to be recognized as one of Norris's major works, though few critics would go so far as Maxwell Geismar who thinks it his 'key' novel.[19] In its youthful crudity, it exposes very clearly the roots of Norris's ambivalence about current theories of social and biological evolution, as well as showing the overwhelming influence of Zola's work, especially *La Bête Humaine* and *L'Assommoir*. Its melodramatic plot traces the decline and fall of a young San Francisco dandy whose brutal, amoral instincts gradually overwhelm both his social training and his aesthetic sensibility. After seducing one of the numerous 'fast' but virtuous girls who populate the city's pleasure spots, Vandover finds his life beginning to disintegrate. The girl commits suicide, Vandover is socially ostracized, and after his father's death, plunges into a life of debauchery, poverty, and indifference, marked by the onset of lycanthropy, a disease which periodically transforms him physically into the animal which he morally resembles. The ironies of Vandover's life are underlined by constant reference to the careers of his boyhood friends, Charlie Geary and Dolliver Haight. Geary's philosophy of the survival of the fittest, together with his amoral business dealings, eventually lead to a situation where, as a slum landlord, he employs Vandover to clean out his filthy cottages. Haight, on the other hand, is a sensitive young man who believes in the purity of women and the superiority of old-fashioned virtues. His life is ruined when he innocently contracts venereal disease from a prostitute's playful kiss on his cut lip.

These examples of determinism, fate, and chance, create a pseudo-philosophical scheme that makes for a naively contrived plot. What redeems the novel, though, is its texture. Norris shows an unerring mastery of physical and psychological detail which he deploys with great vivacity to produce an unforgettable picture of San Francisco in its heyday. Saloons, oyster bars, hotels with their various categories of private rooms, the meals consumed in these colourful places, and the people who eat them before seeking other pleasures, the parties and dances, the rituals of courtship, and the more dubious pursuits of young bachelors out on the town – all are evoked with unusual power to create a dense medium for his melodrama. Here, for example, he is describing Vandover and Ida's moment of weakness in the Imperial Hotel:

> They did not hurry over their little supper, but ate and drank slowly, and had more oysters to go with the last half of their bottle. Ida's face was ablaze, her eyes flashing, her blond hair disordered and falling about her cheeks.
> Vandover put his arm about her neck, and drew her toward him, and as she sank down upon him, smiling and complaisant, her hair tumbling upon her shoulders and her head and throat bent back, he leaned his cheek against hers, speaking in a low voice.
> 'No-no,' she murmured, smiling: 'never – ah, if I hadn't come – no, Van – please –' And then with a long breath she abandoned herself. (5)

For Norris, realism was a term reserved for the depiction of small, everyday detail – 'the things that are likely to happen between lunch and supper'. The seduction of Ida, on the other hand, belongs to his romanticism – 'the unplumbed depths of the human heart, and the mystery of sex, and the problems of life, and the black, unsearched penetralia of the soul of man'. This defence of the romantic in fiction, which probably derived as much from his admiration of Richard Harding Davis as of Zola, was composed after the event and published posthumously with his other essays and articles in *The Responsibilities of the Novelist*. Though V. L. Parrington called the collection 'the textbook of the young naturalist',[20] Norris's criticism is not only full of inconsistences and contradictions, but is also, as Donald Pizer has demonstrated, deeply anti-intellectual and primitivistic.[21] If any coherent critical position can be derived from his essays, it has less to do with mechanism versus organism or realism versus romanticism, than with a sustained attack on the aesthetic decadence of Wilde and Pater and a plea for what Norris called 'manliness' in literature. His championship of life over mere literature also led him to despise the 'tea cup tragedies' of the older realists, and to plead for fiction that takes characters away from the mundane and flings them 'into the throes of a vast and terrible drama that works itself out in unleashed passions, in blood, and in sudden death'.

McTeague (1899) certainly fulfils these requirements. The passions that Norris unleashes in his Polk Street dentist lead inevitably to murder by way of lust, greed, and the most startlingly sadistic rape fantasies. With the creation of McTeague, Norris took American fiction into an entirely new dimension. The lower-middle-class world of San Francisco still provides a medium and ballast for the melodrama, and for many readers the picture of merchants and tradesmen at work and play is the best part of the novel. But all Norris's conscious power went into his story of the fatal events in which McTeague and his wife Trina are enmeshed. There is a remorseless inevitability in the way the two exacerbate each other's obsession: Trina, utterly lost to human satisfaction, can in the end only be moved by the ecstatic sensuality of stripping naked then embracing her precious hoard of gold; McTeague, in pursuit of the same treasure, works himself into a frenzy of hatred for his wife, in trying to control his fury by beating his mattress as he lies prostrate on it in torment. There is only one outcome imaginable, though the sequel to the murder of Trina – McTeague desperately fleeing into the California desert with the worthless money and the equally useless symbolic canary in its gilded cage – provides a surreal and unexpected conclusion.

If Norris's career had ended at this point, or even after the publication of his next three works, the semi-autobiographical romance *Blix* (1899) and his two adventure novels, *Moran of the Lady Letty* (1898) and *A Man's Woman* (1900), there would be some justification for those who see him merely as a disciple of Kipling or a precursor of Jack London. His preoccupation with the type of Nietzschean superman figure results in characters not unlike those found in *The Sea Wolf* (1904), while his confused applications of popular Darwinism also recall London. Moreover, the two authors shared a belief in white racial superiority that most modern readers find unpalatable, though if one reads more widely in the popular literature of the period – Southern novels like *His Red Rock* (1898) by Thomas Nelson Page, for example, *The Clansman* (1905) by Thomas Dixon, or even *The Battle-Ground* (1902) by Ellen Glasgow – it becomes apparent that such attitudes were so widespread as to be taken for granted.

Norris was too ambitious, though, to continue with such potboilers. His ambition was to create an epic novel of America, and as the subject of his projected trilogy he chose 'wheat': its cultivation, sale, distribution, and consumption. The final part, *The Wolf*, which would have had a European setting, was never written, since Norris died of appendicitis in 1902 shortly after completing the second volume, *The Pit*. In any event, he came closest to fulfilling his ambition in the first book of the three, *The Octopus*. Though it suffers from the same kind of muddled logic as his other work, it captures better than any novel both the essence and the feel of the closing period of American westward expansion. Norris based his story on an event that had taken place in 1880, the notorious Mussel Slough affair in which six members of the Settlers' League, ranchers in the San Joaquin Valley, were killed by hired gunmen of the South Pacific Railroad in a dispute over the sale of land. The novel has all the elements of a classic muck-raking work, and, indeed, at the time, Norris was associated with the magazine *McClure's* which was to become famous for its articles by such writers as Ida Tarbell and Lincoln Steffens attacking the monopolistic trusts and corporations. He even wrote to a member of his publisher's editorial department who had urged caution on him retorting that he was firmly 'enlisted upon the other side' from the railroad trust. Norris's subsequent interview with the president of the railroad, incorporated into the novel as an interview between his poet-narrator Presley, the fictional counterpart, and Shelgrim, may have modified his views about the innocence of the settlers and changed the planned direction of the novel, but the philosophical contradictions in *The Octopus* go much deeper. In broad terms, the main story seems designed to show the insignificance of individual men in relation to larger 'forces' whether natural like wheat or industrial like railroads:

Men, Lilliputians, gnats in the sunshine, buzzed
impudently in their tiny battles, were born, lived through
their little day, died, and were forgotten; while the Wheat,
wrapped in Nirvanic calm, grew steadily under the night,
alone with the stars and with God.
   Men were naught, death was naught, FORCE only
existed – FORCE that brought men into the world,
FORCE that crowded them out of it to make way for the
succeeding generation, FORCE that made the wheat grow,
FORCE that garnered it from the soil to give place to the
succeeding crop (2: 9)

At the same time, individual stories, especially that about his chief character Magnus Derrick, imply a belief in the efficacy of moral choice. Derrick who is a lifelong upholder of principle, succumbs to the prevailing corrupt practices of his friends and enemies, and so brings about his own destruction. Similarly, the evil railroad agent, S. Behrman, becomes the victim of poetic justice when he suffocates in the wheat-filled hold of a ship bound for Calcutta. Norris, it seems, was not prepared to forsake sensational irony in the interests of consistency. The most curious strand in the novel, though, is the sub-plot dealing with the life of a mystical shepherd, Vanamee, a Thoreau-like figure living close to nature and shunning society. Vanamee's great love, Angele, had been raped years before and died in childbirth. Now she is restored to him in the guise of her identical daughter, and it is Vanamee the transcendental romantic who sees the connection between man and wheat, and who is allowed to pronounce the final truth that all things inevitably and surely work together for good. It is an embarrassingly sentimental intrusion into what is otherwise a powerful, if flawed, epic.

The Pit is also flawed in its structure, for it sacrifices the logic of its story to a sentimental ending in which Jadwin, the wheat specu-lator, loses his fortune in the wheat pit at the Chicago Board of Trade, and is thereby restored to his errant wife, Laura. Like that of Silas Lapham, Jadwin's fall helps to restore his humanity, but despite this obvious contrivance, The Pit is, as Larzer Ziff claims, the first profound American business novel in that it does more than merely transpose traditional moral problems into the field of commerce.[22] In addition, it examines the psychic consequences of the commercializ-ation of American life. Ziff is surely right to emphasize the social and sexual corollaries of industrialization in the novel, but The Pit is also profound in its perception of an important change that was taking place in American capitalism itself. The old-style, swashbuckling moguls like Jadwin were coming into contact with a new breed of speculator typified by the cold, ruthless financier, Crookes, men whose only interest lay in figures and statistics and whose inhumanity was sure to replace the all-too-human Napoleonic qualities of the independent businessman. Norris captured American business at a significant moment during its shift from one phase to another, which also gives the novel an importance which surpasses its purely aesthetic qualities. If, as Richard Hofstadter claims in his book on Social Darwinism in American Thought, this period of American history was like a vast human caricature of the Darwinian theory of evolution, it is novelists like Norris, and from rather different perspectives in the same city, Henry B. Fuller in The Cliff-Dwellers (1892) and Upton Sinclair in The Jungle (1906), who have enabled us to see that era's developments, conflicts, and mutations more clearly.

Dreiser

Howells, Crane and Norris, for all their considerable literary skills, do not in retrospect relate as clearly as Theodore Dreiser to twentieth-century American literature. Though they guided the novel towards new subjects and made possible a radically new form for it, they, like the cities they wrote about – Boston, New York and San Francisco – were never completely emancipated from European forms and influences. Chicago, on the other hand, was coming to be seen in the 1890s not just as the capital of the Midwest but as the quintessential American city, and Dreiser along with other Midwestern novelists was determined to be its laureate.

Chicago had forced itself upon America's attention during the Columbian Exposition of 1893. To many visitors at the time and to various observers later, the spectacle of the White City in Chicago was the culmination and embodiment of all that America had been and might become, from the celestial city upon a hill to the New Jerusalem. For others, the debates between James Burnham and Louis Sullivan about architecture really masked a struggle between the conflicting forces of business élitism and populism. Turner's famous 'Frontier thesis', first propounded at the fair to members of the American Historical Association, signalled, for many, the end of America's rural past and the official inauguration of its urban future. And yet others thought that the central issues embodied in the exhibition were the principles of Pragmatism, expounded by William James versus those of Idealism and the Genteel Tradition.

James's chief disciple, John Dewey, preferred to call himself an Instrumentalist rather than a Pragmatist. His thought, like Dreiser's fiction, seems to have a particular geographical relevance to Chicago and its central position in the developing nation. What Lewis Mumford says of Dewey can equally well be applied to Dreiser:

> No one has plumbed the bottom of Mr. Dewey's
> philosophy who does not feel in back of it the
> shapelessness, the faith in the current go of things, and the
> general utilitarian idealism of Chicago – the spirit which
> produced the best of the early skyscrapers, the Chicago
> exposition, Burnham's grandiose city plans, the great park
> and playground system, the clotted disorder of
> interminable slums.[23]

Mumford is misleading, though, in suggesting that in both writers 'lack of style is a lack of organic connection'. Reading Dewey may be 'as depressing as a subway ride', just as Dreiser's pages sometimes resemble 'a dumpheap', but these are just the expressive connections between their thoughts and sentences in which we see captured their acceptance of the way things are. In Dreiser especially, a steady, flat, empirical gaze gathers all the various objects of attention into an undifferentiated and democratic flow – a slow, shifting movement of life in which individuals struggle to realize their desires but very seldom succeed in imposing their wills. It is precisely in his style that Dreiser manifests the profound changes that were taking effect in American life around the turn of the century.

Dreiser was not Chicago-born, but like thousands of others, had been drawn there from the vast surrounding land of middle America – in his case, small-town Indiana where he had grown up in an impoverished Roman Catholic family. His own feelings about his initial encounter with the great city can be found in the opening chapters of *Sister Carrie* (1900), though his heroine was ostensibly based on one of his sisters, Emma. He also recalled 'the throb and urge and sting' of his first days in Chicago in his autobiography *Dawn* (1931), when as he says, the spirit of the city flowed into him and made him ecstatic. That was in 1887, and in the years between his arrival and the writing of his first novel he had plenty of time and opportunity to modify those feelings. Working at numerous jobs in a variety of cities, he gradually became familiar with other, darker sides of American urban reality. What he experienced there convinced him that those who had not shared his experiences and vision but had remained loyal to the farm and all it stood for, were at best nostalgic lotus-eaters, suspended in dreams or lost in impossible romances. There is plenty of evidence to support Dreiser's view in the writings of his contemporaries from Indiana. Two immensely popular novels bracket *Sister Carrie* at the turn of the century: Charles Major's *When Knighthood was in Flower* (1898) and Gene Stratton-Porter's *Freckles* (1904). Their accounts of adventures in Tudor England or even in the Limberlost swamps, allowed readers to ignore the social and psychological realities of urban life and to substitute for them the colour of remote or impossible worlds. In the context of such books, it is easy to see why Dreiser's novel caused such a furore in the publishing house of Doubleday, Page and Company.

The story of the novel's publication has become part of American cultural mythology as it concerns the war between the puritanical philistines and the bohemian artists. Both H. L. Mencken in *A Book of Prefaces* (1917) and Frank Harris in his *Contemporary Portraits* (1919) used the story to illustrate this theme, and even though later accounts distort actual events in order to produce more clear-cut heroes and villains, the episode does have its representative characteristics and, at the very least, demonstrates the sharp divisions in taste and morality at the time. *Sister Carrie* had already been rejected by Harpers when Frank Norris, who was employed as a reader by Doubleday, Page and Company, enthusiastically recommended it to his employers as 'a true book in all senses of the word'. Page, in his partner's absence supported this view, but was subsequently persuaded to change his mind by Doubleday himself who was horrified by what he read. Page then attempted to extricate the firm from its obligation on the grounds that Dreiser's characters would not interest the majority of readers. But, supported by Norris, Dreiser insisted on publication. A thousand copies of the novel were printed, and despite the publisher's unwillingness to help in its distribution, a few hundred copies were sold. But it was not until Dreiser issued the book himself when he became part owner of a publishing house in 1907, that the novel began to sell in any quantity. Even then its success was limited compared with the sales of Mrs Porter's sentimental romances, said to stand at eight million during her lifetime.

But the troubled history of the novel's publication did not end there. In order to get it published at all, Dreiser had allowed a variety of friends, relatives, and professional editors to edit his original manuscript for him. In addition to tidying his uncertain grammar and removing instances of coarser language, his friend Arthur Harry and his wife, Jug, also took it upon themselves to rearrange several incidents and remove about thirty thousand words. It was not until 1981 that a text was finally produced corresponding to Dreiser's original version. As Alfred Kazin says, the restored text is not necessarily a better novel, but it is certainly a different one, less reticent about the sexuality of its characters and less cruel in its presentation of their lives.[24] Given that Dreiser always believed that beneath all other desires, whether for wealth, preferment, or distinction, there lay a deep craving for sensory gratification – 'lust moves the seeker in every field of effort' – the restoration of the expurgated passages helps to establish more clearly the forces at work in the lives of Carrie, Drouet, and Hurstwood. The strengthening of these unconscious motivations also sharpens the dialectical play between the striving of the various individuals and the 'vagaries of fortune' which determine the wider structure of the novel. Carrie's undeviating, automatic pursuit of the better life and her lack of interest in or comprehension of any broader significance in the world about her, is apparent from the moment she arrives in Chicago. Here she is looking for a job:

> Through the open windows she could see the figures of
> men and women in working aprons, moving busily about.
> The great streets were wall-lined mysteries to her. The

> vast offices, strange mazes which concerned far-off
> individuals of importance. She could only think of people
> connected with them as counting money, dressing
> magnificently and riding in carriages. What they dealt in,
> how they labored, to what end it all came, she had only
> the vaguest conception. That it could concern her, other
> than regards some little nook in which she might daily
> labor, never crossed her mind. Each concern in each
> building must be fabulously rich. These men in dressy
> suits such as Drouet wore must be powerful and
> fashionable – the men the newspapers talked about. It was
> all wonderful, all vast, all far removed. (2)

Appropriately, Dreiser keeps Drouet in the back of both Carrie's and
the reader's mind, even at this stage in her career when she is hoping
to succeed by her own efforts. Once she sees the futility of menial
work and the meanness of the life endured by people like her sister
who remain trapped in it, she allows herself to be taken up and kept
by the flashy womanizer she first met on the train to Chicago. Drouet,
like Carrie, is caught up by the city's hypnotic influences which play
upon his deepest desires. 'He could not help what he was going to do.
He could not see clearly enough to wish to do differently.' Though
Drouet himself might occasionally feel twinges of conscience about his
behaviour, Dreiser would no more think of judging him than he would
any other predatory animal. Carrie's eventual desertion of him in
favour of her more sophisticated lover, Hurstwood, is also recorded
as a simple, natural, and instinctive act.

With the appearance of Hurstwood, the novel finds its determining
form – the contrasting and unwilled destinies of the helpless couple.
Carrie's successful career that takes her to success on Broadway is as
inexplicable as Hurstwood's slow decline to poverty and suicide a few
blocks away. The precipitating event, one which cost Dreiser a great
deal of thought and labour, shows how radically different is his view
of the human condition from that of all his predecessors, either American or European.

Hurstwood, unhappily married to an ambitious woman who wants
to divorce him, and beset by emotional and financial problems, has the
opportunity to steal ten thousand dollars from the safe of the tavern
he manages. The money would ensure him a comfortable future with
Carrie, but the fear of discovery and prosecution holds him back, as
he crouches by the safe with the money in his hand:

> The wavering of a mind under such circumstances is an
> almost inexplicable thing and yet it is absolutely true.

Hurstwood could not bring himself to act definitely. He
wanted to think about it – to ponder it over, to decide
whether it were best. He was drawn by such a keen desire
for Carrie, driven by such a state of turmoil in his own
affairs, that he thought constantly that it would be best,
and yet he wavered. He did not know what evil might
result from it to him – how soon he might come to grief.
The true ethics of the situation never once occurred to
him. It is most certain that they never would have under
any circumstances. (29)

Dreiser's emphasis on the truth of Hurstwood's psychology,
however redundant it seems, can be better appreciated in the light of
his own experience. As a young man he was accused of stealing
twenty-five dollars from his Chicago employers and was dismissed.
A quarter of a century later he is still preoccupied with the entanglements of accident and will, and sets up an identical situation for the
'murder' of Roberta by Clyde Griffiths in *An American Tragedy* (1925).

In spite of Dreiser's awkward attempts to protect his central characters' instinctive desires from censure in this way, it is significant, as
Maxwell Geismar has pointed out, that such men are usually the
victims of excessive punishment for their attempts to defy convention.
Their fate, Geismar argues, reflects 'civilisation's deep reservoir of
guilt, where indeed we were all caught, tried and convicted for the sins
which we, like the hero, had planned and barely not committed'.[25] The
trap that Clyde Griffiths falls into is much more complicated, however,
both psychologically and sociologically, than anything devised for the
characters in *Sister Carrie* or *Jennie Gerhardt* (1911). Jennie, like Carrie
Meeber, is a 'sinful innocent' caught up in the lives of men who themselves are torn between society's moral codes and their own materialistic desires. A similar philosophy lies behind the creation of
Cowperwood, the hero of Dreiser's 'Trilogy of Desire', *The Financier*
(1912), *The Titan* (1914) and *The Stoic* (1947). In these novels, though,
the earlier formula of 'a waif amid forces' is reversed to show a Nietzschean superman – based on the financier Charles T. Yerkes –
attempting to subjugate society to his will, and women to the demands
of his sexual appetite. More significant than this reversal itself is the
way it leads Dreiser to regard the social medium in which Cowperwood's career unfolds, or at least, the way Cowperwood's consciousness constructs that medium. Both *The Financier* and *The Titan* make
much greater use of imagery drawn from Darwinian biology than the
earlier novels do. The story of Cowperwood's rise and temporary fall
in the Philadelphia jungle of finance capitalism begins and ends with
evolutionary parables. As a boy he learns his most important lesson

by watching the way in which a lobster slowly and cunningly tears a squid apart piece by tiny piece; and at the end of the book, after his term in prison, when he decides to change his field of activity to Chicago, Dreiser gives us the story of the black grouper whose great quality is its ability to change its colour according to its environment – a perfect example of nature's subtlety and chicanery.[26] In *The Titan* Cowperwood's second wife, stung by his cold-hearted infidelities, rails at him: 'What a liar you are, Frank! How really shifty you are! I don't wonder you are a multimillionaire – If you could live long enough you would eat up the whole world.' (57)

At this point in his career Cowperwood resembles Henry James's financier Abel Gaw of *The Ivory Tower*, a novel left unfinished when James died in 1916. James pictures Gaw, an old man, sitting 'like a ruffled-hawk, motionless but for his single tremor, with his beak which had pecked so many hearts out visibly sharper than ever', and says of him that 'He was a person without an alternative . . . and now revolved in the hard-rimmed circle from which he had not a single issue.' (Bk1, 1) It has become a commonplace of later literature to see the triumphs of such moguls as hollow and self-defeating, but Dreiser's superb study of the type is an entirely original exploration of modern dehumanization and alienation. In point of fact, Dreiser did envisage an alternative for men like Frank Cowperwood. In *The Stoic*, for example, he begins to suggest that the antidote to Western materialism might be found in Eastern mysticism. *The Bulwark* (1946), completed during the period of his life when he became interested in Thoreau, is full of yearning for the lost innocence of America. His hero, Solon Barnes, is a Philadelphia banker, too, but also a Quaker who resigns from the bank in order to pursue a life of religious study. Dreiser's revulsion at the sordid world of American capitalism is genuine enough. It led him in the late 1920s to flirt with Russian communism, and in 1931 to write a full-length condemnation of the world he had earlier so lovingly documented, called *Tragic America*. But by the time he wrote *The Bulwark*, he no longer had the energy to embody his beliefs in convincing stories or to relate his characters to their environments.

One of the great achievements of the Realists was to create characters whose lives were so completely identified with their milieux that they illuminated an entire era of American social history. The frenetic turbulence and confusion of the Gilded Age, brought about by America's transformation into a modern industrial democracy of unprecedented proportion, is brilliantly reflected in the dense medium created to support Maggie, Carrie, Vandover, and Bartley Hubbard. In their struggles to ride the powerful currents of late nineteenth-century capitalism, they – and a score of other memorable characters

– unconsciously express the conflicting tensions that were helping to shape a new 'American Ideology'.

Erik Erikson has described these contradictory forces, just as the novelists did, in terms of the personalities produced by them:

> . . . the functioning American, as the heir of a history of extreme contrasts and abrupt changes, bases his final ego-identity on some tentative combination of dynamic polarities such as migratory and sedentary, individualistic and standardized, competitive and cooperative, pious and freethinking, responsible and cynical, etc. . . . To leave his choices open, the American, on the whole, lives with two sets of 'truths': a set of religious principles or religiously pronounced political principles of a highly puritan quality, and a set of shifting slogans which indicate what, at a given time, one may get away with on the basis of not more than a hunch, a mood, or a notion.[27]

If this may be taken as an accurate description of the modern American, then it was the nineteenth-century Realists who first gave us our detailed insights into the phenomenon.

Notes

1. *American Realism: New Essays*, edited by Eric Sundquist (Baltimore and London, 1982), p. 23.

2. Fredric Jameson, 'The Realist Floor-Plan', in *On Signs*, edited by Marshall Blonsky (Oxford, 1985), p. 374.

3. Alan Trachtenburg, *The Incorporation of America: Culture and Society in the Gilded Age* (New York, 1982). p. 7.

4. For further analyses of Dreiser's style see Sandy Petrey, 'Language of Realism, Language of False Consciousness: A Reading of *Sister Carrie*', *Novel*, · 10 (1977), 101–13; Walter Benn Michaels, '*Sister Carrie's* Popular Economy', *Critical Inquiry*, 7 (1980), 373–90; and Rachel Bowlby, *Just Looking: Consumer Culture in Dreiser, Gissing and Zola* (London, 1985).

5. See for example Nina Baym, 'Melodramas of Beset Manhood: How Theories of American Fiction Exclude Women Authors', *American Quarterly*, 33 (1981), 123–39. This essay is reprinted in an excellent collection, *The New Feminist Criticism*, edited by Elaine Showalter (London, 1986).

6. George J. Becker, 'Realism: An Essay in Definition', *Modern Language Quarterly*, 10 (1949), 193.

7. Alfred Kazin, *On Native Grounds: An Interpretation of American Prose Literature*, abridged edition (New York, 1956), p. 13.

8. See H. L. Mencken, *Prejudices: First Series* (New York, 1919). Mencken's criticism of Howells is reprinted in *Howells: A Century of Criticism*, edited by K. E. Eble (Dallas, 1970). Steven Mailloux discusses the problem of irony in *The Red Badge* at some length in his book, *Interpretive Conventions: The Reader in the Study of American Fiction* (Irhaca, NY, 1982), Ch. 7. Mailloux cites this text as an example of the way in which insensitive editing and expurgation have often completely changed the meaning and interpretations of major American novels.

9. Quoted by Harold H. Kolb, jun., *The Illusion of Life: American Realism as a Literary Form* (Charlottesville, 1969), p. 22. See Kolb's book for a fuller account of the 'Realism War'.

10. Michael Davitt Bell suggests that Howells's inability to present Realism as a species of literary *presentation* is not the result of his theoretical naivety. But to have proclaimed an interest in such matters would have involved the admission that he was primarily an artist and therefore irrelevant to the world of men's activities. See 'The Sin of Art and the Problem of American Realism', in *Prospects*, 9 (1984), 115–42. And in a full-length study of *Gender, Fantasy and Realism in American Literature* (New York, 1982), Alfred Habegger conducts a detailed historical investigation of nineteenth-century gender in order to demonstrate the struggle waged by Howells and James to win manhood, and their effort to represent in narrative form just what it meant to grow up male in their time and place.

11. Lionel Trilling, *The Opposing Self* (London, 1955), p. 82.

12. Edwin H. Cady, 'Introduction' to *A Modern Instance* (Harmondsworth, 1984), p. xvi.

13. Howells's conversion to Critical Realism is described more fully by Edwin H. Cady in his two-volume biography, *The Road to Realism* and *The Realist at War* (Syracuse, 1956, 1957), and by Everett Carter, *Howells and the Age of Realism* (Philadelphia and New York, 1959).

14. Harry Levin, *Grounds for Comparison* (Cambridge, Mass., 1972) p. 250.

15. See, for example, Marston LaFrance, 'Stephen Crane's *Private Fleming: His Various Battles*', in *Patterns of Commitment in American Literature*, edited by Marston LaFrance (Toronto, 1967), pp. 113–33.

16. Winterich's edition was published in 1951 and many subsequent editions include the additional material bracketed in the text.

17. John Berryman, *Stephen Crane*, (New York, 1950), p. 279.

18. Warren French, *Frank Norris* (New York, 1962), p. 54.

19. Maxwell Geismar, *Rebels and Ancestors: The American Novel, 1890–1915* (London, 1954), p. 52.

20. Vernon L. Parrington, *The Beginnings of Critical Realism in America: 1860–1920*, Main Currents in American Thought, 3, (New York, 1958), p. 188.

21. Donald Pizer, *Realism and Naturalism in Nineteenth-Century American Literature* (Carbondale and Edwardsville, Ill. 1966).

22. Larzer Ziff, *The American 1890s: Life and Times of a Lost Generation* (London, 1967), p. 273.

23. Lewis Mumford, *The Golden Day: A Study in American Literature and Culture* (New York, 1968), p 131.

24. The Pennsylvania edition of *Sister Carrie*, edited by James L. West III Philadelphia, 1981). An identical text was published in England with an Introduction by Alfred Kazin (Harmondsworth, 1981). References are to this edition.

25. Geismar, p. 361.

26. Walter Benn Michaels has argued that this famous image is curiously inapplicable to the events of *The Financier* itself, which demonstrate nature's instability rather than any organizing force. See 'Dreiser's Financier: The Man of Business as a Man of Letters', in *American Realism: New Essays*, pp. 278–95.

27. Erik H. Erikson, *Childhood and Society* (Harmondsworth, 1965), p. 278.

Chapter 4
The Regional Novelists

If there is any truth in the contention that a writer's 'happiest occasions are those in which there appears to be a sustaining relation between reality and his imagination,[1] the nature of American life in the last quarter of the nineteenth century rendered it difficult for the majority of novelists to work in that situation. Those who could, like Dreiser, and (sporadically) W. D. Howells, exercised their imaginations in the main current of American history and, thereby, helped to create a National Novel. A more common reaction, as we have seen, was one involving some form of temporal or spatial escape. For the expatriate artist, Europe, or occasionally, as in the case of Lafcadio Hearn, Asia, provided the necessary remoteness both literally and figuratively. On a minor scale the various regions of the country performed a similar function for those who either could not or did not wish to uproot themselves from their native soil. It can be argued, of course, and frequently was, that the writer who focuses most closely on his own locality is more likely to produce the true novel of America than those who attempt to catch the national spirit in the artificial air of New York or Boston. In actual fact, the realism of the regionalists was most often a technique employed to create historical or even mythic fictions that bore only an oblique relation to the larger movements of history; and when a regional writer did succeed in coming to terms with the texture and structure of a contemporary locality, it was usually someone like Hamlin Garland whose 'veritism' was only made possible by the fact that he had first of all created the necessary perspective by removing himself to Boston from his native Midwest. For the most part, regional writers, like their expatriate counterparts, were forever looking backwards in the vain hope of resurrecting a vanishing ideal that could somehow be equated with contemporary America.

The Midwest: Eggleston, Kirkland, Howe, Garland

The problem for writers in the Midwest was to reconcile their unshakeable belief in the Adamic virtues of the pioneering farmers – a blend of Republican independence and Protestant morality – with the environmental factors that had, if Frederick Jackson Turner's frontier thesis was correct, helped to produce them. It was true that the existence of free land was rapidly becoming a myth as the western frontier was beginning to close and as thousands of small farmers over-mortgaged their land and sank further into debt. But the idea of the West as a latter-day Eden might still have carried some conviction had it not been for the cruel combination of a protracted drought between 1887 and 1896 together with a steady depletion of the country's gold reserves, culminating in the financial crash of 1893. Unlimited economic expansion, reinforced by a philosophy of the inevitability of progress, had left the farmer ill-prepared to deal with deteriorating conditions, and his only immediate response was to leave the unproductive land and return east. In political terms, however, radical problems called for equally radical solutions, both conservative and progressive, and these were reflected in various forms of romantic and Utopian literature as we have seen.

In addition to the rash of popular medieval romances that sufficiently indicated the degree of disillusionment experienced by authors and readers alike, several Midwestern novelists, writing out of a similar impulse, attempted to rediscover in their own region values comparable to those displayed by the heroes of more exotic romances. Booth Tarkington's *The Gentleman from Indiana* (1899) and Maurice Thompson's *Alice of Old Vincennes* (1900) both assert the natural democratic virtues of inner cleanliness and outer strength in opposition to the degeneration of the Ku Klux Klan and the French respectively, but as Larzer Ziff points out,[2] the characters in the novels who embody these qualities derive them not from the society in which they function, but in one case by virtue of being high-born and in the other by way of a fancy Eastern education. In seeking to perpetuate the frontier myth, they actually help to undermine it. The same is true of the novel that was to become more popular than any of the other Midwestern romances, Charles M. Sheldon's *In His Steps* (1896). Written by a small-town minister in Kansas, it purports to show how a group of citizens defeat the evils surrounding them by basing their lives on that of Christ. Meanwhile, in actuality a large proportion of the state's population, more responsive to the social realities of its situation, was painfully back-trailing east with wagons bearing the ironic legend, 'In God we trusted, in Kansas we busted.' The immense popularity of Sheldon's novel probably owed more to the fact that in his scheme stubborn social problems do not have to be solved, they disappear.

An unwillingness to write about life as it really was in the prairie states unites the two ends of the fictional political spectrum in the Utopian novel and the romance. The search for general panaceas blinded the majority of writers to what was near at hand, and also helped to eclipse the work of those who had persisted in trying to come to terms with the hardships of life along the Middle Border. Yet it eventually proved to be the subdued fiction of the early local colourists rather than the more lurid products of the popular authors that nourished the mainstream of American fiction. E. W. Howe, Joseph Kirkland, Edward Eggleston, and above all, Hamlin Garland, were the writers whose work laid the foundations for later regionalists such as Sherwood Anderson or Sinclair Lewis, and at the same time contributed more generally to the development of a realistic literature in America. Eggleston's *The Hoosier Schoolmaster* (1871) was, according to its author, an attempt to show characters as the logical products of their environment. This makes it sound more like a work of naturalism than what it really is – a genre study influenced by Hyppolite Taine's essay on Dutch painting. Eggleston's interest in the grotesque, the humorous, and the sentimental aspects of rural life, together with his dependence on traditional plot situations, give it a Dickensian quality, despite his attempts to describe honestly the speech and customs of the Hoosiers.

Kirkland's novel *Zury, the Meanest Man in Spring County* (1887), is also derivative, in spite of the fact that it is as true as he could make it, full of literally exact incidents and characters drawn, as he said, from 'my down-state acquaintances'. The 'low life . . . in actual contact with the soil' is, on his own admission, an attempt to reproduce a 'palpable mutation' of Hardy's *Far from the Madding Crowd*, and as with Eggleston, the literary debt sometimes impedes a native spontaneity.

Between these two novels, Edgar Howe published – with some difficulty – *The Story of a Country Town* (1883). Unlike Eggleston and Kirkland, Howe had little education and no literary background, and though his novel is in some respects cruder than theirs, it has a bleak, flat style that creates an impressive medium for the story of John Westlock's grim life. Written when he was the editor of a small newspaper, 'almost entirely at night, on the kitchen table', and printed at his own expense, the book creates an impressive picture of the blighting effect of poverty combined with repressive, fundamentalist religion. This part of the novel is autobiographical, and even though Howe weakened it by grafting on a Gothic murder mystery, his bitter analysis of the spiritual emptiness of rural America has something in common with those of Garland and later, Sinclair Lewis.[3]

What characterizes all these regional works is the attempt to free provincial literature from its ties to Eastern, and ultimately, European cultural values. In various ways, stylistic and thematic, these are works held back by a literary timidity that can be appreciated by comparing them with the one contemporary masterpiece set in the West – *Huckleberry Finn*. Twain achieved exactly what Garland was calling for in *Crumbling Idols* (1894), a series of essays dedicated to the idea that Boston and even New York could not be the centres for a new national literature, and that if American art were not to become sterile or moribund, it must root itself in local soil. In his advice to young Western artists, Garland even mentions the river life of the Mississippi as being a fine subject among dozens of others. He also calls for a manner to be developed by new realists that would involve raising simple, vivid, and unhackneyed language to a higher degree of expression. In order to find out what he had in mind by this, it is helpful to look at his own fiction. Most of Garland's critics have concluded either that he was seduced from his true path by the promise of wealth, popularity, and the recognition of those Eastern arbiters whom he dismissed in *Crumbling Idols*; or that he was always a romantic at heart, more concerned with the myth of a 'Western Garden' than with the bitter reality of life along the Middle Border, and that his masterpiece *Main Travelled Roads* (1891) was a literary sport produced by the immediate shock of returning to the family farm in South Dakota.[4] In later life Garland himself alternated between regret that he had not followed Howells's advice to work out the seam he had made his own – by transforming local colour writing into an instrument of social realism – and relief that he had fled the prosaic plains for the 'silver and purple summits of the Continental Divide'. He always maintained an interest in 'sociological background', but that is exactly what is wrong with his later work which is set in the Rockies. The problems he introduces in novels such as *The Captain of the Grey Troop* (1902) or *Cavanagh, Forest Ranger* (1910), remain in the background and are not really integrated with the romantic adventures that form the foreground of the stories. *Rose of Dutcher's Coolly* (1895), which marks the turning-point of his career and has an autobiographical feel about it, identifies a moment when his heroine makes a leap analogous to that taken by Garland himself. She has been taken to hear Wagner at a Chicago concert:

> When she rose to her feet the girl from the coolly
> staggered, and the brilliant, moving, murmuring house
> blurred into fluid color like a wheel of roses. The real

world was gone, the world of imagined things lay all
about her. She felt the power to reach out her hand to
take fame and fortune. In that one reeling instant the life
of the little coolly, the lonely, gentle old father, and the
days of her youth – all her past – were pushed into
immeasurable distance. The pulling of weeds in the corn,
the driving of cattle to pasture were as the doings of ants
in a dirt-heap. (19)

But Garland has not portrayed even Rose's early life on the farm
in this way. Her later development necessitates an inborn physical and
spiritual superiority that guarantees her an immunity to environmental
pressure quite different from that seen in the blighted lives he evoked
in *Main Travelled Roads*:

Sometimes when alone she stripped off her clothes and ran
amid the tall corn-stalks like a wild thing. Her slim little
brown body slid among the leaves like a weasel in the
grass. Some secret, strange delight, drawn from ancestral
sources, bubbled over from her pounding heart, and she
ran and ran until wearied and sore with the rasping corn-
leaves, then she sadly put on civilised dress once more. (2)

In Garland's earlier stories, men, women and children alike
constantly struggle against the forces of nature and society, and in re-
creating the quality of their lives, he occasionally achieves a vernacular
intensity comparable with Twain's. In 'Under the Lion's Paw', for
example, the defeated farmer, Haskins, tells how he was forced out
of Kansas by plagues of grasshoppers:

'Eat! They wiped us out. They chewed everything that
was green. They jest set around waitin' f'r us to die t'eat
us too. My God! I ust t'dream of 'em sittin' 'round on the
bedpost, six feet long, workin their jaws. They eet the
fork-handles. They got worse 'n' worse till they jest rolled
on one another, piled up like snow in winter. Well, it ain't
no use. If I was t'talk all winter I couldn't tell nawthin'.
But all the while I couldn't help thinkin' of all that land
back here that nobuddy was usin' that I ought o' had
'stead o' bein' out there in that cussed country.'

What gives the story its naturalistic depth, though, is the way the
grasshoppers are used as a grotesque prologue and parallel to the
rapaciousness of Haskin's new landlord. Together with help from his

neighbours and his own and his family's 'ferocious labour', Haskins resurrects a derelict farm. But at the end of it all he is told by the owner that his improvements have served only to put up its price so much that far from being the 'free man' he thought he was, he is faced at the end of the story with the prospect of an endless struggle to pay off his debts. In a moment of murderous rage, he swings his fork at the greedy landlord before subsiding into a more characteristic posture of defeated despair.

Garland wrote this story and the others that make up *Main Travelled Roads* when he was still poor enough to need to work as a farmhand for his father in order to pay his fare back east. But his commitment was theoretical as well as practical. He was also a passionate disciple of Henry George and a campaigner for the single tax and other reforms that would help to ease the plight of the small farmer. Later, when his romantic adventure novels were selling by the hundred thousand, his sympathetic bitterness would lose its edge and his imagination its vital contact with the meanness of rural life. What he achieved, though, in one book helped to make possible the work of Sherwood Anderson, Sinclair Lewis, and John Steinbeck.

The South: Cable, Chopin

According to the historian, C. Vann Woodward,[5] one of the most significant inventions in the New South was the myth of the Old South. While this view has been contested by others, who see the myth's origins as dating from the decline of the Tidewater economy in the 1830s, it was the traumatic experience of the Civil War and its aftermath that really led Southerners to idealize a vanishing aristocratic way of life based upon the old plantation economy. In actual fact, the core of the social structure in the *ante-bellum* South consisted of several million individuals who had little or no connection with the large plantations, and though this aspect of Southern life was not entirely ignored in fiction,[6] the abiding impression created by popular writers in the later nineteenth century is one of chivalric gentlemen and their ladies pursuing romantic, ritualistic pleasures and attended by contented slaves whose lives were almost as leisurely as those of their masters. The two novelists who did most to promulgate this 'moonlight and magnolia' myth were, as it happens, both related to the 'first families' of Virginia – John Esten Cooke and Thomas Nelson Page.

After serving in the Confederate Army, Cooke turned his romantic talents to fiction about the war itself, and produced works such as *Surry of Eagle's Nest* (1866), in which officers – referred to as Cavaliers – take time off from their gallant exploits to foil the designs of melodramatic villains in pursuit of the heroine. It is instructive to contrast Cooke's view of the war with that of the Northern writer, John de Forest, in his *Miss Ravenel's Conversion from Secession to Loyalty* (1867), in order to see just how far apart Southern and Northern views of the conflict were.[7]

Page, whose work was first published in the 1880s, specialized in stories in which elderly Black 'uncles' reminisce about their idyllic lives under slavery, but he also produced in 1898 *His Red Rock*, which along with Thomas Dixon's *The Clansman* (1905), helped to bring into being the Ku Klux Klan by portraying a heroic Southern revolt against reconstruction. His writing, whether about past or present life, is equally unrealistic and falls neatly into place in the swelling volume of contemporary anti-modernistic propaganda.

The emergence of a writer like George Washington Cable in such a literary and social atmosphere is quite remarkable. It is sometimes explained by reference to his New England ancestry which, it is argued, gave him a moral sense quite alien to that of most Southerners and led him eventually to recoil from Southern society and make his home back in New England. Whatever the reason, though, Cable succeeded in antagonizing the whole of the conservative South by the liberal views expressed in his two books of essays, *The Silent South* (1885) and *The Negro Question* (1890). Even before this, however, in his first and best-known novel, *The Grandissimes* (1880), he had begun to express views both on the treatment of slaves and on Southern mores in general, that led to his virtual ostracism in New Orleans, the city in which he lived and about which he wrote. *The Grandissimes* is set in the early years of the nineteenth century, but it is still in Cable's words 'as plain a protest against the times in which it was written as against the earlier times in which its scenes were set'. The effect of the Louisiana Purchase on the Creole population of what was still very much a Franco-Spanish city, can be seen as a parallel to that of the defeat of the South in the Civil War. In both cases, a proud indigenous population reacts against 'invasion' by an alien culture, and at the same time continues to maintain a position of 'superiority' in relation to the Black society in its midst. Cable's realism in the treatment of these subjects is badly flawed by his use of a conventional romantic plot revolving around a long-standing feud between two Creole families. But within this story his treatment of such explosive topics as miscegenation and violence is hardly matched by any writer before Faulkner. He also introduces into the novel the brilliant short story of Bras-Coupé, the African Prince sold into slavery, told in a manner that anticipates Faulkner's many parables and digressions in his novels. The story is intended to turn into flesh and blood 'the truth that all Slavery is maiming', and it is not surprising that when Cable tried to publish the story separately, it was turned down by every magazine editor he approached. Apart from its metaphoric significance within the novel, its evocation of the Louisiana landscape and its exotic inhabitants makes it a fictional *tour de force* in its own right.

It is difficult to judge how Cable's art might have developed beyond *The Grandissimes* had he not been frustrated by the prevailing taste of editors for local-colour prose-pastorals and romances. As it was, he complied with their demands and never reproduced anything as powerful as his first novel. In later life he began to write best-selling romances about the Civil War, spiced with erotic fantasies and comparable, as Edmund Wilson remarks, with those that disfigure Owen Wister's novel *The Virginian* (1902)[8] which testify to what commentators now see as the growing feminization of American culture.

Ironically, the finest novel written from and about a woman's point of view in the nineteenth century, Kate Chopin's *The Awakening* (1899), was universally condemned at the time of its appearance, though it has gradually come to be recognized as a classic, both within the canon of women's writing and of American literature in general. It, too, deals with a woman's erotic fantasies, but unlike Cable's *The Cavalier* (1901) or *The Virginian* the heroine's consciousness is here directly presented as the central theme of the novel, and the consequences of her sexual awakening create its plot.

In realizing her fantasies, Edna Pontellier raises social and moral problems of an urgent, and for many readers, a disturbing nature. Her growing determination to assert her social, economic, and sexual independence openly challenges the patriarchal society in which she is trapped, and by implication, American society in general. It can be argued that *The Awakening* is not really a regional novel in the sense that many of Chopin's short stories about Cajuns, Creoles, and Blacks in *Bayou Folk* (1894) are. She came to believe that American art was hampered by being tied to convention and the past and, therefore, that it was unable to come to terms with 'human existence in its subtle, complex, true meaning, stripped of the veil with which ethical and coventional standards have draped it'. To this extent her work is part of the general modernist reaction against provincial realism, yet both Edna Pontellier's life and the form her rebellion takes are clearly shaped by the wealthy Creole society into which she has married.

The free, flirtatious life-style of the summer colony on Grand Isle, where wives, children and a few young bachelors idle on the beaches while their menfolk make money in New Orleans, disorientates Edna, who mistakenly equates manner with behaviour and falls disastrously in love with Robert Lebrun. Robert, warned off by one of Edna's married friends, leaves for Mexico, but Edna, aroused now from the emotional torpor of her marriage, embarks upon a life of independent sensory and emotional gratification. She takes up painting, neglects her domestic role, and drifts into an affair with a notorious rake.

Eventually she perceives what the inevitable consequences of her revolt will be, especially when Robert returns and confesses his love for her, but refuses to act on it. The rigid conventions of Creole society will not permit her to live respectably as a free woman, so unable either to continue defiantly or to return home submissively, she returns to Grand Isle, takes off her clothes and walks naked into the sea. The description of Edna's last moments, richly sensuous and ambiguous as they are not only show the power of Chopin's prose but also suggest why her novel created such a controversy:

> How strange and awful it seemed to stand naked under the sky! How delicious! She felt like some new-born creature, opening its eyes in a familiar world that it had never known.
>   The foamy wavelets curled up to her white feet, and coiled like serpents about her ankles. She walked out. The water was chill, but she walked on. The water was deep but she lifted her white body and reached out with a long, sweeping stroke. The touch of the sea is sensuous, enfolding the body in its soft, close embrace.(39)

A wider context for *The Awakening* was provided by two influential books published at the same time, Charlotte Gilman Perkins's *Women and Economics* (1898), and Thorstein Veblen's *The Theory of the Leisure Class* (1899). Edna's plight nicely exemplifies the contemporary shift in American society from production to consumerism. The conspicuous consumption satirized by Veblen is the visible corollary of Edna's feelings of uselessness and futility. In order to maintain her husband's financial credibility, her role in their marriage is reduced to that of chief ornament in his display of wealth. The rules of their stylized existence permit her to take but not to make. Her creative instincts are stifled, and the need which Perkins argues is the distinguishing characteristic of humanity – to express one's inner thoughts in some outer form – is denied her. Ironically, Edna's alternative quest for sensual gratification is one that capitalism and consumerism, with all their stress on material acquisition, have encouraged in her.

In exposing her heroine's social victimization, Kate Chopin transcended the narrower preoccupations of regional fiction, and in relating

Edna's plight to her deep biological and emotional needs, moved firmly away from nineteenth-century concerns into the twentieth century. The only contemporary American novelist to make a similar transition was Henry James.

New England: Jewett, Wharton

Writing in the middle of the Great Depression, Granville Hicks suggested in his Marxist account of American literary history that late-nineteenth-century regionalism was inevitably doomed to failure by the unwillingness of sectional authors to progress from a study of the local and familiar to an understanding of the larger issues in American society. Many regional writers, baffled or dismayed by modern developments, removed themselves physically from their chosen localities, as did Twain, Bret Harte, and George Washington Cable. Others, like Eggleston, gave up writing fiction altogether, and turned to history instead. But the great majority, alienated from the world of the railroad, the telegraph, and mechanized agriculture, turned their backs on the present in order to 'recapture the romantic past of boyhood impressions, the sectional life of the vanished era', where they contented themselves with churning out repetitious tales full of stereotyped characters and soggy sentiments.[9] Though this is a harsh oversimplification of the situation, it is true that many of these writers did produce a good deal of sentimental fiction for children. In particular, it is unfair on those novelists who left their regions to write from a broader national or even international perspective. It is also less true of some regions than others, depending on the depth of history involved and the degree to which the 'shock of the new' disturbed an existing social stability.

The Midwest, and to a lesser extent, the South, experienced the traumas of the Gilded Age and Reconstruction more directly than the six New England states, and though the political, economic, and social upheavals there did lead some writers to retreat completely into a mythical or historical alternative, they also provided others with the necessary reality against which to measure their regions' and their own traditional values. The dialectic thus created did not find wholly, satisfactory fictional expression in the South before Faulkner, though there were interesting interim attempts made by Allen Tate and Robert Penn Warren for instance to test the Southern myth. The westward development of American culture has also remained a vital issue for twentieth-century novelists, but as far as fiction is concerned, New England has proved as barren a subject for modern novelists as its soil for modern farmers. Significantly, all the major twentieth-century writers in New England have been poets: Robert Frost, Edwin Arlington Robinson, Wallace Stevens, Charles Olson, and Robert Lowell. To say this is not to imply that poets do not have a vital connection with the life of their region; Wallace Stevens, for one, has eloquently refuted this idea,[10] and Charles Olson's major work vividly re-creates the town of Gloucester, Massachusetts, to prove Stevens's point. Yet poets are not subject to the same spatial and temporal restrictions which limit more 'realistic' novelists, and therefore are not as dependent for subject-matter on the tangible manifestations of change. Van Wyck Brooks has claimed that the overwhelming feeling in New England at the turn of the century was one of disappointment and chagrin, summed up by the literary critic Borrett Wendell in 1893 when he wrote 'We are vanishing into provincial obscurity. America has swept from our grasp. The future is beyond us.'[11] If New England was becoming the 'deserted farm of literature', it is not surprising that its best minds could only retain any vitality at all by developing into 'museums of idols'. The prevalent belief that New England's day was over inevitably led writers towards a preoccupation with lost things, and this is certainly what is most characteristic of the best New England regionalists, Mary E. Wilkins and Sarah Orne Jewett.

Though Mary E. Wilkins did write novels eventually, including one, *The Portion of Labor* (1901), that examines labour problems in a New England mill, her best work was completed earlier and is mainly contained in two volumes of stories, *A Humble Romance* (1887) and *A New England Nun* (1891). Both Howells and James admired her early work, and it is not difficult to see how it relates to theirs. She was apparently not altogether happy with her realistic manner, though, and later confessed that she had adopted it for its 'selling qualities'. As soon as possible she, too, escaped into romance, and it is a nice double irony that in 1926 Hamlin Garland, another fugitive from realism, presented her with the Howells Medal for Fiction.

Her early stories of moral decay and human desolation have much in common with Garland's. They present a world of squalor, poverty, and ugliness where a few ageing individuals struggle for existence in an inhospitable environment, both human and natural. In one sense, the prospect here is even bleaker than in the Midwest. Even if the process of decay could be halted and the seaports and farms revitalized, there is no one left to do it. The young men have mostly gone west, leaving behind the sick and the old, doomed to long spinsterhoods or early death. The quality of their lives is determined, moreover, by a psychological legacy from their Puritan ancestry, which in the absence of a sustaining theological framework has formed into stiff-necked pride, eccentricity, and futile renunciation of experience and a corresponding addiction to failure.

Hayden Carruth – the New England poet – has characterized the later inversions of Puritanism in a way that, broadening the simplistic historiographical myth, illuminates very clearly the nature of literature written under its influence. It is not merely a matter of radicalism changing first to reactionary orthodoxy and then to gentility, nor of its initial revolutionary militancy turning to quietism. In addition, Puritanism's tragic conception of existence and its accompanying heroism are reduced to comedy and irony filtered through fantasy, Utopianism, or even madness. Similarly, the early individualism and sturdy independence of the Puritan shrivels into a fanatical devotion to privacy.[12] These are exactly the features that stand out most clearly in the fiction of Sarah Orne Jewett as well as forming another important element that differentiates her world from that of Mary E. Wilkins. But it is also, according to Carruth, an important residue of the Puritan inheritance: the pride in mere landscape which is a corollary of the exploitation of the land, both of them being a reversal of the earlier custodial tradition of Puritan theology.

Jewett's feeling for and use of the Maine coast in her fiction has nothing to do with the pathetic fallacy. Her better critics have recognized this,[13] while not necessarily seeing that in counterpointing man and nature as she so often does, she tends ironically to distance the lives she writes about. This distancing effect is compounded by her characteristic structural device of using as narrators summer visitors who bring to village life the values of the outside world. In *Deephaven* (1877), for example, the device leads to a pattern of rather obvious and crude contrasts, and there is still something of this in *The Country of the Pointed Firs* (1896), though by this stage in her career she had learned to incorporate perspective so as to achieve subtle complications and ambiguities. A fairly typical scene exhibiting these elements occurs in 'Through the Schoolhouse Window', in which the narrator, having attended a funeral service for one of the village's widows, declines to join the procession to the graveyard and instead watches it from a distance:

> The bay-sheltered islands and the great sea beyond
> stretched away to the far horizon southward and eastward;
> the little procession in the foreground looked futile and
> helpless on the edge of the rocky shore. It was a glorious
> day early in July, with a clear, high sky; there were no
> clouds, there was no noise of the sea. The song sparrows
> sang and sang, as if with joyous knowledge of

immortality, and contempt for those who could so pettily
concern themselves with death. I stood watching until the
funeral procession had crept round a shoulder of the slope
below and disappeared from the great landscape as if it
had gone into a cave. . . . Watching the funeral gave me a
sort of pain. I began to wonder if I ought not to have
walked with the rest, instead of hurrying away at the end
of the service. Perhaps the Sunday gown I had put on for
the occasion was making this disastrous change of feeling,
but I had now made myself and my friends remember that
I did not really belong to Dunnet Landing. (4)

Between this beginning and the narrator's departure by sea at the
end of the summer when the little town sinks from view, 'indistinguishable from the other towns that looked as if they were crumbled
on the furzy-green stoniness of the shore', she opens up the lives of
various villagers as they tell their own histories or those of their neighbours, eccentric or prosaic, pathetic or comic. The stories themselves
are absorbing and give the book its deserved status, but they also
confirm the view of one of her characters that 'we're all turned upside
down, and going back year by year'. (24)

And this, of course, is the general condition that regional literature
illuminates so clearly: an inability to relate to the new forces shaping
American society and a consequent retreat from them into the past.
This can only result in lives lacking authenticity and true social identity, lives that by being wrenched away from social and psychological
norms, become grotesque, no matter how sympathetically evoked.[14]

Perhaps the best example of human wastage in New England
writing is Edith Wharton's short novel *Ethan Frome* (1911). Edith
Wharton was not herself a New Englander, and most of her novels
dealt with a stratum of society very different from what she called 'my
granite outcroppings; but half-emerged from the soil, and scarcely
more articulate'. She has been accused of having little sympathy for
the characters in her novel and of writing a clever but cruel story
lacking in moral reverberations, but such criticism fails to take into
account her deep understanding of rural decay in New England, and
the ways in which the poverty of the land, the harshness of the climate,
and the economic depression are bound to be reflected in the bare,
emotional lives of those who endure them.

The story is pieced together by a young engineer, temporarily
trapped by a strike in a small town in western Massachusetts. It
concerns the history of Ethan Frome, a gaunt, bitter ruin of a man,
whose condition is the result of a momentous event that took place
a quarter of a century before. Unlike the 'smart ones' who got away,

Ethan has stayed on his family's barren farm with its ailing sawmill, both mortgaged to the hilt, to look after first his father, then his mother, and finally his sickly wife. The quality of life in these dying communities is brilliantly captured in Ethan's brief account of his mother's last years:

> 'We're kinder side-tracked here now, . . . but there was considerable passing before the railroad was carried through to the Flats . . . I've always set down the worst of mother's trouble to that. When she got the rheumatism so bad she couldn't move around she used to sit up there and watch the road by the hour; and one year, when they was six months mending the Bettsbridge pike after the floods, and Harmon Gow had to bring his stage round this way, she picked up so that she used to get down to the gate most days to see him. But after the trains begun running nobody ever came by here to speak of, and mother never could get it through her head what had happened, and it preyed on her right along till she died.'
> (Prologue)

After his mother's death, Ethan lives on with Zeenie, his ailing, shrewish wife until her young cousin Mattie comes to live with them. Mattie's vivacity and warmth stir Ethan back to life and they begin to fall in love under the eyes of the jealous Zeenie. He contemplates the possibility of running away to the West with her and even sets out to borrow the money for the fare, but is brought up short by the realization of what his desertion would entail for his wife. Desperate and wretched, he sets off to take Mattie to the train after Zeenie tells the girl to leave. On the way they finally confess their love for each other but admit its hopelessness. Urged on by Mattie, Ethan takes a sled and they recklessly coast down a dangerous hill, 'right into the big elm. . . . So't we'd never have to leave each other any more.'

Ironically, Mattie's wish is granted. She is crippled by the accident and is taken back by Zeenie into the lonely farmhouse where the three of them eke out their sour and loveless existence, described by one of the townsmen: 'Don't see's there's much difference between the Fromes up at the farm and the Fromes down in the graveyard; 'cept that down there they're all quiet, and the women have got to hold their tongues.' (Epilogue)

This remark could almost be taken as a general statement about the life of the region, and Edith Wharton's occasional widening of focus shows her to be fully aware of the 'larger issues of civilisation' that encompass and partly account for these stunted lives. Zeenie's debility is only a more notable instance in a community 'rich in pathological instances', and Ethan's vain desire for change and freedom is matched by the gravestones around his house, each of which seems to bear the legend 'we never got away – how should you?'

Nineteenth-century regional fiction is often regarded as a minor tributary of the Realist movement, but I think it can more profitably be seen as a kind of distorting mirror image of the national novel. The same pressures that moulded the fiction of Dreiser and Norris, can also be discerned in the work of their lesser contemporaries. What makes the regional novelists different, and often accounts for their more limited achievements, is their inability to fuse the disparate ideological strands of contemporary life in the creation of new kinds of characters. In failing to do this, their novels remain structurally and thematically incoherent; testimony no less though to the painful and sometimes tragic upheavals that were ruthlessly obliterating long established life styles and remorselessly severing the present from the past.

Notes

1. See Denis Donoghue, *The Sovereign Ghost* (London, 1976), p. 104.

2. Larzer Ziff, *The American 1890s: Life and Times of a Lost Generation* (London,1967), pp. 89–91.

3. In an interesting essay on the novel, John William Ward suggests that the book has a double importance in the history of American literature. It marked the moment when the myth of America as a garden gave way to the idea of a wasteland of broken dreams. And in terms of technique the novel unsuccessfully attempts to combine primitive naturalism with psychological realism. See his *Red, White, and Blue: Men, Books, and Ideas in American Culture* (New York,1969), pp. 92–105.

4. See, for example, Jay Martin, *Harvests of Change: American Literature 1865–1914* (Englewood Cliffs, NJ, 1967), pp. 124–32, and Ziff, pp. 93–108.

5. C. Vann Woodward, *Origins of the New South, 1877–1913* (Baton Rouge, La., 1951), p. 154.

6. See Merrill Maguire Skaggs, *The Folk of Southern Fiction* (Athens, Ga., 1972).

7. The best study of the literature of the Civil War is by Edmund Wilson, *Patriotic Gore* (New York,1962).

8. Wilson, pp. 595–6.

9. See Granville Hicks, *The Great Tradition: An Interpretation of American Literature Since the Civil War*, revised edition (New York, 1935), p. 61.

10. Wallace Stevens has written poems and prose pieces about Connecticut, and Charles Olson's *Maximus Poems* trace the history of Gloucester in some detail.

11. See Van Wyck Brooks, *New England: Indian Summer, 1865–1915* (New York,1940), Chapter 20.

12. Hayden Carruth, 'The New England Tradition', in *Regional Perspectives: An Examination of America's Literary Heritage*, edited by John Gordon Burke (Chicago, 1973), pp. 2–47.

13. See, for example, Werner Berthoff's essay 'The Art of Jewett's *Pointed Firs*' in *New England Quarterly*, 32 (1959), reprinted in his book, *Fictions and Events: Essays in Criticism and Literary History* (New York, 1971), pp. 243–63.

14. Julia Bader has dicussed this phenomenon and its manifestations in Jewett's fiction. She argues that the occasional loss of solidity, moments when sense perception loses its grasp on what is 'out there', is quite different from similar subversions of reality in Modernist art. For Jewett and her contemporaries it is brought about by social, sexual, and psychological dislocations. See 'The Dissolving Vision: Realism in Jewett, Freeman and Gilman', in *American Realism: New Essays*, pp. 176–98.

Chapter 5
Impossible Futures and Impossible Pasts: Bellamy, Howells, Donnelly, London, Frederic

One phenomenon of the late nineteenth century in America unites the diverse interpretations of a multitude of cultural commentators. All agree that the 1880s and 1890s were marked by deep and irreconcilable divisions between those who accepted Darwin's theory of evolution and its social, political, and moral consequences, and those who propounded alternative possibilities to capitalism, unbridled competition, and the survival of the fittest. With the benefit of a century's hindsight, it is tempting to dismiss all those who reacted against the given realities of the situation as 'escapists', and it is one of the great virtues of recent cultural history that a number of scholars have illuminated the centrality and urgency of the debates which coloured every aspect of intellectual life in those decades. Whether the emphasis is primarily political, as in Peter Cann's *The Divided Mind*; economic, as in Alan Trachtenburg's *The Incorporation of America*; aesthetic, as in Jackson Lear's *No Place of Grace*; or sociological, as in Marcus Klein's *Foreigners*, the picture that emerges is one of crucial struggles between modernists and anti-modernists, or between socialists and capitalists, struggles which took as their ground the village or the city, the past or the future, and the individual or the collective. Inevitably, these issues found their way into the fiction of the time, and though the great debate is often confused by writers shifting their ground or holding contradictory positions within single novels, the way in which novelists responded imaginatively to the situation is a clear indication of the extent to which the theme had pervaded the national consciousness.

Perhaps the most remarkable literary feature of the 1890s was the sudden rise to popularity of the Utopian novel. More than a hundred were published before 1900 – as many, in fact, as there had been actual Utopian communities in the preceding century. Given the circumstances and nature of America's colonization and development, it is not at all surprising that her people have been preoccupied with creating various forms of ideal commonwealths, or as Emerson said in 1840, that there is 'not a reading man but has a draft of a new community in his waistcoat pocket'.[1] Some of these projects for social reform took extreme or eccentric forms and were inevitably doomed to failure, but the impulses behind them lingered on into a period when their practical realization had become less and less possible. Henry James characterized the typical milieu in his realistic reform novel *The Bostonians* (1886) as a 'Frogpondium' inhabited by 'long haired men and short haired women', while at the same time recognizing that his main theme, the position of women in modern society, was of genuine moment. Other major writers, as we shall see, were also diverted by the notions of Utopia, though the majority of such works were produced by men who had more reforming zeal than literary skill.

Common to them all, however, was a deep dissatisfaction with the state of contemporary society. Howells spoke for a great many in 1888 when he confessed in a letter to Henry James that 'after fifty years of optimistic content with "civilisation" and its ability to come out all right in the end, I now abhor it, and feel that it is coming out all wrong in the end'.[2]

Much of this discontent was reflected in hostility to industrial development, the mechanization of labour and life, and their inevitable corollary, the city. The widespread belief that unlimited development could only result in the impoverishment of life is summed up in the title of Henry George's immensely popular critique *Progress and Poverty* (1879), which quickly went through 100 editions. George is best remembered for his theory of the single tax whereby wealth could be taken from the few and redistributed among the community that had created it. Like his fellow economist, Lawrence Gronlund, whose socialist *Co-operative Commonwealth* depended for its realization on a return to the country, George saw the American city as a poisonous tumour which, if left to grow unchecked, would suck all the wholesome juice of the country into its vortex and infect the entire nation. His central solution for the evils of overcrowding, disease, and poverty, a land tax, may or may not have been feasible in practice, but the Utopian novelists influenced by such ideas had no need to concern themselves with the practical problems of implementation. For them, the transition to the millennium could be assumed to have already occurred, as it has in the most popular of all affirmative fictions, Edward Bellamy's *Looking Backward: 2000–1887* (1888).

Boston in the year 2000 – the site of Bellamy's Utopia – has evolved by way of advances in technology and by the development of socialism, into the City Beautiful. Poverty together with money has been abolished, and the abundant wealth of the nation is freely available to all. The end of competition and unregulated profiteering has brought an end to waste so that the country's economy is precisely geared to the needs of its citizens. Into this social paradise Bellamy projects his nineteenth-century hero, Julian West, who had been presumed dead in 1887 when his house burned down but had actually enjoyed thirteen decades of Rip Van Winkle-like hypnotic sleep in a sealed underground vault. Bellamy was a good enough craftsman to portray Julian's awakening to the new world as a mixed blessing. From time to time he suffers from feelings of loneliness and alienation, and Bellamy uses these emotions as the basis for a love-story involving a descendant of the girl who loved him in his former existence. Julian's feelings of doubt about his true identity, cut off as he is from both past and future, lead him back to the womb-like suspension of his underground vault, where he sleeps again and eventually reawakens back in the Boston of 1887. Venturing out into his familiar old world, he is appalled by the 'festering . . . wretchedness' he encounters, and is doubly affected by the knowledge of the ideal alternative of future social felicity. It is this later experience that proves to be the dream, however, or rather the nightmare, and to his vast relief and ours, he comes back to actuality in the paradisal future. Not surprisingly, Henry George accused Bellamy of creating castles in the air, and Bellamy himself denied any more serious purpose in his novel than to build a 'cloud-palace for an ideal humanity'. Even so, the power of Bellamy's fiction had a profound effect, not just on the public and his fellow novelists but also on such economists as Veblen, who was to produce the most biting critique of American society in 1899 in *The Theory of the Leisure Class*.

Looking Backward almost immediately produced a spate of imitations and refutations, but by far the most distinguished of Bellamy's supporters was W. D. Howells (see also Ch. 2), who wrote two Utopian novels, *A Traveller from Altruria* (1894) and *Through the Eye of the Needle* (1907), as well as a series of 'Letters of an Altrurian Traveller', published in the *Cosmopolitan Magazine* between November 1893 and September 1894.

In the year that *Looking Backwards* was published, Howells read and welcomed another testimony 'against the system by which a few men with wealth and luxury, and the vast mass of men are overworked and underfed' – Tolstoy's *What to Do?* And when in 1889 Howells left New York for Boston, he was naturally drawn into the orbit of Christian Socialists like Bellamy who was just launching his Nationalist Clubs, Edward Everett Hale who was forming a group to propound Tolstoy's gospel, and the founders of the People's Party, soon to become the Populist Party. All these, together with Howells's own exploration of Utopian ideas in *The World of Chance* (1893), lay behind his preliminary Altrurian novels. In his earlier work, he created a character, David Hughes, who was a former member of the Brook Farm community, a famous socialist Utopia based on equality. But rather than explore the possibility of such an ideal community, he employs Hughes to examine the alternative of competitive life in the developing capitalist state. Indeed, Hughes is writing a book to be called *The World Revisited*, intended as a criticism of modern life in all its aspects. Hughes's critique would have found good company in the torrent of muckraking literature that was beginning to flow in the early 1890s. In the same year that *A Traveller from Altruria* appeared, Henry Demarest Lloyd published the bible of the muckrakers, *Wealth Against Commonwealth*, based on his sensational earlier study of the Standard Oil Company which Howells himself had bravely accepted for the *Atlantic* in 1881 when he was its editor.

One of the aspects of contemporary life that Hughes singles out is 'the whole architectural nightmare' of the American city, an 'indecent exposure' of the average tasteless man's mind which should not be permitted. It is a subject to which Howells returns in the lectures given by Mr Homos the Altrurian. The form of Howells's romance – and it is one that he had used before – is simply a gathering of middle-class families in a summer hotel, where they are led to expose the shortcomings of their society by the innocent questioning of the Altrurian. Mr Homos quickly sees that present-day America has much in common with the past of his own society and, therefore, must also contain the germ of a better future. He finally describes his own country and the phases of its growth from egoism (Egoria), through Accumulation to altruism (Altruria).

After a bloodless revolution achieved at the ballot-box, it was a simple matter, he says, to transfer all assets from a few monopolies to the State. All it took to initiate the redistribution of wealth and the transformation of life was a single clause in the statute. Under the new dispensation, all the evils brought by competition and greed began to disappear along with the institutions that had nourished them. The cities had been allowed to fall into ruin, and as is fitting for such sites of cruelty and suffering, are now inhabited by ravening beasts and poisonous reptiles. The citizens, meanwhile, have either returned to the villages or to one or other of the regional capitals. In their turn these have become civic and cultural centres, while manufacturing has been removed to the countryside. Here mills and shops rise like temples 'amid leafy boscages beside the streams, which form their only power', dedicated to 'that sympathy between the divine and human which expresses itself in honest and exquisite workmanship' (12).

If this reads like a vision by William Morris, Howells is well aware of it. A member of Homos's audience, the professor, accuses him of plagiarism, and Homos freely admits the influence not only of Morris but also of Thomas More, Francis Bacon, Mazzini, Campanella, and Bellamy. Altruria as an eclectic and whimsical juxtaposition of such technological marvels as the high-speed electric express and the pastoral manufacturing idyll described above, does give the impression, as one of Homos's hearers says, of 'pretty soap-bubble worlds solidified'.

Like many other social critics, Howells discovered to his amazement and delight the actual 'solidification' of his soap bubbles at the 1893 Columbian Exposition in Chicago. One of the 'Letters of an Altrurian Traveller' which formed a kind of supplement to the novel and provided the basis for his later romance, is entirely given to a description of what he calls the 'World's Fair City'. To his fellow Altrurian, Cyril, Homos confides that it would 'be useless trying to persuade most Americans that the World's Fair City was not the effect, the fine flower, of the competition which underlies their economy, but was in fact the first fruits of the principle of emulation which animates our happy commonwealth, and gives men, as nowhere else on earth, a foretaste of heaven'. But the exposition certainly did not give Henry Adams a foretaste of heaven. Writing in *The Education of Henry Adams* (1907), and looking back on the fair, he viewed it with some bitterness – along with the adoption of a single gold standard – as the final triumph of mechanization and centralization. Capitalism, with its corporations, trusts, and the consolidation of forces, had for him put paid for ever to all the eighteenth-century values he held so dear. Though Adams in his customary fashion extracts more implications from the symbol than it will legitimately yield, and though he links his abhorrence of bankers with that of other disagreeable certainties such as age, senility, and death, there can be little question that his view of the exhibition was more prescient than that of Howells. Of course, Adams was writing with the benefit of hindsight in the knowledge that the Populists had finally lost their cause at the turn of the century. Howells's optimism was not so easily quenched, and in 1907 when he was bringing out *Through the Eye of the Needle*, he was encouraged by signs of a resurgence of progressivism. His buoyancy continues throughout the book and is symbolized by the love-affair and marriage of Homos to an American girl, Eveleth Strange. In the second part of the work, Eveleth elaborates on details of Altrurian life and customs in her letters home to America, and though Howells does not make any significant changes in his original Utopian vision, he does allow Eveleth one ironic tribute to the excitement of life under the old regime. She is 'wolfishly hungry' for news of America, and asks her correspondent, 'Do you still keep on murdering and divorcing, and drowning and burning, and mommicking and maiming people by sea and land? Has there been any war since I left? Is the financial panic as great as ever, and is there as much hunger and cold? I know that whatever your crimes and calamities are, your heroism and martyrdom, your wild generosity and self-devotion, are equal to them' (14).

Eveleth's questions indicate one of the inevitable shortcomings of the Utopian state as pictured by Bellamy and Howells: the eventlessness of life in such a perfect setting. The violence and destruction she half hankers after are amply provided though, in the best-known dystopian work of the period, Ignatius Donnelly's *Caesar's Column* (1890). Donnelly, a convinced Populist, does embody a vision of Utopia in his novel, set in an embryonic agrarian community in Africa where his protagonist Gabriel Welstein and his friends have taken refuge after the catastrophic débâcle visited upon American civilization in 1988. Though Donnelly's aims and values were not significantly different from Bellamy's, he belonged to that class of millennialists who were convinced that any real improvement in society would not be brought about by gradual evolution but by revolution and an ensuing period of chaos. The scene in which Caesar Lombellini, the leader of a working-class rebellion, orders the piles of bodies in Union Square to be concreted over in layers, is more reminiscent of Twain's *Connecticut Yankee* published the previous year, than of any other novel. Donnelly's pessimism is rooted in a view of human nature that is much more like Twain's than Bellamy's. In the sermons, for example, that feature in both novels, the two writers manifest their very different ideas about social evolution. Bellamy's minister tells his congregation in a telecast that the human race is gradually returning to God and that the process of evolution will be complete when the divine secret hidden in the germ is perfectly realized. Donnelly's preacher, on the other hand, looks forward to a time when through its superior strength the ruling class will enjoy the full benefits that power confers. Given such a philosophy, it is not surprising that Donnelly can discover no better solution to social conflict than complete annihilation of the ruling plutocrats and oligarchs. This he accomplishes with a great deal of apocalyptic relish, his scenes of lurid slaughter being seasoned with the traditional biblical imagery associated with the harrowing of hell.

An even more unrelieved pessimism pervades Jack London's dystopian novel *The Iron Heel* (1907), a work that was rejected even by' contemporary socialists because of its terrifying picture of the future. London uses the device of a diary written by the converted wife of a proletarian leader and discovered seven centuries later, to describe the collapse of capitalism, the rise of a tyrannical oligarchy, and a savage civil war waged over three centuries of dictatorship. The conditions he predicts are much worse than anything envisaged by either his fellow novelists or contemporary socialists, and they reflect his lifelong belief that it is useless for the working class to fuse rather than fight, if it wishes to avoid the ruthless dehumanization and enslavement portrayed in the novel. The inhabitants of the labour ghettos, the people of the abyss, are seen as the 'refuse and scum of life, a raging, screaming, screeching, demoniacal horde', the degraded waste of society totally abject in its conditioned servitude.

This, one should remember, is in effect London's view of the present, and it is therefore not surprising that he preferred *The Jungle* to *Looking Backward*. He thought that Sinclair's novel was 'brutal with life . . . written of sweat and blood, and groans and tears. It depicts what man is compelled to be in our world, in the Twentieth Century.'

Whereas Jack London projects his imagination back into the present from a possible future in order to illustrate the former's deficiencies, another group of popular novelists took refuge from the same unpalatable present in an equally unreal American or even European, past. Perhaps the most distinguished example of the divided mind at the turn of the century was that of Henry Adams. The record of his own failed attempts to avoid entrapment by conflicting ideologies is most elegantly recounted in his intellectual autobiography *The Education*, but he had outlined part of the problem much earlier in his two novels *Esther* (1884), and *Democracy* (1889), where he had applied his ideas to religion and politics respectively. As a historian, though, he could pose the dilemma more starkly, and in an essay of 1894 entitled 'The Tendency of History' he laid bare the alternatives that also faced contemporary novelists. Historians, he argued, could restrict themselves to revealing the growing evils associated with unrestrained and advancing materialism, or could show the necessary consequences of this trend in the triumph of socialism. In either case, society would be likely to respond negatively, whereas if the scientific historian could prove that society must eventually revert to the Church to save itself, he would have to relinquish his beliefs in science itself, and this would be tantamount to committing suicide.

Novelists less subject to the rigours of scientific proof but equally concerned to direct society towards a better mode of existence, embraced not only religion but all forms of non-rational experience as an antidote to the iron laws of determinism. The more bleak the present and future of industrial society seemed, the more inviting the temporal, spatial, or ideological alternatives to it appeared. For the drabness of life in a mechanized modern city where the individual will had been subsumed by the machine, and man's selfhood subjugated by impersonal forces, the novelist could and did provide an imaginative escape into the colour, heroism, and authenticity of alternative milieux in the past. At its simplest level, this need was satisfied by the immense number of historical romances produced in the last years of the century, and writers such as Winston Churchill, F. Marion Crawford, and Clarence Major were so popular that Howells began to fear for the brutalization of the popular mind and the ruin of taste. He either failed to see or refused to recognize that the phenomenon he so despised was part of a much larger movement which embraced more than just middle-brow pulp literature. It manifested itself, for example, in England in the popularity of Robert Louis Stevenson, Rudyard Kipling, Oscar Wilde, and *The Yellow Book*. The *fin de siècle* ethos on both sides of the Atlantic possessed a number of seemingly disparate elements that had in common a rejection of the realities of the present and a glorification of the past. The activism propounded by Theodore Roosevelt may have had connections with America's imperialist ambitions, but it was also expressed by men like Henry Adams's brother, Brooks, in his *The Law of Civilisation and Decay* (1895), intended as a polemic against the modern merchant class and a plea for the reinstatement of the medieval warrior ideal. The growth of Vitalism as a philosophy can be linked to a new desire for authenticity and selfhood in a world that seemed to deny them, but it also pointed back to a pre-industrial simple life and often beyond it, to medieval mysticism. And in reacting against the banality and ugliness of late Victorian taste, the aesthetes identified vulgarity with the products of the machine, so that the proliferating Arts and Crafts movement often boasted of the complete lack of any modernity in its work.[3]

In such an atmosphere very few writers were able to maintain their commitment to realism and social reform. Even Hamlin Garland, who never ceased to proclaim that his prime aim was to promote truth rather than beauty, and to extend the reign of justice, turned to romantic novels about Indians in the Far West after the commercial failure of *Rose of Dutcher's Coolly* (1895), a realistic precursor of *Sister Carrie*. Others, among them Henry Harland and Henry Fuller, found it easier to repudiate their realism. For his part Harland had two quite distinct careers as a novelist. In the 1880s he wrote novels about Jewish immigrant life in New York, then after moving to England and founding *The Yellow Book* with Aubrey Beardsley, he began to produce witty, lightweight romances such as *The Cardinal's Snuff Box* (1900). Fuller, in contrast, vacillated between writing realistic novels of Chicago life such as *The Cliff-Dwellers* (1893) and *With the Procession* (1895), both of which influenced Dreiser, and romantic excursions into the more exotic aspects of European society in *The Chevalier of Pensieri-Vani* (1890), and *The Chatelaine of La Trinité* (1892). In the earlier book Fuller comes closest to stating his own and many other Americans' Jamesian predicament, when he describes the feelings of Mr Occident, an American visitor to Italy: 'Birth and habit drew him in one direction; culture and aspiration, in another; but he had never been a good American, and he feared he should never make a good European.'

By far the best example of this whole movement, outside the work of Henry James himself, is, as one might expect, a novel in which the issues themselves are foregrounded as the dramatic embodiment of the theme: Harold Frederic's *The Damnation of Theron Ware* (1896). Though Frederic eventually went the way of most American expatriates and ended his career by writing three English romances, *The Damnation* remains one of the best novels dealing with the social, cultural, and psychological conflicts of the late nineteenth century. It is a more complex treatment of the theme dealt with in James's *Roderick Hudson* (1878)[4] and a more interesting dramatization of the subject than that in Mrs Humphrey Ward's *Robert Elsmere* (1888), the novel on which it is reputed to be based.[5] The fact that it was used as ammunition by supporters of both sides in the 'Realism War' testifies to the fairness with which Frederic dealt with the issues involved. Significantly, the novel was published in England under the quite different title, *Illuminations*, a word that suggests an alternative interpretation.

The tension between conflicting philosophies is brought to life in the story of a young Methodist minister whose ambitions are initially thwarted by his appointment to a poor primitive church in Octavius, instead of to the rich, progressive church in Tecumseh for which he and his wife had hoped. Once there, he is driven partly by his own predilections and partly by the bigotry of the local Methodists into the orbit of the three people who will assist in bringing about his damnation (or illumination): Father Forbes, an Irish Catholic priest, Dr Ledsmer, an amateur Germanic scientist, and Celia Madden, a beautiful if somewhat overblown Pre-Raphaelite aesthete. As well as being sexually dazzled by Celia's hedonism, Theron is overwhelmed by the glimpses he is given into undreamed-of worlds which force him to re-examine his own narrow prejudices. The quality of Frederic's work is clearly shown by the way he does this – not as the Utopian novelists might, in a series of dry debates but by animating Theron's consciousness with its luridly sensational images of corruption:

> The foundations upon which its dark bulk reared itself
> were ignorance, squalor, brutality, and vice. Pigs
> wallowed in the mire before its base, and burrowing into
> this base were a myriad of narrow doors, each bearing the
> hateful sign of a saloon, and giving forth from its recesses
> of night the sounds of screams and curses. Above were
> sculptured rows of lowering, ape-like faces from Nast's
> and Keppler's cartoons, and out of these sprang into the

> vague upper gloom, on the one side, lamp-posts from
> which Negroes hung by the neck, and on the other
> gibbets for dynamiters and Molly Maguires; and between
> the two glowed a spectral picture of some black-robed,
> tonsured men, with leering satanic masks, making a
> bonfire of the Bible in the public schools. (5)

Lacking firm moral or spiritual foundations of his own, Theron is utterly unable to resist or evaluate the glamour and false sophistication of his new friends. The final stage in his metamorphosis takes place in a scene of rich comedy as he lolls on an oriental couch in Celia's 'inner sanctum,' dizzy with cigar smoke, drinking Benedictine, and breathing in the air of pagan decadence around him. Celia is playing Chopin to him – 'The Greekiest of the Greeks' – and Theron responds characteristically 'I am interested in Shopang. . . . He lived with – what's his name – George something.' From this moment he is lost, and his fall is ensured when he later kisses Celia in a scene which owes more to Hawthorne than to any realist writer.[6] He mistakenly believes that the whole bewildering world of wealth and beauty, spiritual exaltation and love, is being offered him on a silver salver. He has only to strip off his miserable ecclesiastical bandages and reveal his manliness by pursuing Celia to New York, and his transformation will be complete.

When he does finally confront her with a declaration of love, Celia strips away his illusions about himself in a remorseless analysis of his character and behaviour that also serves as an analysis of her own superficiality. Associating herself with Father Forbes and Dr Ledsmer, she admits that what had appealed to them in Theron was his natural and unsophisticated freshness, and that in attempting to improve himself he had, in fact, degenerated into a bore, a 'donkey trying to play lap-dog'. Rejecting his impulse to murder his tormentress, Theron opts for the traditional alternative, a drunken binge in the city, from which he is rescued by a couple of pragmatic Methodist fund-raisers who, despite their dubious methods and shady background, prove to have more genuine humanity than his erstwhile friends. Theron, unlike the tragic heroes of romance, picks himself up and at the end of the novel is preparing to leave for Seattle and a new career in politics.

The tone of *The Damnation of Theron Ware* is often closer to that of a novel like James's *The Europeans* (1878), even though the plotting is reminiscent of *Roderick Hudson*, but in any case, the comparison with James is certainly appropriate. In dramatizing the central social, intellectual, and cultural debates of the late nineteenth century, Frederic adds an interesting dimension to the International Novel, though James himself would eventually develop the form in even more remarkable ways.[7]

Discussion of Harold Frederic has taken us beyond the limits of the Utopian novel and back towards the mainstream of American fiction. The Utopians, whether more enamoured of the past or the future, have one thing in common: a revulsion from the actual and an inability to deal with it in their novels. Motivated more by political idealism than by the stirrings of imagination they inevitably fail in their attempts to flesh out their alien worlds. It is not surprising that most of their readers end up like Eveleth Strange, 'wolfishly hungry' for more news of the real America.

Notes

1. Letter to Thomas Carlyle in 1840. This letter is quoted in Mark Holloway's excellent history of Utopian communities in America from 1680 to 1880, *Heavens on Earth*, second edition (New York, 1966), p. 19.

2. See *Life in Letters of William Dean Howells*, edited by Mildred Howells, 2 vols (New York, 1968), I, 416–18.

3. For a detailed study of chivalric values in American romantic fiction see John Fraser, *America and the Pattern of Chivalry* (Cambridge, 1982).

4. John Henry Raleigh suggests some points of comparison between the two novels in '*The Damnation of Theron Ware*', in *American Literature*, 30 (1958), 210–27.

5. For a brief study of Frederic's sources see Robert H. Woodward, 'Some Sources for Harold Frederic's *The Damnation of Theron Ware*', *American Literature*, 33 (1961), 46–51.

6. George W. Johnson traces some of the novelist's debts to Hawthorne in 'Harold Frederic's Young Goodman Ware: The Ambiguities of a Realistic Romance', *Modern Fiction Studies*, 8 (1962), 361–74.

7. Frederic despised James and called him 'an effeminate old donkey' whose 'literary admirations serve me generally as warnings what to avoid'. In his Introduction to the Penguin edition of *The Damnation of Theron Ware* (Harmondsworth, 1986), Scott Donaldson discusses the influence of other writers on Frederic.

Chapter 6
Henry James

In 1879, twelve years after writing his famous declaration of spiritual independence to T. S. Perry,[1] James, now in his mid-thirties and more committed both to his career as a novelist and to permanent exile from his native country, once again took stock of what he considered the more important national characteristics of his countrymen. In doing so, he was also tacitly setting out his own qualifications as a critic of the culture he had left behind, and contrasting them with those of his most famous predecessor, Hawthorne:

> . . . the Civil War marks an era in the American mind. It
> introduced into the national consciousness a certain sense
> of proportion and relation, of the world being a more
> complicated place than it had hitherto seemed, the future
> more treacherous, success more difficult. At the rate at
> which things are going, it is obvious that good Americans
> will be more numerous than ever; but the good American,
> in days to come, will be a more critical person than his
> complacent and confident grandfather. He has eaten of the
> tree of knowledge.[2]

America itself was certainly becoming a far more complex society as we have seen, and some of the irreconcilable interests of different sections and classes had begun to be defined by the war between the states. James's own sense of relation and proportion, though, was immeasurably extended by his deepening acquaintance with European society and culture. This innate understanding of America was brought into much clearer focus in the Parisian salons of Madame Viardot and Madame de Blocqueville, where he met Flaubert, Daudet, Maupassant, Zola, the Goncourts, and Turgenev, and was, as he says, admitted to the 'aristocracy of the fine'. But even such a mundane event as breakfast at the Adelphi Hotel in Liverpool nourished not just his body but also his grasping imagination with the kind of images that he loved to probe for significance by comparing them with their American counterparts. For him Europe, from the very beginning, was an inexhaustible 'tree of knowledge':

> the damp and darksome light washed in from the steep,
> black, bricky street, the crackle of the strong draught of
> the British 'sea-coal' fire, much more confident of its
> function, I thought, than the fires I had left, the rustle of
> the thick, stiff, loudly unfolded and refolded *Times*, the
> incomparable truth to type of the waiter, truth to history,
> to literature, to poetry, to Dickens, to Thackeray,
> positively to Smollett and to Hogarth, to every connection
> that could help me to appropriate him and his setting, an
> arrangement of things hanging together with a romantic
> rightness that had the force of a revelation.[3]

As an American, however, James experienced the need to fight against this feeling if he were to avoid making 'a superstitious valuation' of Europe, and in the earlier part of his career he did so well enough to convince another American expatriate, Ezra Pound, that he had 'a desire to square all things to the ethical standards of a Salem mid-week Unitarian Prayer Meeting'.[4]

Pound is wrong, of course, to attribute this kind of moralism even to James's early fiction set in America – *The Europeans* (1879), *Washington Square* (1881), and *The Bostonians* (1886) – in which he was trying to chart the national consciousness and fix it in relation to its environment. The scope of his critical irony in the shorter novels and the subtle exploration of the submerged energies and passions of the central characters in *The Bostonians* are the product of a talent untrammelled by the provincialism that marked even the best of his American contemporaries.

The Europeans was James's first considerable attempt to dramatize conflicting cultural values in a story of Old-World sophisticates coming to visit their American relatives. He had already achieved considerable success with *Daisy Miller* (1879) and would return again and again to the formula in which complex relationships are engendered by the introduction of American innocents to the dangerous world of Europe. His later, horrified protest at the shape taken by his native culture in his travel book *The American Scene* (1907) and in the unfinished novel, *The Ivory Tower* (1917) was made long after he had won his reputation as an international novelist. In 1879, though, he was more concerned to explore the limitations and comic possibilities of the Puritan conscience in characters like Mr Wentworth:

If you had been present, it would probably not have
seemed to you that the advent of these brilliant strangers
was treated as an exhilarating occurrence, a pleasure the
more in this tranquil household, a prospective source of
entertainment. This was not Mr. Wentworth's way of
treating any human occurrence. A sudden irruption into
the well-ordered consciousness of the Wentworths of an
element not allowed for in its scheme of usual obligations,
required a readjustment of that sense of responsibility
which constituted its principal furniture. To consider an
event crudely and baldly in the light of the pleasure it
might bring them, was an intellectual exercise with which
Felix Young's American cousins were almost wholly
unacquainted, and which they scarcely supposed to be
largely pursued by any such human society. The arrival of
Felix and his sister was a satisfaction but it was a
singularly joyless and inelastic satisfaction. It was an
extension of duty, of the exercise of the more recondite
virtues. (4)

The advent of the Europeans, as far as the Americans are concerned,
is in every way beneficial inasmuch as it helps to bring about several
very important changes in their lives. But apart from Gertrude, who
is never in sympathy with the Puritan ethos anyway, it is doubtful if
any of them are made to extend their tolerance to any alien form of
life.

The definition of a Puritan as one who renounces the life of the flesh
in favour of the life of the spirit fails to do justice to the extremism
of Mr Wentworth. His renunciation is more complete, so that he
habitually withdraws from the possibility of any new experience. The
resulting isolation is not an uncommon phenomenon in nineteenth-
century America and it is associated both with New England Puritanism and also with the 'Genteel Tradition' which it favoured. Here
Wentworth is expressing typical caution in the face of 'peculiar' influences: 'You must be careful', he said, 'you must keep watch. Indeed
we must all be careful. This is a great change – we are to be exposed
to peculiar influences. I don't say they are bad; I don't judge them in
advance. But they may perhaps make it necessary that we should
exercise a great deal of wisdom and self-control. It will be a different
tone' (4). Yet in spite of the old man's shortcomings, James's treatment
of Mr Wentworth is more sympathetic than some of the above illus-
trations may indicate. The New England brand of Puritanism may not
be conducive to much pleasure ('amuse ourselves? – we are not chil-

dren'), yet when one considers their obvious virtues: their goodness, honesty, nobility, their own particular refinement, one is made aware that in any product of James's civilization these are the basic American characteristics which may be supplemented but not superseded.

They are also the virtues that James fondly cherished even as he described their disappearance from the New York of *Washington Square*. It is instructive to compare James's treatment of the society with that in Edith Wharton's New York novel *The Age of Innocence* (1920) not merely to demonstrate James's superiority as a writer but also his deeper knowledge of, and warmer affection for, that city.

The Age of Innocence describes the pressures brought to bear by society on two of its members having an illicit affair. In the name of good taste the lovers are forced to separate and return to their drab, empty lives. Edith Wharton's satire of that society is superb. Operas, balls, engagement rites, the ceremonies of dining – all are observed with keenly ironic detachment, thus creating the atmosphere in which a small, ingrown, artificial community once had its being – 'a small slippery pyramid, in which, as yet, hardly a fissure had been made or a foothold gained'. (6) It is as if a tiny fragment of the European aristocracy had been transplanted and allowed to continue its ritualistic way of living, completely divorced from the environment in which it had evolved. But as such it does not provide any kind of answer to James's complaint about the lack of manners and customs in American life. The society described in *The Age of Innocence* may have been a feature of the American scene but it was scarcely an American phenomenon. The distinctly native flavour of *Washington Square*, on the other hand, is powerfully created in the first paragraphs of the novel. The naive vigour and parochialism of mid-century New York is present in every line James writes. In exploring these qualities, he is led to examine fundamental characteristics of American civilization that are quite beyond the reach of Edith Wharton. For him, surfaces are only important inasmuch as they represent life, so that whereas in *The Age of Innocence* manners are an index to nothing beyond themselves, in *Washington Square* they are always tied to the moral climate in which they have their origins.

As well as shifting the location of his story from London where he had first heard it told by Fanny Kemble, the actress, James moved its action back in time to the 1850s, so giving himself a thirty-year perspective on events. The distance obtained in this way allowed him to manipulate the angle of his narrative vision and give an added dimension to his picture of American society poised on the brink of a major upheaval, enjoying the last years of its pre-war, provincial innocence before it was swept into the maelstrom of expansion, immigration, industrialization, finance capitalism, and all the developments that James later came to abhor. The entire novel is pervaded by the sense of an irrecoverable past, a menacing future, and the human and social implications of imminent change.

In 1850 James was a child of seven. His father had recently brought his family back to New York from Albany and purchased a house on West Fourteenth Street. It was here that James spent several years of his childhood, a period that he finally wrote about at length in the first volume of his autobiography, *A Small Boy and Others*.[5] He tenderly recalls the 'small warm dusky homogeneous world' of mid-century New York by weaving together a dazzling skein of sensory impressions. The limits of his childhood world were naturally close ones: Broadway from Union Square to Barnum's great American Museum by the City Hall, and a few blocks east and west. Within this small compass, only extended by visits to the circus, the World's Fair and the more rural reaches of Manhattan, he discovered the normal pleasures of city life. He visited theatres and ice-cream parlours, rode on the new streetcars, and obtained some kind of formal education in various schools, but a much more extensive informal one in casual encounters with his father's broad circle of artistic friends and relations.

James's sense of the compactness of New York society was not just the product of an infant perspective. It was still a small town with a population of only 200,000, though even at this stage the pattern of social history was being laid, enabling him later to make nice discriminations with almost archaeological exactness. The age of 'brown stone' building was just beginning, and he contrasts this 'danger signal' with the quieter harmonies of the earlier time, represented by Washington Square 'so decent in its dignity, so instinctively unpretentious'. This air of established repose and modest luxury is confidently re-created in the early chapters of the novel. James even relaxes his narrative angle to the extent of including an autobiographical digression in his description. Such intrusions are rare in his fiction; they signify his easy familiarity with the material and act as a guarantee of its authenticity.

He is no less aware, in looking back, of the portents of doom. The 'long, shrill city' of the future was rapidly taking shape in the wake of the relentless tide of commercial development rolling inexorably up Manhattan Island. There were occasional setbacks such as the economic depression of 1856, but the unruly riots of that year only strengthened the determination of the State Legislature to create a more efficient city. Order was quickly restored, progress resumed, and, by the time *Washington Square* came to be written, the Gilded Age had obliterated nearly every vestige of James's comfortable childhood world.

It is a mark of his genius that he can so effortlessly create the human concomitants of all this social history. The agent of the Slopers' moral and emotional destruction is, of course, the aptly named Morris Townsend. He is both an outsider and a threat to the solidarity of the complacent bourgeois community, and his difference from the young men of Catherine's social circle, as well as his beauty, are what first fascinate her:

> He was very amusing. He asked her about the people that
> were near them; he tried to guess who some of them
> were, and he made the most laughable mistakes. He
> criticised them very freely, in a positive, off-hand way.
> Catherine had never heard any one – especially any young
> man – talk just like that. It was the way a young man
> might talk in a novel; or, better still, in a play, on the
> stage, close before the foot-lights, looking at the audience,
> and with every one looking at him, so that you wondered
> at his presence of mind. And yet Mr. Townsend was not
> like an actor; he seemed so sincere, so natural. (4)

It does not take Catherine's father, or the reader, very long to see that Morris Townsend does not have the soul of a gentleman but is a 'plausible coxcomb' in search of an easy fortune. Yet the criticisms he makes of Catherine's family and friends are not undeserved either. James is not blinded to the vacuity and hypocrisy of this society by his nostalgia, and Dr Sloper's ironic view of Morris is always finally subject to the author's own. After all, Dr Sloper also married into money, if not for it, and the manner in which he pursues his medical career does not set him so far apart from Morris:

> It was an element in Doctor Sloper's reputation that his
> learning and his skill were very evenly balanced; he was
> what you might call a scholarly doctor, and yet there was
> nothing abstract in his remedies – he always ordered you
> to take something. Though he was felt to be extremely
> thorough, he was not uncomfortably theoretic; and if he
> sometimes explained matters rather more minutely than
> might seem of use to the patient, he never went so far
> (like some practitioners one had heard of) as to trust to the
> explanation alone, but always left behind him an
> inscrutable prescription. There were some doctors that left
> the prescription without offering any explanation at all;
> and he did not belong to that class either, which was after
> all the most vulgar. It will be seen that I am describing a
> clever man; and this is really the reason why Doctor
> Sloper had become a local celebrity. (1)

If Morris Townsend is playing a part, so too is Dr Sloper, and the brilliant comedy in the first half of the novel is produced out of their ironic detachment from the emotional situation they are creating. Throughout the complication of the plot Catherine is seen as a plain, passive pawn in their amusing game, and Aunt Penniman's melo-dramatic misreadings of character and situation only serve further to obscure our view of her. In her attempts simultaneously to create mystery and high drama, she is, as Dr Sloper comments, 'like a revolving lighthouse; pitch darkness alternating with a dazzling brilliancy!'

James himself deliberately does little to illuminate the object of all their attention in the early chapters, being content to provide at first a largely negative description of Catherine:

> She was not ugly . . . was decidedly not clever; she was
> not quick with her book, nor, indeed, with anything else.
> She was not abnormally deficient. . . . Doctor Sloper
> would have liked to be proud of his daughter; but there
> was nothing to be proud of in poor Catherine. (2)

Her total lack of positive characteristics gives little scope for sympath-etic identification even to the most determinedly romantic reader at this stage, who is directed instead to enjoy the manœuvres of her father and lover as they play out their scenes with polished urbanity and wit. Beneath the restrained hostility James allows us to see the joy of conflict and the respect each feels for the other's ability. But above all, what each admires in the other is the display of style.

So, too, does the reader at first. But ultimately *Washington Square* is much more than a social comedy. The points of view maintained throughout the first half of the novel are eventually superseded by that of Catherine herself as she is finally brought to life by 'the clairvoyance of her passion'. It is she who exposes the sorry inadequacies of the players as, one by one, she forces them to step out of their roles, relinquish their masks and reveal their true motives. Like the girl in Fanny Kemble's original story, Catherine is the kind of person who is permanently affected by her impressions. The depth of her poorly articulated emotion in contrast to the superficial, malicious, or merely silly attitudes of her loved ones is what finally moves the reader and enlists his sympathy.

The turning-point for her father occurs some time during their extended trip to Europe. Before their departure he confides to his other sister, Mrs Almond, that Catherine's obstinacy in sticking to Morris Townsend positively excites him, but that he believes he understands her and, having taken the measure of her resistance, is confident of his ultimate triumph. However, when it eventually becomes clear to him after six months of their Grand Tour, that Catherine has not budged an inch, his urbanity completely deserts him, and as genuine anger takes the place of excitement, he attempts to frighten and subdue her by a crude display of passion:

> He stopped in front of her, and stood looking at her with eyes that had kept the light of the flushing snow-summits on which they had just been fixed. Then, abruptly, in a low tone, he asked her an unexpected question,
> 'Have you given him up?'
> The question was unexpected, but Catherine was only superficially unprepared.
> 'No, father,' she answered.
> He looked at her again for some moments without speaking.
> 'Does he write to you?' he asked.
> 'Yes, about twice a month.'
> The Doctor looked up and down the valley, swinging his stick; then he said to her, in the same low tone,
> 'I am very angry.'
> She wondered what he meant – whether he wished to frighten her. If he did, the place was well chosen: this hard, melancholy dell, abandoned by the summer light, made her feel her loneliness. She looked around her, and her heart grew cold; for a moment her fear was great. But she could think of nothing to say, save to murmur, gently, 'I am sorry.' (24)

Sloper continues to show this hardness to her throughout the remainder of his life and eventually alters his will when he realizes that she will never allow him to enjoy the triumph of an empty victory over her. She will neither promise not to marry Morris after her father's death, nor gratify Sloper during his lifetime by marrying a more eligible suitor. The old man dies in the knowledge that he has broken the springs of Catherine's affection for him but not the power of her resistance.

As for Morris, he too gives vent to his anger and cruelty when he sees that he has lost the game and great prize that would have been his. His heartlessness at their parting enables Catherine to see him for the first time without his mask of polished civility, and the scene between them provokes in her the only outburst of visible grief in the novel. It is quickly over and, in a wonderfully economical paragraph, James creates a chilling image of the desolation that follows it:

When it had grown dark, Catherine went to the window, and looked out; she stood there for half an hour, on the mere chance that he would come up the steps. At last she turned away, for she saw her father come in. He had seen her at the window looking out, and he stopped a moment at the bottom of the white steps, and gravely, with an air of exaggerated courtesy, lifted his hat to her. The gesture was so incongruous to the condition she was in, this stately tribute of respect to a poor girl despised and forsaken was so out of place, that the thing gave her a kind of horror, and she hurried away to her room. It seemed to her that she had given Morris up. (30)

Aunt Penniman does not remain unscathed either. She is also subjected to Catherine's revaluation and judgement; one that is final and without appeal. Her manipulation of Catherine's emotions, if less conscious than the others', is hardly less cruel, conducted as it is for her own amusement and gain. When the unhappy girl exposes the casual wickedness behind the old woman's meddlesome folly and demands to be left alone, many readers, I imagine, experience a twinge of conscience brought by their earlier relish of the comedy inherent in the situation.

Nor does James attempt to mitigate his picture of Catherine's isolation. Our last view of her after she has rejected Morris's pathetic attempt to renew his suit years later is one that stays in the memory. She returns to the parlour of the empty Washington Square house, takes up her morsel of embroidery and sits down with it 'for life, as it were'.

It is a stern and sombre note on which to end a novel. But James's consciousness of the amount of life he had had to sacrifice in order to preserve his necessary disinterested spectatorship at least guarantees his sympathy for the succession of characters in his novels who, for whatever reasons, make similar renunciations.

One of James's most penetrating studies of renunciation and self-immolation is that of Olive Chancellor, the crypto-Lesbian feminist in *The Bostonians*. Wanting to write 'a very American tale', he asked himself what was the most salient and peculiar feature of social life in the mid-1880s. His answer was 'the situation of women, the decline of the sentiment of sex, the agitation on their behalf'.[6] It is misleading, however, to read *The Bostonians* merely as a social novel exposing the more bizarre aspects of Boston's Frogpondium. James was well qualified to deal with what he called 'long haired men and short haired women . . . [the] great irregular army of nostrum-mongers, domiciled in humanitary Bohemia'. His own father had been at various times a

Fouerierite and a Swedenborgian, and his portrait of Miss Birdseye – one of the novel's minor characters – was widely recognized as a satiric, if affectionate portrait of Hawthorne's well-known reforming sister-in-law. But at the heart of the novel lies an understanding of the psychological basis of action that goes far beyond the requirements of social realism.

James begins to probe the psychological basis of Olive's puritanism early in the book. We are told that: 'The most secret, the most sacred hope of her nature, was that some day she might have such a change, she might be a martyr and die for something.' We are thus prepared for the fulfilment of her desires in her relationship with Verena Tarrant. Verena's response to the plea that they should 'renounce, refrain, abstain' was to wonder 'what could be the need of this scheme of renunciation'. She is the typical Jamesian innocent, ruthlessly cultivated as a vehicle for the feminist movement, and her connection with it is 'the most unreal, accidental, illusory thing in the world'. Her fickleness towards the cause, and the final rupture between the two women bring Olive a great deal of suffering, but 'The prospect of suffering was always, spiritually speaking, so much cash in her pocket', and she freely avails herself of this supply in the closing scenes of the book. Typically enough, she spares herself no degradation and goes off to face the hisses and boos of the disappointed audience in the Boston lecture hall like 'some feminine firebrand of Paris revolutions erect on a barricade, or even the sacrificial figure of Hypatia whirled through the furious mob of Alexandria' (42).

By the very skilful way in which he juxtaposes private and public themes, James contrives to lay bare the relationship between the feminist movement and the psychology of its members – demonstrating truths which strike us as commonplace today but which were considered startling, if not ridiculous, in a world that had not experienced the Freudian revolution. On other aspects of the problem – for instance on the effect of democratic institutions upon the equality of the sexes – he is not so explicit. De Tocqueville, in his *Democracy in America*, (1835, 1840) had been quite clear in his view that the great social changes would eventually make women the equal of men, but not, he adds, in the way that some people have understood equality. Women, he says, must never be allowed into business or politics but must fulfil their own particular nature in the best possible manner. Nothing could be worse, he believes, than giving men and women the same functions, imposing on both the same duties, and granting to both the same rights. The only result that this could have would be to produce weak men and disorderly women. Nevertheless, he states that if he were asked to what factor the singular prosperity and growing strength of Americans ought mainly to be attributed, he would reply: 'To the superiority of their women.'

These views are just those of Basil Ransome, the hero of *The Bostonians*, and we are not at all surprised to discover that de Tocqueville is his favourite author. Even Ransome's smugness and complacency are a reflection of the Frenchman's, and James seems fully aware of a petty conservative aestheticism that constantly contaminates his hero's moral position.

The dichotomy between the social or the aesthetic on the one hand and the moral or political on the other, reaches right to the heart of the Jamesian dialectic. His imagination ranges continually between these terms, and any civilization, he intimates, must assess correctly the relative weight due to moral and aesthetic considerations. It is a minor theme of *The Bostonians*, but it occupies the forefront of his English novels of the middle period, *The Princess Casamassima* (1886), *The Tragic Muse* (1890), but above all, *The Portrait of a Lady* (1881).

Everything James wrote before *Tha Portrait of a Lady* seems to lead up to and be included in that work, but it is not only included, for everything is 'placed' with unerring rightness. The values he has been weighing against one another in the earlier novels are done full justice here, and though he still tips the scales in the same direction as before, one has the feeling that now he knows better why he does so. He has taken the measure not only of Madame Merle and Gilbert Osmond, but also of Lord Warburton and the English aristocracy; and what is perhaps more important still, he has come to grips with the Americans, Mrs Touchett, Henrietta Stackpole, and Caspar Goodwood.

The centre of James's drama, however, is located in Isabel Archer's consciousness, and it is with her that criticism must begin. Isabel is something more than merely another 'American Girl' – a more finely realized Daisy Miller. Here James is staking a real claim for the superiority of American values, and he does so far more successfully than in any other of his early novels. So confident is he of Isabel's chances of attaining a 'completed consciousness', a state which in her is largely bound up with images of a moral nature, that he makes no more attempt to minimize her deficiencies than George Eliot did with her prototype Dorothea Brooke in *Middlemarch*:

> Altogether, with her meagre knowledge, her inflated
> ideals, her confidence at once innocent and dogmatic, her
> temper at once exacting and indulgent, her mixture of
> curiosity and fastidiousness, of vivacity and indifference,
> her desire to look very well and to be if possible even
> better, her determination to see, to try, to know, her

combination of the delicate, desultory, flame-like spirit and
the eager and personal creature of conditions: she would
be an easy victim of scientific criticism if she were not
intended to awaken on the reader's part an impulse more
tender and more purely expectant. (6)

Her determination to see, to try, and to know, attracts her to European
civilization, yet her moral integrity guarantees her immunity from it.
We recognize James's own dilemma here, and in Isabel's rejection of
Warburton, his implicit recognition of the impossibility of reconciling
his conflicting attitudes towards Europe. If Isobel is to pursue her
policy of 'expansion', she can only satisfactorily do so in Europe.
Gardencourt, the symbol of country-house civilization with its rich
perfection:

at once revealed a world and gratified a need. The large,
low rooms, with brown ceilings and dusky corners, the
deep embrasures and curious casements, the quiet light on
dark polished panels, the deep greenness outside, that
seemed always peeping in, the sense of well-ordered
privacy in the centre of a 'property' – a place where
sounds were felicitously accidental, where the tread was
muffled by the earth itself and in the thick mild air all
friction dropped out of contact and all shrillness out of
talk – these things were much to the taste of our young
lady. (6)

Yet she has been made aware of the ugliness and misery upon which
this social system is based, and also of Warburton's incongruous
radicalism:

Their radical views are a kind of amusement; they've got
to have some amusement, and they might have coarser
taste than that. You see they're very luxurious, and these
progressive ideas are about their biggest luxury. They
make them feel moral and yet don't damage their position.
(8)

There is more to Isabel's relationship with Warburton than this,
though. Marriage with him would represent an escape, a separation
from the 'usual chances and dangers, from what most people know
and suffer'. Such a marriage, with its ease and comfort, would necessi-
tate a renunciation of her ultimate moral responsibilities. When she
finally rejects Lord Warburton after meeting him again in Rome, she

explains to Ralph Touchett that Gilbert Osmond's overriding advantage lies in his appeal to her 'one ambition – to be free to follow a good feeling'. Lord Warburton's strength and power would deny her the exercise of that freedom, as would Caspar Goodwood's. Osmond's 'very poverties, dressed out as honours', constitute a large part of his attraction for Isabel. This problem can be seen as part of a larger one which occupies James's attention throughout the book – the possibility of freeing moral choice from the pressure of one's conditioning. Isabel Archer believes in an inescapable destiny which is predetermined by her particular upbringing and environment, yet she insists on accepting full responsibility for the consequences of her actions.

F. R. Leavis, discussing *Daniel Deronda* in *The Great Tradition*, finds *The Portrait of a Lady* lacking in moral substance by comparison. He finds fault with James for freeing Isabel Archer from the economic and social pressures which force Gwendolen Harleth's choice, and then demanding uncritical homage and admiration for her when all the time we ought to be blaming her for ignoring the advice of Mr Touchett, Ralph Touchett, and Lord Warburton. On the contrary, the admiration and homage James tries to exact are entirely her due; more so, indeed, than in Gwendolen Harleth's case, where the economic and social pressures do, despite what Leavis says, mitigate our critical response. By freeing Isabel from these external pressures, James makes her final choice even more praiseworthy, especially since she has every excuse for evading this responsibility, as Caspar Goodwood points out in his last interview with her:

> Why shouldn't we be happy – when it's here before us,
> when it's so easy? I'm yours for ever – for ever and ever.
> Here I stand; I'm as firm as a rock. What have you to care
> about? You've no children; that perhaps would be an
> obstacle. As it is, you've nothing to consider. You must
> save what you can of your life; you mustn't lose it all
> simply because you've lost a part . . . I swear, as I stand
> here, that a woman deliberately made to suffer is justified
> in anything in life – in going down into the streets if that
> will help her! I know how you suffer, and that's why I'm
> here. We can do absolutely as we please; to whom under
> the sun do we owe anything? What is it that holds us,
> what is it that has the smallest right to interfere in such a
> question as this? (55)

This appeal, which she resists only by making the supreme effort of her life, clarifies her decision: 'She had not known where to turn; but she knew now. There was a very straight path.' Surely Isabel's integrity, preserved in the face of such great provocation, does not, if we are making the correct responses, make for moral incoherence in the book. It can be argued that the actual choice she makes is wrong – that she has the wrong conception of where her duty lies – but even this argument is really untenable.

This discussion has taken us too far ahead, and we must now return to Isabel's attempts to come to terms with European civilization, something she achieves only by what seems like an act of rationalization. It is not that her moral sensibility is submerged by an aestheticism like Osmond's, but that the 'moral retreat' she has hitherto needed when confronted by declarations of love from Warburton and Osmond is no longer necessary, given her changed ideals: 'The desire for unlimited expansion had been succeeded in her soul by the sense that life was vacant without some private duty that might gather one's energies to a point . . . she could surrender to[Osmond]with a kind of humility, she could marry him with a kind of pride; she was not only taking, she was giving' (35). It may be thought that this decision denotes a puritanism far more deeply rooted than that displayed by any of James's conventional puritans in the novel, and that eventually it is detrimental to the 'personal life' and 'completed consciousness' Isabel wishes to cultivate. But what must be insisted on here is her reaction to the European's preoccupation with the 'world' and with 'things'. This comes out best in one of her conversations with Madame Merle. Madame Merle speaks first:

> 'When you've lived as long as I you'll see that every
> human being has his shell and you must take the shell into
> account. By the shell I mean the whole envelope of
> circumstances. There's no such thing as an isolated man or
> woman; we're each of us made up of some cluster of
> appurtenances. What shall we call our 'self'? Where does it
> begin, where does it end? It overflows into everything that
> belongs to us – and than it flows back again. I know a
> large part of myself is in the clothes I choose to wear. I
> have a great respect for *things*! One's self – for other
> people – is one's expression of oneself; and one's house,
> one's furniture, one's garments, the books one reads, the
> company one keeps – these things are all expressive. . . .'
> 'I don't agree with you. I think just the other way. I
> don't know whether I succeed in expressing myself, but I
> know that nothing else expresses me. Nothing that
> belongs to me is any measure of me; everything's on the
> contrary a limit, a barrier, and a perfectly arbitrary one.'
> (19)

What we are presented with by Madame Merle represents the real sterility of European civilization; it is sterile because the moral sensibility abdicates in favour of the aesthetic, and, paradoxically, because of a morbid preoccupation with 'self', totally unlike Isabel's healthy introversion. These defects show themselves most clearly in Gilbert Osmond, who lives exclusively for the aesthetic value of 'forms' while having no conception of the values underlying them. This is the basic situation behind much egotism, where the egotist must depend entirely on the people and things which he so despises. In analysing Osmond's egotism, James writes what is, in his own words, 'obviously the best thing in the book'.[7] At this point he is most closely engaged with his subject, for he is also defining the limitations and shortcomings of a whole society.

It remains only to discuss James's concern with what he calls 'the dusky old-world expedient' of renunciation, and this brings us back to my earlier remarks about the significance of Isabel's choice in returning to Osmond. It is plain that her moral integrity at least must be acknowledged, but James insists that the reader be prepared to go beyond this and accept that her decision implies neither renunciation nor defeat. Isabel herself realizes that: 'Deep in her soul – deeper than any appetite for renunciation – was the sense that life would be her business for a long time to come' (53). And the realization is made even more explicit in her last conversation with Ralph Touchett. He has asked her whether or not she will return to Osmond:

> 'Why should there be pain? In such hours as this what
> have we to do with pain? That's not the deepest thing;
> there's something deeper.' . . . 'It passes, after all; it's
> passing now. But love remains. I don't know why we
> should suffer so much. Perhaps I shall find out. There are
> many things in life. You're very young.'
> 'I feel very old' said Isabel.
> You'll grow young again. That's how I see you . . . I
> don't believe that such a generous mistake as yours can
> hurt you for more than a little.' (54)

Such is Ralph Touchett's view. And we can be certain that it is the one we are meant to endorse.

If we compare this to the ending of The Wings of the Dove (1902), where the dying Millie Theale symbolically turns her 'face to the wall' there can be no doubt about the moral cohesion and artistic integrity of The Portrait of a Lady.

James had hoped that his two realistic novels of the mid-1880s, The Bostonians and The Princess Casamassima, with their overtly social and political subjects, would rekindle his popularity and capture for him a larger share of the market. When this did not happen, he turned to other projects and experiments in the 1890s, producing stories about artists for *The Yellow Book*, ghost stories including his masterpiece in the genre, *The Turn of the Screw* (1898), unsuccessful plays, and novels in which he experimented brilliantly with technique such as *What Maisie Knew* (1897) and *The Awkward Age* (1898). What characterizes most of his writing at this time is a growing preoccupation with the problem of dramatizing the individual consciousness. In his efforts to give more immediate inner life to his characters – efforts which incidentally were being made simultaneously by other Europeans such as Eduard Dujardin who was experimenting with primitive stream-of-consciousness techniques – James temporarily let his larger themes fall into abeyance. But in the early years of the new century, having discovered how to make the vital connections between inner and outer worlds, he created – ten years before Joyce and Proust – the first major modernist masterpieces, *The Wings of the Dove* (1902), *The Ambassadors* (1903), and *The Golden Bowl* (1904).

Critical opinion remains sharply divided by these late, strange novels. There are those opposed to the whole modernist enterprise, who see them as a betrayal of realism, some detect in their author a sentimental surrender to European decadence and thus an even worse betrayal of America itself; others, looking through the texts rather than at them, have discovered archaic religious allegories hidden in them; and for some readers they represent the final consummation, if not of nineteenth-century American fiction, then certainly of James's own extensive life's work.

A desire to tease from the artist's work a coherent and rounded philosophy – the extracted essence of a lifetime's experience or the painstaking translation into art of another's philosophical system – must be counted as one of the major temptations for the literary critic. The temptation is almost irresistible in the case of James's *The Ambassadors*, *The Wings of the Dove*, and *The Golden Bowl*. Quentin Anderson's interpretation is only one of many that make the mistake of looking through James's text rather than at it.[8] What such criticisms usually have in common is an insistence that James intends the opposite of what he appears to be saying, or that his words can be made to mean anything at all. Caroline Gordon provides a nice example of the latter fault in her essay tracing archetypal patterns of Christianity in the late novels:

> 'It is significant, I think, that James turns Mr. Verver into a hero with the same gesture he uses to turn Chad into a villain; the characteristic gesture of hands thrust into the pockets.'[9]

James himself provides the best answer to these critics and the best introduction to the real themes of the novels in his working notes. Though he is writing about *The Ambassadors*, his remarks are true of the others, too. He sees the novel not as a secret history of the Church or as a condemnation of self-righteousness, but rather as a demonstration of one man's moral expansion as he is brought to an awareness that the values entrenched in American puritanism and provincialism are inadequate for full appreciation of the subtle and various qualities of life in a civilized community.

Lambert Strether, a middle-aged American, is sent to Paris from Woollett, Mass., by Mrs Newsome in order to rescue her son Chad from the immoral life they are both sure he must be leading. Success in this enterprise will enable Strether to marry Mrs Newsome and attain the 'consideration and comfort of security' which his life has so far lacked. Thus James creates once more the familiar pattern of the submission of New World innocence to European experience. Strether proceeds by way of a number of crises to a 'total' view of life – which makes it possible for him finally to 'see' Mrs Newsome and evaluate his own experience. His growing awareness of the 'emptiness' of Woollett and all it stands for is concretely rendered at each stage of his initiation into the life of Paris. The first intimation that there may exist a finer, more intuitive existence than he had hitherto imagined is obliquely introduced by way of an architectural image. James juxtaposes the secondary hotel in which Strether is installed – 'all indoor chill, glass-roofed court and slippery staircase' – with Chad's home:

> High, broad, clear – he was expert enough to make out in
> a moment that it was admirably built – it fairly
> embarrassed our friend by the quality that, as he would
> have said, it 'sprang' on him . . . the quality produced by
> measure and balance, the fine relation of part to part and
> space to space, was probably – aided by the presence of
> ornament as positive as it was discreet, and by the
> complexion of the stone, a cold, fair grey, warmed and
> polished a little by life – neither more nor less than a case
> of distinction, such a case as he could only feel
> unexpectedly as a sort of delivered challenge?(5)

James has come a long way in such passages from his early attempts to relate man to his created environment. In all his fiction he tries to avoid using setting as mere backdrop for action. Even as early as *Roderick Hudson* (1876), he does not introduce the 'clear white houses' of New England just for local colour as Rebecca West maintained, but as a reminder of the 'kindness, comfort, safety, the warning voice of duty, the perfect absence of temptation'; in short, of the things his

young artist would have to sacrifice in Europe. Lambert Strether is in
many ways an older version of Roderick, but now James has learned
how to create the moral conflict within his character's consciousness
rather than impose it from outside.

Strether's first real revelation in the novel is also partly a product
of his situation, and the effect upon him of his civilized surroundings.
He uses the occasion for a speech based on an anecdote concerning
W. D. Howells which, as James reminds us in his Preface, contains the
'whole case' of the novel: 'Never can a composition of this sort have
sprung straighter from a dropped grain of suggestion.' The essence of
The Ambassadors is, he says, contained in the following exhortation:

> 'Live all you can; it's a mistake not to. It doesn't so much
> matter what you do in particular, so long as you have
> your life. If you haven't had that, what have you had? . . .
> I see it now. I haven't done so enough before – and now
> I'm old; too old at any rate for what I see.' (11)

This is the vision to which Strether eventually comes. It is the 'precious
moral' of everything, and the interest lies largely in Strether's attempts
to retain that vision in the face of any shock that might win him back
to 'the principles of Woollett'. This shock comes when he discovers
by accident that Chad and Madame de Vionnet are lovers, and they
act out for him the lie 'in the charming affair'. However, his experience
has fitted him now to approach such facts in a new way, and his vision
remains essentially unimpaired. He has participated in and contributed
to 'life' by becoming 'with his perceptions and his mistakes, his concessions and his reserves, the droll mixture, as it must seem to them, of
his braveries and his fears, the general spectacle of his art and his
innocence . . . a common priceless ground for them to meet
upon.'(32) If one's moral vibrations are the test of life, then Strether
has lived, and the fact of his having done so and the importance James
attaches to the point make nonsense of Anderson's contention that
'Strether is the worst of us all'.

So it is that Lambert Strether is on the side of 'life', and the novel
is, in Philip Rahv's words, 'a veritable declaration of the rights of man
– not to be sure, of the rights of the public or the social man, but of
the rights of the private man, of the rights of personality, whose openness to experience provides the sole effective guaranty of its development'.[10] what remains to be examined is the actual quality of the
experience to which Strether submits himself, and the role of the
individual consciousness which become in the late novels the touch-
stone for the testing of all values. These considerations are forced on
us by the subtleties of the late manner, which for some critics at least

represents a 'doing' disproportionate to the issues – 'to any issues that
are concretely held and presented'. There are no objective sanctions
for such judgements, which depend upon individual taste and a sense
of proportion. But it at least helps to clarify the importance of the
issues involved if James's concept of consciousness is historically sited.
This will serve the dual purpose of clarifying his relation to the civilization coming into being during his lifetime, and free him from the
artificial ties with which Anderson seeks to bind him to his father.[11]
It may also throw a little light on the way in which, as James becomes
more immersed in the presentation of individual consciousness, he
relies increasingly on the power of symbol and myth.

Emerson, in his essay 'The Transcendentalist', affirms the overriding
importance of consciousness:

> The idealist takes his departure from his consciousness,
> and reckons the world an appearance . . . [he] has another
> measure, which is metaphysical, namely, the rank which
> things themselves take in his consciousness; not at all the
> size or appearance. Mind is the only reality, of which men
> and all other natures are better or worse reflectors. Nature,
> literature, history are only subjective phenomena.
> (*Miscellanies*)

This last view Emerson illustrates at some length in his essay 'History':

> The world exists for the education of each man. There is
> no age or state of society or mode of action in history, to
> which there is not somewhat corresponding in his life.
> Everything tends in a wonderful manner to abbreviate
> itself and yield its own virtue to him. He must sit solidly
> at home, and not suffer himself to be bullied by kings or
> empires, but know that he is greater than all the
> geography and all the government of the world; he must
> transfer the point of view from which history is
> commonly read, from Rome and Athens and London to
> himself, and not deny his conviction that he is the court,
> and if England or Egypt have anything to say to him, he
> will try the case; if not, let them for ever be silent. He
> must attain and maintain that lofty site where facts yield
> their secret sense, and poetry and annals are alike.

And Thoreau, who retired to the woods in order to 'suck out all
the marrow of life', claimed in *Walden* that: 'if I am overflowing with

life, am rich in experience for which I lack expression, then nature will be my language full of poetry – all nature will fable and every natural phenomenon be a myth'. And as he says elsewhere, 'A fact truly and absolutely stated . . . acquires a mythological or universal significance.' The world as appearance – the poetic and symbolic content of historical fact – and the impressionistic use of these facts all suggest the late novels; the James who, at the very end of his life, became obsessed by the figure of Napoleon, and who images states of consciousness in the language of great public events:

> Strether had all along been subject to sudden gusts of
> fancy in connection with such matters as these – odd starts
> of the historic sense, suppositions and divinations with no
> warrant but their intensity. Thus and so, on the eve of the
> great recorded dates, the days and nights of revolution, the
> sounds had come in, the omens, the beginnings broken
> out. They were the smell of revolution, the smell of the
> public temper – or perhaps simply the smell of blood. (32)

But even when James appears to be disagreeing with the Transcendentalists' view of the world, he does so in imagery curiously akin to theirs. Consider, for example, these two passages, one taken from *The Ambassadors* and the other from Emerson's essay, 'The Transcendentalist':

> The affair – I mean the affair of life – couldn't, no doubt,
> have been different for me; for it's at the best a tin mould,
> either fluted or embossed, with ornamental excrescences,
> or else smooth and dreadfully plain, into which, the
> helpless jelly, one's consciousness is poured – so that one
> 'takes' the form, as the great cook says. (11)

> I – this thought which is called I – is the mould into
> which the world is poured like melted wax. The mould is
> invisible, but the world betrays the shape of the mould.

There is, I think, ample evidence to establish James's dependence not on his father's unique Swedenborgian system but on the native intellectual climate of which they both partook.

There is, of course, another side to James's preoccupation with what he called 'the essence of life'. In an important sense he is a product of the trend discussed elsewhere – the trend in a mass society towards isolation of the individual. R. P. Blackmur has discussed the plight of this individual whose consciousness, he says, we burden beyond our previous measure: 'We make him in our art, especially the art of literature, assume the whole weight of the cultural establishment. . . . There is only the succession of creative consciousness – each of which is an attempt to incorporate, to give body to, to incarnate, as much as it is possible to experience, to feel it, the life of the times.'[12]

Blackmur's point also suggests some of the ways in which modern criticism has attempted to go beyond the formalist interpretations made by the New Critics who rehabilitated James in the 1940s and 1950s. It has done so either by exploring the social complications James anticipated in 1879, and discovering new contexts for his fiction, or, as John Carlos Rowe does, by actually probing the formal aspects of James's art to uncover their underlying significance.[13]

Rowe attempts to combat the narrowness of traditional formalist criticism by using an approach developed by Frederic Jameson in *The Political Unconscious*. This is based upon the idea that a culture's power or ideology is the consequence of a dynamic interrelation of different forces which are given expression in typical forms. It is the 'ideology of form' that thus becomes the ultimate aim of critical understanding. Rowe illustrates this approach in a subtle analysis of *The Princess Casamassima*, but he also explores the limits of Feminist and Psycho-analytic criticism in essays on *The Bostonians, The Spoils of Poynton*, 'The Aspern Papers', and 'The Turn of the Screw'.[14] He also makes use of Harold Bloom's *The Anxiety of Influence* to suggest a more complex relationship between James and Hawthorne on the one hand, and a reinterpretation of Trollope's influence on the other. Rowe argues that James's defence against his fears of being associated with the 'scribbling tribe' of popular women authors who dominated the literary scene prior to his own emergence, was to transpose his 'femininity' or androgyny into an aesthetic quality which he then identified as the most salient feature of the 'modern author'.

Another recent attempt to relate Henry James to 'American mascu-linity, its violent rites of passage, the Civil War, the rough and tumble of primitive capitalism, and female culture in the 1860s and 1870s' occupies a major part of Alfred Habegger's book, *Gender, Fantasy and Realism in American Literature*. Habegger maintains that the day-dreams embodied in domestic novels written by popular women authors presented an ideological challenge to American men that was taken up in the 1870s and 1880s by James and more particularly by Howells. Together they succeeded in pushing back 'the borders of fantasyland' by giving new features to standard character types, and by exhibiting characters in their true relations with one another.

The source of those forces or fantasies that combine to create a culture's dominant ideology, will necessarily be located differently by individual critics according to a variety of factors that condition their particular judgements. Elizabeth Allen, for example, whose book on

James resembles Habegger's methodologically, in that it explores the development of a conflict in the fiction between woman as sign and woman as self, uncovers different sources for the myth of 'true womanhood', against which James's heroines struggle to redefine themselves.[15] Moreover, as she, and other Feminist critics point out, the difficulty of reading or 'decoding' James is further compounded by contemporary myths which continue to distort the vision of 'phallic critics'.[16]

Despite these difficulties the revision of James's fiction and discussion of its place within the canon of American literature, has been given fresh impetus by the proliferation of new critical theories in the 1970s and 1980s. Indeed, the entire map of nineteenth-century fiction, confidently drawn in the post-war period by such critics as Richard Chase, Lionel Trilling, R. W. B. Lewis, and Leo Marx, is beginning to lose authority as new explorers give their accounts of another terrain with quite different features occupying the same historical space. As the Modernist movement itself recedes into the past, it is gradually getting easier to discern more clearly its outlines and dimensions. These will determine the shape and scope of the second part of this study.

Notes

1. *Henry James Letters*, vol 1, 1843–1875, edited by Leon Edel (Cambridge, Mass., 1974), p. 77.

2. Henry James, *Hawthorne* (London, 1879), see ch. 5.

3. *Autobiography: A Small Boy and Others, Notes of a Son and Brother, The Middle Years*, edited by Frederick W. Dupee (London, 1956), p. 549.

4. *Literary Essays of Ezra Pound*, edited by T. S. Eliot (London, 1954), p. 299.

5. See *Autobiography*, Ch. 8.

6. James discussed his own fiction at great length in his notebooks and in the Prefaces to the New York edition of his work. These writings have been published in separate volumes: *The Notebooks of Henry James*, edited by F. O. Matthiessen and Kenneth B. Murdock (New York, 1947), and *The Art of the Novel: Critical Prefaces*, edited by R. P. Blackmur (New York, 1934).

7. *Art of the Novel*, p. 57.

8. Quentin Anderson, *The American Henry James* (New Brunswick, NJ, 1957).

9. Caroline Gordon, 'Adam Verver, our National Hero', *Sewanee Review*, 63 (1955). p. 44.

10. Philip Rahv, *Image and Idea*, (London, 1957), p. 8.

11. In a later essay, 'Henry James's Cultural Office', *Prospects*, 8 (1983), 197–210, Quentin Anderson extends his thesis and discusses James's Emersonian subversion of the nineteenth-century social world.

12. R. P. Blackmur, 'The Loose and Baggy Monsters of Henry James', *Studies in Henry James*, edited with an introduction by Veronica A. Makowsky (New York, 1983). p. 144.

13. John Carlos Rowe, *The Theoretical Dimensions of Henry James* (London, 1985). For a broader application of theory see his earlier book, *Through the Custom-House: Nineteenth-Century American Fiction and Modern Theory* (Baltimore and London, 1982).

14. For an example of a psychoanalytic reading of James that uses modern (Lacanian) theories see Shoshana Felman, 'Turning the Screw of Interpretation', *Yale French Studies*, 55/56 (1977), 94–207.

15. Elizabeth Allen, *A Woman's Place in the Novels of Henry James* (London, 1984).

16. See, for example, Judith Fetterley, *The Resisting Reader: A Feminist Approach to American Fiction* (Bloomington, Ind., and London, 1978).

Part Two:

'The American
Century',
1900–1940

Chapter 7
Introduction

Attempts to reassert traditional American social ideals, particularly those of freedom, equality, and individualism, or their abandonment under pressure from ideologies spawned by the later developments of industrial capitalism and a consumer-orientated society, must feature among the more significant strands of American intellectual life during the first half of the twentieth century. These struggles, sometimes conducted in the abstract and at others given body by political acts and movements, provide particularly illuminating contexts for the study of the novel, making taxonomic sense of a multitude of seemingly diverse, even meaningless, literary events. The map of the second half of this history is designed to show the various streams of realism continuing to flow throughout the modern period and being replenished and revitalized by new tributaries, while at the same time a major literary counterforce develops out of all the minor 'anti-modern' reactions to realism in the 1890s to form a part of the international movement which is paradoxically called Modernism.

The justification for such a name lies in the fact that the writers who embraced its ideals found intellectual support for their world-view in the new ideas propounded by scientists, sociologists, psychologists, and philosophers who were themselves reacting against the accelerating mechanization of life and the progressive dehumanization of the individual. American realists, on the other hand, equally troubled by new social developments, were less willing to abandon traditional values and ideas and sought initially to redefine such concepts as liberty and individualism in the interests of the very real material benefits brought by machine technology and collectivization. The political orientations of such writers, though important, are from our point of view relative, not primary. As Lincoln Steffens noted early in the century, 'big business was producing what the Socialists held up as their goal: food, shelter and clothing for all'. In the 1930s, after the Wall Street Crash and the ensuing economic depression, it became a different matter, and like their counterparts in the Soviet Union, many realists came to place their art in the service of revolutionary politics.

The major social and economic phenomenon, then, determining these responses was the continuation and consolidation of the processes set in motion much earlier by the founding of trusts and corporations; organizations devised to maximize the efficiency of the production, distribution, and sale of goods on an unprecedentedly large scale. Such causal connections are notoriously complex and difficult to establish with any certainty, but it would be futile to deny the close relations obtaining between these large-scale business organizations and almost every significant aspect of American life in the period. Immigration, urbanization, imperialism, consumerism, technological development, the mass media – in short all the features that help to define the distinctive quality of life in modern America – are affected by the demands of capitalism. The history of these various manifestations has been painstakingly described and needs no rehearsal here, but one example will help to establish the kind of connection that I wish to emphasize between society and the products of the individual imagination.

In the winter of 1866–67, when Mark Twain made his momentous decision to quit the west coast, it took him twenty-eight days to travel from San Francisco to New York. In 1870 America was an emptier country than it was to become by the outbreak of the First World War, and despite the existence of the transcontinental railroad, Americans were still living in communities very much isolated both from each other and from the rest of the world. The general conquest of American space, as opposed to the tenuous links set up by the railroad, was made possible first by the invention and then the mass production of the automobile, together with the construction of a huge network of roads. The existence by 1915 of two and a half million cars and thousands of miles of good roads radically changed the individual's perception of his environment and his relation to it, something reinforced even more by the simultaneous development of powered flight which culminated in Lindbergh's historic crossing of the Atlantic in 1927. Even more significant in some respects were the accompanying developments in radio and telephone communication. When New York was connected to San Francisco in 1913, it could be claimed that American technology had conquered both space and time. A month had become a moment, and the conditions now obtained which were to take the world into Marshall McLuhan's 'global village'.

To determine whether these changes came about in order to satisfy the needs of a rapidly expanding business civilization or were consequent upon it, is less important for our purposes than to place them in relation to their effect upon individual consciousnesses. This is not as simple as it may seem and will certainly not result in any neat demarcation between modernists and realists, for example. The best one can hope for is that a few general trends may be discerned which, taken together with many other factors, will help to map the chart of literary history.

The most fundamental aspect of nineteenth-century realism and its essential defining characteristic is the belief in a dynamic relation between man and his environment. The various disputes about realism considered in Chapter 3 do not impinge upon this axiom so much as other different ways of demonstrating the relationship. Empirical philosophy, Newtonian physics, Darwinism, whether biological or social, and Marxist economics, are all indicative of a world-view in which space and time are assumed to have absolute, independent validity. Man's individuality is a product of his social context, and the proper task of literature is to show how changes in one produce changes in the other. For such writers and their successors, the changes brought by scientific and technological advances at the end of the century did not necessarily entail a radical reappraisal of basic philosophy, even though they may have been forced to consider the social effects of man's enhanced ability to manipulate his spatial and temporal context.

When Frederick Winslow Taylor conducted his famous shovelling experiment – an early time and motion study in the Bethlehem Steel Company in Pennsylvania in the 1890s – he not only saved the company a great deal of money by reorganizing the shape of the plant and the movements of workers within it, but also laid the foundation for a new social ethic. 'In the past', he said, 'the man has been first; in the future the system must be first.' The acceptance of this doctrine and its implementation by industrialists who immediately understood that time and space really did mean money, has changed the nature of our world and therefore of human nature, too. Behaviourism in psychology, no less than shifts in population or even changes in architectural styles, can only be properly understood in relation to such ideas.

It will be obvious, for example, that the ideals of freedom and individualism referred to above could only survive with great difficulty in this new intellectual ethos. Taylor himself, reluctant to abandon such cherished concepts, was fully aware of the implications of his work. In his book *The Principles of Scientific Management* (1911) he tried desperately to yoke them to the concept of co-operation, arguing that though the stop-watch and the flow chart demand of each man that he perform 'that function for which he is best suited', nevertheless 'each man at the same time loses none of his originality and proper personal initiative, and yet is controlled by and must work harmoniously with many other men'.[1]

The ways in which these issues are dealt with, different degrees of emphasis being given to the human, social, or political dimensions, lie behind the organization and specialization at all levels of man's life, behind internal migrations whether forced or voluntary, behind continued immigration, the rise of totalitarian states, Fascist or Communist, war, strikes, and poverty; these are the themes that give body to the fiction of Upton Sinclair, Sinclair Lewis, Willa Cather, Henry Roth, James T. Farrell, Richard Wright, and John Steinbeck. What is truly distinctive in their work is not its subject-matter, though; many modernist writers treat the same problems in their fiction. It is rather the common attempt to preserve humane, rational values in opposition to all the forces bent on extinguishing them, and the structural and stylistic strategies adopted to achieve this end. The essentially mimetic art of the realists is the primary evidence for their belief in an objective, independent reality that obeys certain rational laws. It is this belief which distinguishes them from their modernist contemporaries, and as the century wears on, begins to make them appear rather old-fashioned and slightly alien to the main aesthetic and intellectual developments.

The deeper intellectual currents which began to gather strength at the turn of the century and were eventually to erode nearly all the certainties of the past, had many different sources and tributaries. It would be inappropriate to attempt here a description of the intellectual revolution that gave birth to Modernism, but a few examples may serve to indicate how thoroughly nineteenth-century thought was being undermined by physicists, mathematicians, philosophers, and psychologists, who were thus laying the foundations for something new in literature.

At about the same time that Frederick Winslow Taylor was applying the strict laws of causality to time and movement in Pennsylvania, a French philosopher, Henri Bergson, was just as busily rejecting them in an effort to provide a solution to the kind of paradoxes to which they gave rise. His flash of intuition in Clermont-Ferrand helped him to solve Zeno's paradox which states that no matter how fast Achilles runs in an attempt to catch and overtake the tortoise, he cannot succeed because for every unit of space he covers, the tortoise will, in turn, continue to cover a further unit, however small, and will, therefore, always remain ahead. Bergson's solution, which eventually came to involve a sustained attack on mechanistic thinking in general and formed the basis for his life's work, lay in a refusal to express time and motion in terms of space or distance. Instead of binding these concepts inextricably together as Taylor did, for example, he saw that time as experienced in the individual consciousness – duration – was not a feature of the physical world at all, and bore no necessary relation to space. Bergson's first two books on the subject were published in 1889 and 1897, and in 1903, two years before Einstein published his *Special Theory of Relativity*, he wrote an essay on metaphysics in which he pinpointed the significance of his ideas. In it he argued that the only reality we can intuit is determined by our consciousness, and that to achieve such fluid concepts, the world must reverse the direction in which it habitually thinks.

This is exactly what the best contemporary minds were doing in an attempt to impose order on a reality that seemed increasingly impenetrable and chaotic. Godel in mathematics, Heisenberg and Niels Bohr in physics, Heidegger and later Sartre in philosophy, Freud and Jung in psychology, all of them aware of the contradictions inherent in reality, were in a variety of self-conscious hypotheses recharting the world and producing maps in which the normal geographical features were replaced by contour lines of the psyche, measurements by sensations, history by myth.

Bergson was not a particularly original thinker. Indeed, his ideas were to be rejected by almost all his successors except William James. But the direction of his thought is typical of the way in which introspection, intuition, even irrationality were beginning to supplant the confident rationality of earlier thinkers. The scope of this revolution is well indicated in an essay on Modernism by Malcolm Bradbury and James McFarlane:

> It is the art consequent on Heisenberg's 'Uncertainty
> Principle', of the destruction of civilisation and reason in
> the First World War, of the world changed and
> reinterpreted by Marx, Freud and Darwin, of capitalism
> and constant industrial acceleration, of existential exposure
> to meaninglessness or absurdity. It is the literature of
> technology. It is the art consequent on the dis-establishing
> of communal reality and conventional notions of causality,
> on the destruction of traditional notions of the wholeness
> of individual character, on the linguistic chaos that ensues
> when public notions of language have been discredited and
> when all realities have become subjective fictions.[2]

Another indication of the breadth and force of this intellectual upheaval is the bewildering number of different experimental movements in the arts that sprang up in its wake: Expressionism, Cubism, Surrealism, Dadaism, Vorticism, Futurism, and many, many more. As with Realism, however, it would be a mistake to try to describe Modernism in terms of its stylistic varieties. All that can properly be claimed about the various forms of textual and structural experimentation is that they result from a conviction that it had become impossible to employ traditional language or forms to record new perceptions of reality accurately. Nor does it seem satisfactory to label the modernist writers merely as reactionaries whose apocalyptic nihilism had led them into the embrace of various conservative ideologies. While it is undoubtedly true that the metaphysical or moral visions which prompted individual artists towards either realism or modernism also tended to determine their left- or right-wing political alignments, there are enough exceptions on either side to make such classifications suspect.

This is especially true of American writers. Though it is possible without too much Procrustean chopping and stretching, to make Steinbeck or Faulkner fit the political stereotypes associated with radical realism or reactionary modernism, there are others such as John Dos Passos whose refusal to conform demonstrates the superficiality of such easy categorizations. Some critics have been tempted to explain away Dos Passos's combination of modernist technique and radical politics in *U.S.A.* as being somehow less typical or truthful. But this makes nonsense of the commonly accepted judgement that *U.S.A.* is his masterpiece, and that his later works do not have the same integrity or vitality. Dos Passos's own explanation, one that has affinities with Lincoln Steffens's view of shifting socialist alignments, is that neither his vision nor his technique underwent any real change. For Dos Passos, the primary aim was always to combat totalitarian regimes and states of mind, which in the 1920s he associated with capitalist dictatorship, and later with Communist dictatorship.

Another factor that forces the literary historian to modify most generalizations about the American modernist novel is one suggested in Hugh Kenner's recent book on the period, *A Homemade World*. American poets, without any great expectation of a large readership, could afford to experiment with the notorious difficulties of modernist poetry, and some of them, including E. E. Cummings (*The Enormous Room*, 1922) and Conrad Aiken (*Blue Voyage*, 1927) even wrote experimental novels which reached a similarly small public. There were also permanent exiles such as Gertrude Stein, living and working in the international artistic community of Paris, who committed themselves fully to the modernist movement with the same result as far as sales went. The major American novelists of the period, however, were writing for a mass market comprised mainly of native readers, so that whatever affinities they might have felt for James Joyce, Virginia Woolf, or Marcel Proust, were severely modified in their practice by the need to maintain communication and hence sales. As Kenner remarks, 'Later Fitzgerald could be praised for a craft like Conrad's, and Hemingway for writing nearly as well as Hemingway, but neither man's art has been easy to extricate from his years as a public performer.'[3]

Of course, such compromises can be and have been explained as failures of nerve, or by a desire to sell out to the American 'bitch-goddess', success. It is not surprising that the American writer, working in the world's most powerful industrial society and competing with its irresistibly 'realistic' media, advertising, and the movies, occasionally took some protective colouring from their ethos.[4] To a casual observer, for example, Frederick Henry's lonely stand in *A Farewell to Arms* (1929) or Jay Gatsby's in *The Great Gatsby* (1925), may appear to be reassertion of those values of freedom and individialism enshrined by nineteenth-century liberalism. But as we shall see, each is based on so absolute a rejection of the prevailing version of contemporary reality that the traditional concepts become emptied of all their accumulated meanings. In the military and industrial contexts within which they are taken, these retreats represent rejections of history and society just as emphatic as any made by their European contemporaries. American modernism may well be, as Kenner claims, a home-made variety. The same can be said of American realism. This should not be taken as evidence that European forms and ideas were being diluted in crossing the Atlantic, but rather that American literature was beginning to find its own distinctive voice.

The generation of writers at the heart of the movement, Hemingway, Fitzgerald, Dos Passos, Faulkner, and Wolfe, were all born in the years between 1896 and 1900. All of them came to manhood during the First World War, and the American experience of that war and its aftermath was also a crucial factor in determining the shape of their art. Congress did not declare war on Germany until April 1917, and though most of these writers were to put on uniform for at least a short time, their involvement in a foreign theatre must have been at least tinged with detachment or with what Malcolm Cowley has called the 'spectatorial attitude'.[5] Some of them, and others whose names were not to become well known, fought and died on the Western Front, but if compared with French, German, or British losses, American casualties in the war were very slight. The more typical American's experience was one of acting as an ambulance driver for a foreign army or as a correspondent in somebody else's war. It is not surprising, then, that at the Armistice in November 1918, many young American writers felt like Fitzgerald that they had not really had an opportunity to test themselves and apply their energies in the cause. They had watched while European civilization acted out its death-wish on the bloody battlefields of France, before coming home to a country determined at all costs to re-establish its worship of the almighty dollar and cast out the evils of drink, vice, and even revolution. The returning servicemen quite rightly saw themselves as 'forgotten men', and among them was a group of writers who almost gladly accepted the title of the 'Lost Generation'. What they had lost were their roots, and with them their sense of cultural and social identity. Even if the First World War was not the most significant event in determining the end of an era, but one more symptom of a much deeper split between the wholeness of the past and future fragmentation; and even though America and Americans were not as directly involved in it as most Europeans, it would still be wrong to minimize its importance for the writers who witnessed it.

Another unique feature of American modernism, and one that Malcolm Cowley touches on in the epilogue to his book on the Lost Generation, *Exiles' Return*, is the developing awareness among its adherents of a continuity between their writing and that of their nineteenth-century predecessors, Brockden Brown, Poe, Hawthorne, Melville, and even Crane and James. It is a truism of literary history that for whatever reasons, realism came very late to American fiction, disrupting a powerful tradition of allegory, symbolism, and romance. The conditions that alienated modern novelists from their societies and turned them towards the exploration and expression of subjective, eccentric, or even psychopathic states of mind, at least left American modernists with some notable early examples of similar writing in their own literature. The sense of restoring links with a tradition gives their voices a confidence often lacking in the more obviously defiant tones of the European avant-garde.

Finally, the development of American modernism was profoundly affected by what was happening in America in the 1930s. Of course, the Depression was experienced in Europe, too, but the severity of the Crash in 1929 and the contrast produced as the boom years were succeeded by a decade of poverty, privation, and turmoil, made the American experience particularly traumatic. Having, as Cowley says in the essay referred to above, experienced three phases of rebellion – against the Genteel Tradition, against the hypocrisies of the First World War, and against the philistinism of the Harding years in the 1920s – the literary exiles finally returned to their homeland only to find themselves alienated once more. Unwilling or unable to accept collective political or social discipline, they did not join the ranks of any particular party, write proletarian novels, or even suggest any panaceas for the nation's economic ills. There were exceptions to this rule, it is true, but the general pattern was one of private, non-political, or even conservative rebellion against a society that finally left them with no lingering hope in the American Dream. The Spanish Civil War briefly revived their idealism and sense of political purpose, but before the bitter lessons of the liberal defeat could be properly assimilated, another even greater conflict emerged to preoccupy them and bring the era to its close.

Notes

1. Daniel Bell examines 'the cult of efficiency in America' in his book, *The End of Ideology* (Glencoe, Illinois, 1960), pp. 222–62.

2. *Modernism, 1890–1930*, edited by Malcolm Bradbury and James McFarlane (Harmondsworth, 1976), p. 27.

3. Hugh Kenner, *A Homemade World: The American Modernist Writers* (New York, 1975), p. xvii.

4. Some of the connections between Modernism and Consumerism are explored by Matei Calinescu in *Faces of Modernity* (Bloomington, Indi. 1977). See, for example, his chapter on 'Kitsch', pp. 225–62.

5. Malcolm Cowley, *A Second Flowering: Works and Days of the Lost Generation* (New York, 1973), p. 9.

Chapter 8
Realists, Radicals and the City: Sinclair, Poole, Farrell, Halper, Wright, Gold, Levin, Fuchs

In the early autumn of 1933 the management of the Bethlehem Steel Company – the plant at which Frederick W. Taylor had conducted his 'shovelling experiment' forty years earlier – placed a large order for riot guns, grenades, and projectile shells. These armaments were purchased in case they were needed to fight against the firm's employees who were being urged to organize themselves into a single industrial union. In the event, the weapons were not used for that purpose, but on Memorial Day in 1937, at a different steel plant in Chicago, workers engaged in a similar struggle were fired on by police when they attempted to picket their own mill. Several were killed instantly, more died in hospital from their wounds, and over a hundred men, women, and children were injured. In his account of the massacre, the left-wing novelist Howard Fast called it the most shocking event in America since the Haymarket Affair in the 1880s. Even so, it was only one of hundreds of similar, if less dramatic, confrontations scarring American labour relations in this period, and William Leuchtenburg, setting the event in a wider context, remarks of these changes in union organization that 'what was truly noteworthy was the relatively little bloodshed that marked this momentous transfer of social power'.[1]

Appalling as these violent episodes undoubtedly were, Leuchtenburg is surely right to draw attention to the phenomenon of a relatively peaceful shift away from the old craft organization to new mass unions whose leaders were not merely concerned with the 'extra nickel in the pay envelope' philosophy, but also with education, civil rights, welfare, and everything in fact that touched the lives of their members. This was an entirely natural response to similar changes being brought about by the development of massive aggregations of power in industrial mergers, trusts, and corporations. Efficiency 'other-directedness', and managerial skills were the key qualities required in the new consumer-oriented society, and the younger labour leaders were quick to develop them. In the steel industry, for example, the violent strikes took place not against the giant corporation United Steel but against the so-called 'Little Steel' companies – those like Bethlehem and Republic, whose bosses were still clinging to a *laissez-faire* philosophy of freedom and individuality in a situation that had made them more and more obsolete.

Those traditional attitudes and the radical reforming literature based on them have, for modern observers and readers, an old-fashioned if heroic flavour about them. The vehement disputes that raged throughout the 1930s in left-wing magazines and the American Writers' Congress about the nature of proletarian fiction, seemed to many, even at the time, irrelevant to the significant imaginative literature being produced. This is not to deny, though, the quantitative importance of proletarian fiction produced in this period. Fay Blake lists over one hundred and sixty strike novels, for example, published in the years between 1900 and 1940.[2] One of these, actually called *Little Steel* (1938), was written by that indefatigable campaigner for social justice, Upton Sinclair. *Little Steel* was one of the last of his many industrial novels that included *The Jungle* (1906), *King Coal* (1917), and *Oil* (1927), before he turned to a wider stage with his long series of Lanny Budd narratives. They maintain a continuity of documentary realism, social protest, and optimistic socialism from the time of the early Muck-raking movement, through the Progressive period and the succession of novel social panaceas, to the New Freedom, the New Nationalism and the New Deal. Sinclair's attitudes and techniques changed less in four decades than the world he wrote about, but seen within that wide historical context, the progressive marginalization of his themes does suggest the changing fortunes of realism in the period.

The power of *The Jungle*, Sinclair's best novel, comes, as Walter Rideout says, not just from its descriptions of the filth, disease, degradation, and hopelessness of the Chicago meat-packers' lives.[3] Such graphic and sensational passages resulted from Sinclair's own researches and, at least, had the immediate effect of helping to get the laws governing the production of food in the United States changed. But they also read like parts of an investigative essay, complete with footnotes, and like similar passages of documentation in his other novels, they stand somewhat inertly as a mass of information imperfectly assimilated into the consciousness of his characters. His descriptions seem to own more to a realist novel like John de Forest's *Miss Ravenel's Conversion* than to the more sophisticated naturalism of Dreiser. The clumsy way he introduces such set pieces indicates the difficulty he has in fictionalizing his material:

> Anybody who could invent a new imitation had been sure
> of a fortune from old Durham, said Jurgis's informant; but
> it was hard to think of anything new in a place where so

many sharp wits had been at work for so long; where men welcomed tuberculosis in the cattle they were feeding, because it made them fatten more quickly; and where they bought up all the old rancid butter left over in the grocery stores of a continent, and 'oxidised' it by a forced-air process, to take away the odour, rechurned it with skim-milk, and sold it in bricks in the cities! Up to a year or two ago, it had been the custom to kill horses in the yards – ostensibly for fertiliser; but after long agitation, the newspapers had been able to make the public realise that the horses were being canned. Now it was against the law to kill horses in Packingtown, and the law was really complied with – for the present, at any rate. (9)

A more serious fault in the novel, and it is one inherent in a certain kind of protest literature, is the way Sinclair handles his hero's conversion to socialism after his many tribulations. In a succession of essays and speeches, Sinclair abandons fiction for pamphleteering, proving Rideout's point that his imagination was quickened more by the pathos of the poor than by their power. Significantly, this humanitarian strain in Sinclair is just what offends the Marxist critic Granville Hicks. Writing about Sinclair in the depths of the Depression, Hicks quickly passes over Sinclair's own years of poverty and despair – the seed-bed for the growth of his political sympathies – and concentrates instead on his later love of money and his residual religious feelings. He couples Sinclair with Jack London, suggesting that both were unable to transcend their liberal psychologies and were therefore condemned to write from and for the middle classes.[4] Though this criticism is not really applicable to *The Jungle*, it has some force when applied to Sinclair's later work, in which the psychology of the liberal convert comes to occupy the forefront of the fiction.

Hicks's complaint also has some theoretical validity, and it reflects the central debate at the American Writers' Congress in 1935 about whether proletarian literature could or should only be written by members of that class, or whether it was enough for the writer to embrace the interests of the working class whatever his own social origins. The terms of the argument are not unlike those employed in discussions of the Black Aesthetic and Feminist literary theory in the 1960s and 1970s. What made the proletarian issue both more poignant but more abstract than these, though, was the fact that at the time the only people who appeared to be willing to produce such work, and certainly the only ones who wanted to discuss it at conferences, were members of the educated middle classes. This dichotomy between the actual condition of society and the ideologies of those writing about it, lends a similar dimension of unintentional irony to the wider debates about Humanism that were waged so fiercely in literary circles in the 1930s. These took such forms as the famous essay by Michael Gold in *The New Republic*, dissecting the fiction of Thornton Wilder. In it the anti-Humanist proletarian took the member of the genteel bourgeoisie to task for ignoring the reality of cotton-mills and labour racketeers in his novels and substituting for them castles, palaces, and far-off Greek islands where readers may study the human heart when it is nourished by blue blood.[5] The fallacy here, as Hicks perceived in his criticism of Sinclair, comes from the mistaken belief that all the liberal Humanist had to do to create a new form of radical realism was to turn his attention to the right subjects.

One work that ingeniously solves this problem and has frequently been called the best socialist novel in America, is Ernest Poole's novel *The Harbor* (1915). It does so by making the hero's changing attitude to his environmant its primary subject. As a child, Billy learns to love the energy and romance he associates with New York harbour, and these feelings are gradually transmuted into an aesthetic appreciation of its teeming world as he prepares himself to become a novelist. Later, however, under the tutelage of a Taylor-like engineer who is engaged in reforming the port's activities, he changes again and comes to worship the 'God of Efficiency'. He marries the engineer's daughter and, as a journalist, immerses himself in the world of big business corporations and finance capitalism. Blind at this stage of his life to the consequences of attempts to impose order by the application of scientific principles, he needs the help of his radical friend, Joe Kramer, before realizing the inhumanity of the God he worships.

Deep in the bowels of a ship he comes to his ultimate revelation and his conversion to socialism, as he sees the hideously cruel effects of business efficiency on the lives of workers who are responsible for its success. He supports the revolt of the overburdened slaves who have been driven to rebel against the harsh conditions of their employment. The strike fails, but Billy is left with a new god whose feet 'stood in poverty' but in whose head 'were all the dreams of all the toilers of the earth'. Though the novel ends with a demand for freedom and equality for the poor and oppressed, what gives the book its uniqueness is Poole's flat rejection of individualism; and his realization that the power of organized capitalism can only be matched by the collective power of labour.

Poole's novel was one of the last to be written in the buoyant mood of pre-war socialism. After the Armistice it quickly became apparent that as a significant political movement, socialism in America was doomed. From then on, radical novels were less and less likely to express the same affirmative beliefs in a Utopian future. When radicalism eventually re-emerged as a force during the Depression, it had a very different character, one that Leslie Fiedler describes as a kind of self-righteous smugness in being among the excluded and a masochistic wish-fear that welcomed the End of Days.[6]

The terms that Fiedler uses are in themselves suggestive of the individualism seen by orthodox left-wing critics as the root problem of protest literature written by middle-class liberals. Such writers were more often associated with the apocalyptic world of the modernist writer, and as Fiedler goes on to remark, the novels produced in this spirit did not bear much relevance to the actual events of the time: the immense gains made by organized labour, the Wagner Act, and the successes of the Congress of Industrial Organizations (CIO).

The novels that did mirror those realities were more likely to be produced in the tradition of immigrant literature which showed a quite different trajectory. Thomas Bell's *Out of this Furnace* (1941) is not untypical. It deals with three generaticns of Slovak immigrants in a Pennsylvania steel town, and its last section describes the campaign for unionization and collective bargaining brought to a successful conclusion by the Steel Workers' Organizing Committee. For the hero, Dobie Dabrejcak, the end of the fifty-year struggle for justice is linked to an acceptance of his nationality:

'Maybe not the kind of American that came over on the *Mayflower*', he reflected, 'or the kind that's always shooting off their mouths about Americanism and patriotism, including some of the God-damndest heels you'd ever want to see, but the kind that's got *Made in U.S.A.* stamped all over them, from the kind of grub they like to the things they wouldn't do for all the money in the world.' (4.18)

A Pennsylvania steel town is also the setting for a Black migrant novel that was published in the same year, William Attaway's *Blood on the Forge* (1941). Though it also deals with a violent strike and the attempts of workers to discover new identities in an alien, urban environment, these themes are given a different focus from that in *Out of this Furnace*. The Black workers have been brought from the South in order to break the strike, and Attaway, in following the whole process in the lives of three brothers from Kentucky, evokes the hopeless situation of the uprooted peasants, all of them 'green men' who believe it a sin to 'melt up the ground', and are eventually crushed by the anti-human forces, both natural and social, that they are made to serve.

Most of the proletarian novels written by novelists who saw themselves as belonging to the immigrant tradition take the form of what
Rideout calls 'Bottom Dog' novels after the famous example by
Edward Dahlberg. They present realistic pictures of life in the over-
crowded slums and the inhuman conditions of work experienced by
immigrants in large American cities. They may or may not be
primarily inspired by reformist or revolutionary politics, but in any
case they do not have such stereotyped plots as either the strike novel
or the conversion novel, where even in the best examples such as Jack
Conroy's *The Disinherited* (1933), or Robert Cantwell's *The Land of
Plenty* (1934) the major events have a depressing inevitability. Rideout's
final type of proletarian novel, the fiction of middle-class decay, is also
more congenial to the non-doctrinaire realist like James T. Farrell
whose Studs Lonigan trilogy is the best example, though a more
obvious one is Josephine Herbst's trilogy *Pity is Not Enough* (1933),
The Executioner Waits (1934), and *Rope of Gold* (1939).

The immigrant tradition of fiction is itself a divided stream,
reflecting the main dispersal patterns of various national groups. With
such massive numbers of people involved, there are thousands of
exceptions to every rule, but generally what was distinctive about
German and Scandinavian Protestant immigrant groups was their
decision to settle in the great farming areas of the Midwest, whereas
Irish, Italian, and East European Jewish immigrants were much more
likely to be found in the large cities, particularly New York and
Chicago. These immigrants' subsequent experience of the frontier and
the ghetto fed into the existing traditions of realist fiction, and in the
case of Jewish writing, which will be dealt with separately, trans-
formed it. Before considering this phenomenon, though, it might be
useful to establish a different point of view which modifies both the
ethnic divisions and the classifications of proletarian fiction made by
Rideout.

If one looks at the literature of a particular large city such as
Chicago, it is possible to discover good examples of every kind of
realist or proletarian novel written by novelists from a multitude of
racial or social backgrounds, including Richard Wright, the Black
novelist whose *Native Son* (1940) has often been called the finest
proletarian novel of all. Though it may sometimes seem that the Jewish
immigrant writer is a New York phenomenon, Meyer Levin's *The Old
Bunch* (1937), a novel about a group of East Side Jews, is a
distinguished exception; and though his work falls outside the scope
of this study, Saul Bellow was also growing up in Chicago in the
1930s, absorbing the material that would form the basis of *The Adventures of Angie March* (1953) and *Humboldt's Gift* (1975). It is also true
to say that the novels of middle-class decay are not generally set in

large cities at all, but again Farrell's meticulous study of the ecology of the South Side Irish is a major exception.[7]

Farrell, like Dos Passos, defies almost any attempt at classification. Though he is customarily regarded, if not as a proletarian writer, then at least as a realist of the Left, he rejects such affiliations quite specifically in his book *A Note on Literary Criticism* (1936), calling such writing 'a literature of simplicity . . . even of downright banality', while in a later essay, 'Literature and Ideology' (1942), he suggested that American proletarian writers in the 1930s 'wrote with almost total irrelevance to the real situation in America'. What that situation really was he pinpoints in another essay in *The League of Frightened Philistines*, (1945) in which he discusses the composition of his Studs Lonigan trilogy.

It is, he claims, a novel about the way in which the simple social and religious beliefs of hard-working Irish immigrants are undermined in a later generation by the breakdown of the institutions designed to protect them, particularly the home and the Church. The spiritual poverty pervading what Farrell calls 'one of the most insane eras of our history – the Prohibition era', gradually frustrates and defeats the growing adolescent as his values become those of the only world he knows – the streets and the poolroom. Where the original immigrants and their children fleeing from the bitter hardship of life in nineteenth-century Ireland had been fired by the American dream of success and sustained in the New World by the thought of creating a better environment for their families, the younger generation see only the broken promise of American life. All the hopes of the boys in *Young Lonigan* (1932), distorted in the tired clichés of Father Gilhooley's florid speech to the graduation class of St Patrick's School, prove irrelevant in the world described in *The Young Manhood of Studs Lonigan* (1934) and *Judgement Day* (1935). The traditions, whether material or spiritual, that sustained their parents, have lost their validity in a culture dedicated to the shallow pleasures of consumerism. As Studs and his friends drift aimlessly though life experiencing but not enjoying an assortment of chaotic and stultifying encounters in which sex, drink, and violence become ends in themselves, the past becomes their only stable point of reference and premature death the only possible outcome for their stunted lives. Stud's pathetic reveries about his innocent and hopeful childhood which occupy so much of the last novel in the trilogy and are contrasted with his ugly and futile drift towards death, did not appeal to many contemporary left-wing critics, who could accept Farrell's remorseless dissection of American society's shortcomings but not his failure to suggest any political cure for them. Even Dreiser, with whom he is often compared, discovered a vitality and excitement in the city which is quite lacking in Farrell's angry but hopeless tirade against the material density and spiritual aridity of contemporary life.

Another Chicago novelist whose work was approved of for political reasons and who writes from an ecological, or in political terms, a collective point of view, is Albert Halper. His particular focus is much narrower than Farrell's, however, and though the Old Bowman House where the electrotype plant is situated in *The Foundry* (1934), happens to be on Dearborn Street in Chicago, the actual setting is largely irrelevant to his theme. Like Farrell, Halper's anger is fuelled by the social forces that are robbing men of their identities, but in his case these are associated almost exclusively with the machines being used in industry not just to enslave men but also to make them redundant. Both in this novel and *The Chute* (1937), men are portrayed as locked in a constant struggle against the relentless pressures of a mechanized environment that threatens to transform them too into automata and take a terrible toll in the process.

> The clock now showed four-thirty, and still the racket did not let up. The place became a madhouse, and each man was his own insane asylum. Every time Cassius passed the partition windows, he saw the questioning stares of the two partners. 'Can you make it?' their glances seemed to say. . . . Hey, Pinky, saw that cast! The time clock near the office was ticking, ticking; a tremendous press was standing idle with a huge printing contract hanging in the balance. Hey, Pinky, saw that cast! (6)

The plot of the novel involves the men's attempts to defeat and ultimately to come to terms with a new, more frightening machine called The Big Smasher, and it ends with them succumbing to its power and that of the time-stamper which is clocking away the minutes of their regulated lives. The Big Smasher could almost have been the model for those machines satirized in Charlie Chaplin's film *Modern Times* (1936).[8] Chaplin's comedy is based on the notion of the interdependence of man and machine in industrial society. First he shows man as the victim of a 'feeding machine' which goes wrong; then as food for the machine as Charlie gets sucked into one at the end of a conveyorbelt; and finally, both man and machine as elements subordinated to industry's inexorable time-schedules, when Charlie's attempt to rescue a fellow worker from the devouring machine is interrupted by the lunch whistle.

Even in novels where working conditions are not central to the plot, such as Nelson Algren's *Somebody in Boots* (1935), the same atmosphere of defeat and despair characterizes passing references to life in

Chicago's factories, workshops, and mills, Algren introduces each section of his novel with a quotation from the *Communist Manifesto*, and that dealing with Norah Egan's job in the Sunshine Frock Shop on Chicago's South Side is the famous passage describing the conditions of life of the lumpenproletariat as an ideal preparation 'for the part of a bribed tool of reactionary intrigue', rather than as part of a revolutionary movement. The 'hurry-up' sounds of the sewing-machine and the 'hurry-up' routines that dominate even their eating and drinking breaks, make all the girls want to scream and yell at the foreman. Most of them remain cowed and subservient, though, and when Norah does begin to complain, she gradually finds that she is being starved of work until eventually she is quietly squeezed out of her job altogether.

Algren's use of that particular sentence from the *Communist Manifesto* suggests the problem encountered by the better novelists who sympathized with current left-wing political movements. Urged by the official aestheticians of the Party to show the heroic workers in their struggle against the evils of capitalism, they were constrained by what E. M. Forster called a 'moral realism' to depict a more accurate picture of the social and psychological effects of exploitation and oppression. This is true of both Farrell and Algren, but an even more interesting case is that of Richard Wright.

Wright came to Chicago in 1927 as a young man from Mississippi, part of the great migration of Blacks from the rural South to the industrial centres of the North-east and Midwest. He stayed in Chicago for ten years before moving, like many writers before him, first to New York and then to Europe. While in Chicago he had a number of jobs, but more significantly came by way of the local John Reed Club into the Communist Party. The story of his later disillusionment is told in an essay that was printed in the well-known anthology *The God that Failed*,[9] but during his early years as an apprentice writer in Chicago, he remained very much under the influence of Party intellectuals. Even at this stage in his career, though, his artistic integrity was stronger than any political doctrine, and though he held back his first novel, probably on the advice of his political mentors, he did not destroy the manuscript, and it was eventually published as *Lawd Today* in 1963.

It is easy to see why *Lawd Today* would not satisfy the requirements of critics whose main aim was to promote the cause. Its hero, Jake Jackson, is a Black postal worker whose life is a perfect example of the spiritual poverty engendered by the squalid conditions in the Chicago slums and exacerbated by racial discrimination. Jake is, in fact, an anti-hero, a brutal, bigoted victim of his environment whose life is dominated by 'the American "lust for trash"'. We follow his activi-

ties though one bleak winter's day in Chicago – ironically it is
Lincoln's Birthday, 12 February – as he drifts around his neighbourhood, spends eight numbing hours working at his repetitive job in
what he and his fellow workers call the Squirrel Cage, takes part in
a drunken orgy at a night-club where he is robbed, before returning
home to beat up his wife.

Despite occasional awkwardness in handling point of view and
despite traces of literary influence extending from Gertrude Stein and
James Joyce to Dos Passos, *Lawd Today* is in one respect a better novel
than Wright's more famous *Native Son* (1940). He does not avoid the
political implications of his material in *Lawd Today*, but with subtle
irony uses it to show how Jake and his friends are unable to make the
necessary connections between their lives and the actions needed to
change them. Jake's fantasies, nourished by the life he is only dimly
aware of outside the slum, never extend beyond the acquisition of
enough money to realize his dream of joining the 'rich white folks' and
freeing himself from his race and class. Like Algren's characters, Jake
Jackson has been corrupted by the false promises of the capitalist world
and he offers little hope to the revolutionaries.

The same is true of Bigger Thomas in *Native Son*, who bears some
relation to Jake and even more to Dreiser's Clyde Griffith in *An
American Tragedy*. Where he differs from Clyde, though, is in the depth
of the ineradicable bitterness and murderous hatred inspired by his life
as a Black outcast living in a rat-infested slum in the world's richest
society. Black writers who initiated the tradition of urban fiction
during the Harlem Renaissance in the 1920s – Claude Mckay, Wallace
Thurman, Countee Cullen, and Langston Hughes – inhabit a society that
has all the synthetic gaiety of the Jazz Age, and their fiction, like that
of White sympathizers such as Carl Van Vechten, turns the actuality
of Harlem into a bizarre, exotic 'jungle' in which the primitivism of
the Black is contrasted with, but produced for the entertainment of,
an élite, civilized White reader.

Bigger's primitivism takes a totally different form. In his introduc-
tory essay, 'How "Bigger" was Born', Wright suggests that the
'tensity, the fear, the hate, the impatience, the sense of exclusion, the
ache for violent action, the emotional and cultural hunger' in Bigger,
are the same that drove other Biggers in Germany and Russia to
become Fascists or Communists. In America, though, educational
restrictions and economic oppression combine to ensure that the young
urban Blacks cannot find any political expression for their inarticulate
anger. Though Wright says he was fearful about the probable response
to the novel of his friends in the Party and of his fellow Blacks, he
believed that to have made *Native Son* a vehicle for either Communism
or Black Nationalism would have meant losing the truth of Bigger

himself. It is this resolve to cleave to individual realities rather than to political analyses that eventually led Wright away from radical politics towards existentialist fiction.

Bigger's emotional condition is brilliantly prefigured in the lurid opening scene of the novel in which he pursues and kills a huge rat scuttling around the kitchen of the South Side apartment he shares with his mother, sister, and brother. He is deeply ashamed of his inability to provide for them and his shame has turned to hatred:

> He knew that the moment he allowed what his life meant
> to enter fully into his consciousness, he would either kill
> himself or someone else. So he denied himself and acted
> tough. (Bk 1)

His toughness is a response to his fear, and it is fear that leads to the murder of his new boss's daughter, Mary Dalton. Throughout the first section of the novel, Wright has shown Bigger in a variety of situations – in the poolroom, the street, and the movies – sullenly resentful and scared of the White world that is, at the same time, out of reach and yet as he says, 'Right down here in my stomach'. When Mary Dalton and her Communist boy-friend, Jan, attempt to get to know him, he is confused and embarrassed by their intimacy. He is also sexually excited by Mary who has drunk too much and has to be helped to bed. As he leans over her body kissing her, he is disturbed by her blind mother, and in panic smothers the girl with a pillow.

It is after this accidental 'murder', similar to that of Roberta in *An American Tragedy*, and Bigger's gruesome disposal of the body, that his attitudes begin to change. He feels more alive than ever before in that he has at last taken his life into his own hands and is moving towards 'that sense of fulness he had so often but inadequately felt in magazines and movies'. He attempts to pin the blame for the murder on Mary's boy-friend, but after the girl's bones are discovered in the Dalton's furnace, Bigger realizes that the forces of the White world are closing in on him. He confesses his crime to his Black girl-friend, Bessie, who is then forced to flee with him. In a deserted building they make love before Bigger brutally bludgeons her to death with a brick as she sleeps beside him – Bigger once again experiencing the sense of power and freedom that comes with making things happen.

The last third of the novel, again like *An American Tragedy*, deals with Bigger's trial. He is eloquently defended by a Communist, Max, who is allowed to state the case against the American race and class attitudes at great length but, of course, his words are to no avail against the racist prosecutor's charge that what they are dealing with is a 'half-human black ape'. Bigger, too, resists Max's view of him, and in imagery anticipating Ralph Ellison's in *Invisible Man* (1953), he again asserts his need for identity and freedom.

> 'I hurt folk 'cause I felt I had to; that's all. They was
> crowding me too close; they wouldn't give me no room.
> Lots of times I tried to forget 'em, but I couldn't. They
> wouldn't let me . . . I'll be feeling and thinking that they
> didn't see me and I didn't see them.' (Bk 3)

Though he is going to the death predicted for him from the very beginning of the novel, Bigger's life has at last come to have meaning. As he says in his last interview, 'I'm all right. For real, I am.' It is the reality of Bigger that marks the difference between Wright's fiction and that of the general run of protest or proletarian writing. Black writing, like Black society in general, had taken a long time to transcend the stereotypes forced upon it throughout American history, but *Native Son* opened up new worlds for novelists who began writing after the Second World War.

Literary historians and cultural commentators have occasionally been tempted to compare the Black experience in fiction with that of the American Jew. Indeed, Bigger's lawyer, Max, does just this in *Native Son*. But the origins and development of the two traditions are so different, and the societies involved so dissimilar that beyond the shared suffering from racial prejudice there is very little that can usefully be described. It is true, of course, that like Blacks many thousands of Jews came to American cities from rural backgrounds, ill-equipped for life in an urban industrial environment. But the Jew brought with him the advantage and disadvantage of a foreign culture and language reaching far back into European history. His adaptation to American life presented problems of a quite different scale and nature, the repercussions of which extend into the second and third generations.

The size of the emigration of Russian and East European Jews to America during the last decades of the nineteenth century and the first part of the twentieth, making as it did for a significant change in the map of world Jewry, was still only one more chapter in a continuing Diaspora. Those who first wrote about the New Exodus, such as Abraham Cahn in *The Rise of David Levinsky* (1917), used the experience to explore not only American life in general but also a further stage in the progressive secularization of Jewish culture. The novel opens with Levinsky's terse résumé of his life and its meaning for him:

> Sometimes, when I think of my past in a superficial,
> casual way, the metamorphosis I have gone through

strikes me as nothing short of a miracle. I was born and
reared in the lowest depths of poverty and I arrived in
America – in 1885 – with four cents in my pocket. I am
now worth more than two million dollars and recognised
as one of the two or three leading men in the cloak-and-
suit trade in the United States. And yet when I take a
look at my inner identity it impresses me as being
precisely the same as it was thirty or forty years ago. My
present station, power, the amount of worldly happiness at
my command, and the rest of it, seem to be devoid of
significance. (1:1)

His American 'rise' from the Lower East Side ghetto to his suite of
rooms in a high-class hotel, only serves to convince him that 'there
are cases when success is Tragedy'. Levinsky's career describes an
opposite trajectory to that of Silas Lapham, but Cahn's message is the
same as Howells's: the price of success in America is too high. In the
final book of the novel, called 'Episodes of a Lonely Life', Levinsky's
spiritual, emotional, and moral poverty are described in terms of his
estrangement from his religion, from conjugal love, and even from his
own workers: 'Amid the pandemonium of my six hundred sewing
machines and the jingle of gold which they pour into my lap, I feel
the deadly silence of solitude' (14: 7).

Cahn's criticisms are not directed at the American capitalist ethos
as such. His realistic account of the growth of the American garment
industry is coloured with pride and pleasure in what was a uniquely
Jewish achievement in American industrial history. It is the individualism necessary for entrepreneurial success that cuts Levinsky off from
any community and eventually destroys his happiness.

For Mike Gold, on the other hand, the community values of the
Lower East Side described in *Jews Without Money* (1930), are vulnerable
not so much to the isolation of success as to the pressures of poverty,
and his solution to the problem is specifically political. Having
described in a series of loosely structured episodes the filth, vice, and
squalor of his childhood neighbourhood, as well as the heroism of
those who attempt to create a humane society there, he calls for the
creation of a new environment, a Utopia that might provide a 'garden
for the human spirit'. Even though Gold's political commitment to
communism was firmer and more enduring than that of most of his
contemporaries, the Utopian hopes expressed at the end of *Jews
Without Money* do not carry enough conviction to suggest a genuine
alternative to existing American society. All Utopias tend to possess
this 'bloodless' quality, of course, and what is more likely to be
remembered about the novel is the vitality of the teeming East Side

culture that haunted Gold's imagination throughout his life. Despite
the long odyssey which took him first to Harvard, then Europe, and
finally, at the end of his life, to California, he was still writing about
his childhood in the New York slums. In one of these 'sequels' to *Jews
Without Money*[10] he writes rather sadly about his loss of religious faith
and his discovery of new gods. 'The Ghetto walls were thin in
America', he remarks, and though this is true for all practical purposes,
his own need to return to the site of his origins proves that they do
not crumble as easily as all that.

Given the difficulty, and for many, the undesirability, of shrugging
off the burdens of their Jewish inheritance, the question facing many
sensitive first-generation Jews – a class described by Marcus Klein as
'the emerging disestablished'[11] – was one confronted by Meyer Levin,
obliquely in his fiction and directly in his autobiography, *In Search*
(1950). He saw himself as a strange mixture of 'Chicago and Chas-
sidim' and in his best-known novel *The Old Bunch* (1937), he traces
the effects of such combinations on the lives of a group of twenty boys
and girls as they grow to maturity in the 1920s, and in a variety of
ways, involving careers in law, medicine, business, sport, and crime,
seek to come to terms with the discontinuities between their past and
the present. Though the techniques used in the novel may derive from
Dos Passos, Levin uses its structure as a strategy for dealing with the
problem of creating a sufficiently dense milieu to sustain communal
values:

> While novelists emphasised the individual in the family
> unit as the determining human relationship, I saw the
> surrounding group, the bunch, as perhaps even more
> important than the family in the formative years.
> Particularly in the children of immigrants, the life values
> were determined largely through these group
> relationships[12]

Despite superficial similarities with the modernism of Dos Passos
and, at the close with Nathanael West, *The Old Bunch* remains firmly
in the realist tradition. The practical imperatives that impel Levin's
characters to discover viable life-styles in cosmopolitan Chicago, are
too firmly rooted in the realities of class, money, and manners to lend
themselves to modernist ways of thought and writing.

Another contemporary Jewish novelist for whom such realities are
inescapable is Daniel Fuchs. In his case, though, the location of events
in his Williamsburg Trilogy – the poor Jewish section of Brooklyn –
is so insistently present in the foreground of the fiction that it dominates his characters in a more typically naturalistic way. This certainly

is the case in the first novel, *Summer in Williamsburg* (1934), which portrays Philip Hayman hopelessly trapped by his environment, and life as 'a circle without significance'. The second and third novels, *Homage to Blenholt* (1936) and *Low Company* (1937), though still preoccupied with the impossibility of escaping from the realities of a particular social condition, treat such attempts comically by using *schlemiels* whose idealistic aspirations can be ironically juxtaposed with the harsh facts of life in the Jewish ghetto.

It is tempting at this point to draw parallels between Fuchs and the two most celebrated Jewish novelists of the 1930s, Henry Roth and Nathanael West. Neither of them would be at all out of place in a chapter dealing with radicalism and the American city. On the other hand, the quality of their vision, and the structural and linguistic organization of their novels give them stronger affinities with American modernist writers, and their fiction will, therefore, be used to indicate the essential continuity between movements that, far from being mutually exclusive, continuously touch and refresh each other.

This assimilative vigour of twentieth-century American literature is, of course, one of its outstanding characteristics. Not only did the great Black and Jewish migrations immeasurably enrich the American linguistic 'melting pot', but the range of unusual history and experience which their presence made available, gave American realist fiction a much larger and richer lease of life than it enjoyed in Europe. In a more oblique way, the new, exotic cosmopolitanism of the great industrial and commercial centres also spurred another group of writers to turn its attention with mixed emotions back to what seemed like a doomed culture in the heartland of America.

Notes

1. William Leuchtenburg, *Franklin D. Roosevelt and the New Deal, 1932–1940* (New York, 1963), p. 241. Howard Fast's essay, 'An Occurrence at Republic Steel', is reprinted in *The Aspirin Age*, edited by Isabel Leighton (Harmondsworth, 1964), p. 391–409

2. See *The Strike in the American Novel* (Metuchen, NJ, 1972).

3. See *The Radical Novel in the United States* (Cambridge, Mass., 1956), pp. 33–4.

4. Granville Hicks, *The Great Tradition: An Interpretation of American Literature Since the Civil War*, revised edition (New York, 1935), pp. 192–203.

5. 'Wilder: Prophet of the Genteel Christ', *in Years of Protest*, edited by Jack Salzman and Barry Wallenstein (New York, 1967), pp. 233–8.

6. 'The Two Memories: Reflections on Writers and Writing in the Thirties', in *Proletarian Writers of the Thirties*, edited by David Madden (Carbondale and Edwardsville, Ill. 1968), pp. 3–25.

7. Blanche Gelfant uses the term 'ecological novel' in *The American City Novel* (Norman, Okla., 1954), to describe those novels that have as their protagonists, not individuals but spatial units such as apartment houses or city blocks.

8. Daniel Bell includes an excellent essay on this aspect of industrial society, 'Work and its Discontents', in *The End of Ideology* (Glencoe, Ill., 1962).

9. 'I Tried to Be a Communist', Atlantic Monthly, 159 (Aug. 1944), pp. 61–70 (Sep. 1944), pp. 48–56. The essay was later reprinted in *The God That Failed*, edited by Richard Crossman (New York, 1949).

10. Reprinted in *Mike Gold: A Literary Anthology* edited by Michael Folsom (New York, 1972).

11. See 'The Roots of Radicals: Experience in the Thirties', in *Proletarian Writers of the Thirties*. pp. 134–57.

12. M. Levin, *In Search: An Autobiography* (Paris, 1950) pp. 75–6.

Chapter 9

Realists, Liberals and the Village: Anderson, Lewis, Cather, Glasgow, Tate, Caldwell, Steinbeck

The transformation of the structure and texture of American life between 1880 and 1920, and the consequences of that metamorphosis elicited three quite distinct kinds of fictional responses. The most direct reaction to the social upheavals of the period was that shown by the radical novelists and the most obscure was that of the modernists. Between the two, however, an older tradition of non-doctrinal realism reaching back to Twain, the nineteenth-century regionalists, and the local colour novelists, re-emerged after the First World War. Ironically, the beginnings of this new realism in about 1920 coincided with the death of W. D. Howells, the man whose own attempts to maintain that tradition had already been eclipsed by the impact of naturalism. Appropriately enough, the two writers most closely identified with the new development, Sherwood Anderson and Sinclair Lewis, both came from the same Midwestern small town background as Howells; Lewis's father was a country doctor in Minnesota and Anderson's a harness-maker in Howells's native state of Ohio. The movement with which their names have been persistently linked is most often described as a 'revolt from the village',[1] and Sherwood Anderson's abrupt flight from his paint business in Elyria to the literary life of Chicago at a time when most men are settling comfortably into middle age, is seen as a significant symbolic act in this rebellion. Viewed from a longer perspective and in the broader context of twentieth-century realism, though, their revolt seems to have been directed not only against the ethos of village or small town existence as such, but also against all those forces which threatened to stifle and defeat the humanity buried in common everyday life. Though these forces often took the form of moribund Victorian codes of conduct and beliefs, the hypocrisies and deadening routines from which the truths of the human condition cried out to be liberated, they were also represented, if more distantly, by the surrounding pressure of the new industrialized America that was coming into being. Caught between an obsolete heritage and an equally dehumanized future, the characteristic stance of the new realists was decidedly shaky: a curious combination of satire and celebration in the search for an individualistic freedom that was becoming more elusive with every passing year.

Sherwood Anderson's critics have often commented on the contribution made to his art by a unique spatial or temporal environment.[2] Ohio in the 1880s and 1890s when Anderson was growing up, was poised uneasily between the past and the future, a world of small Western farmers and the rapidly expanding industrial towns in the north of the State. Although Clyde, the place in which Anderson lived and the model for Winesburg, his famous fictional small town, never became a part of the great change, there was a moment in the 1880s when it seemed that natural gas and the coming of the railroads would engulf the place in a wave of modernization. Even though these developments were abortive, the novelist, looking back in his *Memoirs* (1942), recognized a more important revolution in the people themselves, 'a kind of fever, an excitement in the veins'. He writes wistfully about the disappearance of old craftsman, such as wagon, buggy, and furniture makers in the village, as men turned to 'the life of the machine', and it is the re-creation of what he calls that 'old individualistic small town life' coexistent with a new desire for freedom, that gives *Winesburg, Ohio* (1919) its special poignancy and makes the book more than a series of sketches connected only by a common location and the continuing presence of George Willard, the young journalist. The theme of a divided world radiates out to touch every aspect of life in the town though it finds its most insistent expression in the sexual frustrations and occasional fulfilments of the characters he calls his 'grotesques'. There are, he says, hundreds and hundreds of 'truths' in the world, the truth of virginity and passion, wealth and poverty, thought and profligacy, carelessness and abandon. It is the need to cling to particular 'truths' and to live their lives by them that makes his characters grotesque and changes their truths into falsehoods. Their dogged determination to pursue an abstract idea to its often tragic conclusion against all the circumstances of their lives, allows Anderson to manipulate the ambivalence he creates in both his characters and readers.

One of the clearest examples of this, is in 'The Untold Lie'. The story is about a farm-hand called Ray Pearson, though it appears at first to focus more on the life of one of his young fellow workers, Hal Winter. Characteristically, though, in a seemingly artless and garrulous way, Anderson no sooner introduces his protagonists than he digresses to tell the story of Hal's father's bizarre death. After getting drunk one evening, the old man had driven his wagon and horses home along the railroad track and straight at an onrushing train, screaming and raving as he careered to certain death. The anecdote bears a thematic relation to the main story, but Anderson also uses it to enforce a larger point. The narrator says that most of the townspeople declared the old drunk would go straight to hell and that the community would be better off without him, but George Willard and his young friends had a secret conviction that he knew what he was doing and showed admirable courage in terminating a humdrum life in so glorious a fashion. Their child-like romanticism and the old man's blind refusal of reality both serve as points of reference for the story Anderson is about to tell.

As the two farm-hands work in the fields, the older one, Ray, muses on the beauty of the landscape in late fall and slips into a reverie about how he was tricked into marriage by a girl who went into the woods with him on just such a day years before. Hal breaks into his thoughts, and after telling Ray that he too has just got a girl pregnant, asks the older man's advice about whether or not to marry her: 'Has a fellow got to do it?' he asked, 'Has he got to be harnessed up and driven through life like a horse?' Full of bitterness as he contemplates his own wretched domestic life, Ray decides he must save his friend from the kind of mistake he made. Escaping from his nagging wife and family, he later races to town to find Hal, but the young man forestalls him by declaring that he will marry the girl after all, that he wants to settle down and have children. It is a moment of release for both men and their separate tensions are dissolved in laughter:

> As the form of Hal Winters disappeared in the dusk that lay over the road that led to Winesburg, [Ray] turned and walked slowly back across the fields to where he had left his torn overcoat. As he went, some memory of pleasant evenings spent with the thin-legged children in the tumble-down house by the creek must have come into his mind, for he muttered words 'It's just as well. Whatever I told him would have been a lie', he said softly, and then his form also disappeared into the darkness of the fields. ('The Untold Lie')

Both Hal and Ray can be seen as examples of what Anderson calls 'the defeated figures of an old American individualistic small town life'. Usually Anderson's 'grotesques' are, by the very nature of their obsessions, lonely and isolated men and women whose stories are only discovered through their need to talk to the book's recording consciousness, George Willard. Occasionally Anderson allows them to reveal their inner selves in ironic confrontations with each other, and sometimes, as in the stories of Kate Swift and the Reverend Curtis Hartman, with George, too. Kate, the sexually frustrated school-teacher, almost seduces George, her former pupil, and when she rushes home in a frenzy of guilt, she is spied on as usual by the Presbyterian pastor who has taken a small piece of stained glass out of his bell-tower window so that he can secretly watch Kate in bed:

> Kate Swift appeared. In the room next door a lamp was
> lighted and the waiting man stared into an empty bed.
> Then upon the bed before his eyes a naked woman threw
> herself. Lying face downward she wept and beat with her
> fists upon the pillow. With a final outburst of weeping she
> half arose, and in the presence of the man who had waited
> to look and to think thoughts, the woman of sin began to
> pray. In the lamplight her figure, slim and strong, looked
> like the figure of the boy in the presence of the Christ on
> the leaded window. ('The Strength of God')

Hartman, of course, sees this as a sign from God. He smashes the window with his fist then rushes headlong to the office of the *Winesburg Eagle* where he blurts out an incoherent confession to George Willard. George, still undergoing his own sexual trauma after Kate's departure, not unnaturally thinks the whole town is going mad.

Occasionally Anderson uses the stories of his grotesques to further the skeletal plot of George's rites of passage to manhood. Throughout the book, for example, we encounter George's mother whose greatest desire is 'to get out of town, out of my clothes, out of my marriage, out of my body, out of everything'. She eventually gets her wish, and her death does help to liberate something in her son who then decides to leave Winesburg.

George's education, like that of Stephen in Joyce's *Portrait of the Artist as a Young Man*, is artistic as well as emotional, and some of the stories are used to explore or illuminate this aspect of his development. Kate Swift's ostensible interest in George, for example, lies in his writing, and their sexual encounter is provoked by her advice to him to 'stop fooling with words' and start living. Though she is thinking here of herself, she also provides a clue to Anderson's art when she says 'The Thing to learn is to know what people are thinking about, not what they say.'

A further hint is provided by Enoch Robinson, the lonely fugitive from Winesburg who wants to explain his paintings to his friends in New York: 'the picture you see doesn't consist of the things you see and say words about. There is something else, something you don't see at all.' It is likely that George, who spends his days as a reporter running about like an excited dog and writing trivial facts in his note-book, would not understand Enoch's ideas any better at this stage in his life than the students in New York do; but the whole point of his experience in Winesburg, whether his own painful groping towards maturity or the vicarious sufferings recounted to him, is to bring him to an understanding of the essential reality of the things 'you don't see at all'.

This is also the important point to be made about Anderson's realism. It marks the shift from what, in simplest terms, can be characterized as the Darwinian world of the naturalists, to the Freudian world of the new realists. In *Winesburg, Ohio*, Anderson succeeds brilliantly in uncovering the inner realities of his characters, and he continues to do so in the first part of *Poor White* (1920). His attempt to carry his characters forward into the new American age, 'into the whirl and roar of modern machines', often results, as in *Many Marriages* (1923) and *Dark Laughter* (1925), in the substitution of naive fantasy for reality. But the story of Hugh McVay's progressive alienation as he becomes a famous inventor trapped in the frame of an inarticulate Missouri country boy, carries a dimension of social density lacking in Anderson's later Laurentian work. As Irving Howe says, *Poor White* is remarkable for its avoidance of the split between humane ideology and aggressive power-hunger that disrupts the work of so many of his socially oriented contemporaries.[3]

Howe may have had Sinclair Lewis in mind when making this judgement, for such comparisons are very difficult to avoid between two writers whose major works appeared almost simultaneously and who both took American provincial life as their subject. Maxwell Geismar calls them a necessary complement to each other, but then goes on to suggest that whereas Anderson, when not looking back nostalgically, is always willing to give 'this democracy thing another whirl yet',[4] Lewis is more concerned to record pessimistically the final step in the industrial triumph: the pillage of the town. Virginia Woolf makes a similar point in contrasting the 'shell-less' Anderson with Lewis whose books are so completely externalized that there is no room left for the snail.[5]

To say these things is not to imply that Sinclair Lewis did not want to make room for the individualistic, humane values that Anderson cherished. He knew just as well as Anderson that 'if a man cannot love his own patch of ground, then he cannot love the street, the city, the state or the country of which it is a part'. For him the trouble was that every little patch was by now either mortgaged to the greed of businessmen or so overworked that it had lost its fertility. Moreover, Lewis was not by any means a lone prophet in this wilderness. In the same year that he published *Babbitt* (1922), Lewis Mumford claimed that in its aridity the average American town was like the Alkali Desert, while H. L. Mencken in his melancholy outpourings throughout the 1920s, continued to lament the fact that in solving most of the material problems of life, America had come no nearer at all to dealing with such immutable problems as sin, or stupidity.[6] He claimed that the irreconcilable antagonism between democratic Puritanism and common decency is what was probably responsible for the uneasiness and unhappiness so prevalent in American life. Mencken's continued attacks on the institutions associated with Puritanism and democracy so impressed Lewis that he was ready to make him 'the Pope of America'. The split that Howe sees between a humane ideology and the hunger for power was becoming a generally recognized fact of American experience. Lewis's importance is that for all his faults as a novelist he gave this fact its most emphatic expression, first in *Main Street* (1920) and then in *Babbitt* (1922).

He had written several novels before *Main Street*, but in them his realism is more often subordinated to Romance than satire as he focuses attention on the lives of his rebellious characters rather than on the Midwestern environment that makes their rebellion necessary. *Main Street* clearly changes this pattern by simply reversing the situation and having its heroine, Carol Kennicott, come to Gopher Prairie from a more sophisticated milieu which allows her to place its essential bleakness. The chasm between her naive idealism and the reality of what she encounters gives Lewis's criticisms a satiric force quite different from the contemporary Midwestern novels with which *Main Street* was constantly compared by reviewers: *Winesburg, Ohio*, Zora Gale's *Miss Lulu Bett* (1920), and Floyd Dell's *Moon-Calf* (1920). In his biography of Lewis, Mark Schorer calls the novel 'a thunderclap that changed the literary atmosphere',[7] and though this is true, as a comparison with those contemporary works and later ones shows, any change brought about by *Main Street* was the result of Lewis's style rather than any new perception; a style that has been repeatedly criticized for its crudity, though it possesses an undoubted power, based as it is on remarkable accuracy in its presentation of detail.

Carol's observations of Gopher Prairie, precipitated by her reading of American sociologists and the English realists, are also formed partly as a counter to the traditions of the small town as they appear in the popular fiction of the day, either as the home of comic old rustics or as 'the one sure abode of friendship, honesty, and clean sweet marriageable girls'. But what Carol actually discovers is:

> A savorless people, gulping tasteless food, and sitting
> afterward, coatless and thoughtless, in rocking-chairs
> prickly with inane decorations, listening to mechanical
> music, saying mechanical things about the excellence of
> Ford automobiles, and viewing themselves as the greatest
> race in the world. (22)

The innocence of the American past has been traded for the promise of a boundless materialistic future, and both have been betrayed by the imposition of a dull conformity:

> Nine-tenths of the American towns are so alike that it is the completest boredom to wander from one to another. Always, west of Pittsburg, and often, east of it, there is the same lumber yard, the same railroad station, the same Ford garage, the same creamery, the same box-like houses and two-storey shops. The new, more conscious houses are alike in their very attempts at diversity: the same bungalows, the same square houses of stucco or tapestry brick. The shops show the same standardised, nationally advertised wares; the newspapers of sections three thousand miles apart have the same 'syndicated features'; the boy in Arkansas displays just such a flamboyant ready-made suit as is found on just such a boy in Delaware, both of them iterate the same slang phrases from the same sporting-pages, and if one of them is in college and the other is a banker, no one may surmise which is which. (22)

Lewis's target is the assembly line and the effect it was having on the individual. E. M. Forster pinpoints Lewis's method of capturing the mechanization of American life when he calls him a photographer rather than an artist.[8] It is Lewis's ability flatly to record what he sees that makes his satire convincing, and when his patience deserts him in his later writing, the shortcomings of his art and his intellect are cruelly exposed. Even in his best work his inability fully to transcend the middle-class conventions he is attacking and to give real substance to Carol Kennicott's yearnings or to George F. Babbitt's vague aspirations, makes for a depressing absence of any positively realized value in the characters he creates. In later life Lewis maintained that Carol's intellectual and artistic deficiencies were part of his design, but the book itself and the things he said about it at the time in a letter to Floyd Dell, do not bear this view out. Moreover, Lewis's other social rebels in Gopher Prairie – Miles Bjornstram, Erik Valberg, Raymond Wutherspoon, and Guy Pollack – are equally inadequate rebels. As Maxwell Geismar says, 'they not only lack the courage of their convictions, they also lack convictions'.[9]

They also lack, as Carol herself does, any sexual potency, and the whole shape of the novel depends upon her need to express herself emotionally and sexually as well as to relate those frustrations to the lack of beauty in her immediate environment. The weakness of her drives can be gauged by the ease with which her rebellion collapses,

and from the complacency with which she eventually rejects the larger
world of Washington for the comforts of the village, the active difficulty of literature for the passive pleasures of the movies, and the
excitement of sexual fulfilment for the routine of domesticity. At the
end of the novel after admitting her defeat by the forces of Philistinism,
she maintains that she has nevertheless kept the faith, and suggests to
her husband that she will bring up their daughter to be 'a bomb to
blow up smugness'. Lewis's hatred of 'tea table gentility' and the stul-
tification of small-town life are genuine enough, but the alternatives
he vaguely proposes – aeroplane trips to Mars and world-wide industrial unions – demonstrate by their irrelevance the limitations of his
own imagination.

In writing *Babbitt* Lewis created an even more difficult fictional
problem for himself by using as his central character a figure who has
to be both the target of his satire and the vehicle for his broader criticisms of society itself. This necessitates so implausible a change in his
hero's attitudes and behaviour that the novel is virtually split in two.
This fatal flaw in *Babbitt's* structure was hardly noticed at the time of
its publication by readers who were overwhelmed by the force of
Lewis's satire, directed this time at the American businessman and the
ethos of a typical Midwestern city, Zenith. Lewis's portrait of Zenith
was so accurate that at least five cities claimed to be its model, and the
word Babbitt was immediately adopted as a term for the archetypal
'boob' who struts and swaggers through the first part of the book.
Edith Wharton, to whom Lewis rather surprisingly dedicated the
novel, was an exception. In a friendly letter to him praising the book,
she makes the point that *Main Street* has unity and depth because its
society is reflected in the consciousness of a woman who suffered from
it because she had points of comparison and was therefore detached
from it. Babbitt, on the other hand, 'is in and of Zenith up to his
chin and over'. Lewis's efforts to extricate his hero in some way by
creating a plot, was apparently an afterthought. It was certainly a
mistake.[10]

His original idea had been to follow Babbitt through the events of
one day 'from alarm clock to alarm clock', and this idea is retained in
the first seven chapters. In order to broaden the scope of his satire,
Lewis then began to add chapter after chapter dealing with such
subjects as clubs, trade conventions, religion and politics, until the
extension of his criticism obliged him to create a 'story' for Babbitt
if he were to prevent the book from becoming a mere series of essays.
So Babbitt is portrayed as a man with an underlying sensitivity who
rebels against the mores of his world, flirts with radical politics and
another woman, and generally asserts his individuality before being
brought to heel in a rather contrived way at the end.

Another reason for not following the original plan – and it is closely linked with the novel's great merit – is connected with the conception of George Babbitt himself. By his very nature he is not large or powerful enough to dominate his world and embody the cultural characteristics which Lewis wanted to expose. The tycoons and entrepreneurs who had filled the fiction of Dreiser and Norris with their power and aggression had given way to the corporation conformist in a grey flannel suit. Babbitt is a little man whose main aim is to be indistinguishable from his fellows, not to rule them. The only way in which Lewis could keep him at the centre of his novel, once he had exhausted the petty details of his hero's dull daily routine, was to have him rebel in some way.

Before this, though, Lewis allows Babbitt to define himself and his culture not only by his actions but also by his speech to the Zenith Real Estate Board, in which he paints a general picture of the Ideal Citizen. Whatever his profession, he says the solid American Citizen will cultivate the characteristics of the businessman, not wasting time in day-dreams, going to society teas, or kicking about things that are none of his business. Even artists can aspire to 'drag down fifty thousand bucks a year' and mingle with executives on equal terms provided they handle their wares with pep and avoid the mistakes of those 'shabby bums' in Europe who live in attics and exist on booze and spaghetti. The artists' contribution to the city's well-being is not to be equated with that of car salesmen, of course, nor of manufacturers of lighting fixtures, but such people are infinitely preferable to the long-haired intellectuals at the State University who masquerade under such sham names as 'liberals', 'radicals', or 'non-partisans'. Babbitt maintains it is as much everyone's duty to get such people fired from their posts 'as it is to sell all the real estate and gather in all the good shekels we can'. The ultimate aim of society is to produce a new generation of standardized Americans, 'fellows with hair on their chests and smiles in their eyes and adding machines in their offices'.

After speeches such as this it is difficult to take Babbitt's defection seriously, though Lewis tries hard to shift the reader's attention to more general targets and to turn his satire to the rest of the 'Boys' as they appropriately call themselves. Babbitt's plausibility is restored by the device of giving his wife an acute attack of appendicitis. Babbitt immediately sees that his 'fling' is over, and with some relief opts for the 'paralysed contentment' of middle age. Basking in the forgiveness of his family, the Elks, the Good Citizen League, the Boosters, and the Athletic Club, he surrenders his synthetic individuality with hardly a whimper, and though, like Carol Kennicott, he makes a speech about the next generation taking things a little further than he had been able to do, we last see him conniving at his son's plan to quit the university and take a job in a factory.

Lewis's career and reputation gathered momentum throughout the 1920s in the wake of his enormous success. He was the first American to be awarded the Nobel Prize for Literature at the end of the decade, and *Main Street* and *Babbitt*, which together sold 2 million copies in forty years, set the pattern for much of his subsequent fiction. The satiric style of *Babbitt* is directed at religious movements and their commercial exploitation in *Elmer Gantry* (1927), and at Fascism in *It Can't Happen Here* (1935). In *Arrowsmith* (1925), on the other hand, though Lewis still criticizes commercial exploiters – in this case of medical research – the temptation to create ferociously satirical caricatures is tempered by a desire to introduce more realistic and sympathetic characters like Martin Arrowsmith himself, Leora Tozer, and his ideal figure, the scientist Max Gottlieb. Lewis does not have the right kind of talent, though, to relate his characters to their environment convincingly, and in this novel, as in *Dodsworth* (1929), there is an emptiness and a lack of cohesion that Lewis tries to offset with a strained sentimentality. When published, *Arrowsmith* was praised for its truth, humanity, and sincerity, but if one compares Lewis's descriptions of Wheatsylvania, Dakota, with those of Black Hawk in Willa Cather's *My Antonia* (1918), his inability to penetrate beyond surface detail and his refusal to subordinate ideas to perceptions, are thrown into sharp relief. If his characters seem like tourists, it is largely because his own descriptions read more like advertising copy than fiction:

All afternoon they drove in the flapping buggy across the long undulations of the prairie. To their wandering there was no barrier, neither lake nor mountain nor factory-bristling city, and the·breeze about them was flowing sunshine.
Martin cried to Leora, 'I feel as if all the Zenith dust and hospital lint were washed out of my lungs. Dakota. Real man's country. Frontier. Opportunity. America!'
From the thick swale the young prairie chickens rose. As he watched them sweep across the wheat, his sun-drowsed spirit was part of the great land, and he was almost freed of the impatience with which he had started from Wheatsylvania. (14)

To introduce Willa Cather's name into a discussion of Lewis's style must again call into question the utility of 'realism' as a critical term. The multitudinous details that Lewis 'photographed' to provide the material for his satire have no place at all in Willa Cather's novels. In an essay she wrote in 1922 entitled 'The Novel Démeublé' she called for a purer type of fiction that would throw out all the 'social furniture' with which it had been cluttered since Balzac's time. In her own later work, and even in that written before this critical moment, she succeeded well enough to convince many critics that she was really more of a lyric poet than a novelist. In the same essay, she even rejected the whole world of 'physical sensation', as well as the banking system and the Stock Exchange, so that if one were to define realism in terms of subject-matter, her place in this chapter would certainly be open to doubt. If, on the other hand, the possibility of treating the spiritual life realistically is conceded, then her inclusion here is legitimate. And even if such a claim seems insubstantial, her evocation of the land, whether it is the Nebraska prairies of *O Pioneers* (1913) and *My Antonia*, or the south-western deserts of her later work, these sources of spiritual value in her world cannot be dismissed as metaphoric projections or mythic landscapes. She herself had grown up in Nebraska during the period she preferred to describe, the 1880s, at a time when the land was barely settled, and her descriptions of farms and small communities come from her most important and ineradicable memories.

Like other Midwestern writers, Willa Cather had at first attempted to escape the narrowness and dullness of her early environment. She was not immune to the restlessness of small-town existence which she describes so well and, tantalized by the glimpses of European history and culture provided by her cosmopolitan neighbours, she eventually arrived in New York. She pursued a successful career as a journalist and produced a volume of short stories called *The Troll Garden* (1905), and a novel, *Alexander's Bridge* (1912), before returning to the past for material that would sustain the fiction of her middle period. An important influence at this time which affected her decision to reject the 'studio picture' writing of her Jamesian period, was that of Sarah Orne Jewett, who advised her to find her 'own quiet centre of life, and write from that to the world . . . to the human heart'.[11]

While it is not a distortion of the truth to see Willa Cather as yet another in a procession of American artists 'who have gone down to defeat before the actualities of American life', Lionel Trilling's observation needs more qualification than he provides by blaming American life itself and placing her in very distinguished company.[12] It is true that the refuges she sought from the petty, crass materialism of the present – first the sanctuary of art and later that of Roman Catholicism – did not always provide sufficient space or serenity to counter her petulant anti-modernism. But between these she discovered in Nebraska her great subject, and in the lives of the pioneers found a great theme to erect on it.

O Pioneers was her first work in the new mode and it is not entirely successful. Her style in it is free of the literariness of her earlier work, and there are real gains in immediacy and concreteness.[13] Where characters in her earlier fiction act against a background, the figures in this novel inhabit their world and are defined by it in a Hardyesque way. Here, for example, is Alexandra Bergson, who will become the novel's central character and the vehicle for Willa Cather's final affirmation. The contrast between Alexandra and her friend Carl sets up the dialectic that will shape the book's main theme:

> Although it was only four o'clock, the winter day was
> fading. The road led southwest, toward the streak of pale,
> watery light that glimmered in the leaden sky. The light
> fell upon the two sad young faces that were turned mutely
> toward it: upon the eyes of the girl, who seemed to be
> looking with such anguished perplexity into the future;
> upon the sombre eyes of the boy, who seemed already to
> be looking into the past. The little town behind them had
> vanished as if it had never been, had fallen behind the
> swell of the prairie, and the stern frozen country received
> them into its bosom. (Part 1)

Alexandra and Carl are driving back to see her dying father, John Bergson. He is one of the many defeated figures in the novel, a Swedish immigrant who unsuccessfully tried to tame the land for eleven years in the hope of recovering his lost family wealth. Others, like the Linstrums are driven back east by the droughts that sent so many others retreating across the Mississippi in the mid-1880s, or like Alexandra's brothers Oscar and Lou, they merely lack the strength and imagination of the successful pioneer. Alexandra herself possesses these qualities in abundance and uses them powerfully and lovingly to create a paradisal garden out of the wilderness. Her feeling for the land, expressed in rich, sensuous imagery is too positive to be regarded as a mere compensation for the fact that, being always surrounded by little men, she finds no real joy in human sexual relationships. Her stoic loneliness that is only slightly tempered by her eventual passionless union with Carl, is seen as the necessary condition of her spiritual identity.

In one of her essays Willa Cather spoke of human relationships as 'the tragic necessity of human life', and a large part of O Pioneers is taken up with the story of such a relationship between Alexandra's brother Emil, and Marie, the estranged wife of Frank Shabata. Their love-affair is spontaneous and idyllic, despite the social and religious transgressions it involves. Willa Cather comes as close here as anywhere to making out a case for sexual fulfilment, but when the two are killed by Frank in a murderous rage, she uses the terrible climax to brood on the destruction and sorrow brought by Marie's warm impulsiveness. The best answer she can find is in the kind of withdrawal from human contact made by character after character in her subsequent fiction, and the varying degrees of emotional and spiritual fulfilment they achieve.

The weakness of O Pioneers derives from a lack of integration between its thematically related stories. In rejecting the artificial form of the well-made novel, Willa Cather never completely mastered the kind of organic structure which her materials demanded, though she came close to it in My Antonia by entangling her heroine's story with that of Jim Burden, the narrator.

Jim and Antonia arrive in Nebraska together, one an orphan from Virginia, and the other in a poor family of Bohemian immigrants. The first third of the novel describing their early experience, the hardships and joys of lives that are intimately bound up with the folklore of the last European settlers, provides not just a superbly realized base for the rest of the work, but also the human values that it will test.

Jim's grandparents take him to live in the nearby small town of Black Hawk, and he is shortly followed there by Antonia, who becomes one of the 'hired girls' that customarily help out their families by finding work in town. In addition to displaying a wonderful awareness of the nuances of social structure and providing a vivid description of the texture of life in those early settlements, this section of the novel explores the major theme of human development on, and away from, the land. The hired girls, all daughters of poor immigrants, are like a race apart. They have a physical ease and grace that distinguishes them from the others, and as well as considering them inferior, the Black Hawk residents see in their bold beauty a threat to social stability. In addition to their natural charm and animal vigour, they are the first to achieve prosperity as a result of their energetic involvement in life, and Jim, though ironically cut off from them himself, finds the attitude of the townspeople towards the hired girls, stupid. The Black Hawk boys and the men, too, are enthralled by Lena Lingard's swelling figure and provocative walk, and Cather creates rich comedy out of Ole Benson's pursuit of Lena in a sequence that must surely have been in Faulkner's mind when he wrote The Hamlet. For all their fascination, though, her admirers, like Jim, are trapped within narrower conventions which dictate that they will eventually marry Black Hawk girls and live in brand-new houses with chairs that must not be sat upon and hand-painted china that must not be used. This attitude sometimes has potentially tragic effects on the girls, as in Antonia's case, when she is deserted by the flashy railroad conductor, Larry Donovan, who fathers her child but then refuses to marry her.

Antonia's story is told in retrospect to Jim by friends, but the event that effectively brings their childhood to an end in the novel is an idyllic picnic shared by Jim and four of the hired girls, including Lena and Antonia. On a hot summer afternoon they chat desultorily but meaningfully about their pasts and possible futures, linking their lives to those of their European ancestors, the Spanish explorers before them, and to the land itself. It is one of the great pastoral scenes in American fiction, culminating in a justly famous image:

> Presently we saw a curious thing. There were no clouds,
> the sun was going down in a limpid, gold-washed sky.
> Just as the lower edge of the red disk rested on the high
> fields against the horizon, a great black figure suddenly
> appeared on the face of the sun. We sprang to our feet,
> straining our eyes toward it. In a moment we realised
> what it was. On some up-land farm, a plough had been
> left standing in the field. The sun was sinking just behind
> it. Magnified across the distance by the horizontal light, it
> stood out against the sun, was exactly contained within
> the circle of the disc, the handles, the tongue, the shape –
> black against the molten red. There it was, heroic in size,
> a picture writing on the sun. (4)

The optical illusions produced by the tricks of light and space heighten but do not destroy reality, either for Jim Burden or the reader. Though Jim leaves Nebraska for a career in law, he always remembers the reality of his past. Antonia, however, continues to create hers in actuality, and in a coda to the main action she is visited years later by Jim on her prosperous farm, surrounded by family, animals, and crops, 'a rich mine of life, like the founders of early races'.

Nothing else in Willa Cather's fiction approaches *My Antonia* in its generous affirmation of life, and her later works, *The Professor's House* (1925), *Death Comes for the Archbishop* (1927) and *Shadows on the Rock* (1931), justify Geismar's lament, 'if only she hadn't needed to go so far afield for her spiritual sanctuary, when a less ornate mode of salvation might have done!'[14] Of course, it can be argued that if Willa Cather had allowed the common people of her tales to experience more of the exquisite torment of life, she might have satisfied Geismar but only at the expense of a parochialism that the same critic perversely claimed elsewhere could have saved Henry James![15] If one compares *My Antonia* with even the best of the Scandinavian pioneer novels such as O. E. Rölvaag's *Giants in the Earth* (1927), Willa Cather's breadth of vision and her ability to project that vision back into the stories she tells is the mark of her superiority. Rölvaag's psychological realism often seems in contrast, dull, unfocused, and repetitive, and his socio-logical extensions of the immigrant theme in *Peder Victorious* (1929) and *Their Father's God* (1931) confirm this view, even if allowances are made for the fact that his novels are translated from the original Norwegian. Similar criticisms could be made of many other contem-porary regional novels which skilfully and sensitively explore the interaction of generations in specific localities; novels such as Glenway Wescott's *The Grandmothers* (1927), Joseph Hergesheimer's *The Lime-stone Tree* (1931), or Louis Bromfield's *The Farm* (1933), all of which, despite their local strengths, lack the aesthetic rigour of *My Antonia*.

The temptation for regional writers to sink back into a narrow provincialism is one that particularly exercised the minds of a group of Southern writers and critics in the 1920s and 1930s. The Southern Agrarians (or 'Fugitives' as they were sometimes called, after the title of a short-lived magazine), met together in Nashville, Tennessee, as young teachers and students of literature, and out of their brief associ-ation came not simply a body of literature sufficiently distinguished to suggest to many a Southern renaissance,[16] but an entire critical movement, the New Criticism, that was powerful enough to dominate the literary academy for thirty years.

Though the critical theories developed by Allan Tate, John Crowe Ransom, Cleanth Brooks, and Robert Penn Warren have much broader significance in the history of modernism, in that they relate to the development of Structuralism in Western thought, they were also devised in a particular place at a particular time, and these local circumstances gave their ideas a connection, if not an affinity, with the various manifestations of the new realism we have been examining. This is particularly true of their attempts to yoke social and moral philosophies to a specific aesthetic. Ransom in *The World's Body* (1938), Tate in *Reactionary Essays on Poetry and Ideas* (1936), and several contributors to the famous symposium *I'll Take My Stand* (1930) emphasized what they saw as a developing contrast in American life between the attitudes induced by Northern, urban industrialism and a more conservative world-view then under attack in the South. The deepening impact of scientific thought and technological development had, they thought, served to estrange men from the land, to foster abstract modes of thought and exploitative, materialistic attitudes; and to exacerbate a split in the already dissociated sensibilities of modern man. The antidote to this spiritual breakdown lay in the reaffirmation of traditional American, agrarian values, so as to bring about man's reintegration with the land and landscape. The sacrifice of material progress to the pleasures of the contemplative life, however unrealistic as a political programme, had a powerful emotional appeal in a period of general disillusionment, and it was manifested at every level of

American culture all the way down to the debased sentimental pastoralism of Hollywood Westerns, and the shallow myth-making of *Gone With The Wind* (1936).

The Fugitives' more immediate aim was the revitalization of Southern literature, and in addition to making their own significant contribution in such novels as Stark Young's *So Red The Rose* (1934), Allen Tate's *The Fathers* (1938), Robert Penn Warren's *Night Rider* (1939), and *All the King's Men* (1946), they instituted a debate about Southern culture that has had far-reaching implications for the interpretation of such writers as Ellen Glasgow, Thomas Wolfe, and William Faulkner. In each of these novels an older, often idealistic way of life is juxtaposed, implicitly or explicitly, with a newer, more realistic, personal or pragmatic life-style, in order to define the values of a culture that had developed and sustained itself always in a hostile environment.

Allen Tate, summing up the achievements of the Southern Renaissance at a time when he believed it had run its course (or rather had been overtaken by the new provincialism), saw quite clearly that it was the passionate conflict of two irreconcilable lifestyles that produced so much artistic energy and work of a high order:

> If the Southern subject is the destruction by war the later
> degradation of the South by carpetbaggers and scalawags,
> and a consequent lack of moral force and imagination in
> the cynical materialism of the New South, then the
> sociologists of fiction and the so-called traditionalists are
> trying to talk about the same thing. But with this
> difference – and it is a difference between two worlds: the
> provincial world of the present, which sees in material
> welfare and legal justice the whole solution to the human
> problem; and the classical-Christian World, based upon the
> regional consciousness, which held that honor, truth,
> imagination, human dignity, and limited acquisitiveness,
> could alone justify a social order however rich and efficient
> it may be; and could do much to redeem an order
> dilapidated and corrupt, like the South today, if a few
> people passionately hold these beliefs.[17]

Among the writers Tate praises for their celebration of the regional consciousness, the most conspicuous is of course Faulkner, whose sagas of Yoknapatawpha County conform perfectly to Tate's description of 'the Southern subject', and who, five years after Tate's essay, echoed its sentiments in his Nobel Prize acceptance speech. There he too spoke of the 'verities and truths of the heart' without which any story is ephemeral – love and honour and pity and pride and compassion and sacrifice. Tate also listed Ellen Glasgow among the traditionalists, though curiously enough he condemned her best novel *Barren Ground* (1925) by faintly praising it as the best of a bunch of novels lacking true universality. He thought that instead of making the frustrations of her Virginian farmers a reflection of moral decay everywhere, she had used them as a simple object-lesson in the lack of American 'advantages'.

It is true that the heroine of the novel, Dorinda Oakley, eventually does become the most successful farmer in the area by applying modern techniques to the intractable land. But to suggest that this is in any sense the 'object-lesson' of the novel is to ignore its real centre of interest: Dorinda's emotional and mental life. In her autobiography, *The Woman Within* (1954), Ellen Glasgow uses the same terminology as Tate to make this point about her novel: 'I had always wished to escape from the particular into the general, from the provincial into the universal . . . I had resolved to write of the South, not, in elegy, as a conquered province, but, vitally, as a part of the larger world.' The same point can be made about Dorinda herself whose retreat from her unhappy love-affair into farming parallels Ellen Glasgow's situation at the time she wrote the novel. But the author uses this autobiographical fact to drive home one of the insights she learned from Tolstoy, that 'the ordinary is simply the universal observed from the surface, that the direct approach to reality is not without, but within'.[18]

The juxtaposition of Dorinda and the landscape is introduced in the first three sentences of the novel – an arresting image of both movement and stasis that anticipates so much of its action:

> A girl in an orange-coloured shawl stood at the window
> of Pedlar's store and looked, through the falling snow, at
> the deserted road. Though she watched there without
> moving, her attitude, in its stillness, gave an impression of
> arrested flight, as if she were running toward life.
> Bare, starved, desolate, the country closed in about her.
> (I. 1)

Throughout the first part of the novel Dorinda searches for love in a story that, in paraphrase, appears unnatural and melodramatic. She is deserted by her lover, Jason Greylock, whom she tries to kill, and after losing her unborn illegitimate child in New York, returns to Virginia where she steadily and coldly triumphs over all the weak, degenerate men who have failed to give her the love she needs. Described in this way, *Barren Ground* might be considered a precursor of Margaret Mitchell's *Gone With The Wind*, and Ellen Glasgow a vengeful feminist, but in fact the centre of the novel, reached through Dorinda's cathartic human pilgrimage, exists behind what Ellen Glasgow called the 'little destinies of men and women' in a Hardy-like evocation of 'that unconquerable vastness in which nothing is everything'.[19] After Jason's pathetic death – the final act of the melodrama – Dorinda turns from the human to discover her permanent self, the reality beneath the actuality: 'The Spirit of the land was flowing into her, and her own spirit, strengthened and refreshed, was flowing out again toward life.' (3.11)

Some critics have seen this 'mystique of the land' as a romantic or sentimental compensation for the failure of human relationship in the novel, rather than as a sign of Ellen Glasgow's 'transcendent maturity' – a point which proves how difficult it is for the Southern novelist to tread the line between romanticism and provincialism. What saves the work from this form of sentimentality and makes Dorinda a heroine comparable to Antonia, is the degree of self-knowledge given to her. As she clears the land to create pasture, burning the inevitable broom-sedge that chokes everything, and grubbing up the pine and sassafras in the process, her meditation on her life – a metaphor for the South as a whole – leaves the reader in no doubt that Ellen Glasgow herself scorned any easy choice between the illusions of the past and the advantages of the progressive future:

> Her nightmare dream of ploughing under the thistles, was translated into the actual event. Perhaps, as the years went by, the reality would follow the dream into oblivion. At thirty, she had looked forward to forty, as the time of her release from vain expectation; but when forty came, she pushed the horizon of her freedom still farther away.
> 'Perhaps at fifty I shall be rid of it for ever', she thought.
> (3:1)

The liberal morality to which Allen Tate objected in Ellen Glasgow is as charged with irony and scepticism as is the romanticism of her good friend and fellow Richmond novelist, James Branch Cabell. In his long series of fantasies, ostensibly removed from contemporary Virginia to medieval Europe, Cabell shows time and again how men fail to serve their various dreams owing to the 'inadequacy of the flesh' and eventually 'dwindle into responsible citizens'. As is apparent from this and many other comments, Cabell despised realism, believing that if it is a form of art, 'the morning newspaper is a permanent contribution to literature'. Yet, for all their dramatic opposition in formal terms, the qualifying ironies of Glasgow and Cabell create a humanist centre where they meet. Louis Rubin in an excellent essay on the two novelists suggests that their irony owes something to the unique ethos of Richmond,[20] which as the besieged capital of the rebellious South during the Civil War, saw itself as the home of lost causes and spent the rest of the century deliberately cultivating the legends of the doomed but heroic Confederacy; forever reminiscing, as Cabell said, 'of womanhood, and of the brightness of hope's rainbow, and of the tomb, and of right upon the scaffold, and of the scroll of fame, and of the stars, and of the verdict of posterity'. By the same token, and precisely because it had been the besieged capital, Richmond had maintained the excellent rail network existing at the time and had developed into a thriving industrial and commercial city that was unique in the South but comparable with many in the Midwest and North. This discrepancy between the cultivated myths of the past and the raw actualities of the present offered rich material for the ironic temper of Cabell and provided a dense social medium for Ellen Glasgow's social satires written after *Barren Ground* was completed.

These novels, *The Romantic Comedians* (1926), *They Stooped to Folly* (1929) and *The Sheltered Life* (1932), treat the follies of romantic love, but their deeper satiric bite comes from the clash of cultures represented by an ageing, obsolete aristocracy in conflict with a young, buoyant *bourgeoisie*. Though Ellen Glasgow's intellectual sympathies are usually with the emancipated middle classes, her deeper feelings extend to those who are vainly trying to cling to the vanishing order and civility of the past. Her ability to balance equally the claims of two ways of life gives her novels of this period a pace and lightness lacking in both her earlier and later work, and it produces a tone quite different from Allen Tate's *The Fathers* (1938), a novel set in northern Virginia during the Civil War and based on a similar theme.

Allen Tate's sensibilities proved just as complex as Ellen Glasgow's, his artistic integrity was just as secure, and his basic sympathies were very similar, if more pronounced. Yet *The Fathers* ends in tragedy and is pervaded by a pessimism that flows from a deep sense of loss as Tate describes the inevitable death of a way of life. Even when he pokes gentle fun at the rituals of the aristocratic Buchans, he uses images similar to those found in his essay quoted above, and then goes on to make a very serious point. After Lacy Buchan, the narrator, describes his mother's 'ritual of utility' as she washes the good china, he comments that if this ritual had been discredited or even questioned, 'she would have felt that the purity of womanhood was in danger, that religion and morality were jeopardised, and that infidels had wickedly asserted that the State of Virginia (by which she meant her friends and kin) was not the direct legatee of the civilisation of Greece and Rome' (Part 2). What Tate is re-creating is a society in which every minute act possesses moral significance and wider meaning. And as in all such rigid societies, historical change cannot be accommodated. For Tate this is the real tragedy of the Civil War: that it opened up an abyss of uncontrolled passion which is exactly what civilization is designed to avoid.

George Posey, the man who marries Lacy's sister and then brings tragedy into their lives, does not understand this compact on which civilization is based. He is the prototype of the modern American, a human being whose life is purely personal. He is a refined man but one who does not understand the rules of the game, and who therefore cannot protect himself from the realities of the abyss: money, sex, and death. Having no social context with which to control his emotion, he is without honour or dignity, and his passions are manifested in brutality, corruption, and greed.

Such men are the legacy of the war and its aftermath, the residue left by the defeat of the old order. Major Buchan, the archetypal Southern aristocrat, cannot cope with George's lack of 'culture', and their encounters in the novel contribute some moments of rich social comedy. The Major is completely bewildered by George's calm response to his intended insults: 'Papa looked as if someone entitled to know all about it had denied the heliocentric theory or argued that there were no abolitionists in Boston. That was the first time I knew the meaning of the word aghast.' (Part 1)

Later, his response to the Yankee officer who has come to burn his home, is similar, and we are left in no doubt that this is also the tragic response of the South as a whole to the destructive forces of modernity. The officer has given him half an hour to leave:

> 'The major looked at him. He held himself up and Mr.
> Posey, you know how he is when he don't like folks.
> Polite. That's what he was. He was polite to that Yankee.
> He come down to the bottom step and said "There is
> *nothing* that you can give to me, sir", and walked back
> into the house.' (Part 3)

Unable either to capitulate, accommodate, or resist, Major Buchan, like the culture he represents, commits suicide.

The distinction Tate makes between the timeless world of the *ante-bellum* South and the fragmentation of modern life is one that preoccupied Faulkner, too, and in the Nobel Prize speech referred to above he argues that if the 'old verities' are forgotten by the modern novelist, he will write 'not of love but of lust, of defeats in which nobody loses anything of value, of victories without hope . . . not of the heart but of the glands'. Faulkner might almost have been describing the work of his own Southern contemporary, Erskine Caldwell.

Caldwell's fictional world is very similar to that of Faulkner's *As I Lay Dying* (1930) – a world of poor, uneducated white farmers eking out a miserable, animal-like existence in the Deep South. Some of their grotesque characters and the bizarre events they devise could even be interchanged. But there the similarities end. In Caldwell there is nothing to equal the metaphysical dimension in which Faulkner brilliantly manipulates his multiple narratives; instead the reader is relentlessly drawn into a series of repetitive situations produced by a combination of intolerable social and natural circumstances.

In his preface to *Tobacco Road* (1932), Caldwell writes of the images that prompted his novel: poor farmers waiting vainly for the cotton crop to mature as their parents had for tobacco, in fields where the impoverished soil will support nothing but broomsedge and scrub oak. In the novel itself we are told that the landowners have departed the region, leaving their tenants to manage as best they can, while the Lesters, deserted by most of their children who have gone to work in the cotton-mills of Augusta, are slowly starving to death, unable to borrow money for seed and fertilizer except at exorbitant interest rates from the city loan sharks. It is a situation that could provide the material for realist fiction, and on the basis of this subject-matter alone, Caldwell's work has often been described in that way. There is, however, a vital connection missing between the foreground and background of the fiction, an omission that frees his characters and allows them to expand into gross caricatures. Like the Bundrens in *As I Lay Dying*, the Lesters are trapped by their individual obsessions, but Caldwell's failure to enter into their consciousnesses leaves them as mechanical grotesques whose activities can only be exploited for sensational purposes. Kenneth Burke has suggested that Caldwell is really a Symbolist whose 'work serves most readily as case history for the psychologist and whose plots are more intelligent when interpreted as dreams'.[21] Such a reading of *Tobacco Road* or *God's Little Acre* (1933) at least satisfies a need to order the pervasive irrationality of Caldwell's world into a logic of dreams, and accounts for his characters' actions by the use of such terms as 'balked religiosity' and 'incest awe'. But there can be little doubt that it does not correspond to the author's conscious intentions, which appear to have been social and are similar to those that inspired his documentary works *You Have Seen Their Faces* (1937) and *Say! Is This the U.S.A.?* (1941).

An explanation of why Caldwell's realistic intentions are not realized in the novels is hinted at by Burke elsewhere in his essay, when he compares the characters to frogs that have had the higher centres of their brains removed for experimental purposes. The resulting decerebrated creatures bear the same relation to frogs, Burke claims, as Caldwell's characters do to real people. Only a cursory examination of *Tobacco Road* is necessary to establish the truth of this observation and to show how such a reductionist version of life militates against realism.

Jeeter Lester, the head of the household, has declined into irreversible apathy. He dreams of clearing his land and planting a crop once more but cannot bring himself to visit any of his children for a loan, or even summon up the energy to sell firewood in town. His wife, Ada, suffering from pellagra, thinks only of obtaining a decent dress to be buried in, while his mother, similarly afflicted, spends her time collecting twigs for a fire on which to cook non-existent food. Of the two children left at home, Dude is apparently mentally retarded, though there is little to differentiate him from the other characters in the novel, while Ella May is disfigured by a harelip which has never been treated.

Around these four characters and Jeeter's son-in-law, Lov, Caldwell builds his famous opening scene which occupies a fifth of the entire novel. Lov is returning home to his thirteen-year-old wife, Pearl, with a bag of turnips which he has bought for fifty cents. He stops at Jeeter's in order to get help from his father-in-law in dealing with Pearl, who has resolutely refused to have anything to do with him since their wedding. The bag of turnips is nominated by Jeeter as the price for his aid, and when Lov refuses the deal, the family resorts to subterfuge. Ella May seduces Lov, and while the two of them copulate in the yard watched by the hungry family and a group of passing Negroes, Jeeter grabs the turnips and makes for the woods. The appropriateness of Burke's description of these characters can be judged not only from their animalistic behaviour but also from the way Caldwell writes about them. Here for example, is Ella May at the end of the episode:

> Dude went to the pine stump and sat down to watch the
> red wood-ants crawl over the stomach and breasts of his
> sister. The muscles of her legs twitched nervously for a
> while, and then slowly the jerking stopped altogether, and
> she lay still. Her mouth was partly open, and her upper
> lip looked as if it had been torn wider apart than it
> naturally was. The perspiration had dried on her forehead
> and cheeks, and smudges of dirt were streaked over her
> pale white skin. (4)

It is possible to argue, as several critics have, that in creating such subhuman characters, creatures of instinct and conditioned reflex, Caldwell is well within the naturalist tradition inaugurated by Zola. Indeed the image of ants crawling over the body of Ella May is faintly reminiscent of a similar one in Stephen Crane's *The Red Badge of*

Courage. However, even if we grant the naturalist's intention in passages like this, it must be said that by the time the novel was written the philosophies that had made naturalism such a potent movement in the nineteenth century had lost impetus, and, as Philip Rahv says in his essay on the subject, had been replaced by new ideas informing a literature with a different problematic: the nature of reality itself.[22] Moreover, the greater part of *Tobacco Road* cannot pretend to any kind of sociological aim. Rahv calls Caldwell a writer of 'rural abandon', and his most memorable scenes – the episode in the brothel and the death of Jeeter's mother – are in the tradition of black comedy. The effect of these scenes depends entirely upon their lack of psychological plausibility. And when Caldwell fails to maintain this 'unreality' in his tall tales, as in Jeeter's story of a rat eating his father's corpse, he lapses into tasteless sensationalism.

Many of the themes and subjects already discussed in this chapter, as well as the attitudes adopted by regional writers towards the land and accelerated urbanization, are taken up in the Californian fiction of John Steinbeck. Apart from Faulkner, whose novels clearly transcend the location of their subject-matter and who will therefore be discussed separately, Steinbeck is the most celebrated regional novelist in American literary history, and also the most widely read. Moreover, it seems clear that the popularity of his work does owe something to its regional qualities. The fiction he published after leaving California – *The Moon is Down* (1942), *The Wayward Bus* (1947), *Burning Bright* (1950), *East of Eden* (1952), *The Short Reign of Pippin IV* (1959), and *The Winter of Our Discontent* (1961) – has not enjoyed the same success as his earlier writing. Even the apparent exception to this rule – *Cannery Row* (1945) – helps to prove its truth, involving as it does an affectionate backward glance at the subject-matter that preoccupied Steinbeck in the 1930s.

After writing two early romances *Cup of Gold* (1929) and *To a God Unknown* (1933), based on the Arthurian myth and the Bible respectively, Steinbeck quickly settled down to produce a series of works dealing with people and events in the same territory to which he had given life in a volume of loosely connected short stories, *Pastures of Heaven*, published between these two in 1932. The region of California he chose to make his own, the Central Valley, has a character quite distinct from either northern California centring on San Francisco, or the area which is sometimes known as Hollywood/Southland. San Francisco had been the literary capital of the West in the late nineteenth century, and Los Angeles was to become an equally strong magnet for writers in the twentieth. Each of these regions produced its own distinctive fiction. Walter Wells in his book *Tycoons and Locusts* characterizes the former as misanthropic and the latter as sardonic or sceptical, and contrasts both with the sanguinity and sentimentality of Steinbeck's fiction.

Such generalizations, with their overtones of ecological determinism, should be treated cautiously. That there is a stream of optimistic sentimentality running through Steinbeck's work is true, and it does often seem to be related to his feeling for the beneficient fertility of the valleys in which he sets his stories. But there are other factors operating upon him too, such as the political climate of the Depression and the New·Deal, which severely modified his sanguinity in novels like *In Dubious Battle* (1936) and *The Grapes of Wrath* (1939). Another major influence which helps to distinguish his work from that of all his contemporaries is the philosophy of his friend and mentor, the biologist Ed Ricketts. The two met in the early 1930s in a dentist's waiting-room in Pacific Grove and immediately became close friends. Ricketts, who owned a laboratory on Monterey's Cannery Row, appears as a slightly disguised character in a number of the subsequent novels, but his more important presence lies in the pervasive reach of his ideas into almost every corner of Steinbeck's fiction. These are expressed most clearly in *The Log from the Sea of Cortez* (1950), a commentary on a biological expedition on which the two men had gone some ten years earlier and which Steinbeck had described in *The Sea of Cortez* (1941). What seems to have impressed him most forcibly about the behaviour of the marine life they studied was the way separate organisms were capable of joining together to create an entity with characteristics quite different from those of its individual members. In traditional naturalistic fashion, Steinbeck translated this knowledge into his studies of the behaviour of men, both as individuals and as social groups. It became a firm element in his general belief that to know man at all, one has to see him primarily as part of an animal species. At the simplest level, this philosophy informs Steinbeck's description of the instinctive behaviour of the *paisanos* in *Tortilla Flat*, and it led Edmund Wilson to link him through his tendency to 'animalise humanity' with a novelist like Erskine Caldwell.[23]

Steinbeck's ideas are developed much more fully and interestingly, though, in novels such as *In Dubious Battle*, where he uses them to explore the psychology of mobs, and in *The Grapes of Wrath*, where they are pushed far beyond the limits of the biological in his suggestion that men's souls have the same capacity to merge holistically as their bodies do. At this point Steinbeck comes very close to Transcendentalist thought, and sometimes appears to be enunciating an eclectic philosophy developed from various incompatible streams of American intellectual history. The unresolved contradictions inherent in these ideas are reflected in Tom Joad's philosophical bewilderment throughout *The Grapes of Wrath*, and more damningly in Steinbeck's apparent unwillingness to pursue the logic of particular ideas in the book's narrative. This results, as Jules Chametzky points out, 'in several possible endings being tentatively tried out in the novel, only to be discarded when their political or philosophical implications become clear to the author'.[24]

There are critics who think that Steinbeck's blend of Transcendentalism and Pragmatism is successful, and that it leads to a modified form of Christianity,[25] but it is difficult to see how such conflicting philosophies can ever be reconciled except in the most superficial way. Steinbeck's attempts to effect such a fusion, like his use of myth in many of the novels, often detracts from the genuine power of his more deeply realized ideas about the biological nature of man.

In so far as the marine life of the Pacific coast tide pools constitutes a viable microcosm for the novelist, the most arresting idea to emerge from Steinbeck's studies, is neither mystical nor transcendentalist. On the contrary, life is seen as a completely non-teleological phenomenon. His own defence of this view in *The Log From the Sea of Cortez* points accurately to the real strengths of his fiction:

> Non-teleological ideas derive through 'is' thinking,
> associated with natural selection as Darwin seems to have
> understood it. They imply depth, fundamentalism, and
> clarity – seeing beyond traditional or personal projections.
> They consider events as outgrowths and expressions rather
> than as results; conscious acceptance as a desideratum, and
> certainly as an all-important prerequisite. Non-teleological
> thinking concerns itself primarily not with what should be,
> or could be, or might be, but rather with what actually
> 'is' – attempting at most to answer the already sufficiently
> difficult questions *what* or *how*, instead of *why*. (14)

This is the firm root of Steinbeck's thought, and when he allows his novels to grow from it freely, he produces powerful naturalistic fiction. He comes closest to achieving this with *In Dubious Battle*, which as a result is the best strike novel written in the 1930s. But even his earlier work, distorted as it often is by alien grafts, contains memorable insights and episodes.

In *Pastures of Heaven*, for example, which Maxwell Geismar thinks is possibly Steinbeck's best novel,[26] the gap between the 'is' and the 'ought' is exploited in order to create tragic irony. The pastures of the title are set in a beautiful, fertile valley, and the stories of the various inhabitants of this paradisal haven are all set in motion by Bert Munroe who has taken over Battle Farm in a last effort to escape the series of defeats that has dogged his earlier career. The farm is said to be cursed, but from the moment of his arrival Munroe's luck appears to change and he jokingly suggests that both his curse and the curse on the farm perhaps 'got to fighting and killed each other off'. The curse is still operative, however, but it has begun to work in a different way. One by one, Munroe's neighbours – somewhat reminiscent of Sherwood Anderson's grotesques – are visited by catastrophe and inadvertently destroyed as a result of the actions of Munroe or his family.

As a device for bringing together the disparate elements of his composite novel, the idea of a curse is obviously artificial, and if it were used seriously as a thematic centre as well, the work would be entirely meretricious. But Steinbeck's interest is not occult, and the curse functions more as a symbol for those elements in life that always prevent people from realizing their dreams – the obstacles that stand between 'is' and the 'ought'. In order to make his general point, Steinbeck changes the angle of focus at the close by having a bus-load of tourists look longingly down on to 'Las Pasturas de Cielo' and, unaware of the tragic lives being acted out in this false Eden, they begin to fabricate their own visions of future happiness. As Geismar says, the unresolved questions at the heart of *Pastures of Heaven* are sufficiently haunting to occupy Steinbeck throughout his career. Their various applications to social, economic, political, and psychological subjects, and the answers he arrives at, form the basic structures of his fiction.

These questions are addressed to more specific issues in *Tortilla Flat*, the first of his novels to achieve wide popularity, though even here they are disguised by a pretentious 'mythical' framework that has led to widespread misinterpretations of the novel. Steinbeck maintained that his stories of the exploits of a group of indolent, happy-go-lucky *paisanos* in Monterey is based on Thomas Malory's version of the Arthurian cycle. And when the first readers of the novel apparently failed to respond to the implanted parallels, he even suggested revising it to make the connections more obvious. As they stand, Steinbeck's attempts at literary inflation can easily be ignored since they do little to obscure the true nature of his tragi-comic satire.

What does weaken the force of his dramatic juxtaposition of conflicting life-styles is a failure to observe his own canons of objectivity. A lack of confidence in his ability to convince readers of the intrinsic worth of the *paisanos* leads him to indulge in the sentimental moralizing that spoils so much of his work. The central structural irony of the novel brings on the destruction of the *paisanos*' idyllic existence, and particularly that of the group's leader, Danny, by his apparent good fortune in inheriting two houses from his grandfather. Danny's status as a tenuous member of the property-owning bourgeoisie allows Steinbeck to treat some of his favourite *bêtes noir* – middle-class respectability, machines, the Church – in a mixture of comic and tragic satire. The *paisanos* live in a shanty-town district at the edge of Monterey, and when Danny and his friends forsake their footloose existence to occupy his newly acquired property, they begin to ape the mores of respectable society in the very act of succumbing to the restrictive practices of civilization.

When, for instance, Danny is attempting the conquest of Sweets Romirez, a voluptuous neighbour who has been attracted to him by his wealth, he buys her a second-hand vacuum cleaner. Despite the fact that there is no electricity in Tortilla Flat, Sweets is delighted with her gift, appreciating its real worth as a status symbol which can be pushed around her house to the envy of her neighbours. Eventually the *paisanos* steal the machine back from her and sell it in order to buy yet another two gallons of wine, and the new purchaser discovers to his chagrin what none of the *paisanos* would have dreamed of verifying – that the machine does not even contain a motor! Stories like this make up the bulk of the novel and create a dense, celebratory account of the *paisanos'* carefree and sensual life-style. Eventually, though, Danny recognizes that he has been fatally infected by the bacillus of civilization, and in a desperate attempt to reassert his true, simple self, he tries unsuccessfully to resume his former way of life. The result is tragic, and the novel ends with the destruction of both the house and the group of friends it has temporarily sheltered.

Steinbeck's deepest feelings, intensified by the economic and social chaos brought by the Depression, were provoked, like those of the other realist writers we have examined in this chapter, by his sense that a simple, spontaneous integrity associated with the land and those close to it, was being sacrificed to the demands of progress, and was being replaced by an uncaring, impersonal society whose members lusted after such abstract goals as wealth and status.

Dispossession and nostalgia are given a wider cultural and political context in Steinbeck's major novels of the 1930s, *In Dubious Battle* and *The Grapes of Wrath*, but he returned to an even simpler expression of those themes in another best-seller of the same period, *Of Mice and Men* (1937). Running like a refrain through this brief, pathetic story is the repeated description, demanded from George by his mentally retarded friend Lennie, of the farm they will buy if they ever manage to save any money from their pitiful wages as migrant labourers. George's ritualistic repetition of the various animals and crops in this Utopian vision is sufficient in itself to establish the hopelessness of the dream, but the latter is also counterpointed by realistic accounts of the actual loss of such smallholdings by characters caught in the same economic trap. Crooks, the Black stable buck, eventually attempts to make

Lennie confront the futility of his hopes, and though his warning is ignored, his general point retains its force in the novel:

> Gradually Lennie's interest came around to what was being said.
> 'George says we're gonna have alfalfa for the rabbits.'
> 'What rabbits?'
> 'We're gonna have rabbits an' a berry patch.'
> 'You're nuts.'
> 'We are too. You ast George.'
> 'You're nuts.' Crooks was scornful. 'I seen hunderds of men come by on the road an' on the ranches, with their bindles on their back an' that same damn thing in their heads. Hunderds of them. They come, an' they quit an' go on; an' every damn one of 'em's got a little piece of land in his head. An' never a God damn one of 'em ever gets it. Just like Heaven.' (4)

In speeches such as this Crooks sounds like one of Steinbeck's more cynical labour agitators or 'reds', but the political implications of his thought are not dwelt on in the novel; and the death of Lennie, though similar in some respects to that of Jim described *In Dubious Battle*, carries none of the social reverberations of the episode in the longer novel. When George sorrowfully shoots his friend, the act is reminiscent of the way Lennie kills the animals he loves, but like other literary expressions of *liebestod*, this can only elicit pathos in the reader.

Jim, the hero of *In Dubious Battle* is also the innocent victim of corrupt forces, but they are forces which he has begun to understand and to resist. The novel is designed to show his gradual education as an apprentice agitator during a strike of apple-pickers in the Torgas Valley in California. Though the strike itself dominates the action for most of the book's length, and though it contains some discussion of Communist theory and practice, *In Dubious Battle* is neither a proletarian novel nor even primarily a political one.[27] There is no doubt that Steinbeck's anger was aroused by the fraudulent and brutal practices of the huge Californian land monopolists, just as Frank Norris's had been earlier. The exploitation and intimidation of the small farmers and the migrant workers by the rulers of such empires as Kern County land and the Irvine Corporation is constantly referred to in both this novel and in *The Grapes of Wrath*. The stranglehold taken upon the land by absentee financiers, and maintained by violence, threatened individual freedom and democracy itself. Steinbeck wrote a piece for *The Nation* in the same year that he published *In Dubious Battle* in which he specifically identifies the political issues. And two years later he collected various essays he had contributed to the San Francisco *News* on the same subject, in a pamphlet called *Their Blood Is Strong*. His understanding of the situation is quite clear, as is his sympathy for the victims of the system. What he cannot accept, though, are the solutions offered by the revolutionary Left, and this accounts for the apparent evasiveness of his fiction at certain crucial moments. Even the essay referred to above ends rather lamely with Steinbeck, after describing the appalling conditions of the workers, and the techniques used to enforce them, fervently hoping that the migrant workers 'may be given the right to live decently' and that the bosses will stop tormenting and starving them.[28]

The reasons for Steinbeck's unwillingness to endorse the tactics of the Communist Party during the strike, can be inferred from his portrait of the seasoned Party member, Mac, of *In Dubious Battle*. Like the ruthless employers he is fighting, Mac openly uses every situation he can to further his aims in the 'war'. Consequently, he is shown to be just as inhuman and exploitative as they are, and the dubiety of the title refers not to the outcome of the strike but to the methods used by both sides. The most damning examples of this attitude are emphasized by being placed at the beginning and end of the campaign. On the night Mac and Jim arrive at the apple-pickers' camp they discover a young girl about to give birth, and Mac offers to deliver the baby. Only later does he confess that he had never even seen a birth before but that he had decided he could not miss such a lucky break, 'Course it was nice to help the girl, but hell, even if it killed her – we've got to use anything' (4). His willingness to do just that is demonstrated again at the end of the novel. Jim has his face shot away as he runs into a trap prepared by the enemy, and Mac immediately carries his friend's corpse back to the clearing where the strikers have gathered for a meeting:

> The clearing was full of curious men. They clustered around, until they saw the burden. And then they recoiled. Mac marched through them as though he did not see them. Across the clearing, past the stoves he marched, and the crowd followed silently behind him. He came to the platform. He deposited the figure under the handrail, and leaped to the stand. He dragged Jim across the boards and heaved him against the corner post and steadied him when he slipped sideways.
> London handed the lantern up, and Mac set it carefully on the floor, beside the body, so that its light fell on the head. He stood up and faced the crowd. His hands gripped the rail. His eyes were wide and white. In front

he could see the massed men, eyes shining in the
lamplight. Behind the front row, the men were lumped
and dark. Mac shivered. He moved his jaws to speak, and
seemed to break the frozen jaws loose. His voice was high
and monotonous. 'This guy didn't want nothing for
himself –' he began. His knuckles were white, where he
grasped the rail, 'Comrades! He didn't want nothing for
himself –' (15)

The detached, objective style of this passage is characteristic of the
entire novel, and it is this, as much as anything else, that guarantees
its emotional power. Steinbeck resists the temptation to intrude into
his characters' consciousness, and even if Warren French is correct in
seeing Jim Nolan as a modern Parsifal at the centre of an ironic and
pessimistic allegory of the fate of the chivalric spirit,[29] parallels with
Wagner's opera are never forced, or even alluded to. This gives the
characters and the events they are involved in an autonomy unique in
Steinbeck's work. The only major lapse from dramatic objectivity
occurs in those parts of the novel dominated by Doc Burton, a
character based on Ed Ricketts, who represents the humane, non-
teleological position of the scientist. Doc Burton may be free of
ideological manipulation but his role as a philosophical mouthpiece for
the author is so blatant that his disappearance and presumed death
come as something of a relief. The absence of sentimental editorializing
and choric sententiousness in the climactic moments of the action give
In Dubious Battle a stark power that is lacking even in Steinbeck's most
famous work, *The Grapes of Wrath*.

The qualities of the later novel that enable it to transcend its
manifest flaws, are products of a greatly enlarged scale and perspective.
In writing the story of the Joads's epic migration to California, Steinbeck concentrates his attention on the immediate, local conditions of
their lives, creating a simple but emotional saga of individual courage
and endurance with which it is impossible not to empathize. The
social, economic, and political context that gives broader significance
to the Joads's journey is provided in a series of interchapters in which
Steinbeck is free to engage his readers' attention at a different and more
philosophical level. This double perspective means that when the
various members of the Joad family are moved to speculate on the
meaning of their tribulations and to voice many of Steinbeck's own
vague – even contradictory – ideas about such matters as the Oversoul,
the nature of Women, or the essential superiority of the Poor, these
notions do not necessarily make for intellectual confusion in the novel,
or even, as some critics believe, for a rich, philosophical eclecticism.[30]
On the contrary, their inadequacy acquires poignant irony in juxtaposition with the factual framework constructed around the inner

characters. Steinbeck's ability to sustain his readers' emotional identification with the Joads, while at the same time keeping an intellectual distance from them, is one of his major achievements.

Unfortunately, the inner story and outer world have to be brought together at the close of the novel, when Steinbeck is describing the migrants' experiences in the various camps where they take refuge at the end of their journey. During the first two sections of the book (those describing the drought that causes the Dust Bowl, and the journey along Highway 66), the interchapters are used to illuminate and extend the meaning of the dramatic events, but the various episodes that take place once the family has reached California do not lend themselves to the same kind of coherent interpretation in the interchapters. If, for example, one accepts that the primary cause of the miseries endured by the Joads is the ruthlessly exploitative greed of Eastern financiers, encouraged by a capitalist economy, one obvious solution to the particular situation they face is that symbolized by Weedpatch, the federal camp in which the worst features of the free-enterprise system are replaced by co-operation, compassion, and rational organization. Here in the camp, the Joads begin to rediscover their lost dignity and sense of communal values. Ideologically, this moment might have provided a fitting climax to the novel, and Steinbeck's rejection of what has been called the 'New Deal ending'[31] indicates an ambivalence in his social philosophy. So, too, does his failure to end the book with what the same critic calls the 'Proletarian' solution: the later occasion during the great rains when the workers gather to protect Rosasharn as she is about to go into labour, by collectively building a dike against the flood. Though Steinbeck accepts the need for collective action, whether organized by the State or the workers, he is temperamentally opposed to what he feels is an authoritarian, dehumanizing social system, and instead concludes his novel with an individual symbolic act in which Rosasharn offers her breast – full of milk for her stillborn baby – to a starving old man. Steinbeck's essential conservatism leads him away from radical political solutions towards an agrarian pastoralism which seems at odds with the implications of both the main story and the interchapters. It is in the manipulation of these final events that he betrays his political uncertainty, rather than in the depiction of his characters' conflicting interpretations of experience.

Though these tensions and inconsistencies flaw the novel's structure, *The Grapes of Wrath* remains one of the most powerful indictments of twentieth-century social trends, and an equally powerful affirmation of faith in the individual's ability to endure oppression and win some kind of victory over it. As in most of his novels, Steinbeck erects his fiction on a mythic substructure – in this case, the Old Testament story of the Israelites' exodus from Egypt and their sojourn in Canaan. The parallels indicated not only in events during the Okies' migration westward but also in the deliberately constructed resonances of his style, enable Steinbeck to hint at a spiritual significance in the epic journey and to suggest a human development more profound and enduring than any represented by either the family or the social group:

> In the evening a strange thing happened: the twenty families became one family, the children were the children of all. The loss of home became one less, and the Golden time in the West was one dream. And it might be that a sick child threw despair into the hearts of twenty families, of a hundred people; that a birth there in a tent kept a hundred people quiet and awestruck through the night and filled a hundred people with the birth-joy in the morning. A family which the night before had been lost and fearful might search its goods to find a present for a new baby. In the evening, sitting about the fires, the twenty were one. They grew to the units of camps, units of the evenings and the nights. (17)

The simplicity and balance of the diction, and the repetition of concrete detail and numbers in grammatical units, suggest an archaic, elemental form capable of imposing order on the chaos of contemporary life. In the use of such literary devices Steinbeck goes beyond the realism of his fellow regionalists, just as Dos Passos does by employing very different cultural myths in *U.S.A.* But by separating the interchapters in which he practises these techniques, from his central story, Steinbeck avoids compromising the novel's realistic sections as he had in his earlier works of the 1930s. Nevertheless, when taken as a whole, *The Grapes of Wrath* shows the extent to which the principles of modernism had by this time been incorporated into realistic fiction. In the next three chapters we shall see more extreme examples of the same trend.

Notes

1. The phrase was coined by Carl Van Doren in an essay, 'Revolt from the Village: 1920', *The Nation* (1921).

2. See, for example, Irving Howe, *Sherwood Anderson: A Biographical and Critical*

Study (1951) (Stanford, Calif., 1966) pp. 5–10, and Alfred Kazin, *On Native Grounds: An Interpretation of American Prose Literature*, abridged edition (New York, 1956), p. 67.

3. Howe, p. 123.

4. Maxwell Geismar, *The Last of the Provincials: The American Novel, 1915–1925*, third edition (New York, 1959), p. 24.

5. Virginia Woolf, *The Moment* (London, 1947), pp. 97–100.

6. See, for example, Mencken's *Notes on Democracy* (New York,1926).

7. Mark Schorer, *Sinclair Lewis: An American Life* (New York, 1961), p. 288.

8. E. M. Forster's essay, 'Our Photography: Sinclair Lewis', appeared earlier in the New York *Herald Tribune Books* in 1929 as 'A Camera Man', and is reprinted in *Abinger Harvest* (London, 1936), and in *Sinclair Lewis: A Collection of Critical Essays*, edited by Mark Schorer (Englewood Cliffs, NJ, 1962).

9. *Last of the Provincials*, p. 86.

10. The letter is quoted from at length in *Schorer*, p. 346.

11. See the *Letters of Sarah Orne Jewett*, edited by Annie Fields (Cambridge, Mass., 1911), p. 245.

12. Lionel Trilling, 'Willa Cather' in *After the Genteel Tradition*, edited by Malcome Cowley (Carbondale and Edwardsville, Ill. 1964).

13. For a comparison of passages in *Alexander's Bridge* and *O Pioneers* see David Daiches, *Willa Cather* (Ithaca, NY, 1951), pp. 19–21.

14. *Last of the Provincials*, p. 220.

15. See his *Henry James and his Cult* (London,1964).

16. The most recent study of this movement is by R. H. King, *A Southern Renaissance* (New York, 1980), in which psychoanalytic concepts are used to explore the South's preoccupation with its own past.

17. Allen Tate, *The Man of Letters in the Modern World* (London, 1957) p. 330. The essay from which the quotation is taken, 'The New Provincialism', was first published in 1945.

18. Ellen Glasgow, *The Woman Within: An Autobiography* (1954) (New York, 1980), p. 128.

19. Ellen Glasgow, *A Certain Measure: An Interpretation of Prose Fiction* (New York, 1943), pp. 158–9.

20. 'Two in Richmond: Ellen Glasgow and James Branch Cabell', in *South: Modern Southern Literature in its Cultural Setting*, edited by Louis D. Rubin jun., and Robert D. Jacobs (New York, 1961). The essay is reprinted in Rubin's book, *The Curious Death of the Novel* (Baton Rouge, La., 1967). pp. 152–82.

21. 'Caldwell: Maker of Grotesques', in Kenneth Burke, *The Philosophy of Literary Form* (Baton Rouge, La., 1941). Reprinted in *Psychoanalysis and American Fiction*, edited by Irving Malin (New York, 1965), pp. 245–53.

22. 'Notes on the Decline of Naturalism', in Philip Rahv, *Image and Idea* (London, 1957), p. 152.

23. See *Classics and Commercials: A Literary Chronicle of the Forties* (London, 1951). p. 41.

24. Jules Chametzky, 'The Ambivalent Endings of *The Grapes of Wrath*', in *A Casebook on The Grapes of Wrath*, edited by Agnes McNeill Donohue (New York, 1968), pp. 232–44.

25. See, for example, Frederick I. Carpenter, 'The Philosophical Joads', in *Steinbeck and his Critics: A Record of Twenty-five Years*, edited by E. W. Tedlock, jun., and C. V. Wicker (Albuquerque. N. Mex, 1957), pp. 241–49.

26. See *Writers in Crisis: The American Novel, 1925–1940* (New York, 1947), p. 242.

27. Walter Rideout deliberately excludes *In Dubious Battle* from his discussion of proletarian fiction in his book *The Radical Novel in the United States, 1900–1954* (New York, 1956), p. 325. Joseph Blotner rejects its claims to be classified as a political novel. See *The Modern American Political Novel, 1900–1960* (Austin, Tex., 1966), p. 9. It is briefly discussed, however, by Fay M. Blake in *The Strike in the American Novel* (Metuchen, NJ, 1972).

28. 'Dubious Battle in California', *The Nation* (12 September 1936). The essay is reprinted in a collection of writings from the 1930s, *Years of Protest*, edited by Jack Salzman and Barry Wallenstein (New York, 1967), pp. 66–71.

29. See *John Steinbeck* (New Haven, 1961), p. 64.

30. See Carpenter, pp. 241–9.

31. See Chametzky, pp. 232–44.

Chapter 10

Epics of America: Wolfe, Dos Passos

A great many American novels have been characterized by what can only be called an 'epic quality'. Dreiser's *An American Tragedy*, Steinbeck's *The Grapes of Wrath*, and Faulkner's Yoknapatawpha saga are only a few of the more prominent examples. There are obvious reasons why twentieth-century American writers – and this is even more true of poets than novelists – should continue to celebrate the national spirit long after such manifestations virtually disappeared in Europe. The need arises partly from a desire to affirm that there is such an entity as America – a proposition by no means self-evident to many observers in the early decades of the twentieth century – and partly from an even stronger desire to create an identity for Americans, distinct from their European, Asian, or African inheritance. One way of attempting this – as in the above novels – was through the creation of microcosmic groups or representative individuals whose lives could be used to symbolize essential American experience. What distinguishes the fiction of Thomas Wolfe and John Dos Passos, on the other hand, is its inclusiveness. Each of them, in very different ways, set out with much larger ambition, to capture the totality of life on the continent in all its bewildering variety and complexity. In trying to fulfil such grandiose aims, they were faced with almost insuperable difficulties of form and technique, and the manner in which they coped, or failed to cope, with these problems constitutes another chapter in the history of American Modernism.

It is customary for critics for describe Wolfe's career in terms of failure. Most have dismissed him as a writer of undisputed genius who' lacked the necessary discipline or skill to order his incessant, uncontrolled verbal outpourings. The fact that four of his novels eventually found their way into print is, according to this view, due mostly to the labours of his editors, Maxwell Perkins and Edward Aswell, who throughout Wolfe's career and after his death, exercised all their skill to cut and reorganize his immense output into some kind of sensible shape. There is a good deal of truth in this view, for without the help of his commercial editors, Wolfe's work would probably not have been published at all. It is especially true of his first two novels, *Look Home-ward Angel* (1929) and *Of Time and the River* (1935), and Bernard de Voto is at least partly right when, in reviewing Wolfe's *The Story of a Novel* (1936), he says:

> For five years the artist pours out words like burning lava from a volcano – with little or no idea what their purpose is, which book they belong in, what the relation of part to part is, what is organic and what irrelevant, or what emphasis or coloration in the completed work of art is being served by the job in hand. Then Mr. Perkins decides these questions – from without, and by a process to which rumor applies the word 'assembly'.[1]

Wolfe *was* undisciplined. His gargantuan appetite for experience and his prodigious energy habitually outran his critical sense. He was, to a degree, the victim of his romantic genius and a form of logorrhoea that drove him quite mercilessly to record everything that impinged upon his undiscriminating consciousness. His novels and notebooks are full of lists: hotels, cities, numbers, meals, textures, even a list of the women with whom he had sexual relations in the USA together with the states in which they were born. He frequently interrupts his narrative to recount anecdotes, stories, and even short novels. Charac-ters appear and disappear, interspersed among hundreds of more anonymous figures, drifting from one location to another throughout the work. And at the centre of all this, the only constant factor is the autobiographical recorder – Eugene Gant in the early work, George Webber in the later – whose consciousness lends the fiction the only semblance of form it possesses.

Such observations are based, however, upon the novels in their present published form. Wolfe must, naturally bear responsibility, at least for his earlier work, though there is some evidence in his letters to show that, like most young writers, he often agreed to the changes demanded by Perkins mainly to see himself in print, even while not necessarily agreeing with his editor's critical judgements.

As regards the later work, the situation was very different.[2] In May, 1938, the year of his death, Wolfe delivered a huge manuscript of more than a million words to his new editor. He called it 'The Web and the Rock' and it covered the entire history of America from the arrival of the first Europeans, right up to the New Deal. He claimed that though it was not yet finished, in carefully assembling the sections he had at last begun to feel a sense of wholeness in it. It is this manuscript that E. Aswell worked on after Wolfe's death, producing from it two 'novels', *The Web and the Rock* and *You Can't Go Home Again*, as well as a book of short pieces, *The Hills Beyond*. A large amount of material which Aswell could not fit into any of these volumes was rejected altogether, and it still remains unpublished. It is quite possible that no one – not even Wolfe himself – could have given satisfactory shape to this sprawling mass of work, but until the text is restored and published in the form in which Wolfe left it, we can only glimpse the 'tremendous structure' of his epic.

It does seem clear, however, from Wolfe's notes and letters as well as from research undertaken on the archives, that he did have a definite design in mind when he came to put various pieces of writing together.[3] His difficulty had always been that of relating his inner life to the outer world of experience. Lacking Scott Fitzgerald's sense of irony though, he was quite unable to maintain an equilibrium between the two, and resorted in his first two novels to the desperate expedient of sending his hero into the world to devour it. It is probably true, as Maxwell Geismar asserts, that 'the orgies of tremendous feeding and the hunger for sensation that pervade the early work, denote their absence in Wolfe's early life, just as his hero's inability to establish meaningful relationships with other people and places has its source in his lack of a home, of a place and people to love.[4] But whatever the psychological cause, Eugene Gant's frantic efforts to reclaim the memory of his Southern childhood or to satisfy his desire for reality in the cities of the North end in failure. Despite the sheer weight of images and the welter of topographical detail, neither *Look Homeward Angel* nor *Of Time and the River* succeeds in making viable connections between the hero and his world. They are essentially lyric or expressionist works, whereas what Wolfe wanted to create was an epic.

In order to do so he had to find a way not only of exorcizing the past and objectifying the present, but also of finding a form which would allow him to unite his hero's consciousness with the world in ways that would allow both to survive. Even though he did not finally succeed in this, there is sufficient evidence in his later work to show that he was moving towards a solution. In one of his letters to Aswell, he elaborates on the complications of his belated recognition that 'You can't go home again':

> to your family, back home to your childhood, back home
> to romantic love, back home to a young man's dreams of
> glory and of fame, back home to exile, to escape to
> Europe and some foreign land, back home to lyricism, to
> singing just for singing's sake . . . back home to the ivory
> tower, back home to places in the country, to the cottage
> in Bermuda, away from all the strife and conflict of the
> world, back home to the father you have lost and have

been looking for, back home to someone who can help
you, save you, ease the burden for you, back home to the
old forms and systems of things which once seemed
everlasting but which are changing all the time – back
home to the escapes of Time and Memory.[5]

The implications of Wolfe's painful discovery form the basis of all his
later work. At the end of *The Web and the Rock* George Webber talks
of making 'the true discovery of America', and in one sense that is
what *You Can't Go Home Again* is really about.

It is quite likely that Wolfe's travels in Europe helped him more
than anything else to see America in better perspective, just as Fitzgerald's had, and Henry James's before them. There is a revealing
passage in the last novel in which George Webber, taking stock of his
life, comes to the conclusion that he no longer believes himself to be
'a rare and special person . . . doomed to isolation', but rather a man
'concerned passionately with reality', 'a man who worked and who,
like other men, was a part of life'. He tells, too, of the criticism of
his earlier work which saw it as a 'barbaric yawp', and of his determination to progress beyond such mere utterance, the 'impassioned
expletive of youth':

> In his effort to explore his experience, to extract the
> whole, essential truth of it, and to find a way to write
> about it, he sought to recapture every particle of the life
> he knew down to its minutest details. He spent weeks and
> months trying to put down on paper the exactitudes of
> countless fragments – what he called: 'the dry, caked
> colours of America' – how the entrance to a subway
> looked, the design and webbing of the elevated structure,
> the look and feel of an iron rail, the particular shade of
> rusty green with which so many things are painted in
> America. Then he tried to pin down the foggy colour of
> the brick of which so much of London is constructed, the
> look of an English doorway, of a French window, of the
> roofs and chimney-pots of Paris, of a whole street in
> Munich – and each of these foreign things he then
> examined in contrast to its American counterpart. (4:27)

If Wolfe had not died so young, it is more than likely that he would
have created the appropriate form for his American epic. Towards the
end of his life he was experimenting with interesting techniques and
structures that are not so very different from some of those used by

Dos Passos in *U.S.A.* Given time to perfect them and order his vast materials into an integrated whole, he just might have fulfilled his life-long ambition to produce the Great American Novel. Instead, that honour fell to John Dos Passos.

Dos Passos's best fiction has a pessimism different in kind and more profound than that found in Wolfe or in the work of any of his American contemporaries. His attitudes to life in general and to American society in particular derive from the Naturalists, of course, and his novels have many superficial features in common with those of Crane, Norris, and Dreiser. In this passage, taken from the Introduction to the one-volume edition of *U.S.A.*, some of his characteristic techniques are easily recognizable as he swiftly paints a picture of a society dehumanized by the mechanical pressures of an indifferent material environment:

> The streets are empty. People have packed into subways,
> climbed into streetcars and buses; in the stations they've
> scampered for suburban trains; they've filtered into
> lodgings and tenements, gone up in elevators into
> apartment houses. In a show window two sallow window-
> dressers in their shirtsleeves are bringing out a dummy girl
> in a red evening dress, at a corner welders in masks lean
> into sheets of blue flame repairing a cartrack, a few drunk
> bums shamble along, a sad streetwalker fidgets under an
> arclight. From the river comes the deep rumbling whistle
> of a steamboat leaving dock. A tug hoots far away.
> (*Modern Library*, p. v)

People in the mass are seen packing, climbing, scampering or filtering away from the city, and what remain behind – store window dummies, masked welders, drunken bums and prostitutes – typify the isolated, subhuman or broken detritus of industrial civilization.

In the next paragraph, though, the focus of our attention is shifted as we are brought gradually into the consciousness of a young man, aware of his exclusion and pathetically anxious to embrace and affirm experience in its varied particulars:

> The young man walks by himself, fast but not fast
> enough, far but not far enough (faces slide out of sight,
> talk trails into scattered scraps, footsteps tap fainter in
> alleys); he must catch the last subway, the streetcar, the
> bus, run up the gangplanks of all the steamboats, register
> at all the hotels, work in the cities, answer the wantads,

learn the trades, take up the jobs, live in all the
boardinghouses, sleep in all the beds. One bed is not
enough, one job is not enough, one life is not enough. At
night, head swimming with wants, he walks by himself
alone.

No job, no woman, no house, no city. (p. vi)

This young man is a recurrent type in Dos Passos's fiction. He appears
as Jimmy Herf in *Manhattan Transfer*, Vag in *U.S.A.*, and as Martin
Howe in Dos Passos's first novel, *One Man's Initiation, 1917*. Into these
various characters Dos Passos pours all his democratic, Whitmanesque
passion for total immersion. Typically, these heroes spend their lives
struggling against the crushing power of machines, variously depicted
as the Army, the Law, the Corporation, the Party or the City.
Occasionally, small victories are achieved, if only temporary ones; and
the hero is able, like Andrews when he breaks free from the routine
of army existence to immerse himself into 'the misty, sparkling life of
the streets'.

These minor triumphs of individual freedom are always quickly
squashed, and only serve in the plots of the novels to underscore the
inevitable defeat of the anarchic individual. More importantly, they
introduce into American fiction subtler techniques for representing life
in its subjective/objective states. Sartre, who comes closer than anyone
else to understanding the significance of Dos Passos's major novels,
maintains that Dos Passos's man is a hybrid creature, an interior-
exterior being. We go on living with and within him, with his vacil-
lating, individual consciousness, when suddenly it wavers, weakens,
and is diluted in the collective consciousness.[6] A growing awareness of
the failure of the individual consciousness to resist usurpation by the
machine led Dos Passos to say in 1936 – the year of the Spanish Civil
War – that the world had arrived at 'one of the damnedest tragic
moments of history'. if the 1920s were years which, for Dos Passos,
stripped the bunting off the great illusions of our time and laid bare
'the raw structure of history' beneath, they were also years in which
he learned to create a fiction of impassioned objectivity possessing
some of the quality he so admired in *The Last Tycoon* – the 'quality
of detaching itself from its period while embodying its period'.[7]

The quality of this detachment underwent a radical change at the
end of the 1920s, undoubtedly brought about by Dos Passos's political
experiences in general, and as Alfred Kazin argues, more particularly
as the result of his bitter involvement in the Sacco and Vanzetti affair.[8]
Whatever the reason, it made possible the writing of his masterpiece,
U.S.A., in which the ineffectual struggles against the world of his
earlier aesthete-romantic heroes are superseded by a more complex and

subtle dialectic. The phenomenology of *U.S.A.* is unique; not only in Dos Passos's oeuvre, but also in twentieth-century fiction as a whole. To argue, as many critics have, that Dos Passos mechanically applies the superficial tricks of neo-modernist technique to a Naturalist novel, is to miss completely the point of his structural and stylistic innovations. The relationship between individual characters (there are, of course, no heroes in *U.S.A.*) and the historical and environmental forces they shape and are shaped by, does not admit of any but an artificial separation. In contrast, the prose poems of *District of Columbia* which precede each chapter, are not only crudely written themselves but are also related to the book's fictional and historical structure, in the crudest possible way.

The poise and balance of *U.S.A.* had not been easily achieved, nor was it to be maintained in the novels that followed. Dos Passos's gradual loss of passion as he abandoned the romantic radicalism of his earlier years has been both documented and lamented by Irving Howe and Granville Hicks, among others.[9] What is of more interest to anyone concerned with Dos Passos's major achievements, is the way in which he takes the fictional techniques of Naturalism – particularly those used by Crane and Dreiser – and from them develops a mode uniquely successful in its capacity to relate character to environment and to subsume both to the large shifts and pressures of history.

The first major traumatic experience of Dos Passos's life, and the most enduring in his memory, was that of the First World War. His service with the Norton–Harjes Ambulance Unit and the Medical Corps in France provided the material for two novels, *One Man's Initiation: 1917* and *Three Soldiers*. The first of these, written on the ship returning to America and published in 1920, is manifestly the work of a young Harvard aesthete, tricked out with what Dos Passos was later to call 'twenty-one-year-old rhetoric'. His descriptions of battle and his attempts to order his hero's experiences symbolically do not represent a significant advance on the *fin-de-siècle* verse he had earlier contributed to an anthology of *Eight Harvard Poets*. In reading it, one gets the sense of a mind beginning to grapple with the larger problems of war and social disintegration, but not coming very close to any understanding of them, and ultimately falling back on the inadequate devices of ironic contrast and the juxtaposition of vivid impressions. Dos Passos was to admit later with disarming simplicity that 'the high point for me of the Avocourt offensive was the day I caught myself quietly opening a can of sardines for my lunch in the rear of a dressing station while some poor devil of a poilu was having his leg sawed off on the operating table up front'.[10] Even when he does try to embody larger ideas in his writing, they are laboriously contrived out of a literary or aesthetic background:

It was the fifth time that day that Martin's car had passed
the crossroads where the cavalry was. Someone had
propped up the fallen crucifix so that it tilted dark
despairing arms against the sunset sky where the sun
gleamed like a huge copper kettle lost in its own steam.
The rain made bright yellowish stripes across the sky and
dripped from the cracked feet of the old wooden Christ,
whose gaunt, scarred figure hung out from the tilted
cross, swaying a little under the beating of the rain. . . .
He stared curiously at the fallen jowl and the cavernous
eyes that had meant for some country sculptor ages ago
the utterest agony of pain. Suddenly he noticed that where
the crown of thorns had been about the forehead of the
Christ someone had wound barbed wire. He smiled, and
asked the swaying figure in his mind: 'And you, what do
you think of it, old boy? How do You like Your
followers? Not so romantic as thorns, is it, that barbed
wire?' (6)

The political and social significance of the events he witnessed did
not escape Dos Passos entirely. He could hardly have failed, for
example, to see the growing signs of mutiny among front-line soldiers,
and he became convinced that the real aim of American intervention
was to quell the European revolution. In the novel he includes a
chapter of discussion between various French radicals in which the
hero, Martin Howe, makes a speech about the 'dark forces' at work
enslaving the minds of Americans. Howe makes a feeble effort to
locate the evil spirits – 'America, as you know is ruled by the press.
And the press is ruled by whom? Who shall ever know what dark
forces bought and bought until we should be ready to go blinded and
gagged into war?' Later he was to see that malevolence cannot be
isolated like this and that its effects must be studied in the impersonal
operation of man-made institutions.

Given the conventional form of the novel, it is not easy to see how
the experiences of the hero could have been meaningfully related to
the patterns of history of which he was a part, even had Dos Passos
been able to perceive such a relation. His failure to find a form which
would allow him to express the war's general significance can be seen
in the fact that, while he was still engaged on the novel, his mind was
busy with plans for a series of 'Junius' letters as propaganda for peace.
Nothing came of them, however, and after his discharge from the
Army he made his way to Spain and started work on his second novel.

Three Soldiers is not entirely successful, whether judged as a war
novel or a novel of social protest. It is possible to believe that Dos

Passos was attempting to do for the First World War what Stephen Crane had done for the Civil War, but it makes more sense to restrict the comparison to that section of Dos Passos's book which deals with Chrisfield, the Indiana farm-boy turned soldier who, in his actions and responses, certainly does suggest a critique of Henry Fleming. Viewed as a whole, and especially in the perspective of the later work, one can see Dos Passos in this novel working towards the complexity of structure that gives *U.S.A.* its great density. He obviously wanted to show the crushing effect of the Army on those made to serve in it, at every possible level of their lives. Rather than follow the fortunes of one chosen 'hero', though, who would have had to be the articulate and highly sophisticated autobiographical figure, John Andrews, he shows in the first two sections, 'Making the Mould' and 'The Metal Cools', how a malleable and ingratiating second-generation San Franciscan is inducted into the organization and quickly cowed by it. Chrisfield's section, 'Machines', which is written in a more opaque style and is therefore more like *The Red Badge of Courage*, deals with actual warfare in France; while the three sections in which Andrews figures most prominently, 'Rust', 'The World Outside', and 'Under the Wheels', allow us to penetrate more fully the consciousness of the individual rebelling against the system.

In its conception this is an interesting structure, and Dos Passos had by this time developed enough basic skill to manipulate his characters and their actions within it. The novel fails, though, because Dos Passos, while still passionately believing in the 'dark forces' behind the war, fails utterly in his attempts to locate them, and so takes refuge in one or other aspect of what Edmund Wilson calls his 'stubborn sentimentalism'.[11] That is to say he falsifies his picture of life either by introducing melodramatic values into it or by introducing values into it in a melodramatic way. This results in the creation of three characters who relate to each other and to their common environment only disjunctively, and who come to life only in so far as they are made to serve the novel's general theme. As might be expected, Andrews provides the best example. By profession he is a composer, or at least plans to be, and Dos Passos uses his stilted meditations on music to illustrate and symbolize his spiritual development. One of the first tasks he is given in the Army is to wash windows, and as he performs this mechanical chore he discovers his first theme, 'Arbeit und Rhythmus'. Later other themes supersede this one. First, when he is wounded, Andrews toys with voluptuous images of the Queen of Sheba, derived directly from Flaubert's *La Tentation de Saint Antoine*, and dreams of composing a romantic work on the subject of liberty. Then, when he has finally gone AWOL he actually begins work on a piece which by this time has come to be called the 'Soul and Body of John Brown'. The last image of the novel is that of the score blowing around his empty, desolate room after he has been dragged back to prison by the military policemen.

Chrisfield, on the other hand, is a man without any accessible interior life, although under the influence of Andrews even he begins to dream of his youth back in Indiana. His more typical reaction to the Army and war, however, is purely physiological, and Dos Passos controls the ironies implicit in his behaviouristic responses far more subtly than he does with the more articulate Andrews. Two incidents in particular combine to show the degrading and dehumanizing effects of war. The first, reminiscent of Henry Fleming's encounter in the forest 'chapel', serves ultimately to empty Chrisfield of his conditioned hatred for the enemy. He encounters a dead body in the woods:

> He kicked the German. He could feel the ribs against his
> toes through the leather of his boot. He kicked again and
> again with all his might. The German rolled over heavily.
> He had no face. Chrisfield felt the hatred suddenly ebb out
> of him. Where the face had been was a spongy mass of
> purple and yellow and red, half of which stuck to the
> russet leaves when the body rolled over. Large flies with
> bright shiny green bodies circled about it. In a brown
> clay-grimed hand was a revolver. (3.2)

After this, all his rage is redirected at the man who comes arbitrarily to symbolize the amorphous inhumanity of the Army as a whole – Sergeant Anderson. Eventually, in the midst of battle, he joyfully seizes the opportunity to blow the man to pieces with a grenade before sinking back into a torpor of confused and guilty conformity. Chrisfield, like Andrews, is a recurring type in Dos Passos's fiction, later to be generally associated with the violence of revolutionary politics.

Many of the elements in *Three Soldiers*, while not cohering within the particular work, have an economy and imaginative vigour suggestive of Dos Passos's mature fiction. What is still lacking is the differential focus achieved in the later novels by a more subtle manipulation of the novelist's, and thus the reader's, aperture of attention. *Three Soldiers* induces monotony because Dos Passos has not yet learned to create perspective within fictional space.

Between the appearance of *Three Soldiers* and his next novel, *Streets of Night* (1923), Dos Passos published his book on Spain, *Rosinante to the Road Again* (1922). It remains interesting chiefly for his meditations on the art of fiction which come out of his essays on Pio Baroja and Blasco Ibáñez. In their work, and in Balzac's, he discovered a fictional technique which is more like 'natural history' than 'dramatic creation', and he obviously began to realize that his pictures of American life would have to develop another dimension in order to be related to the gradual evolution and decay of such American ideals as agrarianism, puritanism, and the business ethic.

Streets of Night goes some way towards enlarging Dos Passos's historical perspective by bringing to bear on a group of Bostonian intellectuals the pressure of their common New England past. Again, he uses the Italian Renaissance as a point of contrast with the sterility of a decaying puritanism, but he also chooses to mediate this sense of cultural disintegration at second hand, this time through the sensibilities of T. S. Eliot and Hawthorne, and the principal characters in the novel have only the most tenuous connection with either their immediate or more general environment. Fanshaw Macdougan's Prufrockian brooding over his failure to break free from the invisible constraints of the Genteel Tradition is so vague and literary that one suspects it has its origins in Dos Passos's undergraduate notebooks rather than in his post-war experience.

> And I'll go back and go to and fro to lectures with a
> notebook under my arm, and now and then in the
> evening, when I haven't any engagement, walk into
> Boston through terrible throbbing streets and think for a
> moment I have Nan and Wenny with me, and that we are
> young, leansouled people out of the Renaissance, ready to
> divide life like a cake with our strong hands.

Streets of Night does not make much of a contribution to Dos Passos's development and hardly prepared the way for *Manhattan Transfer*, a novel which seems to belong to a different era altogether.

By far the most extensive and intelligent discussion of *Manhattan Transfer's* aesthetic design is Blanche Gelfant's in *The American City Novel*. Her analysis of the work, in terms of its abstract impressionist techniques and the narrative and thematic use of urban symbols, goes a long way towards answering the complaints of critics like Edmund Wilson and Delmore Schwartz, who apply to Dos Passos's fiction what, are, in effect, Naturalistic canons of judgement, and condemn him for failing to express the 'whole truth' about American life. Gelfant's analysis, on the other hand, is based on the more valid assumption that Dos Passos is primarily concerned to lay bare the *essential* features of his society: the drift towards monopoly capitalism and all that it entails in human terms. The fictional technique, therefore, has little in common with, say, Dreiser's; it is as much, if not more, concerned with exclusion than with inclusion.

Even so, this realization is not in itself sufficient to account for the radically different form of a synoptic novel like *Manhattan Transfer*. After all, Dos Passos had used most of the same devices before in his attempts to present immediacy of texture and a complex structure. What makes *Manhattan Transfer* so different is that it is the product of a new mode of apprehension, a different way of looking at the world. Its exclusiveness is based more on philosophical and psychological principles than on political ones. Marshall McLuhan hints at this difference when he claims that '*Manhattan Transfer* and the *U.S.A.* trilogy are not novels in the usual sense of a selection of characters who influence and define one another by interaction. The novel in that sense was a by-product of biological science and as such persists today only among book-club practitioners'.[12] McLuhan traces the origins of this new vision back through Joyce, Whitman, and Scott to the discovery of the artistic possibilities of discontinuous landscape in the eighteenth century. Without going quite so far, it is easy to see that whereas *Leaves of Grass*, on Whitman's own admission, owes many of its techniques to the art of still photography, *Manhattan Transfer* could not have been written without the example of the movies, and more particularly of *The Birth of a Nation* (1915) and *Intolerance* (1916).

In a campaign to publicize his own achievements, D. W. Griffith bought a full-page advertisement in the *New York Dramatic Mirror* and listed his contributions to the art of the cinema: 'close-up figures, distant views as represented first in *Ramona*, the "switch-back" (i.e. cross-cutting to parallel or past action), sustained suspense, the "fade-out", and restraint in expression'. Almost every page of *Manhattan Transfer* reads like part of the script for one of Griffith's films. For example, the novel's first chapter, 'Ferryslip', is composed of five short sections grouped thematically around the subject of birth and arrival. In the epigraph, after a brief glimpse of gulls wheeling over the floating detritus of a modern industrial city, the angle of vision shifts to the arrival in dock of a ferry-boat and the hourly re-enactment of the birth trauma as 'gates fold upwards, feet step out across the crack, men and women press through the manuresmelling wooden tunnel of the ferryhouse'. Immediately, Dos Passos cuts to a picture of a nurse holding at arm's length, a basket containing a new-born baby who lies in the cotton wool squirming 'feebly like a knot of earthworns'. In the next section, he introduces his first-named character (though the baby in the basket was, in fact, Ellen), Bud Korpenning, in a synechdochic shift involving a movement away from imagistic montage to close-ups, fast cutting and tracking shots:

> The Young man's glance moved up from Bud's road-
> swelled shoes to the red wrist that stuck out from the
> frayed sleeves of his coat, past the skinny turkey's throat

and slid up cockily into the intent eyes under the broken-visored cap.

'That depends where you want to get to.'

'How do I get to Broadway? . . . I want to get to the centre of things.'

'Walk east a block and turn down Broadway and you'll find the centre of things if you walk far enough.'

'Thank you sir. I'll do that.'

The violinist was going through the crowd with his hat held out, the wind ruffling the wisps of gray hair on his shabby bald head. Bud found the face tilted up at him, the crushed eyes like two black pins looking into his.

'Nothin'', he said gruffily and turned away to look at the expanse of river bright as knifeblades. The plank walls of the slip closed in, cracked as the ferry lurched against them; there was rattling of chains, and Bud was pushed forward among the crowd through the ferryhouse. . . .

EAT on a lunchwagon halfway down the block. He slid stiffly onto a revolving stool and looked for a long while at the pricelist.

'Fried eggs and a cup of coffee.' (1)

This section is followed by the first dramatic scene of the novel, though this too is compressed and thematically dense. In it Ed Thatcher visits his wife after the birth of Ellen and later gets involved in a sentimental discussion of his ambitions for his daughter with a German printer, who calmly cheats him out of the price of a beer. Finally, we eavesdrop on the self-imposed initiation rites of a Jewish immigrant who shaves off his beard after seeing an advertisement for Gillette safety razors. The section, and the chapter, end with his being reborn as a true American – 'a face with a dollarbland smile'.

It is easy to see why the substitution of a camera for the mediating reflective narrator appealed so strongly to Sartre, and led him to overrate Dos Passos; he called him the greatest writer of our time. The creation of 'characterless characters' in an 'authorless novel' fortified Sartre's belief in the deceptive nature of self-consciousness, and helped to pave the way not only for his own fiction but also for that of novelists such as Natalie Sarraute and Robbe-Grillet.

If we pursue the implications of the techniques used in *Manhattan Transfer*, it should be possible to resolve the paradoxical phrase used to describe Dos Passos's novels at the beginning of this chapter, where I wrote of his 'impassioned objectivity'. Sartre talks of an indeterminacy of detail and lack of fictional freedom in Dos Passos's world. The impersonal recording lens presents images which are, in the strict sense of the word, meaningless: 'acts, emotions and ideas suddenly settle within a character, make themselves at home and then disappear without his having much to say in the matter. You cannot say he submits to them. He experiences them. There seems to be no law governing their appearance.'[13] This is not to say, however, that the novels are without significance; that they are not open to interpretation, or that because Dos Passos uses techniques of maximum objectivity, he does not write out of passionately held convictions. The condition of the world he describes expresses his most general and pervasive belief that in modern society men do not have lives but what Sartre calls 'destinies'. The most striking and representative image in *Manhattan Transfer* comes at the moment when Ellen makes her 'decision' to marry George Baldwin:

> Ellen stayed a long time looking in the mirror, dabbing a little superfluous powder off her face, trying to make up her mind. She kept winding up a hypothetical dollself and setting it in various positions. Tiny gestures ensued, acted out on various model stages. Suddenly she turned away from the mirror with a shrug of her toowhite shoulders and hurried into the diningroom. . . .
> Through dinner she felt a gradual ice coldness stealing through her like novocaine. She had made up her mind. It seemed as if she had set the photograph of herself in her own place, forever frozen into a single gesture. An invisible silk band of bitterness was tightening round her throat, strangling. Beyond the plates, the ivory pink lamp, the broken pieces of bread, his face above the blank shirtfront jerked and nodded; the flush grew on his cheeks; his nose caught the light now on one side, now on the other, his taut lips moved eloquently over his yellow teeth. Ellen felt herself sitting with her ankles crossed, rigid as a porcelain figure under her clothes, everything about her seemed to be growing hard and enameled, the air bluestreaked with cigarettesmoke, was turning to glass. His wooden face of a marionette waggled senselessly in front of her. She shuddered and hunched up her shoulders.
> (3:5)

It is a superb example of the annihilation of consciousness and the loss of identity, as she becomes an object, submerged in the materiality of her environment.

Dos Passos evidently still felt the need to oppose this pessimism with some kind of affirmation, and in a rather feeble gesture of romantic anarchy he allows Jimmy Herf to escape his own particular destiny: 'If I'd had a decent education and started soon enough I might have been a great scientist. If I'd been a little more highly sexed I might have been an artist or gone in for religion. . . . But here I am by Jesus Christ almost thirty years old and very anxious to live.' We last see him escaping back to life up the ferry-slip which has now become 'a black mouth with a throat of light'. But this is the exception, fictionally unconvincing, that proves the rule; human life cannot prevail against the machine.

The operation of this law is relentless in Dos Passos's next novel, *U.S.A.* The titles of the first two books in the trilogy locate the pivotal coordinates in space and time of his fictional world. The Forty-second Parallel slices the North American continent in two with Chicago as its hub, while 1919, the year of the Versailles Peace Conference, marks for Dos Passos, the historical moment when it became certain that America had become not a new Greece but merely a latter-day Rome; while the struggle for a humane republic finally lost out to the force that dominates the third novel of the trilogy, *The Big Money*.

The problem of extending and sustaining a fiction through large areas of space and time was not a new one. The Picaresque, Epic and Psychological novelists of the eighteenth and nineteenth centuries had shown how it could be accomplished, and indeed, one of the major impulses behind the novel as a distinct genre has been the need continually to redefine character as an identity of consciousness through extension in space and time. Dos Passos, however, despite his ability to create more vividly than most novelists the sense of life as movement and flux, clearly regards geography and duration as illusory, and contrives in *U.S.A.* to sacrifice the portrait of 'life in time' to 'life by value'. E. M. Forster, whose terms these are, claims that 'the allegiance to time is imperative; no novel could be written without it'.[14] But even granting this, one can see that the extraordinary skill displayed by Dos Passos in moving characters through large areas and epochs is used not primarily in order to guarantee their 'reality' but to suggest the rootlessness and restlessness that characterize man's existence in modern civilization.

Similarly, the twenty-six short biographies inserted into the novel are seen by most critics as an attempt to buttress the general historical accuracy of the whole. They have, in fact, a much more complex function in terms of the novel's overall structure and vision. Each is a carefully composed portrait designed to illuminate one or other of the two faces of American civilization. On one side are the Greeks (Dos Passos goes to some lengths to include appropriate allusions in each sketch) – artists, humanitarians, inventors, philosophers; and on the other, the

Romans – politicians, imperialists, industrialists. These figures have an obvious correspondence with the fictional characters in the novel, but whereas Dos Passos makes no attempt to go behind the creatures of his imagination and interpret their actions directly, the subjects of his biographies have, at best, only a representative existence, and it is this that often leads critics to complain of their 'incompleteness'. In Sartrean terms, the fictional characters portray the *en-soi*, and the biographies the *pour-soi*. In terms of literary modes, the fiction is presented dramatically, the fact as lyric. In this way Dos Passos manages to convey both substance and significance without having to resort to the reflective techniques of narrative. The biography of J. Pierpont Morgan is typical of the way Dos Passos creates an objective correlative for his hatred of finance and financiers. The whole section is composed around a few reiterated images and refrains designed to make the great Wall Street moneymaster appear stupid, crude, vulgar and ugly – his magpie eyes and his bull neck, his love of display, and his special gesture of the arm meaning 'What do I get out of it?' Here is a short passage from the middle of the piece which, if one attends to the connotations of the images, effectively serves to reduce its subject to a brutal and grasping social climber:

> Every Christmas his librarian read him Dickens' *A Christmas Carol* from the original manuscript.
> He was very fond of canarybirds and pekinese dogs and liked to take pretty actresses yachting. Each *Corsair* was a finer vessel than the last.
> When he dined with King Edward he sat at His Majesty's right; he ate with the Kaiser tête-à-tête; he liked talking to cardinals or the pope, and never missed a conference of Episcopal bishops;
> Rome was his favourite city.

The whole biography ends with a repetition of the central motif:

> (Wars and panics on the stock exchange,
> machinegunfire and arson,
> bankruptcies, warloans,
> starvation, lice, cholera and typhus:
> good growing weather for the House of Morgan)
> (*1919*, pp. 338–40)

In contrast, this is how the editor of *Vanity Fair* described Morgan when nominating him to the magazine's Hall of Fame in 1921:

Because, like his father, he is the banker of the widest
vision and soundest ability in America; because he is a
lover, collector and connoisseur of art; because he is a
sportsman of the best type, and has kept the America's
Cup in America; but chiefly because he is ever ready to
help a friend, a worthy civic movement, or a deserving
work of charity.

The use of the Newsreels and Camera Eye sections has also been
widely misunderstood by Dos Passos's critics. They stand in a similar
relation to each other as do the fact and fiction in the rest of the novel.
On the one hand, the inappropriately named Camera Eye represents
a disembodied sensibility interpreting experience in a pure stream of
consciousness:

> revolution round the spinning Eiffel Tower
> that burns up our last year's diagrams the
> dates fly off the calendar we'll make everything
> new today is the Year I Today is the sunny morning
> of the first day of spring We gulp our coffee
> splash water on us jump into our clothes run downstairs
> step out wideawake into the first morning of the first
> day of the first year (p. 344)

The Newsreels, on the other hand, pile up a montage of unmediated
and meaningless dramatic incident, collected from contemporary newspapers, and interspersed with snatches of popular songs:

> TO THE GLORY OF FRANCE ETERNAL
> *Oh a German officer crossed the Rhine*
> *Parleyvoo*

> Germans Beaten at Riga Grateful Parisians Cheer Marshals
> of France

> *Oh a German officer crossed the Rhine*
> *He liked the women and loved the wine*
> *Hankypanky parleyvoo*

> PITEOUS PLAINT OF WIFE TELLS OF RIVAL'S
> WILES
> Wilson's arrival in Washington Starts trouble. Paris
> strikers hear harangues at picnic. Cafe wrecked and bombs
> thrown in Fiume streets. Parisians pay more for meat. Il

serait Dangereux d'Augmenter les Vivres. Bethmann
Holweg's Blood Boils. Mysterious Forces Halt
Antibolshevist March. (p. 344)

Those who believe that the bizarre events in the Newsreels are there
to give credibility to the fictional parts of the novel are as misguided
as those who complain that they are not in themselves 'interesting'.
On the contrary – what they induce in the reader – and are surely
meant to induce – is nausea, defined by Sartre as the subject's inability
to digest his experience by reflecting on it. The random, indeterminate,
and neutral presentation reflects a world which is in itself impenetrable,
unalterable, and devoid of essential meaning.

The supreme technical virtuosity of *U.S.A.* is much more, then,
than a flamboyant exercise in novelistic craft by a lesser Joyce. As with
all genuine works of art, the expressive devices are made rigorously
to serve a particular end; in this case the presentation of a truth that
is massive yet easy to overlook, simple in itself but complex in its
ramifications. Any judgement of the novel must come to terms with
that truth. To see Dos Passos as an author of social protest, inspired
by democratic or even revolutionary zeal, is to see him altogether too
narrowly. What his image of America in the 1920s compels us to see
and believe, is a truth become so evident that even *Life* magazine
propounds it now. Twentieth-century man has created physical and
spiritual environments for himself which will not allow him to go on
living, as a human being. Dos Passos's world has no interesting or
memorable characters in it, it is true. Dick Savage, Eveline Hutchins,
Charley Anderson, and the rest are all in the process of becoming
automata. But so was everyone else in the 1930s, according to Dos
Passos. That was the social tragedy of his time.

Notes

1. Bernard DeVoto, 'Genius is not Enough', *Saturday Review of Literature*, 13
   (April 1936). Malcolm Cowley gives a different account of Maxwell Perkins's
   contribution to *Of Time and the River*. He says that Perkins worked with
   Wolfe on the manuscript 'every evening for the better part of a year'. See *A
   Second Flowering* (New York, 1973), p. 168.

2. In the following account I am indebted to the work of John Eldergill who
   has prepared a critical edition of Wolfe's last manuscript, '*The Web and the
   Rock*' (unpublished doctoral dissertation, University of Nottingham, 1972). In
   his Introduction, Eldergill traces the history of this manuscript in some detail.

3. See *The Notebooks of Thomas Wolfe*, edited by Richard S. Kennedy and Pascal Reeves (Chapel Hill, NC, 1970).

4. Maxwell Geismar, *Writers in Crisis: The American Novel, 1925–1940* (New York, 1947), p. 201.

5. *The Notebooks of Thomas Wolfe*, p. 939.

6. Jean-Paul Sartre, 'John Dos Passos and *1919*', in his *Literary and Philosophical Essays* (London, 1955), p. 96.

7. See F. Scott Fitzgerald, *The Crack-Up*, edited by Edmund Wilson (New York, 1945), p. 343.

8. Alfred Kazin, *On Native Grounds: An Interpretation of American Prose Literature*, abridged edition (New York, 1956), p. 275.

9. Irving Howe, 'John Dos Passos: The Loss of Passion', *Tomorrow*, 7 (1949), 54–57, and Granville Hicks, 'The Politics of John Dos Passos', *Antioch Review*, 10 (1950), 85–98.

10. *The Best Times: An Informal Memoir* (New York, 1968), p. 55.

11. Edmund Wilson, 'Dos Passos and the Social Revolution', in *The Shores of Light: A Literary Chronicle of the Twenties and Thirties* (New York, 1952), p. 433.

12. Herbert Marshall McLuhan, 'John Dos Passos: Technique vs. Sensibility', in *Fifty Years of the American Novel*, edited by Harold C. Gardiner, SJ (New York, 1968), p. 162.

13. *Sartre*, p. 91.

14. E. M. Forster, *Aspects of the Novel* (London, 1927), p. 29.

Chapter 11

Modernism: Stein, Hemingway, Miller, West, Roth, Fitzgerald

Like any other large-scale literary movement, modernism cannot be defined solely in terms of its specific literary dynamic, nor can it be adequately explained merely by reference to the social or intellectual pressures that bore upon it. For the purpose of tracing the American contribution to the international movement, however, the more formal aspects of modernist fiction exemplified by the work of such novelists as James Joyce, Marcel Proust, Virginia Woolf, Robert Musil, and D. H. Lawrence will be taken for granted here, so making space for an examination of developments or deviations of a specifically national kind.

Most of the formal characteristics found to varying degrees in the fiction of these major European writers – an emphasis on the primacy of the linguistic medium, a rejection of causality and plots, a destabilization of character, a distortion of perception, and a use of non-linear, discontinuous narrative – have been held to stem from a loss of belief either in the meaning of external reality itself, or at least in the individual's ability to discover any such meaning there. Modernism derives from a subjectivity so radical that it easily leads its practitioners into solipsism or nihilism; and though they will sometimes grudgingly acknowledge the central social and moral issues that sustained the nineteenth-century realist novel, they do so only to deny their validity in the face of overwhelming metaphysical and epistemological doubt. Throughout the early decades of this century it was widely believed that the novel had finally run its course, killed off by *Ulysses* and buried by *Finnegans Wake*. But the form proved more difficult to dispose of than critics imagined. For good or ill, the novel's capaciousness enabled it to absorb and transform the modernist implant without changing its essential nature.

Indeed, it has been convincingly argued that exactly the opposite is true: that the endlessly assimilative character of bourgeois art allowed it to domesticate and vulgarize the avant-garde, its welcoming embrace serving as a cover behind which a successful emasculation took place. According to this view, Modernism in its pure or 'high' form could only be maintained as an oppositional, if not a revolutionary stance, and when that position was threatened by its incorporation into middle-class realism, its followers had no alternative but to abandon their literary and philosophical isolation and re-enter the arena of history.[1]

A different interpretation of the same process is given by Hugh Kenner, whose history of American Modernism referred to above (see p. 116–17) celebrates the achievement of Hemingway, Fitzgerald, and Faulkner, among others, in adopting the insights and craft of their European predecessors to make them available for use in a 'real' American world. Kenner argues that the American novelists managed somehow to give their reading public what it thought it wanted, while at the same time embarking on no less a project than a fifty-year reshaping of the American language.[2] A more cynical explanation of their work – and it is one that Kenner acknowledges – might see in it evidence of their dependence on a large readership and a consequent unwillingness to risk the more extreme difficulties and obscurities associated with the literature of high modernism.

In this connection it is instructive to look at the career of Gertrude Stein, the one American novelist in the period who steadfastly refused to make any concessions to bourgeois taste and who remained as loyal to her difficult art as any of her European contemporaries. The fact that she spent her entire working life abroad, only returning once to the United States for a lecture tour in the early 1930s, has led some critics to belittle her contribution to the national literature. But as she herself pointed out, though Paris might be her home town, America remained her country. It always irritated her that the American public showed great interest in her personality but none at all in her work, and Ernest Hemingway, writing in *A Moveable Feast* (1954) about Paris in the 1920s, recalls her longing to have her work published in the *Atlantic Monthly*, and her more general desire for public recognition. In his comments on her fiction he also indicates why such recognition was never likely to be forthcoming. He praises one of her early stories, 'Melanctha' (which had formed part of *Three Lives* (1909)) for its intelligibility, but goes on to say of her massive novel *The Making of Americans* (1925) that a more conscientious and less lazy writer would have cut the text's endless repetitions and thrown them in the waste basket. This, in effect, is just what her publisher did in 1934 by printing a severely abridged version of the work to coincide with her visit to the United States. The novel was reduced to half its original length, and a comparison of the two versions shows just how damaging such editing was and how crass Hemingway's critical judgement.

Hemingway's comment is based on the assumption that the

repetitions in Stein's prose are merely irrelevant elaborations that obscure the central story, and the failure of the abridged version of *The Making of Americans* to lay bare such a core, helps to prove the inadequacy of such a judgement. Gertrude Stein herself, though, gives the fullest possible explanation of why she found it necessary to reject all the traditional elements of fiction in her search for a new, deeper reality. She does so both in the novel itself and in her famous lecture 'The Gradual Making of *The Making of Americans*'.[3]

As a student and ardent admirer of William James at the Harvard Annex, Gertrude Stein could hardly have failed to be influenced by the famous psychologist's ideas about the nature of mental processes. James's notion of consciousness as a function rather than an entity leads directly to Stein's abandonment of neatly differentiated and demarcated 'characters', just as his metaphor of consciousness as a stream rather than a chain underlies her unique mode of representation. Her abiding concern was to express the essential qualities of people rather than the merely contingent. This preoccupation with what she called 'bottom nature' is the opposite of the realist's interest in the unique and particular, and accounts for the drive towards abstraction in her prose. A person's 'reality' is discovered by stripping away the superficial trivia of life and laying bare the fundamental rhythms of existence. This is how she explains it in her novel:

> When you come to feel the whole of anyone from the
> beginning to the ending, all the kinds of repeating there is
> in them, the different ways at different times repeating
> comes out of them, all the kinds of things and mixtures in
> each one, anyone can see then by looking hard at any one
> living near them that a history of everyone must be a long
> one. (3)

The history of the Herland family in *The Making of Americans* is not only long, but it also becomes the basis for what Stein calls 'a description of every way one can think of men and women, in their beginning, in their middle living, and their ending'. The novel is just as much about the nature of Gertrude Stein's thought and creative processes as it is about any other subject. In shattering surface illusion in this way and substituting for it a layered text in which the workings of her own consciousness and the processes of perception and representation are frankly identified, she was obviously influenced by contemporary developments in the art of French painters whom she knew and whose works she and her brother Leo collected. In *The Autobiography of Alice B. Toklas* (1933) , a book written by Stein about herself, she associates her efforts to achieve a new form of writing with

Picasso's difficult path towards Cubism in his famous portrait of her. She claims that 'Melanctha', which she was composing at the time she sat for the painting, represented the first step taken by literature away from the nineteenth and into the twentieth century. Her subsequent work, with its techiques of verbal collage and the abolition of perspective, also relates very closely to what was happening in the painting of Matisse and Braque.

At the same time, Stein claimed that despite its place in international modernism, her work remained very American. In the first place, she was deeply aware, living as she did among non-English-speaking people, of her efforts to re-create the English language as a new medium, just as for different reasons her American predecessors had been obliged to do centuries earlier.[4] In *The Autobiography of Alice B. Toklas* she suggests that had she not felt so intensely alone with her eyes and her English, language would never have become so 'all in all' to her. In foregrounding the medium in this way, she recalls those American writers, discussed by Richard Poirier, who created linguistic environments as substitutes for the supportive social contexts that were lacking in nineteenth-century America.[5]

Secondly, Gertrude Stein believed and reiterated the belief in both her fiction and essays that Americans have a quite different relation to space and time from that of Europeans. In 'The Gradual Making of *The Making of Americans*' she tries very hard to explain her sense of it:

> this thing is an essentially American thing this sense of a
> space of time and what is to be done within this space of
> time not in any way excepting in the way that it is
> inevitable that there is this space of time and anybody who
> is an American feels what is inside this space of time and
> so well they do what they do within this space of time,
> and so ultimately it is a thing contained within. . . . Think
> of anything, of cowboys, of movies, of detective stories,
> of anybody who goes anywhere or stays at home and is
> an American and you will realise that it is something
> strictly American to conceive a space that is filled with
> moving, a space of time that is always filled with
> moving.[6]

Her reference to the movies – the quintessential American art form – is perhaps the most helpful in explaining this idea. Unlike all other narrative forms, film has no past tenses. Everything that happens on the screen – even flashbacks and montage sequences – takes place in the present tense. Despite the ingenuity of film-makers in devising techniques to show the passage of time, the entire action of any film takes place in the present. When Greta Garbo laughs or Charlie Chaplin eats his bootlaces, they always do so *now*, for audiences who watch in an eternally recoverable and replayable moment. According to Stein, Americans as a race have a personal and internalized time sense that relates to their own actions rather than to any absolute sense of history, and this subjective quality of a 'space of time' is the primary feature of modern American fiction. Many other affinities have been traced between novels and films in the modern period,[7] but the combination of immediacy and ellipsis is one of the more remarkable unifying aspects in the work of writers as different as Dos Passos, Faulkner, Hemingway, and Gertrude Stein herself.

In *The Making of Americans* she uses this technique to explore the 'bottom nature' of her characters, showing just as Faulkner later did in *The Sound and the Fury* (1929), how early incidents in a person's life continue to live on within them. Unlike Faulkner, though, who uses the device to dramatize Benjy's arrested mental development and confused chronological sense, Stein explains and seeks to generalize her ideas about characterology before going on to show them in action in a representative event. Martha Hersland is one of those who 'have their real being in them in young living', and this is brilliantly exemplified by an incident in her childhood, in which Stein's notion of an individual's continuity in time is captured by the juxtaposition of subjective and objective moods and tenses, the child's sense of future and past being contrasted with the continuous flow of time in the narration.

> This is a little story of the acting in her of her being on
> her very young living, this one was a very little one and
> she was running and she was in the street and it was a
> muddy one and she had an umbrella that she was dragging
> and she was crying. 'I will throw the umbrella in the
> mud,' she was saying, she was very little then, she was
> just beginning her schooling, 'I will throw the umbrella in
> the mud.' (4)[8]

Eventually, after several repetitions of this sequence in subtly changing contexts of frustration and rising anger, she bursts out, 'I have throwed the umbrella in the mud', and the narrator concludes 'it was the end of all that to her'. But of course it isn't, and the incident serves as a key to much of what happens to Martha in the novel.

The above quotation – typical of the prose style of the whole book – may suggest why *The Making of Americans* remains one of the great unread masterpieces of American literature. Edmund Wilson, who praises Stein in his book on Symbolism, admits that he has not read the whole novel and wonders whether it is even possible to do so. Ben Reid in a critique of Stein goes further by doubting whether a score of people could be found who have even read the shorter version.[9] If these critics are right, their claims throw an interesting light on the way in which literary influence operates. There is no doubt that Stein – who herself was powerfully influenced by another little-read master-piece, Richardson's *Clarissa* – did have an important effect on later American novelists. Of these, Hemingway is perhaps the best example, and we have seen how he, who certainly had read *The Making of Americans*, appeared to misunderstand its aims and techniques. At the same time it can be argued that the younger writer knew instinctively what he wanted from Stein and was able to assimilate those things without necessarily understanding or even caring how they functioned in her very different art.

Superficially, the methods employed by Hemingway and Stein seem radically opposed; where he endlessly pared his sentences down to reach a core of irrefutable truth, she tirelessly accumulated repetitions to create hers. Yet, as Michael J. Hoffman has demonstrated, there is just as much 'leaving-out' in Stein's style as there is in Hemingway's, and both writers can be seen to engage in a form of 'Abstractionism'[10] One of the qualities that Hemingway praised unstintingly in 'Melanctha' was the truth of its rhythms, and this provides a clue to the most valuable lesson Stein taught him. It is one that helps to illumi-nate her idea about American representations of time and the distinc-tiveness of modern American writing. Hemingway begins his famous book about bullfighting, *Death in the Afternoon* (1930), with a memory of Gertrude Stein talking about her admiration for the matador Jose-lito, from which he quickly moves to the book's other subject – style. The juxtaposition may not be as arbitrary as it seems, though. The time, he recalls, was that of his apprenticeship as a writer in the early 1920s:

> I was trying to write then and I found the greatest
> difficulty, aside from knowing truly what you really felt,
> rather than what you were supposed to feel, and had been
> taught to feel, was to put down what really happened in
> action; what the actual things were which produced the
> emotion that you experienced . . . the sequence of motion
> and fact which made the emotion. (1)

It was a difficult lesson to learn, and one that was only fully mastered in one of his novels and a handful of short stories. Throughout the 1930s the pristine quality of Hemingway's writing gradually began to elude him, and by the end of his career, after the Second World War, manifested itself only as a sad form of self-parody when style or technique became a substitute for, instead of an index to, emotion.

The connection with Stein's remarks about the American sense of moving within a space of time, is made through the concept of 'style'. What the cowboy, the movie star, and the private detective have in common both with each other and with bullfighters like Joselito, is a self contained concept of their inner being, a concept that is projected externally as an unmistakable style. It is this outward manifestation that Hemingway wants to express in order to make plain the spiritual core within. He is quite explicit about this in *The Sun Also Rises* (1926), or, at least, his hero, Jake Barnes is: 'I did not care what it was all about. All I wanted to know was how to live in it. Maybe if you found out how to live in it you learned from that what it was all about.' This could almost be taken as the credo of the modern American existentialist hero (or anti-hero), describing 'the basic' philosophy of a wide range of characters from Jake himself and Jay Gatsby, through Faulkner's Joe Christmas to Norman Mailer's anti-hero Rojack in *An American Dream*, and many others. All of these have the uniquely American belief that if they can learn 'how to live in it', they will perhaps find out what it is all about. The particular 'it' might be war, sexual love, murder, or, in Jake Barnes's case, the ethos of post-war Europe, but in every instance, the clue to essential meaning comes from being and from the sequence of motion and fact, as characters move forward in the space of their own time.

Scott Fitzgerald understood this concept too, and his advice to Hemingway about how to revise *The Sun Also Rises* makes it clear. Fitzgerald wanted him to cut the first thirty pages of his typescript up to the point where, as he says '(after a false start on the introduction of Cohn) it really gets going'. In the event Hemingway deleted 40,000 words in all, amounting to a third of the original, and though the novel still begins with the introduction of Robert Cohn, he did at least remove the 'merely recounted' history of his heroine, Brett Ashley. The original opening, Fitzgerald pointed out, did not even possess Hemingway's usual rhythm and the fact that it may be 'true' is immaterial.[11]

The 'truths' to which Fitzgerald objected in the early part of the original manuscript – an account of Brett's marriage, her character and drinking habits – are what he called 'shopworn'. Manufactured separately, they have to be asserted rather than created in the novel's action, and they consist of what Henry James called mere 'seated information'. Fitzgerald evidently thought the same was true of the sections introducing Robert Cohn, and he would have done away with these too. As we shall see, Fitzgerald himself had similar difficulties with the beginning of *Tender is the Night* (1934). It is true that Hemingway

introduces Cohn with three pages of equally inert history, but at least
in Cohn's case it can be argued that this is appropriate to his character.
In the novel's complex value-system Cohn represents the type of
outdated romantic hero who fails to adjust to the new realities of the
post-war world. He asserts himself and his old-fashioned opinions in
ways that are shown to be inimical to the code which Jake and Brett
are creating and which is perfectly exemplified by the young matador,
Romero. Cohn is introduced in the first three sentences of the book
as a man with the wrong qualifications and the wrong values:

> Robert Cohn was once middleweight boxing champion of
> Princeton. Do not think that I am very much impressed
> by that as a boxing title, but it meant a lot to Cohn. He
> cared nothing for boxing, in fact he disliked it, but he
> learned it painfully and thoroughly to counteract the
> feeling of inferiority and shyness he had felt on being
> treated as a Jew at Princeton. (1)

Cohn's skill as a boxer and his inability to use that skill authentically
are the elements Hemingway uses to create the climax of the novel.
Cohn has developed a romantic passion for Brett, a nymphomaniac
who, like Jake, carries her sexual wound like a symbol of the death
of all the old values, including love. When Cohn learns that Brett has
gone off with Romero, he first knocks down Jake and his friend Mike
Campbell before attacking the matador. Romero, true to his code, gets
up from the floor over a dozen times so as to defeat the boxer in the
only way he can: 'Cohn was crying and telling [Brett] how much he
loved her, and she was telling him not to be a ruddy ass. Then Cohn
leaned down to shake hands with the bull-fighter fellow. No hard feelings, you know. All for forgiveness. And the bull-fighter hit him in
the face again.' (17)

Romero is a perfect example of the hero whose style completely
expresses his inner being: Hemingway, in attempting to define this
quality in him, significantly thinks back to the days of Joselito, and
says that Romero is the only matador since who does not simulate the
appearance of danger in order to give a fake emotional feeling. Like
his creator who knows that he can only begin from 'one true sentence',
the matador stands out among his contemporaries because he can hold
the purity of his line through the maximum exposure. This is the
essence of the code: 'grace under pressure'.

It is what Hemingway's narrator, Jake, is trying to achieve, too, but
without possessing the superb skills of the matador, or even an arena
– like that of war – in which ordinary men can find themselves in their
encounters with danger, violence, and death. In the absence of such

things, and having lost both his sexual potency and his religious faith, Jake is left with a hard-boiled, understated stoicism that can only resist the spectatorial cynicism of dwelling on what might have been, by immersion in the immediate experience of a few concrete universals – bread, wine and nature.

On the way from Paris to the annual fiesta at Pamplona,[12] Jake and Bill Gorton take a side trip for a few days' fishing at Burguete, and it is here, away from the corruption of Paris and the emotional strain generated by Cohn, that Jake discovers his inner poise. In the chapter describing this pastoral moment, Hemingway is clearly trying very hard to establish a fusion between the outer and inner man, and the effort makes great demands on his prose. The simple, realistic style in which the activities of the two friends are described has to carry a heavy burden of meaning, and it operates without the benefit of any overt symbolism, most of its meaning coming from the rhythmical repetition of the rituals of fishing and eating. This is accompanied by an ironic, pseudo-religious litany delivered by the two men, in which Hemingway shows how precariously he wavers between eroticism and sentimentality. The episode is then summarized in a passage in which the universal elements of nature are allowed to dominate any concrete detail:

> We stayed five days at Burguete and had good fishing.
> The nights were cold and the days were hot, and there
> was always a breeze even in the heat of the day. It was
> hot enough so that it felt good to wade in a cold stream,
> and the sun dried you when you came out and sat on the
> bank. We found a stream with a pool deep enough to
> swim in. (12)[13]

Hemingway never suggests that nature itself has any immanent or transcendent meaning. It does, however, provide a neutral ground for man to test his unmediated sensations and values. Indeed, in stories such as 'A Natural History of the Dead' and in his next novel *A Farewell to Arms* (1929), he goes to some lengths to refute the idea of nature as an expression of either God's design or his beneficence. In the story he brutally answers Mungo Park's rhetorical questions about the intentions of a divine creator by describing what death on the battlefield is really like; while in the novel, as the hero Frederick Henry waits for Catherine to die in childbirth, he muses on the meaningless-ness of life and recounts a traditional naturalist parable. He recalls placing a log full of ants on a blazing fire, and watching as they fall off into the flames. Rather than act as a messiah by saving the ants, he throws the water from his whisky cup over them and steams them to death: 'Now Catherine would die. That was what you did. You died. You did not know what it was about.' (41)

In the context of their love-affair, in which they have created a meaningful if temporary existence amid a war-torn world, that last sentence reads like a pessimistic rejection of Jake Barnes's tenuous existential hope. And it is true that there is a deep strain of anti-intellectualism in Hemingway that will not permit him to create characters who are capable of conceptualizing their experiences in the way the reader does. To that extent his heroes never do 'know' what 'it' is about, and this is precisely what creates the special poignancy of his early fiction.

Frederick Henry has volunteered to serve with the Italian Army during the First World War, just as Hemingway did. Like his creator, he gradually becomes disillusioned about the value of the civilization being fought for, and this disillusionment is defined mainly in terms of his responses to the various characters whom he encounters in the period leading up to the Army's defeat at Caporetto and his decision to desert. From the moment Frederick takes up the narration, however, he shows a detachment from everything around him that is more than simply the product of his foreignness. In his initial description of the Italian countryside during the early years of the war, his style – typical of all Hemingway's anti-heroes – is that of someone who registers everything yet interprets nothing:

> In the late summer of that year we lived in a house in a
> village that looked across the river and the plain to the
> mountains. In the bed of the river there were pebbles and
> boulders, dry and white in the sun, and the water was
> clear and swiftly moving the blue in the channels. Troops
> went by the house and down the road and the dust they
> raised powdered the leaves of the trees. The trunks of the
> trees too were dusty and the leaves fell early that year and
> we saw the troops marching along the road and the dust
> rising and leaves, stirred by the breeze, falling and the
> soldiers marching and afterward the road bare and white
> except for the leaves. (1)

Hemingway's succession of co-ordinate clauses and his refusal to discriminate or evaluate imply, as Robert Penn Warren has remarked,[14] a dislocated world in which men live a precarious existence perceptually, and hardly live at all conceptually.

Frederick Henry eventually comes closest to an understanding of his feelings after months of meaningless conflict in which he narrowly escapes death when he is hit in the legs by a trench mortar shell. He has also met and fallen in love with Catherine Barkley, an English volunteer nurse, and after a period of recuperation returns to the front. The summer is over now and the rains are beginning. The war has moved into the mountains and things are going badly for the Italians. After discussing the situation with an Italian patriot who refuses to admit the possibility of defeat, maintaining that their earlier efforts cannot have been in vain, Frederick muses on the discrepancy between his actual experience of war and the words others use to describe it:

> I had seen nothing sacred, and the things that were glorious had no glory and the sacrifices were like the stockyards at Chicago if nothing was done with the meat except bury it. There were many words that you could not stand to hear and finally only the names of places had dignity. Certain numbers were the same way and certain dates and these with the names of the places were all you could say and have them mean anything. Abstract words such as glory, honor, courage, or hallow were obscene beside the concrete names of villages, the numbers of roads, the names of rivers, the numbers of regiments and the dates. (27)

In the confusion of the retreat one of Frederick's companions is shot dead by his own troops and Frederick himself is arrested by the battle police who suspect him of being a German in Italian uniform. He escapes across the Tagliamento River and, cutting the insignia from the sleeves of his jacket, finally decides to make his own separate peace. His efforts to discover meaning in the war or in life itself in his religious discussions with his fellow soldiers, have literally come to nothing, so he turns to his love-affair with Catherine to seek a significance that the wider world cannot provide.

Emerging from the river as a new man – an 'Othello with his occupation gone' – Frederick takes Catherine to a mountain retreat in Switzerland where they pursue a romantic idyll similar in function to that enjoyed by Jake Barnes in Burguete in the earlier novel. As they wait for their child to be born, they retreat into nature and into each other, deliberately disengaging themselves from society so as to concentrate on the intensity of their emotional life. What saves this section of the novel from the banality that threatens to overwhelm it – especially in the lovers' dialogue – is the sense of doom they share, 'as though something were hurrying us and we could not lose any time together'. This feeling pervades the silences between their sentimental declarations of love and helps give the lie to Catherine's final pronouncement that her death is 'just a dirty trick'. Like Frederick's 'defeat', it is a tragic necessity that lifts the novel above its superficial naturalism. There is no 'clean, well-lighted place' where men and women could practise a nobler code.

This conclusion, implicit in *A Farewell to Arms*, is articulated more openly in Hemingway's novels set in the 1930s: *To Have and Have Not* (1937) and *For Whom the Bell Tolls* (1940). For those American writers whose talents had been developed abroad in the 1920s, the return to America in the Depression was a traumatic experience and one that was likely to be damaging to their art. The current preoccupation with economic and social collapse could hardly fail to affect the imaginations of writers like Hemingway and Fitzgerald, but the fiction that resulted from their attempts to come to terms with the domestic crisis – novels such as *To Have and Have Not* and *The Last Tycoon* (1941) – forced them not only into new subject-matter but also into a manner of writing that was alien to them. Fitzgerald never finished his Hollywood novel, and in the notes he left seemed unable to decide on a proper form for it. Hemingway, on the other hand, having told the story of Harry Morgan in *To Have and Have Not*, the typical anti-hero who tries to make it alone as a smuggler, leaves him bleeding to death on a borrowed boat, surrounded by the corpses of the Cubans he has shot, to insert a chapter of social satire as he describes the occupants of yachts at anchor in the basin to which Harry is being returned. The sudden switch in narrative technique to a Dos Passos-like montage undermines the reader's belief in the world that has previously been created, even though Hemingway tries to prepare for this switch by gradually moving out of Harry's consciousness as the novel progresses, towards a more impersonal form of narration. The lives that are briefly described in this chapter, and the generalized social commentary that is appended are so remote from the real concerns of the story that it is impossible to take them as anything but cleverly constructed cameos paying lip-service to fashionable concerns. This passage, for example, describing a ruthless business tycoon would not seem at all out of place in *U.S.A.*:

> He did not think in any abstractions, but in deals, in sales, in transfers and in gifts. He thought in shares, in bales, in thousands of bushels, in options, holding companies, trusts, and subsidiary corporations, and as he went over it he knew they had plenty, enough so he would have no peace for years. If they would not compromise, it would be very bad. In the old days he would not have worried, but the fighting part of him was tired now, along with the other part, and he was alone in

all of this now, and he lay on the big, wide, old bed and could neither read nor sleep. (16)

Hemingway betrays his lack of interest in this kind of social fiction in the satirical portrait of another peripheral character, Richard Gordon; a novelist whose life is going to pieces in Key West in a series of drunken debauches while he attempts to write a proletarian novel about the Gastonia textile strike. References to the contents of Gordon's book make it apparent that Hemingway is once again attacking Sherwood Anderson who had written a rather poor proletarian novel, *Beyond Desire*, in 1932. What provokes Hemingway's ironic contempt in the minor characters he creates, and what sets them apart from Harry Morgan with whom they are contrasted, are the contradictions between the appearance and the reality of their lives – the hypocrisies that flower when the American Dream turns into a nightmare.

Harry Morgan is a victim of the Depression too. In an attempt to provide a living for his family he has been driven to ever more dangerous forms of smuggling, and his last adventure with Cuban revolutionaries leads to his death. But like all Hemingway's previous heroes he resolutely refuses to involve others in the dangers to which he subjects himself. At the point of death, however, he belatedly sees the inadequacy of the philosophy he has lived by, and his last words suggest the change of direction brought about in Hemingway's thought by his return to America:

'A man,' Harry Morgan said, looking at them both.
'One man alone ain't got. No man alone now.' He
stopped. 'No matter how a man alone ain't got no bloody
chance.'
He shut his eyes. It had taken him a long time to get it
out and it had taken him all of his life to learn it. (15)

Even as late as 1937, though, Hemingway's commitment to America was less than total. As John Peale Bishop remarked, the Key West that Hemingway described and chose to live in might still be political America but it is its 'uttermost island', unattached to the native continent.[15] The setting of *To Have and Have Not* is really Cuba, and Hemingway's reluctance to involve himself in the social life of his own country is also suggested by Leslie Fiedler, who observed that by this time in his career Hemingway was talking to himself in pidgin Spanish.[16] Besides, like most American radicals he was more interested in the Spanish Civil War which he had seen at first hand as a correspondent, than in the more mundane battles being fought at home by the New Dealers. There are those who believe that some of the work he produced as a result of that experience – though not his play 'The Fifth Column' or the short stories written in Madrid – is among his best.[17]

What makes *For Whom the Bell Tolls* profoundly different from *A Farewell to Arms*, despite their many superficial similarities, is that its hero, Robert Jordan, having travelled the same path to disillusionment as Frederick Henry, and having partially escaped into an all-consuming love-affair, retains enough selflessness to remain behind after completing his mission, facing certain death at the hands of Fascist troops so that his companions and lover can make their escape. Like Frederick, too, he has been wounded in the leg, though in his case the bone is broken when his horse is shelled and collapses under him. As he waits, machine-gun by his side for the enemy soldiers, he reflects on the significance of the life he has led – life which began to take on meaning when he left his teaching job in America and which reached its climax in the three days that comprise the action of the novel:

> I have fought for what I believe in for a year now. If
> we win here we will win everywhere. The world is a fine
> place and worth the fighting for and I hate very much to
> leave it. And you had a lot of luck, he told himself, to
> have had such a good life. (43)

It is this affirmative conclusion – the suggestion that Hemingway had finally worked his way out of the pessimistic nihilism that had characterized his earlier work – that won over so many critics. Even those like Cleanth Brooks who are not inclined to see any genuine social commitment in the novel, are attracted by Jordan's spirituality which is taken as a form of embryonic Christianity.[18] Brooks argues that Hemingway is too honest and too good a writer to attribute all the evil in his story to the Fascists and all the good to the Loyalists, and that sections such as the one in which he describes Loyalist atrocities show how unwilling he was to subjugate his art to the demands of political propaganda. It is hardly necessary to strain after religious meanings, though, in order to justify Jordan's famous last stand. As the above quotation makes clear, what finally gives his life meaning is his ability to retain his belief in a political cause despite all the cruelties and betrayals that are associated with it.

Brooks is right, however, in pointing out that there is no necessary connection between the quality of a writer's best work and the strength of his social conscience. And the same is surely true of an artist's spiritual conscience. The flaws in *For Whom the Bell Tolls*, apparent even at the level of style and tone, can on the contrary be seen to result directly from Hemingway's acquisition of a more positive philosophy in the 1930s. In his best work, written earlier, Hemingway creates what Hugh Kenner has termed a 'rhetoric of evasion',[19] a style in which his real subject is hidden beneath a surface of events characterized by an almost meaningless banality. It is in the interstices between the ritual performance of humdrum actions or in the lengthening gaps in his characters' mundane conversations that the reader begins to perceive the appalling truth being kept at bay – the ever-present threat of an encroaching 'nada' or non-being. And it is the tension between these two levels, sometimes stretched to almost unendurable limits, that lifts Hemingway's fiction beyond the 'sociological simplicities' of most of his contemporaries.

In *For Whom the Bell Tolls*, on the other hand, his characteristic hard-boiled style gives way to a form of pidgin English – the result of his attempts to simulate the demotic Spanish of Pilar, Pablo, Anselmo, and Maria, the peasants who support Jordan in his dangerous mission. Jordan, who before the war had been an instructor in Spanish at the University of Montana, speaks the same language as they do when he is with them but is not defined by it as they are. In the interior monologues where he develops his more sophisticated ideas about love and life, he is able to isolate himself by reverting to his native American speech patterns. The novel's dialogue, however ingenious it is in reproducing Spanish language patterns, is too artificial for Hemingway to create any subtle nuances, and the way in which Jordan switches from one mode to the other only serves to remind the reader of the quaintness of Hemingway's Spanish characters. Hemingway never found it easy to appreciate the independent reality of anyone who was not a white Anglo-Saxon American male, and his novels are considerably weakened by his patronizing portraits of women, Jews, Blacks, and European peasants. In *For Whom the Bell Tolls* this weakness is most marked in his handling of Robert's lover, Maria, and the sections describing the development of the affair are embarrassingly bad. Here, for example, is part of their conversation just after their famous love-making that 'made the earth move':

> 'I love you rabbit', he said to the girl. 'What was it you were saying?'
> 'I was saying,' she told him, 'that you must not worry about your work because I will not worry you or interfere. If there is anything I can do you will tell me.'
> 'There's nothing,' he said. 'It is really very simple.'
> 'I will learn from Pilar what I should do to take care of a man well and those things I will do,' Maria said. 'Then, as I learn, I will discover things for myself and other things you can tell me.'
> 'There is nothing to do.'

'Que va, man, there is nothing! Thy sleeping robe, this morning, should have been shaken and aired and hung somewhere in the sun. Then, before the dew comes, it should be taken into shelter.'

'Go on rabbit.'

'Thy socks should be washed and dried. I would see thee had two pair.'

'What else?'

'If you would show me I would clean and oil thy pistol.'

'Kiss me,' Robert Jordan said. (13)

The flaw here is not simply that Hemingway fails to create a convincing woman, but that he creates a man who cannot believe in her reality either. This inability to appreciate or even imagine lives that are not governed by the code his heroes live by, nor are directed to the satisfaction of their basic needs, lies behind the failure of Hemingway's later fiction. Having finally recognized in *To Have and Have Not* that 'a man alone ain't got no bloody chance', and in *For Whom the Bell Tolls* that 'No man is an *Iland*, intire of it his selfe',[20] his misfortune was that he could not see how to make the connections between equals that would bring his heroes back into a viable community.

Some of Hemingway's contemporaries, though equally aware of the social and political pressures of the 1930s, made no attempt at all to make any rational adjustment, but instead embraced even more extreme versions of apocalyptic nihilism or individualistic fantasy. Novelists such as Henry Miller and Nathanael West, whose fiction was either ignored or condemned by the majority of socially conscious critics, only gained widespread recognition in America long after their best work had been completed, and in West's case, not until after his death. From his first two novels West earned only $780, and though Miller was told in 1946 by his French publisher that he had accumulated the equivalent of $40,000 in royalties, his books were for many years unavailable in America except to those who smuggled them in from Europe. And when *Tropic of Cancer* (1934) was eventually published in the USA in 1961, though it sold almost one and a half million copies in the first year, it also became the subject of a number of court actions during which its literary and pornographic features were hotly debated by both critics and lawyers.[21]

Characteristically, Miller went to live in Paris at the age of thirty-eight, just when the conditions that had attracted thousands of young Americans there in the previous decade – a buoyant economy at home and a favourable exchange rate – had disappeared. George Orwell, writing about the city in the late 1920s in 'Inside the Whale', contrasts the earlier ethos in which 'gruff-voiced lesbians in corduroy breeches and young men in Grecian or medieval costume hardly attracted a glance,' with the society of the lumpenproletarian fringe that Miller made his own: 'bug-ridden rooms in workingmen's hotels, cheap brothels, cobbled alleys full of reeking refuse and bistros with greasy zinc counters'.[22] This was a milieu in which Miller could finally escape the sense of failure produced in him by prolonged subjection to the American success ethic. Living in extreme poverty, dependent on the sporadic generosity of friends like Alfred Perlés and Anaïs Nin, his creative energies were finally liberated during a productive decade that saw the publication of *Tropic of Cancer* (1934), *Black Spring* (1936), *Max and the White Phagocytes* (1938), and *Tropic of Capricorn* (1938). In the last of these he felt able to return to America for his subject-matter, and began his long and vitriolic attack on the spiritual aridity responsible for producing what he called 'the air-conditioned nightmare'. But in his first years in Paris, the influences that shaped his work were European; stylistically he owes much to Surrealism and Dada. The content of his early fiction resembles that of Louis-Ferdinand Céline whose *Voyage, au bout de la Nuit* (1932) was published when Miller was revising the drafts of his first novel; and Céline's bitter tirades against civilization were buttressed philosophically for Miller by his discovery of Oswald Spengler's apocalyptic meditation *The Decline of the West*, and by his conversations with Michael Frankel whose philosophy of death introduces *Tropic of Cancer*:

> Boris had just given me a summary of his views. He is a weather prophet. The weather will continue bad, he says. There will be more calamities, more death, more despair. Not the slightest indication of a change anywhere. The cancer of time is eating us away. Our heroes have killed themselves, or are killing themselves. The hero, then, is not Time, but Timelessness. We must get in step, towards the prison of death. There is no escape. The weather will not change.
>
> (London, 1963, p. 1)

Miller, who is the autobiographical hero of all his fiction, continues in the belief that the whole world is caught in an inevitable process of dissolution – he pictures it as an enormous cancer eating itself away – and that only when everything has been drawn into the Womb of Time will Chaos be restored and Reality finally be written. The novel combines, then, overpoweringly realistic descriptions of this cancerous decay with the hero's ecstatic introspection as he joyfully welcomes the entropic drift towards non-being. The worse things become, as Miller burrows deeper and deeper into the squalor and animality of the Parisian underworld, the happier he grows. It is the unconditioned pleasure found in the most nauseous and degrading situations that makes *Tropic of Cancer* such a shocking novel. Miller himself calls it 'a gob of spit in the face of Art, a kick in the pants to God, Man, Destiny, Time, Love, Beauty . . . what you will'. His iconoclasm knows no limits, and if, as Orwell claims, this is an accurate dramatization of 'the real-politik of the inner mind', it is not difficult to understand why so many readers have found its truths hard to accept. In his determination to break through the 'illusions' with which men blind themselves to the 'hideousness of reality' – or as he puts it, 'create roses out of this dung-heap' – he gleefully blasphemes against every god that men have chosen to worship. For instance, after encouraging a young Hindu companion to defecate in a prostitute's bidet, much to the disgust of the girl and the other occupants of the cheap brothel they are visiting, Miller takes great pleasure in using the incident as the basis for one of his fantastic tirades against Christianity:

> And so I think what a miracle it would be if this
> miracle which man attends eternally should turn out to be
> nothing more than these two enormous turds which the
> faithful disciple dropped in the *bidet*. What if at the last
> moment, when the banquet table is set and the cymbals
> clash, there should appear suddenly, and wholly without
> warning, a silver platter in which even the blind could see
> that there is nothing more, and nothing less, than two
> enormous lumps of shit. That, I believe would be more
> miraculous than anything which man has looked forward
> to. (p. 97)

Faced with passages such as this, the question critics have tried to answer is posed directly by Frank Kermode when comparing the Baroque cast of Miller's thought with that of the English poet, Crashaw. How can one tell whether this kind of writing is art or piffle? he asks, and concludes that though Miller himself would see the question as unanswerable, his curious stylistic gifts do make him an artist of sorts, even if only a minor one.[23]

In the passage in which Miller speaks of his work as 'a gob of spit in the face of art', he also writes 'I am going to sing for you, a little off key perhaps, but I will sing. I will sing while you croak, I will dance over your dirty corpse. . . .' The dance of Miller's prose, like an elegant pirouette over a black abyss, suggests a partial answer to the question of his artistic worth. He is a painstaking craftsman but one whose writing retains the sense of a spontaneous charge of surrealist energy as he appears to move effortlessly from the scatological to the metaphysical:

> Slime wash and sapphires slipping, sluicing through the
> gay neurons, and the spectrum spliced and the gunwales
> dipping. Soft as lion-pad I heard the gun carriages turn,
> saw them vomit and drool: the firmament sagged and all
> the stars turned black. Black ocean bleeding and the
> brooding stars breeding chunks of fresh-swollen flesh
> while overhead the birds wheeled and out of the
> hallucinated sky fell the balance with mortar and pestle
> and the bandaged eyes of justice. (pp. 251–52)

Like his favourite American poet, Walt Whitman, of whom he says in *Nexus* (1960) that there will never be another like him in all the land, Miller is a visionary, and it is probably futile to try to judge him by conventional artistic standards. The fierce passions which he provokes in both his supporters and detractors are usually of a moral rather than an aesthetic intensity. They are conditioned more by basic affinities for or revulsion at the extreme romantic primitivism which is such an important element in Miller's work – one which unites him to the mainstream of modernist art while at the same time cutting him off completely from the narrower social world of America in the 1930s.

Nathanael West was in some ways equally at odds with the American ethos of the 1930s, though unlike Miller he chose to live and work in the USA and was even involved in the major social and political events that fuelled the imaginations of his contemporaries. As a member of the Screen Writers' Guild he took part in typical left-wing activities, was an ardent advocate of the American Writers' Congress in 1935, and of the Loyalist cause in the Spanish Civil War. His commitment to radical politics was as strong as that of any of his fellow writers, but in his case the economic upheavals and political conflicts of the Depression and the New Deal never found their way into his fiction. Stanley Edgar Hyman suggests that West was luckily unable to use such material for his art,[24] but this implies that he would have done so had he had the talent of Michael Gold or Daniel Fuchs. The truth is that he flatly rejected current ideas about proletarian writing and with them the whole tradition of documentary realism, choosing instead to render his world through the distorting prism of a complex and fragmented imagination. As Leslie Fiedler says, 'West's novels are a deliberate assault on the common man's notion of reality; for violence is not only his subject-matter, but also his technique'.[25]

West's literary apprenticeship, like Miller's, was served in Paris where he spent two years in the mid-1920s and, as Fiedler's comment suggests, his masters were the same Dadaists and Surrealists who influenced Miller so strongly. His antagonism to every American institution was every bit as violent as Miller's and was even exacerbated by a hatred of his American-Jewish inheritance. He was born Nathan Weinstein, but after experiencing the prejudices of snobbish fraternities at Brown University, decided to take Horace Greeley's advice literally to 'Go West, young man', and promptly changed his name. In his first novel, *The Dream Life of Balso Snell* (1931), completed during the late 1920s when he worked nights as an assistant manager in a New York hotel, West's alienation and consequent nihilism express themselves in episodes and images not unlike Miller's. Like *Tropic of Cancer*, the book is little more than a series of loosely related picaresque stories held together by a sketchy journey and a common interest in the more degrading and revolting aspects of the human condition. Like Miller, West effectively dehumanizes his characters by concentrating his attention on their animality, but where the two writers differ is in their tone. West's bald descriptions of the bizarre sexual and physiological elements of life have none of Miller's serenity but are pervaded by a deep, Swiftean hatred. At best, these powerful feelings are shaped by a mordant, ironic wit, but just as often this gives way to uncontrollable nausea, and the result is a series of juvenile scatalogical and sexual jokes as West contemplates the putrefaction of flesh – especially female flesh.

The novel is set in the bowels of the Trojan horse, which the hero has entered, appropriately enough, through its anus. As he journeys through the wooden horse's intestines he encounters a variety of characters whose different stories form the basis of West's wide-ranging satiric attacks on Judaism, Christianity, art, philosophy, and love. One after another these characters are made to reveal the nature of the dung-heap on which their respective 'roses' grow, and the novel ends when Balso has an apocalyptic wet dream in which his body finally breaks free from his mind in a death-like release that he calls 'the mechanics of decay'. Like Miller and the Dadaists, West's ultimate satiric thrust, undermining the very activity he is engaged in, is aimed at literature itself. In the course of his travels Balso reads a pamphlet written by a schoolboy, John Gilson, in which both the overt motivation of writers and the responses of their readers are exposed as hypocrisies, conditioned only by social or literary training and devoid of genuine spontaneity. Gilson confesses that as an artist he is only genuinely moved by sexual fantasies of a sado-masochistic kind or by a desire for revenge on his readers. He imagines himself writing a play for 'the discriminating few: art-lovers and book-lovers, schoolteachers who adore culture, lending librarians, publishers' assistants, homosexualists and homosexualists' assistants, hard-drinking newspapermen, interior decorators, and the writers of advertising copy'. The cast of this avant-garde play will end the evening by marching to the front of the stage to harangue the audience with Chekhov's famous dictum that 'It would be more profitable for the farmer to raise rats for the granary than for the bourgeois to nourish the artist, who must always be preoccupied with undermining institutions.' After this 'the ceiling of the theatre will be made to open and cover the occupants with tons of loose excrement. After the deluge, if they so desire, the patrons of my art can gather in the customary charming groups and discuss the play.'

Gilson's project reads like an early example of the Happenings which became so popular in the 1960s, in which audiences were often physically or sexually assaulted, splattered with paint, or pursued up the aisles of theatres by tractors. It is not surprising that West's work enjoyed its greatest success at that later time when it was seen as the first major contribution to the popular tradition of black humour. It was in the 1960s that his novels began to sell in large numbers, and even as early as 1962 Hyman noted that *Miss Lonelyhearts* (1933) had sold 190,000 copies in paperback and *The Day of the Locust* (1939) 250,000.[26]

In the year that *Miss Lonelyhearts* was published West wrote some notes on his second novel that make clear the work's modernist intentions and attack the concept of realism. Despite all the criticism and explication of West's work since, these notes are still the most helpful guide to his fiction available. He suggests that the book could be subtitled 'A novel in the form of a comic strip', and goes on:

> The chapters to be squares in which many things happen
> through one action. . . . Each chapter instead of going
> forward in time, also goes backward, forward, up and
> down in space like a picture. Violent images are used to
> illustrate commonplace events. Violent acts are left almost
> bald.

In typical modernist fashion he deserts diachronic narration in search of synchronicity, and in so doing dismisses the entire realist tradition:

> Forget the epic, the master work. In America fortunes do
> not accumulate, the soil does not grow, families have no
> history. Leave slow growth to the book reviewers, you
> only have time to explode.[27]

In remorselessly stripping away from the novel all its realistic appar-
atus, West finally rejects psychology, arguing that it 'has nothing to
do with reality' and dismissing it as a plausible motivation for his
characters. What we are left with, then, is a comic strip without any
discernible resemblance to the real world either in its characters or its
actions. Yet *Miss Lonelyhearts* has been universally acclaimed as a
masterpiece of modernist art and favourably compared with the work
of Kafka and T. S. Eliot. Indeed, Eliot's poem *The Waste Land* is a
probable source for the novel and it provides a clue to its essential
themes.

Like Eliot, West sees modern life – and possibly all life – as
manifesting the world's 'tropism for disorder, entropy'. His protagonist is a 'Lonely Hearts' columnist who has been driven almost to
despair and the edge of madness by the vision of pointless suffering
and evil which he encounters every day in the letters written by those
seeking his advice. The novel opens with three examples which make
it clear why he no longer finds such letters funny and feels 'heavy with
shadow'. The first is from 'Sick-of-it-all', a woman who, after bearing
seven children in twelve years, has been told by her doctor that another
may kill her, but whose Catholic husband does not believe in birth-
control or abortion and will not practise restraint. The second is from
'Desperate', a sixteen-year-old girl born with no nose – 'just a big hole
in the middle of my face' – who asks 'What did I do to deserve such
a terrible bad fate?' Finally, there is a letter from 'Harold S.', whose
thirteen-year-old sister has been raped and who dares not tell their
mother about it in case she beats the little girl up or locks her in the
closet. For Miss Lonelyhearts the answer to all this suffering and
wickedness is Christ, just as it was for Eliot. But West goes on to show
in the novel that the redemption promised by Christianity is just as
futile and illusory as the other forms of escape which men pursue: sex,
alcohol, art, or even love. Miss Lonelyhearts seeks temporary relief
from his despair in each of these, and West succeeds in generating
sympathy for him in his painful quest, but he also makes it perfectly
plain that the spiritual aridity of the modern Waste Land is too extreme
to be touched by such human palliatives. It has become part of nature,
itself, and the imagery used to describe this ideal land is very like
Eliot's:

> As far as he could discover, there were no signs of
> spring. The decay that covered the surface of the mottled
> ground was not the kind in which life generates. Last
> year, he remembered, May failed to quicken these soiled
> fields. It had taken all the brutality of July to torture a few
> green spikes through the exhausted dirt. (2)

Throughout the novel's action, Miss Lonelyhearts resists what he calls the 'Christ business', fearing the power of the emotions that are unleashed in him when he invokes the name of 'the Miss Lonelyhearts of Miss Lonelyhearts'. He knows that the people who write to him and think of him as their last hope do not share his inability to believe in the 'Christ dream', and he is cruelly torn between his scepticism and his need to assuage the suffering around him.

At the novel's climax, after he has failed in his efforts to help an embittered cripple, Peter Doyle, and his sadistic, nymphomaniacal wife, Miss Lonelyhearts finally accepts his role as Christ: 'He submitted drafts of his column to God and God approved them.' Full of humility, certain of his final conversion, and anxious to perform the miracle that will restore Doyle to wholeness, he rushes downstairs to embrace the cripple, only to be accidentally shot by him in what is perhaps the most pessimistic ending of any modern American novel. For West, man's need to discover an order with which to counter universal entropy, remains no more than that – a *need*, for which there is no objective correlative. Nevertheless, his recognition of the strength of man's desire for transcendence and his sympathetic exploration of the possibilities of achieving it, combine with an intellectual rejection of all the a alternatives to produce in *Miss Lonelyhearts* a minor satiric masterpiece.

West never again achieved a similar balance in his writing. His next novel, *A Cool Million* (1934), is at the same time his least realistic work and his most overtly political. It is constructed as a parodic inversion of the Horatio Alger 'rags to riches' myth, in which the hero, Lemuel Pitkin, is rewarded for his sobriety, honesty, and thrift by being cheated, robbed, beaten up, mutilated, and finally killed. His death comes as he is making a speech in support of American Fascism and serves to ensure the triumph of Shagpoke Whipple's Leather Shirt party. Whipple is partly based on Calvin Coolidge, whose famous pronouncement that 'the business of America is business' seemed particularly insensitive and callous at a time when millions of Americans were unemployed, and partly on William Dudley Pelley, whose 'Silver Shirts' was just one of a number of semi-Fascist organizations that sprang up in the Depression. Though West's treatment is parodic and farcical, the history of such totalitarian groups in America, committed as they were to super-patriotic isolationism and prepared to promote their ideals by violent means, testifies to a genuine threat to American democracy – one that seriously disturbed West, as it did most liberals at the time.

West's last novel, *The Day of the Locust* (1939), is set in Hollywood, the ultimate 'dream dump', a perfect microcosm for his final onslaught on the American nightmare. He called Hollywood 'a Sargasso of the imagination' and took delight in describing the unreal world of both the studio lots and the environments created for themselves by those who worked in them:

> He went through the swinging doors of the saloon. There
> was no back to the building and he found himself in a
> Paris street, He followed it to its end, coming out in a
> Romanesque courtyard. He heard voices a short distance
> away and went toward them. On a lawn of fiber, a group
> of men and women in riding costume were picnicking.
> They were eating cardboard food in front of a cellophane
> waterfall. (18)

It is a perfect setting for West's grotesque characters who are just as surreal as their surroundings: Faye Greener, the seventeen-year-old starlet, beautiful but hard and brainless; Earle Shoop, a cowboy with a two-dimensional face that a talented child might have drawn with a ruler and compass; a Hollywood Indian called Chief-Kiss-My-Towkus; and a vicious dwarf called Abe Kusich. These, together with Tod Hackett, a painter who dreams of executing one great work, 'The Burning of Los Angeles', and Homer Simpson, an innocent from the Midwest, act out a violent scenario which culminates in riot and murder. West makes no attempt in *The Day of the Locust* to create characters even as convincing as those in *Miss Lonelyhearts*, and no single figure in the novel elicits human interest, let alone sympathy. His original title for the book was *The Cheated*, by which he meant the anonymous mob of people who have come to California to die, and who stand on street-corners with their eyes full of hatred, staring at passers-by. In a sense these people remain at the centre of the novel and West's treatment of them is not at all comic. Nevertheless, they probably represent most accurately his final feelings about the achievements of American civilization:

> Their boredom becomes more and more terrible. They
> realise that they've been tricked and burn with resentment.
> Every day of their lives they read the newspapers and
> went to the movies. Both fed them on lynchings, murder,
> sex crimes, explosions, wrecks, love nests, fires, miracles,
> revolutions, wars. This daily diet made sophisticates of
> them. The sun is a joke. Oranges can't titillate their jaded
> palates. Nothing can ever be violent enough to make taut
> their slack minds and bodies. They have been cheated and
> betrayed. They have slaved and saved for nothing. (27)

West's art came full circle to end where it began – in a vision of overwhelming nihilism and despair. His own violent death in an automobile accident in 1941 brought his career to a sudden end in a sadly apposite manner.

West's Jewish contemporary, Henry Roth, whose single novel *Call it Sleep* was published in 1934, was also rediscovered in the 1960s after years of neglect. So completely had he been forgotten since his withdrawal from the American literary scene that his name was simply omitted from a massive encyclopaedia of American literature published in 1962.[28] In the following year, however, when his book was finally reissued, it quickly established itself as a work of genius and was generally hailed as such by major American and European critics. Within a few years it had sold almost a million copies.

It is not difficult to understand why *Call it Sleep* failed to satisfy the taste of the literary establishment in the 1930s. Though it bears all the marks of a proletarian novel – descriptions of the poverty and brutality of life in a New York ghetto – it is in fact anything but that, and a contemporary reviewer in the *New Masses* was fairly typical in lamenting that young writers such as Roth chose to make no better use of their working-class experience than as material for 'introspective and febrile' novels. Praising the book almost thirty years later for those same qualities, Leslie Fiedler goes on to generalize interestingly about the common threads that held modernist writing together at the time, and also served to make it so unpopular: 'one realises suddenly how in the time of the Great Depression all the more serious fictionists yearned in secret to touch a religious note, toying with the messianic and the apocalyptic but refusing to call them by names not honored in the left-wing journals of the time.'[29]

This perfectly describes the central issue of *Call it Sleep*, just as it does that of *Miss Lonelyhearts*. Fiedler might in fact have had West in mind when formulating his statement, for in trying to define the uniquely Jewish combination of materialism and idealism in Roth, he quotes C. M. Doughty's epigram that West also uses in *Balso Snell*: 'The Semites are like to a man sitting in a cloaca to the eyes, and whose brows touch heaven.'

Though Roth's vision of life is not at all scatological, nor his purpose satiric, like West, he does insist on rooting his characters' lives in their own physicality. What he is most concerned to create, though, is the disordered consciousness of a child, crammed with the fragmented images of a coarse and brutal world which he can neither properly relate to nor understand. Apart from a passage of objective description at the beginning of the novel recounting the boy's arrival in America, and a Joycean montage of voices at the end, everything in the book is filtered through the consciousness of young David

Schearl. Unlike his elders, who are busy trying to make their dreams real, David can hardly tell where reality ends and dreams begin. He inhabits a sharply perceived but dimly understood territory between the cellar and roof of his tenement block – rats, violence, and the terrors of sexuality below, and God, magic, and beauty above – though the two extremes are never entirely distinct:

> The immense heavens of July, the burnished, the
> shining fathom upon fathom. Too pure the zenith was,
> too pure for the flawed and flinching eye; the eye sowed it
> with linty darkness, sowed it with spores and ripples of
> shadow drifting. (– Even up here dark follows, but only a
> little bit.) And to the west, the blinding whorl of sun, the
> disk and trumpet, triple-trumpet blaring light. He blinked,
> dropped his eyes and looked about him. Quiet. Odor of
> ashes, the cold subterranean breath of chimneys. (– Even
> up here cellar follows, but only a little bit.) And about
> were roof-tops to the scarred horizon. Flocks of pigeons
> wheeled. Where they flew in lower air, they hung like a
> poised and never-raveling smoke; nearer at hand and
> higher, they glittered like rippling water in the sun. (4:5)

The quality of Roth's prose is itself sufficient to distinguish his work from that of most of his contemporaries, but it is also the vehicle which, while not ignoring social actuality, subsumes it in darker and more primitive aspects of existence.

The dialectical tension which we have observed in the fiction of West and Roth between various manifestations of materialism and idealism, is not the prerogative solely of Jewish thought. Twentieth-century Americans in general appear to experience a similar ambivalence toward their society and its spiritual goals. And though Jewish tradition has had a powerful impact on American culture, many modernist writers have also drawn on other sources to flesh out similar philosophical structures. It is, for example, a truism of recent literary criticism that Scott Fitzgerald's *The Great Gatsby* achieves its remarkable poise through a delicate balance between celebration and denigration of the American Dream; its author moving confidently back and forwards between his descriptions of vulgar materialism and romantic idealism, and proving what a fine line often separates the two. Edwin Fussell goes further than this in claiming that Fitzgerald's ability to juxtapose the two kinds of sensibility involved is the very source of his excellence, reaching its full maturity when individual aspiration is elevated to the level of national destiny.[30]

There is some evidence, too, that Fitzgerald himself held views like these, at least in so far as he thought of his art as the product of intellect. His characteristic love of ambivalence can be seen in his paraphrase of Keats's idea of 'negative capability': 'The test of a first-rate intelligence', he maintained, 'is the ability to hold two opposed ideas in the mind, at the same time, and still retain the ability to function.'

In his first novel, *This Side of Paradise* (1920), he showed little ability to do this, though towards the end when his autobiographical hero, Amory Blaine, is taking stock of his mental and emotional education, Fitzgerald tries very hard to initiate an interior debate that will somehow link Amory's adolescent musings to larger intellectual and cultural concerns. Having likened himself to Goethe and Conrad, in contrast to Plato and H. G. Wells, Amory quickly loses the thread of his argument, decides that 'Life was a damned muddle', and sinks back into his customary romantic melancholy. The young Fitzgerald seems equally unwilling or unable to pursue the line of thought he has started, and instead abruptly terminates the passage with one of his characteristic images:

> Another dawn flung itself across the river; a belated taxi
> hurried along the street, its lamps still shining like burning
> eyes in a face white from a night's carouse. A melancholy
> siren sounded far down the river. (2:5)

The chapter from which this quotation is taken is misleadingly entitled 'The Egotist becomes a Personage'. Amory Blaine remains a simple egotist to the end, and though this partly helps to account for the novel's failure, it also suggests why *This Side of Paradise* became something of a cult work for young people in the 1920s, its popularity having been likened to that of Salinger's *The Catcher in the Rye* in the 1960s. Amory's unceasing fascination with his own emotional states, together with Fitzgerald's marvellous eye for what has since been called 'status detail' – the various elements that make up a subculture's lifestyle – helped contemporary college boys and flappers to acknowledge their feelings more easily and confirmed their adolescent experiences as being somehow more 'authentic'. In 'The Author's Apology', distributed with early editions of the novel, Fitzgerald said his theory was that authors should write for the youth of their own generation and for critics of the next. And in reply to an accusation made by John Peale Bishop that he appeared to take seventeen as the norm and see all subsequent life as a falling away from perfection, Fitzgerald is reputed to have retorted: 'If you make it fifteen I will agree with you.'[31]

Fitzgerald's artistic credo had not really changed by the time he wrote his next novel, *The Beautiful and Damned* (1922). Though the glitter of the Jazz Age is presented now as somewhat tarnished and his hero and heroine are a little older and the worse for wear, the air of exuberant celebration that pervaded his earlier work is still the most arresting feature of his style, as contemporary reviewers were quick to point out. One of them, writing a piece anonymously for the *Philadelphia Public Ledger* under the heading '"The Beautiful and Damned" Reveals One Phase of Jazz-Vampire Period in Gilded Panorama of Reckless Life', describes Fitzgerald's achievement fairly accurately when he says, 'He has ended by making vice, loose living, sex, red liquor and twelve cylinder cars much less hateful than he intended, or maybe not. Certainly, he spares no intimate touch of bedroom, lingerie, sex contacts, perfume, alcohol and other excitants.'[32]

What is perhaps more interesting in view of Fitzgerald's later development is that most of those same reviewers also read *The Beautiful and Damned* as a work of naturalism, and made unfavourable comparisons between Fitzgerald's attempts to dramatize the decline of his hero and heroine and Dreiser's story of Carrie and Hurstwood or Edith Wharton's *The Custom of the Country*. If the novel is judged in this way as a pseudo-social document, it certainly does have both moral and aesthetic shortcomings. Fitzgerald is too impatient to create characters who are slowly moulded and motivated by their continuing relationships and the environments in which they move. On the contrary, Anthony Patch and his wife, Gloria, rush headlong towards their 'damnation' in what Fitzgerald calls a 'glamorous confusion':

> Outwardly they showed no sign of deterioration. Gloria
> at twenty-six was still the Gloria of twenty; her
> complexion a fresh damp setting for her candid eyes; her
> hair still a childish glory, darkening slowly from a corn
> colour to a deep russet gold; her slender body suggesting
> ever a nymph running and dancing through Orphic
> groves. Masculine eyes, dozens of them, followed her with
> a fascinated stare when she walked through a hotel lobby
> or down the aisle of a theatre. Men asked to be introduced
> to her, fell into prolonged states of sincere admiration,
> made definite love to her – for she was still a thing of
> exquisite and unbelievable beauty. And for his part
> Anthony had rather gained than lost in appearance; his face
> had taken on a certain intangible air of tragedy,
> romantically contrasted with his trim and immaculate
> person. (2:3)

It is quite in keeping with this tone when Fitzgerald finally rescues the young couple at the end of the novel, bestowing thirty million dollars on Anthony and leaving them to sail away in a fairy-tale ending on the *Berengaria*.

It must be said, too, that Fitzgerald himself could not always decide just where his true talents lay, and even after the publication of *The Great Gatsby* he was still inclined occasionally to revert to his earlier and more pedestrian mode of realism. Part of the difficulty he had with the structure of *Tender is the Night* (1934) stemmed from his desire to give it a more realistic form, and similar uncertainties are apparent throughout his notes for *The Last Tycoon*.

Even when writing *The Great Gatsby*, Fitzgerald had toyed with the idea of including one of his early stories in order to fill out the picture of his hero's early life. Luckily he preferred to retain the sense of mystery that is so essential to the character and allows him to take on representative or even mythic significance. Eventually the reader *is* allowed to piece together something of Gatsby's real background from remarks dropped by a variety of witnesses and speculators, but only after Gatsby has presented his own romantic version of it – 'a Platonic conception of himself' – to the narrator, Nick Carraway.

They are driving to Manhattan in Gatsby's cream Rolls-Royce, a fit setting for Gatsby's memoirs which comprise an education at Oxford – 'a family tradition'; travels in Europe and Africa hunting jewels and big game; war service for which he was decorated by 'every Allied government – even Montenegro'; and all of this time spent 'trying to forget something very sad that happened to me long ago'.

This sad event – the only true part of Gatsby's account – was his rejection by Daisy Fay, and we learn more about this later in the novel from Jordan Baker, herself not an entirely reliable narrator. Gatsby had unsuccessfully wooed Daisy years before in Louisville, but true to type she had retreated back to her 'rich, full life' to marry Tom Buchanan who, the day before their wedding, gave her a string of pearls worth three hundred and fifty thousand dollars. Gatsby is now determined to buy back his lost love, wipe out the intervening years, and start all over again. His attempts to do so form the plot of the novel, and the means by which he gets the money to undertake his romantic quest constitute his true history. It is yet another version of the Horatio Alger myth, with Gatsby, then James Gatz, learning how to take advantage of the main chance under the tutelage of tycoons like Dan Cody and crooks such as Wolfsheim, a denizen of Broadway and the man who fixed the World Series in baseball in 1919.

All this information is presented with superb economy as it filters through the consciousness of Nick Carraway, a Midwesterner who represents an older, more stable, and more innocent American society. Nick, who tells us that he had returned from the First World War demanding that the world remain for ever at 'a sort of moral attention' admits that 'if personality was a series of uninterrupted gestures, there was something gorgeous about Gatsby'. And he goes on to identify this quality more specifically as 'a romantic readiness for hope' greater than any he had ever seen.

At first, Nick, and the reader whose responses he guides, is critical of Gatsby's preposterous gesturings, though he gradually comes to appreciate the sheer spiritual power of the man and his incorruptible illusions. However vulgar or meretricious the object of Gatsby's quest and however much 'foul dust' floats in the wake of his dreams, he is, Nick finally discovers, worth the whole bunch of his hangers-on put together.

It is Fitzgerald's triumph in the novel not only to convince the reader of this truth but also to link it with a larger one about America itself. The 'foul dust' surrounding Gatsby is of course identified with Jazz Age society as a whole, and in his evocation of it Fitzgerald brilliantly satirizes its shallow materialism, creating the layered ironies so conspicuously missing in his earlier fiction. He can, for example, suggest the grotesque, surreal life of the American upper class more tellingly than Nathanael West and without lapsing into farce:

> Even when the East excited me most, even when I was
> most keenly aware of its superiority to the bored,
> sprawling, swollen towns beyond the Ohio, with their
> interminable inquisitions which spared only the children
> and the very old – even then it had always for me a
> quality of distortion. West Egg, especially, still figures in
> my more fantastic dreams. I see it as a night scene by El
> Greco: a hundred houses, at once conventional and
> grotesque, crouching under a sullen, overhanging sky and
> a lustreless moon. In the foreground four solemn men in
> dress suits are walking along the sidewalk with a stretcher
> on which lies a drunken woman in a white evening dress.
> Her hand, which dangles over the side, sparkles cold with
> jewels. Gravely the men turn in at a house – the wrong
> house. But no-one knows the woman's name, and no-one
> cares. (9)

Through symbolism, he can also, like T. S. Eliot, suggest the aridity of the waste land that modern society was becoming, and his famous image of Dr T. J. Eckleburg's blank eyes brooding over the Valley of Ashes from an oculist's advertising billboard, also hangs over the entire novel.

Fitzgerald's unique ability, though, is shown best in the way he employs camera-like techniques in such scenes as the one in which he rapidly surveys and unerringly places the individuals who make up Gatsby's famous parties:

> The large room was full of people. One of the girls in
> yellow was playing the piano, and beside her stood a tall,
> red-haired young lady from a famous chorus, engaged in
> song. She had drunk a quantity of champagne, and during
> the course of her song she had decided, inaptly, that
> everything was very, very sad – she was not only singing,
> she was weeping too. Whenever there was a pause in the
> song she filled it with gasping, broken sobs, and then took
> up the lyric again in a quavering soprano. The tears
> coursed down her cheeks – not freely, however, for when
> they came into contact with her heavily beaded eyelashes
> they assumed an inky colour, and pursued the rest of their
> way in slow black rivulets. . . .
> Most of the remaining women were now having fights
> with men said to be their husbands. Even Jordan's party,
> the quartet from East Egg, were rent asunder by
> dissension. One of the men was talking with curious
> intensity to a young actress, and his wife, after attempting
> to laugh at the situation in a dignified and indifferent way,
> broke down entirely and resorted to flank attacks. (3)

Images such as these provide the essential ballast of the novel, against which the reader is invited to judge Gatsby himself.

Gradually, however, it becomes apparent that Gatsby's ability to transcend the sordid materialism of his world, and even to annihilate time itself, is a romantic illusion that had begun to crumble at the very moment he first took Daisy in his arms to make his dream come true:

> His heart beat faster and faster as Daisy's white face
> came up to his own. He knew that when he kissed this
> girl, and forever wed his unutterable visions to her
> perishable breath, his mind would never romp again like
> the mind of God. So he waited, listening for a moment
> longer to the tuning fork that had been struck upon a star.
> Then he kissed her. At his lips' touch she blossomed for
> him like a flower and the incarnation was complete. (6)

Gatsby's innate aristocracy – his fineness of soul – eventually proves an insufficient protection against the brutal carelessness of people like the Buchanans. He dies in his own swimming-pool, shot by the husband of Tom's mistress, who in turn had been accidentally killed by Daisy. Gatsby's dream had become a nightmare. Like the American Dream itself, it had failed to withstand the terrible pressure of reality:

> Most of the big shore places were closed now and there were hardly any lights except the shadowy, moving glow of a ferryboat across the Sound. And as the moon rose higher the inessential houses began to melt away until I became aware of the old island here that flowered once for Dutch sailors' eyes – a fresh, green breast of the new world. Its vanished trees that had made way for Gatsby's house, had once pandered in whispers to the last and greatest of all human dreams; for a transitory enchanted moment man must have held his breath in the presence of this continent, compelled into an aesthetic contemplation he neither understood nor desired, face to face for the last time in history with something commensurate to his capacity for wonder. (9)

In the nine years that separate *The Great Gatsby* from *Tender is the Night*, Fitzgerald's life changed dramatically in a way that now seems symptomatic of the larger changes that were transforming the very nature of American society. In the 1920s Scott and his wife Zelda had somehow contrived always to stay at the leading edge of the Jazz-Age generation, gay and frivolous exemplars of a certain kind of post-war abandon. It hardly seemed to matter whether they were in New York, riding on top of taxi-cabs and jumping into the Washington Square fountain, or getting up to similar tricks in Paris or on the Riviera; wherever they went they took with them a whole generation's idea of itself. All this changed in 1930, when Zelda had her first schizophrenic breakdown – the first of several she was to suffer during that decade. Fitzgerald was haunted by a sense of guilt, believing that their former life-style had been a contributory factor, and he too began to deteriorate both physically and mentally. He described his own breakdown or 'crack-up' as he called it, in a series of essays written for *Esquire*, and in his letters of the time he confessed to friends that his life had dwindled into a round of 'gin, cigarettes, bromides and hope'. It is hardly surprising that such legendary lives as these should have attracted the attention of so many biographers,[33] but apart from its intrinsic interest, Fitzgerald's life is also the essential source material for *Tender is the Night*.

In his excellent essay on the novel Arthur Mizener makes a general comment about Fitzgerald that should be considered beside that of Fussell, cited earlier: 'The tension', Mizener argues, between Fitzgerald's 'inescapable commitment to the inner reality of his imagination and his necessary respect for the outer reality of the world is what gives his fiction its peculiar charm and is the source of his ability to surround a convincing representation of the actual world with an air of enchantment that makes the most ordinary occasions haunting.'[34] The predominance of one or other of these two aspects of Fitzgerald's personality and art – commitment to inner or outer reality – is the root cause of the two different versions we possess of *Tender is the Night*. In its original form Fitzgerald trusts the reader to cope with mystery and the distortions of a subjective point of view, just as he had in *The Great Gatsby*. Book One affords an impressionistic glimpse of Dick Diver's world through the eyes of a young Hollywood starlet, Rosemary Hoyt, with whom he is about to start an affair. It is a world held together only by the force of Dick's incredible charisma, which is highlighted by contrasting satiric portraits of the rich and envious expatriates excluded from his magic circle. Fitzgerald's quick 'snapshots' of these people – for example, that of Al McKisco, a writer working on a novel based on *Ulysses*, 'Only instead of taking twenty-four hours [he] takes a hundred years' (1:2) – are, if anything, even harsher than those in his earlier fiction.

At this stage we have no objective information about the background to the events we witness, no knowledge of Dick's history or that of his wife, and few clues as to the nature of their relationship. Like Gatsby, and, if Mizener is right, like Fitzgerald too, Dick imparts his own values and sense of reality to everything within his orbit:

> . . . to be included in Dick Diver's world for a while was a
> remarkable experience: people believed he made special
> reservations about them, recognising the proud uniqueness
> of their destinies, buried under the compromises of how
> many years. He won everyone quickly with an exquisite
> consideration and a politeness that moved so fast and
> intuitively that it could be examined only in its effect.
> Then, without caution, lest the first bloom of the relation
> wither, he opened the gate to his amusing world. So long
> as they subscribed to it completely, their happiness was his
> preoccupation, but at the first flicker of doubt as to its all-
> inclusiveness he evaporated before their eyes, leaving little
> communicable memory of what he had said or done. (1:6)

In his revision of the book, undertaken shortly before he died, Fitzgerald rearranged the material drastically, so that the episodes involving Rosemary come at their correct chronological place, and the novel begins with a straightforward account of Dick Diver's early career as a psychiatrist and the events which led to his being 'bought' by the wealthy Warren family as a doctor-cum-husband for the mentally ill Nicole. Dick's life in Europe thus becomes part of his long decline, as his energy and talents are ruthlessly used up by the egotistical Nicole and as she gradually recovers to free herself of her need for him.

When he made these changes, Fitzgerald felt that he had restored the novel's 'true' beginning, and Malcolm Cowley, who eventually put them into effect in a 1951 edition, suggests in his introduction to it that the later version is a more 'effective' novel. It is certainly a more conventional one, but what is lost in the new text is the way in which Dick Diver's magical vitality, so concretely rendered in the Rosemary Hoyt section, is made to account not only for his initial act of undertaking Nicole's cure, but also for doing so as her husband against the advice of his medical colleagues. In the original version, seeing Dick's power first through the eyes of Rosemary, we can better appreciate the impulses that led him to choose the life he did. This remains true even when we realize that the very act of allowing himself to fall in love with the girl signals one of those 'lesions of vitality' that will eventually destroy him. Indeed, this realization actually helps us to sympathize even more with him and to understand what some readers find inexplicable: Fitzgerald's insistence on the causal connection between Dick's emotional and spiritual generosity and his inevitable fate.

For those critics who reject Fitzgerald's notion of a reservoir of finite, expendable talent and energy, or his general ideas about psychology, Nicole's return to mental health in the novel is just as unconvincing as Dick's decline. What she represents, however, is the materialism on the opposite side of Fitzgerald's habitual equation. Where Dick creates value and reality in his world, she uses the outer world to create value and a sense of reality in herself. Like Tom and Daisy Buchanan, Nicole embodies all the crass materialism of modern life – a materialism that will always kill the spirit. She is, Fitzgerald says, 'a person to whom nothing need be explained and one to whom nothing *could* be explained':

> Nicole was the product of much ingenuity and toil. For her sake trains began their run at Chicago and traversed the round belly of the continent to California; chicle factories fumed and link belts grew link by link in factories; men mixed toothpaste in vats and drew mouthwash out of copper hogsheads; girls canned tomatoes quickly in August or worked rudely at the Five-and-Tens on Christmas Eve; half-breed Indians toiled on Brazilian coffee plantations and dreamers were muscled out

of patent rights in new tractors – these were some of the
people who gave a tithe to Nicole, and as the whole
system swayed and thundered onward it lent a feverish
bloom to such processes as hers as wholesale buying. . . .
She illustrated very simple principles, containing in herself
her own doom, but illustrated them so accurately that
there was grace in the procedure. (1:12)

Dick Diver's 'doom' is, appropriately enough in a novel published
in the middle of the Great Depression, not so dramatic as Gatsby's,
nor is it in any way heroic. He has, like many Americans at the time,
become part of the slow drift towards obscurity, in his case practising
medicine in small towns in up-state New York, moving from one to
another as he is pursued by petty sexual scandals and professional
lawsuits.

Scott Fitzgerald's own career never fully recovered, either, after his
crack-up. He worked sporadically in Hollywood, wrote some fine
short stories, and began, but never finished his Hollywood novel, *The
Last Tycoon*. He died in California, one day before Nathanael West,
on 21 December, 1941.

Notes

1. See Irving Howe, *The Decline of the New* (London, 1971), pp. 3–33.

2. Hugh Kenner, *A Homemade World: The American Modernist Writers* (New York, 1975).

3. Reprinted in *Look at Me Now and Here I Am: Writings and Lectures 1909–1945*, edited by Patricia Meyerowitz (Harmondsworth, 1971), pp. 84–98.

4. William Gass's essay, 'Gertrude Stein and the Geography of the Sentence', treats this aspect of her language. It is reprinted in his collection, *The World Within the Word* (New York, 1978), pp. 63–123.

5. Richard Poirier, *A World Elsewhere: The Place of Style in American Literature* (London, 1967), pp. 3–49.

6. *Look at Me Now and Here I Am*, p. 98.

7. See for example Claude-Edmonde Magny, *The Age of the American Novel: The Film Aesthetic of Fiction Between the Two Wars*, translated by Eleanor Hochman (New York, 1972).

8. Quotations are taken from the abridged version of the novel as this is the only one currently available.

9. See Edmund Wilson, *Axel's Castle* (New York, 1931), and Ben Reid, *Art by Subtraction: A Dissenting Opinion of Gertrude Stein* (Norman, Okla., 1958).

10. Michael J. Hoffman, *The Development of Abstractionism in the Writings of Gertrude Stein* (Philadelphia, 1965).

11. The hitherto unpublished chapters of *The Sun Also Rises*, and the 'Letter to Ernest Hemingway on *The Sun Also Rises*' by Scott Fitzgerald, are printed together in *Antaeus*, 33 (Spring 1979), 7–18.

12. In England the novel was published under the title, *Fiesta*.

13. See David Lodge's essay on Hemingway's use of metaphor and metonymy and the relation of these devices to elements of modernism and realism in his fiction, *The Modes of Modern Writing* (London, 1979), pp.155–9.

14. See his Introduction to the *Modern Standard Authors* edition (New York, 1962), p. xxix.

15. See his 'Homage to Hemingway', in *After the Genteel Tradition: American Writers 1910–1930*, edited by Malcolm Cowley (Carbondale and Edwardsville, Ill. 1964), pp. 147–58.

16. Leslie Fiedler, *Waiting for the End: The American Literary Scene from Hemingway to Baldwin* (Harmondsworth, 1967), p. 37.

17. See, for example, Malcolm Cowley, who calls *For Whom the Bell Tolls* Hemingway's richest and best novel, *A Second Flowering: Works and Days of the Lost Generation* (New York, 1973), p. 251, and Claude-Edmonde Magny who praises its 'multi-dimensional prose' and claims it is 'a true novel in which the instant gets denser in duration', *Age of the American Novel*, p. 150.

18. Cleanth Brooks, *The Hidden God* (New Haven and London, 1963), p. 18.

19. Kenner, p. 151.

20. Hemingway uses this passage from John Donne as the epigraph for the novel.

21. An account of the novel's history in America, together with extracts from the testimonies of literary critics in various trials are published in *Henry Miller and the Critics*, edited by George Wickes (Carbondale and Edwardsville, Ill. 1963), pp. 149–86.

22. Orwell's essay is reprinted in *Henry Miller and the Critics*, pp. 31–43.

23. 'Henry Miller and John Betjeman: Puzzles and Epiphanies', reprinted in *Henry Miller: Three Decades of Criticism*, edited by Edward Mitchell (New York, 1971), pp. 85–95.

24. See *Nathanael West*, University of Minnesota Pamphlets on American Writers, no. 21 (Minneapolis, 1962), p. 10.

25. See *Love and Death in the American Novel*, revised edition (Harmondsworth, 1984), p. 486.

26. Hyman, *Nathanael West*, p. 11.

27. These notes were originally published in *Contempo*, 3, no. 9 (May 1933) and are reprinted in *Nathanael West: A Collection of Critical Essays*, edition by Jay Martin: (Englewood Cliffs, NJ, 1971), pp. 66–7.

28. Max J. Herzberg, *The Reader's Encyclopedia of American Literature* (New York, 1962).

29. Leslie Fiedler, 'Henry Roth's Neglected Masterpiece', in *Unfinished Business* (New York, 1972), pp. 79–87.

30. Edwin Fussell, 'Fitzgerald's Brave New World', *ELH*, 19 (December 1952). The essay is reprinted in *F. Scott Fitzgerald: A Collection of Critical Essays*, edited by Arthur Mizener (Englewood Cliffs, NJ, 1963), pp. 43–56.

31. Quoted by Charles E. Shain, '*This Side of Paradise*', in F. Scott Fitzgerald: A Collection of Critical Essays, p. 79.

32. A selection of review is reprinted in a collection of documents, *F. Scott Fitzgerald in His Own Time: A Miscellany*, edited by Matthew J. Bruccoli and Jackson R. Bryer (Kent, Ohio, 1971).

33. See, for example, Arthur Mizener, *The Far Side of Paradise* (Boston, 1951), Andrew Turnbull, *Scott Fitzgerald* (New York, 1962), and Andre le Vot, *F. Scott Fitzgerald* (Paris, 1979; Harmondsworth, 1985).

34. Mizener's essay, originally published in his *Twelve Great American Novels* (New York, 1967), is reprinted in *Tender is the Night: Essays in Criticism*, edited by Marvin J. LaHood (Bloomington, Ind., 1969), pp. 102–16.

Chapter 12
William Faulkner

The fact that Faulkner has been singled out from other twentieth-century novelists, and his work allocated an entire chapter, is not intended primarily as an indication of his literary pre-eminence. It is true that, since his death in 1962, his reputation has continued to grow steadily and that there are many critics who now think of him as his country's greatest modern writer. The quality of his fiction then, together with its massive volume, would justify separate treatment as would its notorious difficulty. In the context of this particular history of the American novel, however, Faulkner presents additional problems which can best be tackled by separating him from his contemporaries.

At the same time, it should be borne in mind that Faulkner could fit – if not comfortably – into any one of a number of categories. As a Southern regionalist, his fiction has definite affinities with that of Erskine Caldwell, Ellen Glasgow, and even Thomas Wolfe. Its connections reach back, moreover, into an older tradition of Southern folk art, of nineteenth-century oratory, and even of the frontier 'tall tale'. Faulkner is first and foremost a Southerner who spent his entire life chronicling his own region, and, for a great many readers, Yoknapatawpha County, Mississippi, is as synonymous with the South as Hardy's Wessex is with nineteenth-century rural England.

Such comparisons sufficiently indicate, too, Faulkner's links with an American tradition of realism. But when seen in a broader focus, his art relates more naturally to the style and techniques of international Modernism. As a young poet, he came under the spell of the French *Symbolistes*, and there are aspects of his prose that retain those traces as well as echoes of the European Decadents whose influence continued to exert itself in America well into the twentieth century. More importantly, Faulkner came to maturity in the decade which saw the publication of James Joyce's *Ulysses* and Marcel Proust's *Remembrance of Things Past*. Faulkner's first major works, *The Sound and the Fury* (1929) and *As I Lay Dying* (1930), could hardly have achieved their characteristic structuring of space and time or their fragmented narrative techniques without these or similar precedents. Later, Faulkner would absorb these powerful influences more thoroughly and combine them with others to produce his unique masterpieces of the 1930s, *Light in August* (1932) and *Absalom, Absalom!* (1936); but even as a 'home-made' variety of modernism, his fiction still shares more similarities with that of his European contemporaries than does that of his fellow American modernists.

As well as all this, Faulkner's work – especially when seen in its totality as a continuous saga – can' legitimately claim to constitute another 'epic of America', even though some critics would deny this on grounds of its narrow, insistent focus on a microcosmic 'postage stamp of native soil' in provincial Mississippi. If one accepts, however, that there was more than a little truth in Hawthorne's contention that the North and the South were two distinct nations in the nineteenth century, and remembers, furthermore, that for Faulkner there is no separation possible between past and present, such geographical or temporal limitations lose their significance and Malcolm Cowley is right to call him 'an epic or bardic poet in prose'.[1] The myths he weaves into a legend of the South also serve to give substance to what can properly be called a national spirit. Faulkner later came to make even more grandiose claims for himself, and said in an interview towards the end of his life: 'I like to think of the world I created as being a kind of keystone in the universe; that, small as the keystone is, if it were ever taken away, the universe itself would collapse.'[2] In elevating his work from epic to cosmic proportion, Faulkner has been followed by a multitude of critics who see in it much larger symbolic meanings similar to those he deliberately incorporated into one of his weaker novels, *A Fable* (1954), where he attempted for once to move outside his familiar local territory.

For all these reasons, then, Faulkner is hard to categorize. But there are further difficulties too. For one thing, his career did not come to an end neatly at the beginning of the Second World War but was energetically pursued during and after it. This, in itself, is not significant but it does suggest a greater problem, which is hinted at in Hugh Kenner's description of Faulkner as the 'Last Novelist'.[3] Though he lived and worked on into a period now designated as 'post-modern', Faulkner was, Kenner believes, the last American writer whose procedures still retained traces of their roots in the nineteenth century's 'confident positivism'; the last of a long line who believed that, whatever else they were doing, they were also bringing 'news' to their readers, that their work contained in its distillations of style and point of view an essential residue of factual information about the actual world. But even as Faulkner was completing his life's work – so the argument goes – a new form of writing was appearing; a 'literature of exhaustion', in which the epistemological doubts of the modernists were taken to their logical conclusions in texts which pointed to nothing beyond themselves, or at best possibly to other texts; but in either case having no more 'significance' or meaning than books of random-number tables generated by computers. After Faulkner, the novel came to an impasse, either a temporary resting-place or possibly a permanent dead end, in the linguistic games played by Vladimir Nabokov, John Barth, and Thomas Pynchon.

A very different view, which is hinted at in John Irwin's recent study of Faulkner,[4] sees him not so much as the last representative of a tradition, but as one of those – perhaps even the first – completely to substitute structure for substance in his fiction, to pursue shadows instead of acts, and to subsume the world to the word. Irwin reads Faulkner's novels as literary analogues of Freud's psychology and Nietzsche's philosophy, in which doubling, repetition, recollection, repression, mediation, reversal, and substitution are used to describe not the world as it is, but only the ways in which our unconscious minds perceive it and our consciousness expresses it. In writing about meaning or its absence in Faulkner's work, he argues, for example, that the relation between the author and his book is like that between his narrator and his story, embodying 'the always deferredness' of meaning; an act of narration to produce a story that almost makes sense but not quite. No doubt Irwin had in mind here Faulkner's own comments about the composition of *The Sound and the Fury*, and his remarks accurately describe the author's continuous urge to revise and extend his text. There are many, however, who would argue that the published works, in spite of all – or indeed because of – their broken narratives, do create meanings, though not of course just in the events of their stories.

The equal plausibility of these various interpretations indicates sufficiently well the difficulty of assigning Faulkner a definitive place in literary history. There is also the problem mentioned earlier that he creates even for readers who are not concerned to relate him to other writers or literary movements, but simply to understand him. Not only does his narrative technique, with its complex strategies for concealing one person's story within another's, make for difficulties of comprehension, but these are exacerbated by his constant urge 'to put everything into one sentence – not only the present but the whole past on which it depends and which keeps over-taking the present, second by second'. The structural and stylistic intransigence of Faulkner's prose is often greater, even, than that of Henry James, and it is compounded by an even more eccentric vocabulary, syntax, and punctuation. The opening sentence of *Absalom, Absalom!* has some of these peculiarities, though there are many more obscure ones scattered throughout the works, sometimes extending to more than a thousand words:

> From a little after two o'clock until almost sundown of
> the long hot weary dead September afternoon they sat in
> what Miss Coldfield still called the office because her
> father had called it that – a dim hot airless room with the
> blinds all closed and fastened for forty-three summers
> because when she was a girl someone had believed that
> light and moving air carried heat and that dark was always
> colder, and which (as the sun shone fuller and fuller on
> that side of the house) became latticed with yellow slashes
> full of dust motes which Quentin thought of as being
> flecks of the dead old dried paint itself blown inward from
> the scaling blinds as wind might have blown them. (1)

In this passage we are only brought into one of the two characters' consciousnesses after a digression into the past which tells us something of Miss Coldfield's relations with her father and with anonymous folk superstition. And when we do finally share Quentin's perception, it is a confused, erroneous one. Reading this in retrospect with the entire novel in mind, it is possible to see in it anticipatory thematic images and hints about the two characters that will continue to enrich the texture of the story progressively as it unfolds. But the features of Faulkner's prose which are likely to make an initial impact are also those which repel any easy comprehension. His simplified or omitted punctuation, the uncertain relations between subject, verb, noun and object, the suspension of action and time in a participial stasis, and the qualification of statements by incremental repetition, negation or alternatives, form an impenetrable web of words which might, as one critic argues, create 'a rapt and mystic state in which the reader is held within a dynamically vibrant continuum',[5] but which also undermines our confidence in the capacity of literature to reflect or illuminate the tangible world or the objects in it.

The problem is not so acute in Faulkner's early fiction, *Soldiers' Pay* (1926), *Mosquitoes* (1927), and *Sartoris* (1929), though there are other reasons why these books lack much sense of reality. The strongest influence on Faulkner in 1925 when he was working on his first novel in New Orleans, was undoubtedly that of Sherwood Anderson. It was Anderson who suggested he write about 'that little patch up there in Mississippi', but at the time Faulkner was only just emerging from his own apprenticeship as a poet, and *Soldiers' Pay* shows all the marks of his immersion in Romantic mythology, together with a more specific influence – one felt by many writers more experienced than Faulkner – of T. S. Eliot's *The Waste Land*.

Soldiers' Pay is Faulkner's attempt to portray the 'lost generation' on native soil. It deals in a fairly oblique way with the problems of post-war disillusionment, seeing them in sexual rather than social terms, just as Hemingway does in *The Sun Also Rises*. But, unlike Hemingway, whose novel was published in the same year, Faulkner resorts to the mythology of nymphs, fauns, and satyrs in order to differentiate his various types of men and women, and the novel's complicated plot, fleshed out with self-consciously fine writing, therefore lacks psychological or social authenticity. It is true that, when closely examined, some of Faulkner's later preoccupations can be glimpsed at in embryo, together with some of his recurring characters such as those foreshadowed by Donald Mahon, the maimed idealist returned from the war to die, and by Januarius Jones, an unreal mechanical figure with yellow, goat-like eyes, 'obscene and old in sin'. But taken in isolation, *Soldiers' Pay* does not really suggest the true direction of Faulkner's development.

Nor does *Mosquitoes*, his second novel, in which he seems more intent on working out his own artistic credo and freeing himself from the influence of Sherwood Anderson. The most interesting part of it is not that dealing with the sexual relationships of his various characters who are almost as poorly motivated as those in *Soldiers' Pay*, but the sections in which he broods on the shortcomings of the novel of regional manners in which he finds nothing but 'trivialities in quantities'. Without necessarily rejecting Anderson's advice to cultivate his own soil, Faulkner employs the voice of a critic, Julius Kauffmann, to insist that the true artist must be prepared to dig down to a deeper stratum:

> Life everywhere is the same, you know. Manners of living it may be different – are they not different between adjoining villages? Family names, profits on a single field or orchard, work influences – but man's old compulsions, duty and inclination: the axis and circumference of his squirrel cage, they do not change. (Liveright, New York 1927, p. 243)

In his next work, he actually took Anderson's advice, but at the same time tried to ensure that the 'old compulsions', or what he later referred to in his Nobel Prize acceptance speech as the 'verities and truths of the heart', were not hidden beneath a patina of quaint local colour. If *Sartoris* has a fault it is that Faulkner strains too hard to universalize his hero's feelings of despair and does so in passages of awkward rhetorical excess. Here, for instance, is Bayard accusing himself of having caused his brother's death:

> Then again something bitter and deep and sleepless in him
> blazed out in vindication and justification and accusation:
> what he knew not, blazing out at what, whom he did not
> know: *You did it! You caused it all.* You killed Johnny. (4:4)

Bayard Sartoris is not a convincing character, nor are the minor figures who surround him or the dead ones who occupy his consciousness and memory. But Faulkner is beginning here to approach his major themes: the interaction between past and present, nature and society, man and woman, and to find ways of articulating them dramatically. *Sartoris* is, as one critic describes it, a 'threshhold novel'.[6]

To continue with that metaphor for a moment, it could be said that what Faulkner discovered in his reading of Joyce and put to good use in *The Sound and the Fury* was how to create all the significant features of the 'House of Compson' entirely from inside, without having to cross its threshhold to act as a well-informed guide pointing out the novel's interesting nooks and crannies and giving the reader an objective account of its history. He had learned, in other words, the art of indirection, or how to present what Irwin calls the 'always deferred-ness' of meaning.

In this respect, it is significant that in all his accounts of the genesis of *The Sound and the Fury*, which, as critics point out, vary with every telling, Faulkner insists that the germ from which the novel grew was not a concept but an image – that of 'the muddy seat of a little girl's drawers in a pear tree'.[7] By the time he had explained what she was doing there, how her drawers had got that way and what was happening to her brothers on the ground below, he had already launched into a rich and complicated interpretation of events that then radiated outwards like ripples on a pond. It was at some later point, he insists, that he realized the symbolic possibilities in the soiled pants, and this led him to make associations through time as well, carrying the reverberations of family doom backward and forward into different generations.

The point about starting with an image rather than an idea is that such pictures as that of the girl in the pear tree do not readily yield any circumcribed or exhaustible meaning, either for the novelist or his readers. The implications of this are far-reaching and affect the structure of the entire novel. The book comprises four sections: three blocks of interior monologue delivered in turn by each of three brothers, and a final part which focuses on Dilsey, the family's Black servant. The first of these (and in his interviews Faulkner says he spent a lot of time deciding the best order for them) takes us directly into the chaotic consciousness of an idiot, Benjy; a man with the mind of an infant, incapable of ordering all his teeming sense-impressions, or of differentiating past events from those that have just occurred. Benjy's section is a brilliant but bewildering *tour de force*. It enables Faulkner to present all the essential elements of his story imagistically, without the interference of any conceptualizing or moralizing consciousness, and without the temperamental bias of an adult mind. These are provided in full measure in the following parts by Jason, the cynical materialist whose opening words are: 'Once a bitch, always a bitch, what I say', and by Quentin, the neurotic idealist whose monologue is set eighteen years before the others, just prior to his suicide. These two sections, and the history of the family, are then placed in a different perspective by Dilsey, who contributes a primitive but humane choric conclusion to the Compsons' tragic fall.

Within this framework, Faulkner tells a fairly simple story. The little girl in the tree is Caddy, whose life and its consequences determine almost everything that happens in the novel. In a declining aristocratic Southern family, headed by a gentle but ineffectual man with a neurasthenic wife, Caddy is the only vital member, surrounded by brothers who are 'dead' in various ways and whose lives are distorted by their violent or neurotic reactions to her sexual growth and activity. Caddy's life, too, is eventually spoiled by her family's inability to accept reality. She loses the man she loves, is made pregnant by another, and marries a third who discards her when he discovers that her child is not his. In order to provide a home for her daughter (the 'bitch' of Jason's section), Caddy leaves the girl with her brother, but continues to support her financially. These events trigger Quentin's deep guilt feelings about his sister and lead to his suicide. They also provoke an uncontrollable fixation in Benjy which ultimately causes him to be gelded after molesting a child he mistakes for Caddy.

Stated as baldly as this, the patterning of events and the values attached to them might appear obvious or crude, but the effect of Faulkner's subjective narration is to eliminate any easy moral judgement. Quentin's anguish, for example, might appear from outside to be very similar to Bayard Sartoris's theatrical self-pity, but in fact the monologue is immeasurably enriched so that what remains an adolescent's neurotic preoccupation with his own emotions also becomes a critical metaphysical speculation on the nature of Time, linking Quentin's doom to that of his family and beyond it to that of the South as a whole. Jason's monologue has a similar universality in that his mean-spirited, cynical materialism has a much larger significance for Faulkner. It is a quality that troubles him throughout his career and later comes to be called 'Snopesism', indicating something completely repugnant in the New South, contrasting with the traditional values of personal integrity, family, and community. In *The Sound and the Fury*, though, Jason is himself a product of the old aristocratic ethos, and Faulkner avoids making the easy sociological equations that disfigure so much political fiction. He can even allow himself a measure of sympathy for Jason, bringing him vividly to life in the language of his raw, callous humour. In the sentences which follow the one already quoted we glimpse the seeds of many other comic tall tales, told by or about a succession of Faulknerian innocents who are duped or bested by horse-traders, con-men, and most often of all, by women:

'I says you're lucky if her playing out of school is all that
worries you. I says she ought to be down there in that
kitchen right now, instead of up there in her room,
gobbing paint on her face and waiting for six niggers that
can't even stand up out of a chair unless they've got a pan
full of bread and meat to balance them, to fix breakfast.'
(Modern Library, 1946, p. 198).

Faulkner's deepest sympathy, though, and its expression is one of the novel's great triumphs, is for Benjy. In the description of the incident which leads to his castration, Benjy is allowed to convey all the poignancy of his feeling for Caddy, as well as the impossibility – not just for him but for Faulkner too – of finding adequate words for it:

'They came on. I opened the gate and they stopped,
turning. I was trying to say, and I caught her, trying to
say, and she screamed and I was trying to say and trying
and the bright shapes began to stop and I tried to get out.
I tried to get it off my face, but the bright shapes were
going away. They were going up the hill to where it fell
away and I tried to cry. But when I breathed in, I
couldn't breathe out again to cry, and I had to keep from
falling off the hill into the bright, whirling shapes.' (p. 72)

Faulkner's most powerful feelings are always released by those inarticulate characters whose emotions can only find an outlet in action. He seems to share with other American writers – predictably Ernest Hemingway, but more surprisingly Henry James – a deep distrust of words and, by extension, of his own chosen profession. As one of the characters in a later story says: 'those who can, do, those who cannot and suffer enough because they can't, write about it'.[8]
One of the themes of Faulkner's next novel, *As I Lay Dying*, is

centred in this conflict between saying and doing, or more generally, between acts and consciousness:

> 'I would think how words go straight up in a thin line,
> quick and harmless, and how terribly doing goes along the
> earth, clinging to it, so that after a while, the two lines are
> too far apart for the same person to straddle from one to
> the other; and that sin and love and fear are just sounds
> that people who never sinned nor loved nor feared have
> for what they never had and cannot have until they forget
> the words.' (Modern Library, 1946, p. 475)

The speaker here is Addie Bundren, the 'I' of the novel's title who is actually dead, lying in her coffin with two auger holes that have been bored into her face by Vardaman, one of her sons, who did it to give her some air. Her corpse has just been rescued from a flooded river which her family is crossing in order to fulfil a promise made by her husband, Anse, to bury her in Jefferson. During the course of the action we learn that Addie did not really care where she was buried and only extracted the promise as a form of posthumous revenge. The heroic – or mock-heroic – six-day journey during which the members of her family fight fire and flood, suffer injury and madness, and are ostracized by nearly everyone they encounter because of the corpse's smell, is thus rendered futile. Except that Anse, like the others, has his own reasons for wanting to go to Jefferson, and begins the return journey, not just with a new set of teeth but accompanied by a new Mrs Bundren – a duck-shaped woman with pop-eyes carrying a little 'graphophone'.

It is not surprising that one critic should say of *As I Lay Dying*: 'One is uncertain about the qualities of some of the important characters and about how to feel toward them; one is puzzled by the meanings of many of the events; one is far from sure what the book is chiefly about, and above all one is uncertain to what extent one has been watching an epic or tragedy or farce.'[9] What prevents the reader from making confident judgements about the value of the characters or their actions is the complete absence of any authorial voice in the novel, mediating these bizarre incidents and directing our responses to them. Faulkner, like the ideal artist described by James Joyce in *A Portrait of the Artist as a Young Man*, has withdrawn 'God-like' behind the fifty-nine monologues that make up the book. Meaning is not deferred in the interplay of these many voices, but neither is it abandoned to an overriding vision of the world's absurdity, as some critics believe.[10] If Addie is right – and though hers is only one opinion among many, she does seem to speak from a more privileged position than the rest – meaning, if it is to be found at all, resides in actions themselves rather than in the words people use to interpret them. And so it is in the *act* of taking her corpse to Jefferson and accomplishing the task of finally laying her ghost that Cash, Jewel, Dewey Dell, Darl, Anse, and even young Vardaman, discover something about their individual identities and ultimately about Addie's too. The 'truths' of *As I Lay Dying* are not eternal. It was not until much later that Faulkner came to believe in such things and in his own access to them. But they are truths which have been tested and have been seen to be tested, and are much more convincing as a result.

Except for Darl, whose clairvoyant sanity leads to his incarceration in the Jackson Insane Asylum, there is no character in *As I Lay Dying* who is anything like the young tortured idealist of Faulkner's early fiction. In *Sanctuary* (1931), the novel he published just before his next major work, *Light in August* (1932), such a man, Horace Benbow – a little older than the earlier avatars but cut from the same cloth – stands at the centre of the action and, like Quentin in *The Sound and the Fury*, reflects people and events through the warped lens of his hypertrophied sensibility. The novel was drafted several years earlier as a 'potboiler', and Faulkner's main revision in 1931 consisted of adding a final chapter – an ironic coda in which the syphilitic, impotent murderer Popeye is hanged for a crime he hasn't committed. The ones he *is* responsible for in the novel, raping a young college girl with a corncob, other forms of torture and cold-blooded murder, together with the indifference, aquiescence, or connivance of most of those involved with him, constitute the pattern of overwhelming evil that makes *Sanctuary* such a profoundly shocking and despairing work. This is Faulkner's blackest picture of the human condition, and the presence of the ineffectual idealist, Horace Benbow, does little to relieve it. Indeed, as Horace himself points out, men of this sort are more vulnerable than most and offer scant protection against the world's wickedness: 'there's a corruption about even looking upon evil, even by accident; you cannot haggle, traffic with putrefaction'.

It would be a mistake, then, to see *Sanctuary* as a development from the position Faulkner had reached in *The Sound and the Fury* and *As I Lay Dying*. Despite the power with which his vision is expressed, its bitter, absolute disillusionment, cosmic rather than social, mark it as being essentially less mature than that of the novels published just before it.

The next stage in the evolution of Faulkner's art and thought is represented better by *Light in August*, which comes almost exactly in the middle of what he called his 'hot' period, the seven years between 1929 and 1936 which were for him a 'matchless time' when he wrote one great work after another in a sustained burst of creative energy.

What is remarkable about the novels written at this time is their ostensible difference in form despite their unmistakable common source.
Not only does each of his major novels present quite different solutions
to the problems he set himself, but each one embodies clearly distinct,
if not contradictory aspects of his mature philosophy. What probably
liberated Faulkner's imagination at this time was a recognition of the
need to 'sublimate the actual into the apocryphal'. This freed him from
any obligation he might have felt towards history or consistency in his
treatment of Yoknapatawpha County, and certainly from the need to
pile up 'trivialities in quantities'. The major novels are self-contained
works of art whose place in an extensive saga is of secondary importance, and more of a critical convenience than a literary fact. This
remains true even when the critic is Faulkner himself, the 'sole pro-
prietor' of Yoknapatawpha, who later allowed himself to share others'
views of his achievement and even helped to fill in some of the gaps
in his 'rambling genealogy of the people' in order to give it a retro-
spective coherence.

The weakness of this kind of holistic approach to the fiction is that
it is essentially reductive, the novels being judged not on their own
merits but in terms of how well they fit into some overall pattern. For
example, those critics who simplify Faulkner's moral scheme into a
protracted battle between the forces of 'Sartorism' and 'Snopesism' –
humane ethical responsibility and traditional values versus naturalistic
amorality and modernism – find great difficulty in accommodating
Light in August to their views, and more often than not dismiss it on
the grounds that the 'Snopes' figure in it, Joe Christmas, is made the
protagonist instead of being left as the mere antagonist. Faulkner, it
is argued, has allowed himself to be taken over by the 'Snopes' world,
and this results in a 'malproportioned fiction, wavering between
realism and allegory.'[11]

Nothing could be further from the truth. Joe Christmas's domi-
nation of the novel derives from a determination on Faulkner's part
to explore in detail all the forces that shape and motivate such a man,
rather than to take him at face value. If this allows the reader to identify better with him, it indicates not Faulkner's warped values but
rather the breadth of his imaginative sympathy. Joe Christmas is an
empty man, in some ways as transparent as the nameless hero of Ralph
Ellison's Invisible Man, a novel written twenty years later. Christmas
is a person without either racial or family identity, and without even
a proper name. He is an orphan, tortured by doubts about his
paternity, a man 'things are done to', whose only alternative responses
to the intolerable pressures of the world are either flight or violence.
Those pressures – a malevolent mixture of Calvinism and racism – are
given their full weight in an account of the brutal treatment Joe

Christmas receives at the hands of his grandfather and his foster-father, two life-denying absolutists whose racial and religious fanaticism push him inexorably towards his doomed sexual encounter with Joanna Burden. She is a middle-aged white woman descended from New England Abolitionists, who combines within herself (though in a very different form) all the forces, sexual, racial, and religious, that have so completely dehumanized Joe Christmas; forces which inevitably release in him the dread and rage that lead to her murder.

Joe Christmas is hunted down by the 'super-patriot', Percy Grimm, before being castrated and shot. His end, horrible in itself, is also the occasion for Faulkner to brood on its wider significance and impact, in images which have inevitably led some commentators to see Joe Christmas as a Christ figure:

> When the others reached the kitchen they saw the table
> flung aside now and Grimm stooping over the body.
> When they approached to see what he was about, they
> saw that the man was not dead yet, and when they saw
> what Grimm was doing one of the men gave a choked cry
> and stumbled back into the wall and began to vomit.
> Then Grimm too sprang back, flinging behind him the
> bloody butcher knife. 'Now you'll let white women alone,
> even in hell,' he said. But the man on the floor had not
> moved. He just lay there, with his eyes open and empty
> of everything save consciousness, and with something, a
> shadow, about his mouth. For a long moment he looked
> up at them with peaceful and unfathomable and unbearable
> eyes. Then his face, body, all, seemed to collapse, to fall
> in upon itself, and from out the slashed garments about
> his hips and loins the pent black blood seemed to rush like
> a released breath. It seemed to rush out of his pale body
> like the rush of sparks from a rising rocket; upon that
> black blast the man seemed to rise soaring into their
> memories forever and ever. (19)

The transfiguration Faulkner writes of here is that sought by so many of his characters who furiously rush to their doom in an effort to escape the past. It is the moment when 'was' becomes 'is', and as Alfred Kazin says, Joe Christmas's stillness allows him at last to be seen, to take on an identity.[12]

Light in August contains other, quite complex stories which are linked to this one, sometimes by rather slender threads in the plot. In his later work, such as *The Unvanquished* (1938), *The Wild Palms* (1939), and *Go Down Moses* (1942), Faulkner develops different strategies to create unity out of his short-story cycles, though the weakness of the Gail Hightower sections of *Light in August* is not just the result of such artificial connections. Hightower's entrapment by the romantic Southern past and his withdrawal from the 'loud harsh world' of the present into a dream of 'eternal youth' and 'virginal desire' is an obvious relic of Faulkner's earlier preoccupation with the problems of anguished, introspective idealists, and fits awkwardly into this fictional world.

The same is not true, though, of Lena Grove. It is she who provides the real antithesis to Joe Christmas in the novel, and it is significant that her story frames and contains the others. The qualities celebrated in Lena – innocence, serenity, and fecundity – are set firmly against the sterility and corruption of the lives that touch but cannot affect hers. She arrives from Alabama, heavily pregnant, in search of the man she is sure will marry her. She has been on the road for a month, riding in farm wagons or walking up long dusty tracks with her shoes in her hand. Her natural simplicity appeals to the better nature of everyone she meets, except the father of her child. It inspires the love of the Bunyanesque Christian labourer, Byron Bunch, and our last sight of Lena at the end of the novel embraces a calm affirmation of her life-enhancing durability as she resumes her steady progress along the road, this time accompanied by her baby and her man. Lena is one of Faulkner's earlier versions of the 'earth-mother', a figure that came to preoccupy him more and more and upon which he expended a great deal of his creative energy. The opening chapter of *Light in August* is one of Faulkner's most moving yet least sentimental evocations of all that is natural, of everything that the other characters in the novel either lack or deliberately deny in themselves:

> She begins to eat. She eats slowly, steadily, sucking the rich sardine oil from her fingers with slow and complete relish. Then she stops, not abruptly, yet with utter completeness, her jaw stilled in midchewing, a bitten cracker in her hand and her face lowered a little and her eyes blank, as if she were listening to something very far away or so near as to be inside her. Her face has drained of color, of its full, hearty blood, and she sits quite still, hearing and feeling the implacable and immemorial earth, but without fear or alarm. 'It's twins at least,' she says to herself, without lip movement, without sound. Then the spasm passes. She eats again. The wagon has not stopped; time has not stopped. The wagon crests the final hill and they see smoke. (1)

Faulkner's next major work, *Absalom, Absalom!*, is in some ways the richest, and certainly the densest and most complicated of all his novels. Yet it also focuses more closely on the events of a single story, the rise and fall of Thomas Sutpen's doomed dynasty. Its complications derive from a narrative technique by which events that took place up to forty years earlier are recounted, interpreted, or guessed at by four separate story-tellers: Rosa Coldfield, Sutpen's sister-in-law: Mr Compson and his son Quentin; and Shreve McCannon, Quentin's Harvard room-mate. The density of Faulkner's text owes something to his narrative method, too, in that everything in the novel is coloured by the personalities of those who reconstruct the events in it, and by the degree of their involvement in them. But the details of Sutpen's life and those of his descendants are also used to illuminate much larger social, moral, and metaphysical themes. In keeping with these large ambitions, Faulkner's prose style is stretched to its idiosyncratic limits to convey the subtle nuances of his interconnected patterns of thought. Here, for example, is Rosa Coldfield expressing an idea not unlike Addie Bundren's quoted earlier. But in this case the contrast between physical and mental dominion goes much further than Addie's simple juxtaposition of saying and doing, to embrace in addition ideas of class difference and miscegenation; themes which lie at the very heart of the novel:

> Because there is something in the touch of flesh with flesh
> which abrogates, cuts sharp and straight across the devious
> intricate channels of decorous ordering, which enemies as
> well as lovers know because it makes them both – touch
> and touch of that which is the citadel of the central I-Am's
> private own: not spirit, soul; the liquorish and ungirdled
> mind is anyone's to take in any darkened hallway of this
> earthly tenement. But let flesh touch with flesh, and watch
> the fall of all the eggshell shibboleths of caste and color
> too. (5)

Rosa's rhetoric is coloured, of course, by her own preoccupations which are primarily romantic and sexual. For her, the central fact of the story is the violation of her integrity by Thomas Sutpen. He had suggested to her many years ago that they should mate with each other, and that if the issue was a son he would incorporate her into his grand design by marrying her. In making this callous proposal, Sutpen was merely repeating the pattern of rejection that had begun to dehumanize him as a child, and which he subsequently projects upon the rest of the world. To Rosa, however, who as a young girl had seen herself as 'all polymath love's androgynous advocate', this ruthless disregard of her humanity is sufficient to embitter her whole life, and she withdraws from society to nurse her hatred of the monster who had brought her to life only to trample on the central core of her being.

Quentin Compson, on the other hand, rivets his appalled attention not on the tragic fate of Sutpen himself but on that of his children: Henry and Judith, born to Rosa's sister, and Charles Bon, the son of Sutpen's first wife who had been discarded years before when Sutpen dicovered that she was part Negress. Henry Sutpen kills Charles, his half-brother and closest friend, at the gate of Sutpen's Hundred in 1865, after their return from the Civil War. This act, and the motive behind it, constitute the novel's central mysteries. As those who have read *The Sound and the Fury* know, Quentin is able to contemplate incest if not with equanimity, then as a form of lesser evil. So too is Henry Sutpen, and the proposed marriage between his half-brother and his sister is not the main reason for his dreadful act. What he cannot condone is miscegenation, and it is on account of Charles's Negro blood that Henry feels impelled to shoot him.

These tangled events of a family's tragic history, and the tortuous interpretations of them by those whose lives are affected either directly or by implication, are gradually unravelled to reveal a gaping moral void at their centre. Behind them hovers the colossal figure of Thomas Sutpen, representing (pre-eminently for Mr Compson, who sees in him a reflection of a more general fate) the failure of Southern culture to protect itself against destruction by a society dedicated to the ruthless acquisition and brutal exploitation of power. It is customary in Southern mythology to attribute these characteristics to Northern industrial capitalism, but Faulkner, with a greater sense of moral realism, locates the seeds of future decay in native soil. Thomas Sutpen has his origins in a family of Southern 'poor whites'. So too does Flem Snopes, Faulkner's most notorious evil exemplar and the central figure of his last pre-war novel, *The Hamlet* (1940).

There are some critics who do not believe that *The Hamlet* is a novel, and there would probably have been many more had Faulkner not written two sequels, *The Town* (1957) and *The Mansion* (1959), in which Flem Snopes's history is completed and Snopesism as a social and moral phenomenon is exhaustively explored. *The Hamlet* belongs to that period in Faulkner's life when, as he confessed, 'the speed slows' even though 'the talent doesn't necessarily have to fade at the same time'. Later still, some of his talent would actually desert him, resulting in such relatively artificial and empty novels as *Intruder in the Dust* (1948), which sold more copies than any of his previous books, and *A Fable* (1954), which won the Pulitzer Prize.

Between *Absalom, Absalom!* and those later novels Faulkner devoted

WILLIAM FAULKNER 241

much of his energy to work on his short stories, revising and re-arranging old material and writing linking passages in order to create building blocks for the Yoknapatawpha saga. This must have gradually been taking shape in his mind as it certainly was in Malcolm Cowley's, who worked with Faulkner on an anthology published just after the war, *The Portable Faulkner*. He was probably encouraged, too, by George Marion O'Donnell's essay published in the *Kenyon Review* in 1939, where it is suggested that: 'In a rearrangement of the novels, say for a collected edition, *The Unvanquished* might well stand first; for the action occurs earlier, historically, than in any other of the books, and it objectifies, in the essential terms of Mr. Faulkner's mythology, the central dramatic tension of his work.'[13] O'Donnell's over-simplified account of the mythology, and particularly his identification of Ab Snopes, the poor-white horse-trader, as the chief antagonist of the Sartorises, uncannily anticipates the focus of Faulkner's attention in *The Hamlet*, the novel he was just then 'pulling together' for publication the next year.

He uses a story in it about one of Ab Snopes's horse-trading exploits to introduce the head of the Snopes clan to the, as yet, unwary residents of Frenchman's Bend, the hamlet of the title. It is told by an itinerant sewing-machine agent, Ratliff, one of Faulkner's humane, ironic observers who are used throughout the trilogy to comment on and occasionally to block temporarily the spread of Snopesism. Ratliff tells it to explain to his listeners sitting on the verandah of Littlejohn's Hotel, how Ab, who had already been soured by his dealings with the Sartorises in the Civil War, was finally 'curdled' when he crossed swords with Pat Stamper, the notorious horse-dealer. Like all tall tales, it is incredibly complex, involving a multitude of intricate deals in which each man believes he is getting the better of the other. One of them is always mistaken in his belief, and for the story to have its maximum effect, the audience should know which one that is, but not exactly how he is being tricked. This particular story reaches its climax with Ab Snopes staring in incredulous rage at the fat, black animal he has finally bought from Stamper, as it changes before his eyes into the same thin, bay horse which he originally owned and sold off at the start of the devious proceedings.

Of course, the fact that Ab Snopes's bitterness can be explained at all, let alone in this light-hearted way, makes him unsuitable for Faulkner's larger purposes in the novel, and he only serves here to bring in his wake one whose malign power defies all rational explanation – his son Flem. Elements from many earlier characters, including Januarius Jones, Popeye, and Joe Christmas, find their ultimate resolution and extension in Flem Snopes. Like the evil genius he is, Flem arrives in Frenchman's Bend out of nowhere:

> One moment the road had been empty, the next moment
> the man stood there beside it, at the edge of a small copse
> – the same cloth cap, the same rhythmically chewing jaw
> materialised apparently out of nothing and almost abreast
> of the horse, with an air of the completely and purely
> accidental. (1)

Though he appears banal and nondescript in his soiled city clothes, his eyes 'the colour of stagnant water' and his face 'as blank as a pan of uncooked dough', there is nothing accidental or casual about his actions. He moves through the community like a plague, infecting everything he touches and leaving a trail of blight behind him. Flem hasn't got a single friend on earth, recognizes no allegiance to anyone, even to the members of his own family; he gives no sign, in fact, of feeling anything at all. His impotence and sterility are absolute, and his sympathy for the needs and passions of others non-existent. He sees and treats people literally as objects, to be bought, sold, or exchanged in the pursuit of his blind, implacable drive to power.

Against such a non-human force, a man like Ratliff, shrewd and worldly as he is, has no chance at all. He fights a holding action against Flem for a time and even wins a few small victories, but is inevitably defeated in the end, partly by his own humanity but also by the spreading corruption that ultimately reaches out to touch him too. As well as defeating Ratliff, Flem also does what no other man in Frenchman's Bend can, by resisting the sexual allure of Eula Varner, the storekeeper's daughter. Eula is one of Faulkner's great comic creations. She is distantly related to such earth-mothers as Lena Grove, and though she is later symbolically inflated in order to serve a very serious purpose, her initial manifestations and the 'priapic hullabaloo' she excites are anything but serious or symbolic. Introducing her as a young schoolgirl riding back and forth through the village on the back of her brother's horse, Faulkner joyfully adapts his elaborate rhetoric for comic effect. The tone of his account, if not his syntax, is still relaxed and easy:

> It had been almost five years now since this sight had
> become an integral part of the village's life four times a
> day and five days a week – the roan horse bearing the
> seething and angry man and the girl of whom, even at
> nine and ten and eleven, there was too much – too much
> of leg, too much of breast, too much of buttock; too
> much of mammalian female meat which, in conjunction
> with the tawdry oilcloth receptacle that was obviously a
> grammar-grade book-satchel, was a travesty and paradox

on the whole idea of education. Even while sitting behind
her brother on the horse, the inhabitant of that meat
seemed to lead two separate and distinct lives as infants in
the act of nursing do. There was one Eula Varner who
supplied blood and nourishment to the buttocks and legs
and breasts; there was the other Eula Varner who merely
inhabited them, who went where they went because it was
less trouble to do so, who was comfortable there but in
their doings she intended to have no part, as you are in a
house which you did not design but where the furniture is
all settled and the rent paid up. On the first morning
Varner had put the horse into a fast trot, to get it over
with quick, but almost at once he began to feel the entire
body behind him, which even motionless in a chair
seemed to postulate an invincible abhorrence of straight
lines, jigging its component boneless curves against his
back. He had a vision of himself transporting not only
across the village's horizon but across the embracing
proscenium of the entire inhabited world like the sun
itself, a kaleidoscopic convolution of mammalian ellipses.
(2:1)

Eventually, after her years in school during which she transforms
'the very desks and benches themselves into a grove of Venus' and
drives her teacher away seething with sexual despair, Eula is inevitably
impregnated by one of the youths who constantly swarm around her
like 'wasps about the ripe peach'. With equal inevitability she also falls
into the clutches of Flem Snopes, who buys her as part of a deal and
takes her off to Texas to give birth to the baby. The image of Flem
as he leaves with her – one that recurs in the novel – brings the episode
to a chilling end: 'Snopes turned his head once and spat over the wheel.
He had the straw suitcase on his knees like the coffin of a baby's
funeral.'

Another facet of Faulkner's stylistic virtuosity, also parodic, is
revealed in a later, potentially nauseating anecdote about rural sodomy,
which involves another of the Snopeses, the idiot Ike who falls in love
with a cow. The story is used to show Ratliff attempting to preserve
the moral fabric of the community, but in doing so utilizing the greed
and corruption of Ike's relatives. At this point Ratliff himself is beginning to lose his moral footing, though he expresses his uncertainties
in terms of his own dubious motives for depriving Ike of his loved
one, when this is not really the point at issue. In order to give this
whole episode any semblance of plausibility, Faulkner has to suggest
somehow the essential purity of the idiot's feelings, and he tackles the

problem quite differently from the way he dealt with a similar one in *The Sound and the Fury*. Ike's bestial passion is elevated by Faulkner's description to the level of courtly love:

> The rapid twilight effaces them from the day's tedious
> recording. Original, in the womb-dimension, the
> unavoidable first and the inescapable last, eyeless, they
> descend the hill. He finds the basket by smell and lifts it
> down from the limb and sets it before her. She nuzzles
> into it, blowing the sweet breath-reek into the sweetish
> reek of feed until they become indistinguishable with that
> of the urgent and unimpatient milk as it flows among and
> about his fingers, hands, wrists, warm and indivisible as
> the strong inexhaustible life ichor itself, inherently, of
> itself, renewing. Then he leaves the invisible basket where
> he can find it again at dawn, and goes to the spring. Now
> he can see again. Again his head interrupts, then replaces
> as once more he breaks with drinking, the reversed
> drinking of his drowned and fading image. It is the well
> of days, the still and insatiable aperture of earth. It holds
> in tranquil paradox of suspended precipitation dawn, noon,
> and sunset; yesterday, today, and tomorrow – star-spawn
> and hieroglyph, the fierce white dying rose, then gradual
> and invincible speeding up to and into slack-flood's
> coronal of nympholept noon. (3:1)

Ratliff's final defeat in the novel at the hands of Flem involves another crooked deal in which Ratliff exchanges his share in a Jefferson restaurant for part of the old Frenchman's ruin which Flem owns. His partner in this venture is Henry Armstid, who is motivated by both greed and revenge. They are both tricked into believing that there is treasure buried in the grounds, though long after Ratliff realizes the truth, Armstid goes on digging, 'his gaunt unshaven face . . . completely that of a madman'. Flem is passing the old place on his way to a new life in Jefferson and he stops to stare impassively at the men he has duped: 'Snopes turned his head and spat over the wagon wheel. He jerked the reins slightly. "Come up," he said.'

By the time Flem Snopes re-emerged in Faulkner's fiction in 1957, the twenty miles he had travelled to Jefferson had begun to seem much more. The world of the 1930s had disappeared for ever, its outlines obscured by an intervening evil of far greater import. If we did not have such novels as *The Hamlet* to remind us – 'scratches on the wall of oblivion', as Faulkner called them – it would be difficult to believe that such a world ever existed.

Notes

1. Malcolm Cowley, *A Second Flowering: Works and Days of the Lost Generation* (New York, 1973), p. 152.

2. Jean Stein, 'William Faulkner', *Paris Review*, 12 (1956), 28–52. Reprinted in *Writers at Work: The Paris Review Interviews*, edited by Malcolm Cowley (London, 1958) pp. 109–27.

3. See *A Homemade World: The American Modernist Writers* (New York, 1975), pp. 194–221.

4. John Irwin, *Doubling and Incest/Repetition and Revenge: A Speculative Reading of Faulkner* (Baltimore and London, 1975). For an earlier study of Faulkner's technique which in some ways anticipates Irwin's see Conrad Aiken, 'William Faulkner: The Novel as Form', in *William Faulkner: Four Decades of Criticism*, edited by Linda Welshimer Wagner (East Lansing, Mich., 1973), pp. 134–40.

5. Frank Baldanza, 'Faulkner and Stein: A Study in Stylistic Intransigence', *Georgia Review*, 13 (1959), 274–86 (p. 286).

6. Edmond L. Volpe, *A Reader's Guide to William Faulkner* (London, 1964), p. 76.

7. See *Writers at Work*, p. 118.

8. See 'An Odor of Verbena', the final story in *The Unvanquished*. Hemingway expresses similar sentiments in his story, 'The Snows of Kilimanjaro', as does James in 'The Lesson of the Master'.

9. Walter J. Slatoff, *Quest for Failure: A Study of William Faulkner* (Ithaca, NY 1960), p. 159.

10. See, for example, Volpe, p. 126.

11. George Marion O'Donell, 'Faulkner's Mythology', in *William Faulkner: Four Decades of Criticism*, p. 90.

12. Alfred Kazin, 'The Stillness of *Light in August*', in *Faulkner: A Collection of Critical Essays*, edited by Robert Penn Warren, Twentieth Century Views (Englewood Cliffs, NJ, 1966), pp. 147–62.

13. Reprinted in *William Faulkner: Four Decades of Criticism*, p. 83. Arnold Goldman has written an interesting essay which also deals with these issues, 'Faulkner and the Revision of Yoknapatawpha County', in *The American Novel and the Nineteen Twenties*, edited by Malcolm Bradbury and David Palmer, Stratford-upon-Avon Studies, 13 (London, 1971), pp. 165–95.

Chronology

Note: Dates refer to date of first publication unless otherwise stated; (p) refers to poetry, (d) to drama.

DATE	AMERICAN FICTION	OTHER WORKS	HISTORICAL/CULTURAL EVENTS
1865		Whitman *Drum Taps* (p) Thoreau *Cape Cod*	General Lee surrenders at Appomattox to end war President Lincoln assassinated Johnson's administration (1865–69)
1866	Cooke *Surry of Eagle's Nest*	Howells *Venetian Life* Whittier *Snow-bound* (p)	Civil Rights Bill Second Atlantic cable First oil pipeline laid in Pennsylvania
1867	De Forest *Miss Ravenel's Conversion*	Emerson *May-Day* (p)	First Reconstruction Act Purchase of Alaska Ku Klux Klan formally organized at Nashville
1868	Alcott *Little Women* Harte 'The Luck of Roaring Camp'		President Johnson impeached and acquitted Robert Herrick b. (d. 1938)

DATE	AMERICAN FICTION	OTHER WORKS	HISTORICAL/CULTURAL EVENTS
1869	Harte 'Outcasts of Poker Flat'	Twain *Innocents Abroad*	Grant's administration (1869–77) Union Pacific railroad completed Booth Tarkington b. (d. 1946) 'Black Friday' financial panic First professional baseball team founded
1870		Howard *Saratoga* (d) Emerson *Society and Solitude*	Population 40 million Frank Norris b. (d. 1902) Standard Oil Co. formed
1871	Eggleston *Hoosier Schoolmaster* Howells *Their Wedding Journey*	Whitman *Democratic Vistas* *Passage to India* (p)	Chicago Fire Stephen Crane b. (d. 1900) Theodor Dreiser b. (d. 1945) Campaign of 'Apache extermination' ends
1872		Twain *Roughing It* Holmes *Poet at the Breakfast Table*	Crédit Mobilier scandal First commercial production of celluloid
1873	Howells *A Chance Acquaintance* Twain and Warner *The Gilded Age*		Silver rush in Nevada Bethlehem Steel Co. begins manufacturing in Pittsburgh
1874	Eggleston *The Circuit Rider*	Fiske *Outlines of Cosmic Philosophy*	Zona Gale b. (d. 1938) Ellen Glasgow b. (d. 1945) Gertrude Stein b. (d. 1946) First electric streetcar in New York City

DATE	AMERICAN FICTION	OTHER WORKS	HISTORICAL/CULTURAL EVENTS
1875	Howells *A Foregone Conclusion*		Civil Rights Act Gold Rush in South Dakota
1876	James *Roderick Hudson* Twain *Tom Sawyer*	Centennial edition of *Leaves of Grass*	Battle of Little Big Horn Sherwood Anderson b. (d. 1941) Willa Cather b. (d. 1947) Jack London b. (d. 1916) O. E. Rölvaag b. (d. 1931) Bell's telephone demonstrated
1877	James *The American* Jewett *Deephaven*	Lanier *Poems*	Hayes's administration (1877–81) Edison's phonograph
1878	James *The Europeans*		Joseph Pulitzer buys *Saint Louis Dispatch* Upton Sinclair b. (d. 1968)
1879	Howells *Lady of the Aroostook*	Henry George *Progress and Poverty*	Edison's incandescent lamp James Branch Cabell b. (d. 1958) Woolworth opens first 'five-cent' store
1880	Adams *Democracy* Cable *The Grandissimes*	Twain *A Tramp Abroad*	Population exceeds 50 million Ernest Poole b. (d. 1950) Carl Van Vechten b. (d. 1964)

DATE	AMERICAN FICTION	OTHER WORKS	HISTORICAL/CULTURAL EVENTS
1881	Harris *Uncle Remus* James *Washington Square*		Garfield's administration (1881) Arthur's administration (1881–85) Carnegie establishes his libraries Booker T. Washington establishes industrial institute for Negroes (Tuskegee Institute)
1882	Howells *A Modern Instance* Twain *The Prince and the Pauper*	Whitman *Specimen Days*	First Labor Day celebrated in New York City
1883	Howe *Story of a Country Town*	Twain *Life on the Mississippi*	Brooklyn Bridge completed Metropolitan Opera House opens
1884	Twain *Huckleberry Finn*		Mergenthaler patents his linotype machine
1885	Howells *Rise of Silas Lapham*		Cleveland's first administration (1885–89) Ring Lardner b. (d. 1933) Sinclair Lewis b. (d. 1951) First true American skyscraper built in Chicago

DATE	AMERICAN FICTION	OTHER WORKS	HISTORICAL/CULTURAL EVENTS
1886	Burnett *Little Lord Fauntleroy* Howells *Indian Summer* James *The Bostonians* *Princess Casamassima* Jewett *A White Heron*		Haymarket Riot Elizabeth M. Roberts b. (d. 1941) Emily Dickinson d. Statue of Liberty dedicated American Federation of Labor founded
1887	Frederic *Seth's Brother's Wife* Kirkland *Zury*		Floyd Dell b. (d. 1969) Interstate Commerce Act
1888	Bellamy *Looking Backward* Howells *Annie Kilburn*	Bryce *The American Commonwealth*	First Kodak Land camera 400 people die in New York blizzard
1889	Twain *A Connecticut Yankee*	Carnegie 'Gospel of Wealth' Theodore Roosevelt *The Winning of the West*	Harrison's administration (1889–93) Montana and Washington become 41st and 42nd states First safety bicycles produced in quantity
1890	Howells *A Hazard of New Fortunes* James *The Tragic Muse*	Dickinson *Poems* W. James *Principles of Psychology* Riis *How the Other Half Lives*	Sherman Anti-Trust Act Chief Sitting Bull killed by soldiers Population 63 million

DATE	AMERICAN FICTION	OTHER WORKS	HISTORICAL/CULTURAL EVENTS
1891	Garland *Main Travelled Roads*		First International Copyright Act Henry Miller b. (d. 1980) Melville (b. 1819) died
1892		Page *The Old South*	Lizzie Borden case Ellis Island becomes an immigrant station Homestead and Coeur d'Alene strikes Whitman (b. 1819) died
1893	Ambrose Bierce *Can Such Things Be* Crane *Maggie*	Turner 'The Significance of the Frontier in American History'	Cleveland's second administration (1893–97) Financial panic, depression and widespread unemployment World's Columbian Exposition at Chicago
1894	Howells *Traveller from Altruria* Twain *Pudd'nhead Wilson*	Lloyd *Wealth Against Commonwealth* Dickinson *Letters*	Coxey's Army reaches Washington Pullman strike
1895	Crane *The Red Badge of Courage*	Crane *Black Riders* (p)	Sears Roebuck opens mail-order business Latham demonstrates his moving-picture projector, the Panoptikon

DATE	AMERICAN FICTION	OTHER WORKS	HISTORICAL/CULTURAL EVENTS
1896	Crane *George's Mother* Jewett *The Country of the Pointed Firs* Frederick *The Damnation of Theron Ware*		US athletics team wins 9 out of 12 gold medals at first modern Olympic Games Dos Passos b. (d. 1970)
1897	Crane *The Third Violet* Bellamy *Equality* James *What Maisie Knew* *The Spoils of Poynton*		Klondike Gold Rush Boston subway completed Mckinley's administration Faulkner b. (d. 1962)
1898	Crane 'The Open Boat'		USS *Maine* blown up in Havana harbour US and Spain declare war
1899	Chopin *The Awakening* Howells *Their Silver Wedding Journey* James *The Awkward Age* Norris *McTeague*	Markham 'The Man with the Hoe' (p) Veblen *The Theory of the Leisure Class* William James *Talks on Psychology*	Sullivan designs Schlesinger and Mayer department store in Chicago Hemingway b. (d. 1961)
1900	Dreiser *Sister Carrie* Twain 'The Man that Corrupted Hadleyburg'		Gold Standard Act Population exceeds 75 million Immigration since 1820–19 million 8,000 automobiles registered

DATE	AMERICAN FICTION	OTHER WORKS	HISTORICAL/CULTURAL EVENTS
1901	James *The Sacred Fount* Norris *The Octopus*	Washington *Up From Slavery*	Theodore Roosevelt's administration First transatlantic radio Citizenship granted to Indians of Five Civilized Tribes Glenway Wescott born
1902	Glasgow *The Battle-Ground* James *Wings of the Dove* Wharton *Valley of Decision* Wister *The Virginian*	W. James *Varieties of Religious* *Experience*	US Steel Corporation formed Steinbeck b. (d. 1968)
1903	James *The Ambassadors* London *Call of the Wild* Norris *The Pit* Wiggin *Rebecca of Sunnybrook* *Farm*	Dubois *Souls of Black Folk*	Wright brothers' aeroplane First transcontinental car journey First Western movie, *The Great Train* *Robbery* Caldwell b. Cullen b. (d. 1946)
1904	Cabell *The Eagle's Shadow* Churchill *The Crossing* Glasgow *The Deliverance* Howells *Son of Royal Langbrith* James *The Golden Bowl* London *The Sea-Wolf* Stratton-Porter *Freckles*	Adams *Mont-Saint-Michel and* *Chartres* Steffens *The Shame of the Cities*	Pacific cable completed Socialist National Convention nominates Debs for President Farrell b. (d. 1979)

DATE	AMERICAN FICTION	OTHER WORKS	HISTORICAL/CULTURAL EVENTS
1905	Dixon *The Clansman* Wharton *House of Mirth*	Santayana *Life of Reason*	IWW (Industrial Workers of the World) founded First Rotary Club founded
1906	Churchill *Coniston* Sinclair *The Jungle*		San Francisco earthquake Pure Food and Drug Act
1907	London *The Iron Heel*	Adams *The Education* H. James *The American Scene* W. James *Pragmatism* Fitch *The Truth* (d)	Ziegfeld Follies
1908	Fox *The Trail of the Lonesome Pine* Herrick *The Master of the Inn*		Immigration from Japan restricted Model T Ford introduced 'Ashcan school' of painters established First nickelodeon
1909	London *Martin Eden* Stein *Three Lives* Stratton-Porter *Girl of the Limberlost*	Pound *Personae* (p)	Taft's administration (1909–13) Bakelite patented Wright b. (d. 1960) Welty born
1910		Addams *Twenty Years at Hull House*	Population 92 million Mann Act Twain (b. 1835) died

DATE	AMERICAN FICTION	OTHER WORKS	HISTORICAL/CULTURAL EVENTS
1911	Dreiser *Jennie Gerhardt* Wharton *Ethan Frome*	Bierce *The Devil's Dictionary*	Standard Oil Trust dissolved *The Masses* (later *New Masses*)
1912	Dreiser *The Financier* Grey *Riders of the Purple Sage* Johnson *The Autobiography of an Ex-Colored Man*	Antin *Promised Land*	Progressive Party *Titanic* sinks *Poetry*, a magazine of verse
1913	Cather *O Pioneers* Glasgow *Virginia*	Frost *A Boy's Will* (p) James *A Small Boy and Others* Wilson *The New Freedom*	Wilson's administration (1913–21) The Armory Show Rockefeller donates $100 million to start charitable foundation
1914	Tarkington *Penrod*	Frost *North of Boston* (p) James *Notes of a Son and Brother*	Panama Canal opened
1915	Cather *Song of the Lark* Dreiser *The Genius* Poole *The Harbor*	Masters *Spoon River Anthology* (p)	First transcontinental telephone First taxis ('jitneys')
1916	Twain *Mysterious Stranger* Wharton *Xingu*	Frost *Mountain Interval* (p) Sandburg *Chicago Poems* Dewey *Democracy and Education*	254,000 miles of railroad. Mileage steadily declined after this peak H. James (b. 1843) died

DATE	AMERICAN FICTION	OTHER WORKS	HISTORICAL/CULTURAL EVENTS
1917	Phillips *Susan Lenox* Sinclair *King Coal*	Eliot *Prufrock* (p) Garland *Son of the Middle Border* Robinson *Merlin* (p)	US enters the First World War *The Dial* McCullers (d. 1967)
1918	Cather *My Antonia* Tarkington *Magnificent Ambersons*	O' Neill *Moon of the Caribbees* (d)	Armistice First instalments of James Joyce's *Ulysses* burnt by US Post Office
1919	Anderson *Winesburg, Ohio* Cabell *Jurgen*	Mencken *Prejudices The American Language* Reed *Ten Days that Shook the World*	Treaty of Versailles Black Sox scandal Volstead Act (Prohibition) Alcock and Brown fly the Atlantic American Communist Party formed
1920	Anderson *Poor White* Dell *Moon-Calf* Fitzgerald *This Side of Paradise* Lewis *Main Street* Wharton *Age of Innocence*	Sandburg *Smoke and Steel* (p)	Population 105 million First commercial radio broadcasting Nineteenth Amendment (Women's Suffrage)
1921	Anderson *Triumph of the Egg* Cabell *Figures of Earth* Dos Passos *Three Soldiers* Hecht *Erik Dorn*	O'Neill *Anna Christie* (d)	Harding's administration (1921–23) Sacco–Vanzetti trial Quota Act to limit immigration

DATE	AMERICAN FICTION	OTHER WORKS	HISTORICAL/CULTURAL EVENTS
1922	Cather *One of Ours* Cummings *The Enormous Room* Lewis *Babbitt* Van Vechten *Peter Whiffle*	Eliot *The Waste Land* (p) O'Neill *The Hairy Ape* (d)	Lincoln Memorial dedicated in Washington, DC
1923	Atherton *Black Oxen* Cather *A Lost Lady*	Stevens *Harmonium* (p) Lawrence *Studies in Classic American Literature*	Coolidge's administration (1923–29) *Time* magazine
1924	Hemingway *In Our Time* Melville *Billy Budd*	O'Neill *Desire Under the Elms* (d)	New immigration quotas Hoover appointed head of FBI
1925	Anderson *Dark Laughter* Cather *Professor's House* Dos Passos *Manhattan Transfer* Dreiser *American Tragedy* Fitzgerald *Great Gatsby* Glasgow *Barren Ground* Lewis *Arrowsmith*	Pound *Cantos* (p)	Scopes (Evolution) trial *New Yorker*

DATE	AMERICAN FICTION	OTHER WORKS	HISTORICAL/CULTURAL EVENTS
1926	Faulkner *Soldiers' Pay* Hemingway *Sun Also Rises* Loos *Gentlemen Prefer Blondes* Van Vechten *Nigger Heaven*	Hughes *The Weary Blues* (p)	Byrd flies over North Pole National Broadcasting Co. organized
1927	Aiken *Blue Voyage* Cather *Death Comes for the Archbishop* Faulkner *Mosquitoes* Hemingway *Men Without Women* Rolvaag *Giants in The Earth* Sinclair *Oil* Wilder *Bridge of San Luis Rey*	Sandburg *American Songbag* (p)	Lindbergh's flight from New York to Paris Sacco and Vanzetti executed First talking picture, *The Jazz Singer*
1928	Sinclair *Boston*	Benét *John Brown's Body* (p) Frost *West-Running Brook* (p) O'Neill *Strange Interlude* (p)	First Mickey Mouse cartoon released by Walt Disney

DATE	AMERICAN FICTION	OTHER WORKS	HISTORICAL/CULTURAL EVENTS
1929	Faulkner *Sound and the Fury* Glasgow *They Stooped to Folly* Hemingway *Farewell to Arms* La Farge *Laughing Boy* Lewis *Dodsworth* Wolfe *Look Homeward Angel*	Lynd *Middletown*	Hoover's administration (1929–33) Stock market collapse Museum of Modern Art
1930	Dos Passos *42nd Parallel* Faulkner *As I Lay Dying* Gold *Jews Without Money* Porter *Flowering Judas*	*I'll take my Stand* Crane *The Bridge* (p) Eliot *Ash Wednesday* (p)	Population 123 million Lewis receives Nobel Prize Television broadcasting begins
1931	Buck *The Good Earth* Cather *Shadows on the Rock* Faulkner *Sanctuary* West *Dream Life of Balso Snell*	O'Neill *Mourning Becomes Electra* (d)	Trial of Scottsboro Boys 'Star-Spangled Banner' adopted as national anthem

DATE	AMERICAN FICTION	OTHER WORKS	HISTORICAL/CULTURAL EVENTS
1932	Caldwell *Tobacco Road* Dos Passos *1919* Farrell *Young Lonigan* Faulkner *Light in August* Fisher *In Tragic Life* Glasgow *Sheltered Life*	MacLeish *Conquistador* (p) Hemingway *Death in the Afternoon*	War veterans Bonus march to Washington
1933	Caldwell *God's Little Acre* Cozzens *The Last Adam* Halper *Union Square* Hemingway *Winner Takes Nothing* West *Miss Lonelyhearts*	Stein *Autobiography of Alice B. Toklas* Crane *Collected Poems*	F. D. Roosevelt's administration (1933–45) National Industrial Recovery Act Tennessee Valley power project
1934	Cantwell *Land of Plenty* Farrell *Young Manhood of Studs Lonigan* Fitzgerald *Tender is the Night* Fuchs *Summer in Williamsburg* Miller *Tropic of Cancer* Young *So Red the Rose*	Sherwood *Petrified Forest* (d)	Upton Sinclair's EPIC campaign in California Catholic Legion of Decency begins censorship of films John Dillinger shot

DATE	AMERICAN FICTION	OTHER WORKS	HISTORICAL/CULTURAL EVENTS
1935	Glasgow *Vein of Iron* Steinbeck *Tortilla Flat* Wolfe *Of Time and the River*	Odets *Waiting for Lefty* (d)	Works Progress Administration Federal Writers Project American Writers Congress
1936	Dos Passos *The Big Money* Faulkner *Absalom, Absalom!* Mitchell *Gone With the Wind* Santayana *The Last Puritan* Steinbeck *In Dubious Battle*	Frost *A Further Range* (p) Sandburg *The People, Yes* (p)	Roosevelt re-elected O'Neill receives Nobel Prize Federal Theatre Project
1937	Hemingway *To Have and Have Not* Marquand *The Late George Apley* Roberts *Northwest Passage* Steinbeck *Of Mice and Men* Williams *White Mule*	Odets *Golden Boy*	Memorial Day Massacre in South Chicago
1938	Hemingway *The First Forty-Nine Stories*	Hemingway *The Fifth Column* (d) Wilder *Our Town* (d)	Pearl Buck receives Nobel Prize Orson Welles radio broadcast 'War of the Worlds' causes panic

DATE	AMERICAN FICTION	OTHER WORKS	HISTORICAL/CULTURAL EVENTS
1939	Faulkner *The Wild Palms* Steinbeck *Grapes of Wrath* Wolfe *The Web and the Rock*	Hellman *The Little Foxes* (d)	Regular transatlantic air service
1940	Cather *Sapphira and the Slave Girl* Clarke *The Ox-Bow Incident* Faulkner *The Hamlet* Hemingway *For Whom the Bell Tolls* McCullers *The Heart is a Lonely Hunter* Wolfe *You Can't Go Home Again* Wright *Native Son*	Cummings *Fifty Poems*	Population 132 million Conscription

General Bibliographies

Note: Each section is arranged alphabetically. Place of publication is New York unless otherwise indicated.

(i) The social, cultural and intellectual contexts

Allen, F. L. — *The Big Change: America Transforms Itself, 1900–1950* (1952).

Banner, L. W. — *Women in Modern America: A Brief History* (1974). (From the 1890s to the present.)

Beer, T. — *The Mauve Decade: American Life at the End of the Nineteenth Century* (1926).

Cash, W. J. — *The Mind of the South* (1941).

Conn, P. — *The Divided Mind: Ideology and Imagination in America, 1898–1917* (Cambridge, 1983).

Curti, M. — *The Growth of American Thought* 2nd edn (1951).

Earnest, E. — *The Single Vision: The Alienation of American Intellectuals* (1970).

Flexner, E. — *Century of Struggle: The Woman's Rights Movement in the United States*, rev. edn (Cambridge, Mass. and London, 1979) (Standard work covering the period 1800–1920.)

Hale, N. G. — *Freud and the Americans: The Beginnings of Psychoanalysis in the United States, 1876–1917* (New York, 1971).

Hays, S. P. — *The Response to Industrialism, 1885–1914* (Chicago, 1975).

Hofstadter, R. — *Anti-Intellectualism in American Life* (1963). *Social Darwinism in American Thought* (Philadelphia and London, 1944). (Excellent account of social theories in the late nineteenth and early twentieth centuries.)

Horton, R. W., and H. W. Edwards — *Backgrounds of American Literary Thought* 2nd edn (1967).

King, R. H. — *A Southern Renaissance: The Cultural Awakening of the American South, 1930–1955* (New York and Oxford, 1980).

Lasch, C.	*The New Radicalism in America, 1887–1963: The Intellectual as a Social Type* (1965). (Biographical essays on social reformers.)
Lears, T. J. J.	*No Place of Grace: Antimodernism and the Transformation of American Culture, 1880–1920* (1981).
Leighton, I., ed.	*The Aspirin Age, 1919–1941.* (Good collection of essays on various aspects of American social history.)
McCoy, D. R.	*Coming of Age: The United States During the 1920s and 1930s,* The Pelican History of the United States (Harmondsworth, 1973).
McKelvey, B.	*The Urbanization of America, 1860–1915* (New Brunswick, NJ, 1963).
Manuel, F. E., ed.	*Utopias and Utopian Thought* (Boston, 1966). (Essays by Lewis Mumford, Northrop Frye, Mircea Eliade, and others.)
May, H. F.	*The End of American Innocence: The First Years of Our Own Time, 1912–1917* (1959).
May, L.	*Screening Out the Past: The Birth of Mass Culture and the Motion Picture Industry* (New York and Oxford, 1980). (Analyses aspects of the shift in America from Victorian to modern life.)
Morgan, H. W.	*Unity and Culture: The United States, 1877–1900.* The Pelican History of the United States (Harmondsworth, 1973).
Mumford, L.	*The Brown Decades: A Study of the Arts in America, 1865–1895* 2nd edn (1955). *The Golden Day: A Study in American Experience and Culture* (1932, reprinted 1968).
Parry, A.	*Garrets and Pretenders: A History of Bohemianism in America* rev. edn (1964). (Two new chapters added to the 1933 edition.)
Pells, R. H.	*Radical Visions and American Dreams* (1973). (Intellectual History of the 1930s.)
Rosenberg, B., and D. Manning, eds	*Mass Culture: The Popular Arts in America* (Glencoe, Ill., 1957).
Sklar, R.	*Movie-Made America* (1975). (Examines American films in relation to contemporary social issues.)
Smith, H. N.	*Virgin Land: The American West as Symbol and Myth* (Cambridge, Mass., 1950).
Stott, W.	*Documentary Expression and Thirties America* (1973).
Taylor, P. A. M.	*The Distant Magnet: European Migration to the U.S.A.* (London, 1971). (Surveys the general pattern of immigration.)

Terkel, S.   *Hard Times: An Oral History of the Great Depression*
(1970).

Trachenberg, A.   *The American Image: Photographs from the National
Archives, 1860–1960* (1979).
*The Incorporation of America: Culture and Society in
the Gilded Age* (1982).

Voss, A.   *The American Short Story: A Critical Survey*
(Norman, Okla., 1973). (The most comprehensive
general survey available.)

White M., and L. White   *The Intellectual Versus the City* (Cambridge, Mass.,
1962). (Excellent chapters on Adams, James,
Howells, and the Naturalists.)

White, M.   *Science and Sentiment in America* (1972).
(Philosophical thought from Jonathan Edwards to
John Dewey.)

Wish, H.   *Society and Thought in America* 2nd edn, 2 vols
(1962). (Vol. II deals with America from 1865 to
the present.)

(ii) References and bibliography

American Literary Scholarship: An Annual (Durham,
NC, 1965–   ).

Blanck, J. N.   *Bibliography of American Literature*, 7 vols (New
Haven, Conn., 1955–   ).

Gohdes, C.   *Bibliographical Guide to the Study of the Literature of
the U.S.A.* 3rd edn (Durham, NC, 1970). (Lists of
books to aid the student in acquiring information
and techniques of research.)

Hart, D. J.   *The Oxford Companion to American Literature* (New
York and Oxford, 1965).

Herzberg, M. J., ed.   *The Reader's Encyclopaedia of American Literature*
(1962).

Jones, H. M., and R. M.
Ludwig   *Guide to American Literature and Its Backgrounds Since
1890*, 4th edn (Cambridge, Mass., 1972).

Leary, L.   *Articles on American Literature, 1900–1950* (Durham,
NC, 1954).
Articles on American Literature, 1950–1967 (Durham,
NC, 1970).

Mottram, E., M.
Bradbury, and J. France,
eds   *The Penguin Companion to Literature: U.S.A. and
Latin America* (London, 1971).

Nevius, B.   *The American Novel: Sinclair Lewis to the Present*
(1970). (Lists criticism of major authors.)

(iii)　History and criticism

Aldridge, J. W.
After the Lost Generation: A Critical Study of the Writers of Two Wars (1951). (Hemingway, Dos Passos, and Fitzgerald are the subjects of the first half of the book.)

Bradbury, J. M.
Renaissance in the South: A Critical History of the Literature, 1920–1960 (Chapel Hill, NC, 1963).

Bradbury, M.
The Modern American Novel (Oxford and New York, 1983). (Treats American fiction decade by decade from the 1890s to the present.)

Brooks, V. W.
America's Coming of Age. (The period of literary revolt leading to the 1920s.)

Brooks, V. W.
The Confident Years, 1885–1915 (1952). (The last volume in his history of the writer in America, 1800–1915. The other volumes are: *The World of Washington Irving; The Flowering of New England; The Times of Melville and Whitman;* and *New England: Indian Summer.*)

Carter, P. A.
Another Part of the Twenties (1977) (American society seen from a perspective different from that normally adopted.)

Cowley, M. ed.
After the Genteel Tradition: American Writers Since 1910 (1937). (Excellent collection of essays on major figures.)

Cowley, M.
The Dream of the Golden Mountains: Remembering the 1930s (1980). (A chronological sequel to *Exile's Return.*)
Exile's Return: A Literary Odyssey of the 1920s (1951). (Classic account of the 'lost generation'.)
A Second Flowering: Works and Days of the Lost Generation (1973). (Commentary on eight representative writers.)

Donald, M.
The American Novel in the Twentieth Century (London and New York, 1978).

Duffey, B. I.
The Chicago Renaissance in American Letters: A Critical History (E. Lansing, Mich., 1954).

Fiedler, L. A.
Waiting For the End: The American Literary Scene from Hemingway to Baldwin (1964).

Geismar, M.
The Last of the Provincials, the American Novel 1915–1925 (Boston, Mass., 1947). (Anderson, Cather, Lewis, Fitzgerald.)
Rebels and Ancestors, 1890–1915 (Boston, Mass., 1953). (Norris, Crane, London, Glasgow, and Dreiser.)

	Writers in Crisis: The American Novel Between Two Wars (Boston, Mass., 1942). (Hemingway, Dos Passos, Faulkner, Wolfe, and Steinbeck.)
Gurko, L.	*The Angry Decade: American Literature and Thought from 1929 to Pearl Harbor* (1947).
Hicks, G.	*The Great Tradition: An Interpretation of American Literature Since the Civil War* (1933). (A Marxist interpretation.)
Hoffman, J. F.	*The Modern Novel in America, 1900–1950* (Chicago, 1951). *The Twenties: American Writing in the Post-War Decade* (1955). (Seven themes illustrated by analyses of important texts.)
Howe, I.	*Decline of the New* (London, 1971). (Traces the break-up of modernist culture.)
Kazin, A.	*On Native Grounds: A Study of American Prose Literature from 1890 to the Present* (1942).
Kenner, H.	*A Homemade World: The American Modernist Writers* (1975). (On Faulkner, Hemingway, Fitzgerald, and others.)
Klein, M.	*Foreigners: The Making of American Literature, 1900–1940* (Chicago and London, 1981).
Krammer, D.	*Chicago Renaissance: The Literary Life in the Midwest, 1900–1930* (1966).
Levin, H.	*Memories of the Moderns* (London, 1981). (Comparative study of modernism.)
McCormick, J.	*American Literature, 1919–1932: A Comparative History* (London, 1971).
Martin, J.	*Harvests of Change: American Literature, 1865–1914* (Englewood Cliffs, NJ, 1967).
Rosenfeld, P.	*Port of New York* (Urbana, Ill. and London, 1966). (Reprint of Rosenfeld's essays on fourteen modern artists, originally published in 1924.)
Straumann, H.	*American Literature in the Twentieth Century* (London, 1951). (European view of American conceptions of life.)
Van Doren, C.	*The American Novel, 1789–1939* (1940).
Wilson, E.	*The American Earthquake* (1958). (Documentary of the Jazz Age and the Great Depression.) *The Shores of Light: A Literary Chronicle of the Twenties and Thirties* (1952). *The Twenties* (London, 1975). (Illuminating extracts from notebooks and diaries.)
Ziff, L.	*The American 1890s: Life and Times of a Lost Generation* (1966).

(iv) Special topics

Aaron, D.	*Writers on the Left: Episodes in American Literary Communism* (1961). (Concentrates on the period between 1912 and the Second World War.)
Ahnebrink, L.	*The Beginnings of Naturalism in American Fiction: A Study of the Works of Hamlin Garland, Stephen Crane, and Frank Norris with Special Reference to Some European Influences, 1891–1903.* (Uppsala and Cambridge, Mass., 1950).
Atterby B.	*The Fantasy Tradition in American Literature: From Irving to Le Guin* (Bloomington, Ind., 1980).
Berthoff, W.	*The Ferment of Realism: American Literature, 1894–1919* (1965). (Excellent account of the contexts within which America's realism developed.)
Blake, F. M.	*The Strike in the American Novel* (Metuchen, NJ, 1972). (Includes a large annotated bibliography of strike novels.).
Blake, N. M.	*Novelists' America: Fiction as History, 1910–1940* (Syracuse, NY, 1969).
Blotner, J. L.	*The Modern American Political Novel, 1900–1960,* (Austin, Tex., 1966).
Bluefarb, S.	*The Escape Motif in the American Novel: Mark Twain to Richard Wright* (Columbus, Ohio, 1972). (Traces the theme in eight major novels.)
Bluestone, G.	*Novels Into Film* (Baltimore, 1957).
Bowden, E. T.	*The Dungeon of the Heart: Human Isolation and the American Novel* (1961). (Traces the theme in twelve major novels from Cooper to Faulkner.)
Everson, W.	*Archetype West: The Pacific Coast as a Literary Region* (Berkeley, Calif., 1976).
Fiedler, L. A.	*Love and Death in the American Novel* (1960). (A brilliant balance of psychological and sociological analysis.) *The Return of the Vanishing American* (1968). (Takes the history of the Western novel up to the 1960s.)
Folson, J. K.	*The American Western Novel* (New Haven, Connecticut: 1966). (Deals with popular literature as well as the 'classic' Western novels.)
Franklin, H. B.	*Future Perfect: American Science Fiction of the Nineteenth Century* (1966).
Fraser, J.	*America and the Patterns of Chivalry* (Cambridge, 1982). (Interesting discussion of chivalric values in American fiction.)

Frohock, W. M.   *The Novel of Violence in America*, 2nd edn enlarged (Dallas, 1957). (Concentrates on the period between the two world wars.)

Glicksberg, C. I.   *The Sexual Revolution in Modern American Literature* (The Hague, 1971). (From Dreiser to Mailer.)

Gross, T. L.   *The Heroic Ideal in American Literature* (New York and London, 1972). (Good on Southern and Black heroes.)

Guttmann, A.   *The Jewish Writer in America: Assimilation and the Crisis of Identity* (1971).

Habegger, A.   *Gender, Fantasy, and Realism in American Literature* (1982).

Hilfer, A. C.   *The Revolt from the Village, 1915–1980* (Chapel Hill, NC, 1969).

Hoffman, F. J.   *Freudianism and the Literary Mind* (Baton Rouge, La., 1958). (See chapter on Anderson, Waldo Frank, and Fitzgerald.)

Howe, I.   *Politics and the Novel*, (1957). (See Ch. 7, 'The Politics of Isolation'.)

Huggins, N. I.   *The Harlem Renaissance* (1971).

Jones, A. G.   *Tomorrow Is Another Day: The Woman Writer in the South, 1859–1936* (Baton Rouge, La., and London, 1981). (Discusses seven writers including Kate Chopin, Ellen Glasgow, and Margaret Mitchell.)

Kaplan, H.   *Henry Adams and the Naturalist Tradition in American Fiction* (Chicago, 1981).

Kolodny, A.   *The Lay of the Land: Metaphor as Experience and History in American Life and Letters* (Chapel Hill, NC, 1975). (Traces the repetitions of the 'land-as-woman' symbol in American literature.)

Lee, L. L., and M. Lewis, eds   *Women, Women Writers, and the West* (1980). (Essays on Cather, Rölvaag, Garland, and others.)

Lee, R. E.   *From West to East: Studies in the Literature of the American West* (Urbana, Ill., 1966).

Leisy, E.   *The American Historical Novel* (Norman, Okla., 1950). (Relevant sections on The Westward Movement, The Civil War, and National Expansion.)

Lively, R. A.   *Fiction Fights the Civil War: An Unfinished Chapter in the Literary History of the American People* (Chapel Hill, NC, 1957).

Love, G. A.   *New Americans: The Westerner and the Modern Experience in the American Novel* (London and Toronto, 1982). (Chapters on Norris, Garland, Cather, Anderson, and Lewis.)

Lynn, K. S.   *The Dream of Success: A Study of the Modern American Imagination* (Boston, Mass., 1955).

Madden, D., ed.   *Proletarian Writers of the Thirties* (Carbondale and Edwardsville, Ill. 1968).
Tough Guy Writers of the Thirties (Carbondale and Edwardsville; Ill. 1968). (Essays on Hemingway, Cain, Hammett, Chandler, and others.)

Magny, C.-E.   *The Age of the American Novel: The Film Aesthetic of Fiction Between the Two Wars* (1972). (Dos Passos, Hemingway, Steinbeck, and Faulkner.)

Malin, E., ed.   *Psychoanalysis and American Fiction* (1965). (Essays on Twain, James, Norris, Cather, Caldwell, and others.)

Margolies, E.   *Native Sons: A Critical Study of Twentieth-Century Negro Authors* (Philadelphia, 1968).

Mellard, J. M.   *The Exploded Form: The Modernist Novel in America* (Urbana, Ill., 1980). (Traces Modernism through Naive, Critical, and Sophisticated phases.)

Miller, W. C.   *An Armed America, Its Face in Fiction: A History of the American Military Novel* (New York and London, 1970). (Covers the period from the American Revolution to the Second World War.)

Millgate, M.   *American Social Fiction: James to Cozzens* (1964).

Pinsker, S.   *The Schlemiel as Metaphor: Studies in the Yiddish and American Jewish Novel* (Carbondale, Ill., 1971).

Pizer, D.   *Realism and Naturalism in Nineteenth Century American Literature* (Carbondale, S. Ill., 1966).

Poirier, R.   *A World Elsewhere: The Place of Style in American Literature* (London, 1967). (Excellent on James, Twain, and Dreiser.)

Rideout, W. B.   *The Radical Novel in the United States, 1900–1954: Some Interrelations of Literature and Society* (Cambridge, Mass., 1956).

Rubin, L. D. jun., ed.   *The Comic Imagination in American Literature* (New Brunswick, NJ, 1973). (Good collection of essays on various themes and individual authors.)

Skaggs, H. M.   *The Folk of Southern Fiction* (Athens, Ga., 1972). (Relates local colour literature to social and political context.)

Spindler, M.   *American Literature and Social Change: William Dean Howells to Arthur Miller* (London, 1983).

Sundquist, E. J., ed.   *American Realism: New Essays* (Baltimore and London, 1982). (An excellent collection of essays on all the major Realists.)

Taylor, W. F.   *The Economic Novel in America* (Chapel Hill, NC, 1942).

Walcutt, C. C.   *American Literary Naturalism: A Divided Stream* (Minneapolis, 1956).

Walsh, C.   *From Utopia to Nightmare* (London, 1962). (An account of modern dystopian fiction.)

Weintraub, S.   *The London Yankees* (New York and London, 1979). (Portraits of American expatriate writers between 1874 and 1914.)

Weiss, R.   *The American Myth of Success* (1969). (Social history based on popular success literature.)

Wells, W.   *Tycoons and Locusts: A Regional Look at Hollywood Fiction of the 1930s* (Carbondale and Edwardsville, Ill. 1973). (Fitzgerald, McCoy, Cain, West, and Chandler.)

Westbrook, P. D.   *Free Will and Determinism in American Literature* (Rutherford, NJ, and London, 1979). (Good account of the Determinists and their opponents.)

Wickes, G.   *Americans in Paris, 1903–1939* (1969). (From Gertrude Stein to Henry Miller.)

Wilson, E.   *Patriotic Gore: Studies in the Literature of the American Civil War* (1962). (Excellent section on novelists of the post-war South.)

Individual Authors

Notes on biography, major works, and criticism

ANDERSON, Sherwood (1876–1941), born in Camden, Ohio, but spent his early life moving from one small Midwestern town to another as his father's various business ventures failed. He left high school without graduating, worked briefly in Chicago, and after marrying the daughter of a wealthy businessman, settled down to his own business interests in Ohio. In 1912 he suffered a mental collapse, abandoned his wife and his career, and moved to Chicago to become a full-time writer. His early novels, *Windy McPherson's Son* (1916), *Marching Men* (1917), and especially *Winesburg, Ohio* (1919), established him as a leading writer of the Chicago Renaissance. In the 1920s, living in New Orleans with his second wife, Anderson exerted a considerable influence on such men as Hemingway, Dos Passos, and Faulkner, and continued to produce such novels as *Poor White* (1920), *Many Marriages* (1923), *Dark Laughter* (1925), *Beyond Desire* (1932), and *Kit Brandon* (1936). His early short stories, collected in *The Triumph of the Egg* (1921) and *Horses and Men* (1923) were also popular at the time, but Anderson's reputation declined rapidly in the 1930s and he died in almost complete obscurity while on a tour of South America.

> Schevill, J., *Sherwood Anderson: His Life and Work* (Denver, 1951).
> Jones, H. M. and W. J. Rideout, eds, *Letters of Sherwood Anderson* (1953).

> See: Howe, I., *Sherwood Anderson* (1951). (Rejects much of Anderson's work as muddled or minor but writes well about *Winesburg* and the best short stories.)
> Burbank, R., *Sherwood Anderson* (1964). (Good on the sources of the novels and their intellectual framework.)
> Anderson, D. D., *Sherwood Anderson: An Introduction and Interpretation* (1967).

BIERCE, Ambrose Gwinnet (1842–1914?), born in Meigs County, Ohio, the son of a farmer. He had no formal education, but after serving in the Civil War he worked in the Mint in California and had his first short story published in 1871. Between 1872 and 1876 he worked as a journalist in London before returning to America to write for Hearst's *Examiner*. He had published two collections of sketches, but his best stories are contained in two later volumes, *Tales of Soldiers and Civilians* (1891) and *Can Such Things Be* (1893). As he grew older he became increasingly disillusioned with life. This is exemplified in the bitter irony of his definitions in *The Devil's Dictionary* (1911), and by his disappearance in

Mexico where he had gone to find 'the good, kind darkness', and where he met an uncertain end.

Fatout, P. *Ambrose Bierce, the Devil's Lexicographer* (Norman, Okla., 1951).

O'Connor, R. *Ambrose Bierce: A Biography* (London, 1968).

CABELL, James Branch (1879–1958), born in Richmond into one of the first families of Virginia. He was educated at William and Mary College, and after graduating in 1898, spent some time as a college instructor in Greek and French, and short periods as a journalist in New York and Richmond. After his marriage to Priscilla Bradley in 1913 he lived quietly in Richmond as a Virginia gentleman, preoccupied with his genealogical studies and the creation of his romantic fictional world called Poictesme, in which his hero Dom Manuel strives to achieve unattainable ideals. These novels were subsequently arranged by Cabell in the following genealogical order: *Figures of Earth* (1921), *The Silver Stallion* (1920), *Domnei* (1920), *The Music From Behind the Moon* (1926), *Chivalry* (1909), *Jurgen* (1919), *The Line of Love* (1905), *The High Place* (1923), *Gallantry* (1907), *Something About Eve* (1927), *The Certain Hour* (1916), *The Cards of Vanity* (1909), *From the Hidden Way* (1916), *The Jewel Merchants* (1921), *The Rivet in Grandfather's Neck* (1915), *The Eagle's Shadow* (1904), and *The Cream of the Jest* (1917). An attempt to suppress *Jurgen* on the grounds of sexual immorality led to a brief spell of popularity for Cabell and a considerable increase in income, but his mannered style and disdain for the contemporary world ('Tell the rabble, my name is Cabell') led to almost complete neglect in the 1930s.

Van Doren, C., *James Branch Cabell* (1932).

Davis, J. L. *James Branch Cabell* (1962).

Wells, A. R., *Jesting Moses: A Study in Cabellian Comedy* (Gainsville, Fl., 1962).

Tarrant, D., *James Branch Cabell: The Dream and the Reality* (Norman, Okla., 1967).

CABLE, George Washington (1844–1925), born in New Orleans though he was descended from an old Virginia family. In the Civil War he served with the 4th Mississippi Cavalry and used this experience to write *The Cavalier* (1901). After the war he tried different occupations but was most successful as a humorous columnist for the New Orleans *Picayune*. As a Calvinist, however, he refused to write drama criticism and was dropped from the newspaper. The success of his first short stories, collected in *Old Creole Days* (1879), encouraged him to write *The Grandissimes* (1880), and this was followed by *Dr. Sevier* (1885), *Bonaventure* (1885), and *Bylow Hill* (1902). Though he was popular as a local colourist, Cable's reforming zeal angered many Southerners, and he eventually moved to Massachusetts where he wrote *The Negro Question* (1888) and *The Southern Struggle for Pure Government* (1890).

Turner, A., *George W. Cable: A Biography* (Durham, NC, 1956).

Turner, A., *Mark Twain and George W. Cable: The Record of a Literary Friendship* (East Lansing, Michi., 1960).

See: Butcher, P., *George W. Cable* (1962).

CALDWELL, Erskine (1903–   ), born in Coweta County, Georgia, the son of a

Presbyterian minister whose post as secretary of his denomination involved his family constantly moving throughout the South. This prevented Caldwell from receiving any regular education and he spent his early years in a variety of places following different casual occupations. After his marriage to Helen Lannigan in 1925, Caldwell settled for five years in Maine, where he wrote his two best-known works, *Tobacco Road* (1932) and *God's Little Acre* (1933). He continued to produce fiction throughout the 1930s and 1940s, including *Journeyman* (1935), *Trouble in July* (1940), and *Tragic Ground* (1944). The best of his later work, however, is contained in volumes of short stories such as *Kneel to the Rising Sun* (1935), *Southways* (1938), and *Georgia Boy* (1943). He also collaborated with his second wife, the photographer Margaret Bourke White, to produce documentary studies such as *You Have Seen Their Faces* (1937).

Korges, J. *Erskine Caldwell* (Minneapolis, 1969). (University of Minnesota Pamphlets on American Writers, 1978).

CATHER, Willa Sibert (1873–1947), born in Virginia, but moved with her family to a ranch in Nebraska when she was eight years old. She was educated locally, paying her way through the University of Nebraska by working as a newspaper correspondent, and graduating in 1895. After several years spent as a journalist and teacher in the provinces she was appointed managing editor of *McClure's Magazine* in New York. She remained in this post for six years until 1912 when she resigned to become a full-time writer. She had already published a book of poems in 1903 (*April Twilights*) and one of short stories in 1905 (*The Troll Garden*), but after her resignation she concentrated more on longer fiction. *O Pioneers* (1913) was her first great success, and this was followed by *My Antonia* (1918) and *A Lost Lady* (1923). After her conversion to Roman catholicism she wrote about different themes and locations, *Death Comes for the Archbishop* (1927) being set in the Spanish South-west and *Shadows on the Rock* (1931) French Quebec.

Brown, E. D., and L. Edel, *Willa Cather: A Critical Biography* (Chicago, 1963). (James's biographer completed this scholarly study.)
Woodress, J., *Willa Cather: Her Life and Art* (1970). (Based on letters and other materials not available earlier.)
See: Daiches, D., *Willa Cather: A Critical Introduction* (Ithaca, NY, 1951). (Still the best general introduction.)
Stouck, D., *Willa Cather's Imaginations* (Lincoln, Neb., 1975).

CHOPIN, Kate (O'Flaherty) (1851–1904), born in St Louis, Missouri. Her father was an Irish immigrant and her mother was descended from French Creole stock. At the age of nineteen Kate married a Louisiana Creole, Oscar Chopin, with whom she lived in New Orleans, bearing him six children before his death in 1883. At this time she moved back to her native city and began to write fiction. *At Fault* (1890) is a novel about Creole life, and this was followed by two volumes of stories with similar subjects, *Bayou Folk* (1894) and *A Night in Acadie* (1897). *The Awakening* (1899) caused a storm of controversy and brought her literary career to an end.

Seyerstad, P., *Kate Chopin: A Critical Biography* (Baton Rouge, La., 1969).

See: Wolff, C. G., 'Thanatos and Eros: Kate Chopin's *The Awakening'*, *American Quarterly*, 25 (1973), 123–33. (Interesting psychological analysis of Chopin's heroine.)

         Jones, A. G., *Tomorrow is Another Day: The Woman Writer in the South*, 1859–1936 (Baton Rouge, La., 1981). (Good chapter on Chopin's career.)

CLEMENS, Samuel Langhorne ('Mark Twain') (1835–1910), spent his childhood in the Mississippi valley town of Hannibal, where after the death of his father he became a printer's apprentice. He had a long and varied connection with newspapers as both a journalist and an owner, but before he became a full-time man of letters he also spent some time as a riverboat pilot, recording his experiences in *Life on the Mississippi* (1883). He also tried his hand at mining in Nevada, and this period of his life is reflected in *Roughing It* (1872). His first published story, however, 'The Celebrated Jumping Frog of Calaveras County', appeared in a California newspaper in 1865. It won him immediate fame, and another newspaper financed a trip to Europe where he wrote a series of travel sketches later republished as *The Innocents Abroad* (1869). In 1870 he married Olivia Langdon with whom he settled down in the East to become a professional writer, though he still undertook arduous lecture tours for a number of years both in America and abroad. He collaborated with one of his neighbours in Hartford, Connecticut, to produce his first full-length novel, *The Gilded Age* (1873). Throughout the 1870s and 1880s Twain occupied himself with his writing and various business ventures, bringing the two activities together in 1883 by founding his own publishing firm. His major works of this period were *The Adventures of Tom Sawyer* (1876), *A Tramp Abroad* (1880), *The Prince and the Pauper* (1882), *The Adventures of Huckleberry Finn* (1884), and *A Connecticut Yankee in King Arthur's Court* (1889). In 1894 Twain's publishing firm went bankrupt and Twain himself, shattered by this and other domestic tragedies, endured a period of personal unhappiness and philosophical pessimism from which he never fully recovered. He continued to write, though, and to travel the world. His later works include *The American Claimant* (1892), *Tom Sawyer Abroad* (1894), *The Tragedy of Puddn'head Wilson* (1894), *Personal Recollections of Joan of Arc* (1896), *Tom Sawyer, Detective* (1896), *The Man That Corrupted Hadleyburg and Other Stories and Essays* (1900) and *The Mysterious Stranger* (1916).

         Paine, A. B., *Mark Twain: A Biography*, 3 vols (1912). (The first, indispensable account of Twain's life.)

         Brooks, V. W., *The Ordeal of Mark Twain* (1920). (Argues that Twain's true talent was thwarted by his background, his ambition, and his literary advisers.)

         DeVoto, B., *Mark Twain's America* (Boston, Mass., 1932).

         DeVoto, B., *Mark Twain at Work* (Cambridge, Mass., 1942). (In these two books, reprinted in one volume (Boston, 1967), DeVoto attacks Brooks's thesis.)

         Kaplan, J., *Mr. Clemens and Mark Twain* (Cambridge, Mass., 1966; reprinted Harmondsworth, 1970). (Less polemical than previous accounts, also benefits from the availability of new material.)

See: Bellamy, G. C., *Mark Twain as a Literary Artist* (Norman, Okla., 1950). (A general critical survey claiming considerable conscious artistry in Twain's work.)

Lynn, K. S., *Mark Twain and Southwestern Humor* (Boston, Mass. and Toronto, 1959).

Blair, W., *Mark Twain and Huck Finn* (Berkeley and Los Angeles, 1960). (Centres on his masterpiece but ranges widely to explore the influence that made it possible.)

Smith, H. N., *Mark Twain: The Development of a Writer* (Cambridge, Mass., 1962). (The best critical account of how the tensions and paradoxes of Twain's life affected his art.)

Budd, L. J., *Mark Twain: Social Philosopher* (Bloomington, Ind., 1964).

Cox, J. M., *Mark Twain: The Fate of Humor* (Princeton, NJ, 1966). A serious, sensitive study of the scope, implications and development of Twain's humour.)

Spengemann, W. C., *Mark Twain and the Backwoods Angel: The Matter of Innocence in the Works of Samuel L. Clemens* (Kent, Ohio, 1966).

Gibson, W. M., *The Art of Mark Twain* (1976). (A general survey which places greater emphasis on Twain's shorter works, believing them to be his best.)

Harris, Susan K., *Mark Twain's Escape from Time: A Study of Patterns and Images* (Columbia, Missouri, and London, 1982). (Uses the ideas of Gaston Bachelard, the French phenomenologist to explain how Twain's preferred images help him make an imaginative escape from time and despair.)

CRANE, Stephen (1871–1900), fourteenth child of the Rev. J. T. Crane; educated at several New Jersey schools where he demonstrated a talent for baseball and the theatre. He spent one semester at Syracuse University during which time he wrote the first draft of *Maggie: A Girl of the Streets*. He continued to write fiction and poetry as well as newspaper sketches and war reports as he travelled widely in the United States and abroad. *The Red Badge of Courage*, originally published in a short newspaper version in the Philadelphia *Press* in 1894 made him famous when it appeared in book form the following year. In 1897, after being shipwrecked *en route* to cover a military expedition to Cuba, he came to England with Cora Taylor, the former proprietress of a brothel in Jacksonville. They spent the last years of Crane's life in Surrey and Sussex, interrupted by his nine-month stint as a war correspondent in Cuba. This adventure failed to alleviate his increasing financial difficulties or his deteriorating health. He continued to write, though, and was at the centre of a distinguished literary circle which included Conrad and Henry James. Ill health forced him to seek a cure for his tuberculosis in Germany where he died, at Badenweiler, in 1900.

Berryman, J., *Stephen Crane* (1950). (More valuable for the critical insights of a fellow poet than for the Freudian interpretation of Crane's life.)

Stallman, R. W. and L. Gilkes, eds, *Stephen Crane: Letters* (1960).

Stallman, R. W., *Stephen Crane: A Biography* (1968). (The most informative account of Crane's life, though not as well written as Thomas Beer's earlier biography (1923).)

See: Solomon, E., *Stephen Crane: From Parody to Realism* (Cambridge, Mass., 1966). (Demonstrates the connection between Crane's fiction and the forms of popular nineteenth-century writing.)

Gibson, D. B., *The Fiction of Stephen Crane* (Carbondale, Ill.,
1968). (Psychological analyses of Crane's characters.)
La France, M., *A Reading of Stephen Crane* (Oxford, 1971).
(Explores Crane's ironic techniques.)
Holton, M., *The Fiction and Journalistic Writing of Stephen Crane*
(Baton Rouge, La., 1972). Examines combination of naturalism
and impressionism.)
Gullason, T. A., ed., *Stephen Crane's Career: Perspectives and
Evaluations* (1972). (A large collection of critical essays from the
1890s to the present, celebrating the centennial of Crane's
birth.)
Nagel, J., *Stephen Crane and Literary Impressionism* (Philadelphia,
1980).

DELL, Floyd (1887–   ), born in Barry, Illinois, of poor parents, he left school
early and soon moved to Chicago where he established a reputation for his
literary journalism. Later in New York he served as an editor of *The
Masses* and *The Liberator*. Before turning to fiction he wrote one-act plays
and a study of child psychology. His first novel, *Moon-Calf* (1920) is one
of the first to document the mores of the disillusioned post-war
generation. This was a subject he continued to treat in *The Briary-Bush*
(1921), *Janet March* (1923), and *Runaway* (1925). He also wrote comic
novels such as *An Unmarried Father* (1927).

Hart, J., *Floyd Dell* (1971)

DOS PASSOS, John (1896–1970), born in Chicago, the son of a successful
lawyer descended from Portuguese and American Quaker stock. Educated
at Harvard where he contributed to several magazines, some of his college
verse being published later in *Eight Harvard Poets* (1917). His father who
had fought in the Civil War, prevented him from joining an American
ambulance unit in 1916 by financing a year of architectural study in Spain.
When his father died, however, Dos Passos enlisted in the Norton–Harjes
unit and served in Italy and France. These experiences provided the
background for his first novels, *One Man's Initiation: 1917* (1920) and *Three
Soldiers* (1921). Throughout the 1920s he travelled extensively and wrote
about Europe, the Near East, and Russia. He found time to also produce
two novels, *Streets of Night* (1923) and *Manhattan Transfer* (1925); two
plays, *The Garbage Man* (1926) and *Airways Inc.* (1928); and a defence of
Sacco and Vanzetti, *Facing the Chair* (1927). He also helped found and
wrote for both *The New Masses* magazine and The New Playwrights
Theatre. Throughout the 1930s Dos Passos continued his career as
novelist, playwright, and political reporter, though his major literary effort
went into the writing of the three volumes of *U.S.A. – The 42nd Parallel*
(1930), *1919* (1932), and *The Big Money* (1936). During and after the
Second World War he became increasingly interested in the roots of
American culture and produced a number of historical studies relating to
the problems of American democracy.

Landsberg, M., *Dos Passos' Path to 'U.S.A.'* (Boulder, Col., 1970).
(A political biography covering the years 1912–36.)
Ludington, T., ed., *The Fourteenth Chronicle: Letters and Diaries of
John Dos Passos* (Boston, 1973). (Includes correspondence with
Hemingway, Fitzgerald, Anderson, and other major figures.)

See: Ludington, T., *John Dos Passos: A Twentieth Century Odyssey* (1980).
        Sartre, J-P., 'John Dos Passos and *1919*', in his *Literary and Philosophical Essays* (London, 1955).
        Wrenn, J. H., *John Dos Passos* (1961).
        Brantley, J. D., *The Fiction of John Dos Passos* (The Hague, 1968).
        McLuhan, M., 'John Dos Passos: Technique versus Sensibility', in *Fifty Years of the American Novel*, ed. by H. C. Gardiner, SJ (1968). (This essay and Sartre's contain the most perceptive criticism of Dos Passos written to date.)
        Colley, I., *Dos Passos and the Fiction of Despair* (London, 1978).
        Wagner, L. W., *Dos Passos: Artist as American* (Austin, Tex., 1979).
        Rosen, R. C., *John Dos Passos: Politics and the Writer* (Lincoln, Neb. and London, 1981).

DREISER, Theodore Herman (1871–1945), son of poor immigrants in Terre Haute, Indiana. He broke off his high school education in 1887 to seek work in Chicago. Until 1894 when he moved to New York he worked for numerous newspapers in the Midwest. With help from his brother, the song-writer Paul Dresser, he became a successful magazine editor and also began to write novels and short stories. After his difficulties with the publication of *Sister Carrie* (1900) he suffered a mental breakdown and did not publish any serious fiction until 1911, *Jennie Gerhardt*. With that novel and *The Financier* (1912) and *The Titan* (1914) his reputation was assured. He separated from his first wife, Sarah, at this time and settled in California with his mother's grand-niece, Helen Richardson whom he married in 1944. The final volume of his trilogy, *The Stoic*, appeared posthumously in 1947. His other works include *The 'Genius'* (1915), *An American Tragedy* (1925), and *The Bulwark* (1946). In the later part of his life he travelled widely, visiting Russia in 1928 and Spain during the Civil War in 1938. He applied for membership of the Communist Party shortly before his death in Hollywood.

        Elias, R. H., ed., *Letters of Theodore Dreiser*, 3 vols (Philadelphia, 1959).
        Swanberg, W. A., *Dreiser* (1965). (Great wealth of documentary material.)
        Moers, E., *Two Dreisers* (1969). (Critical biography concentrates on *Sister Carrie* and *American Tragedy*.)

See: Matthiessen, F. O., *Theodore Dreiser* (1951). (Excellent analyses of Dreiser's style.)
        McAleer, J. J., *Theodore Dreiser* (1968) (Explore the tensions between the 'Natural' and the 'Social' in Dreiser's work.)
        Pizer, D., *The Novels of Theodore Dreiser: A Critical Study* (Minneapolis, 1976). (Excellent study of Dreiser's Naturalism.)

EGGLESTON, Edward (1837–1902), born at Vevay, Indiana, the son of a lawyer. After a period as a Methodist minister, he founded his own church in Brooklyn and became an enthusiastic social, religious, and literary reformer. His novels are based upon his close observation of life and memories in Indiana and include *The Hoosier Schoolmaster* (1871), *The End of the World* (1872), *The Circuit Rider* (1874), and *Roxy* (1978).

        Randel, W. P., *Edward Eggleston* (1963).

FARRELL, James Thomas (1904–79), born in Chicago's South Side, an area he lived in until 1931 and wrote about all his life. He was educated at a Catholic high school and attended classes at Chicago University where he wrote the first parts of his famous trilogy, *Young Lonigan* (1932), *The Young Manhood of Studs Lonigan* (1934), and *Judgement Day* (1935). After moving to New York City where he received various prizes and fellowships in recognition of his early work, Farrell remained loyal to his original social ideas and his theories of literary Naturalism. These are discussed in his critical works, *A Note on Literary Criticism* (1936), *The League of Frightened Philistines* (1945) and *Literature and Morality* (1947). They are also exemplified in his later fictional cycles dealing with the life of Danny O'Neill in five books and Bernard Carr in three. In addition to these, Farrell has also published over 200 short stories and several more novels, the best known being *Gas-House McGinty* (1933).

Wald, A. M., *James Farrell: The Revolutionary Socialist Years* (1978)
Branch, E. M., *James T. Farrell* (1971).

FAULKNER, William (1897–1962), born in New Albany., Mississippi, and brought up in Oxford where his father owned a livery stable and was also Treasurer of the University of Mississippi. Faulkner left school early, joined the Royal Flying Corps in Canada in the First World War but was prevented by the Armistice from seeing active service. He returned to Oxford, attended a few courses at the university and, supporting himself by various odd jobs, began to write poetry. After a short period in France and New York City he settled down to write his first novel, *Soldiers' Pay* (1926), in New Orleans, where he was befriended and encouraged by Sherwood Anderson. *Mosquitoes* (1927) was set in New Orleans but Faulkner soon decided to take Anderson's advice to write about the country he knew best and in which he now made his permanent home. With his next work, *Sartoris* (1929), he began the long series of novels set in the mythical Yoknapatawpha County, loosely based on the history of his own and neighbouring Mississippi families. He married Mrs Estelle (Oldham) Franklin in 1929, published *The Sound and the Fury*, but decided that in order to make money from fiction he needed to write a 'pot-boiler'. The result was *Sanctuary* (1931), his first popular success. It was bought by a film studio and Faulkner himself helped to adapt it for the screen. Financial security enabled him to write what he pleased thereafter and he produced his best novels in a steady stream during the 1930s. These include *As I Lay Dying, Light in August* (1932) and *Absalom, Absalom!* (1936). In 1939 Faulkner won the O'Henry Memorial Award and in 1950 the Nobel Prize. His later work which includes the 'Snopes Trilogy' – *The Hamlet* (1940), *The Town* (1957), and *The Mansion* (1959), *Intruder in the Dust* (1948), and *The Reivers* (1962), lacks the sustained intensity of his earlier fiction but helps to fill out the myth of Yoknapatawpha County.

Cowley, M., *The Faulkner-Cowley File: Letters and Memories, 1944–1962* (1966).
Blotner, J., *Faulkner: A Biography*, 2 vols (London, 1974).

See: Howe, I., *William Faulkner: A Critical Study*, 2nd edn (1952). (One of the earlier and more perceptive critical estimates.)
Brooks, C., *William Faulkner: The Yoknapatawpha Country* (New

Haven, Conn., 1963). (Explores the complex background of the fourteen major works.)

Vickery, O. W., *The Novels of William Faulkner: A Critical Introduction*, rev. edn (Baton Rouge, La., 1964). (Good analysis of structure in the major novels.)

Millgate, M., *The Achievement of William Faulkner* (1966). (Best introduction to the life and works.)

Irwin, J. T., *Doubling and Incest/Repetition and Revenge: A Speculative Reading of Faulkner* (Baltimore, 1975). (A good example of modern approaches to Faulkner using Structuralism and Psychoanalysis.)

Matthews, J. T., *The Play of Faulkner's Language* (Ithaca, NY, and London, 1982).

Brooks, P., *Reading for the Plot* (Oxford, 1984). (Excellent chapter on 'Incredulous Narrative: *Absalom, Absalom!*' in which Irwin's methods are extended to explore epistemological problems.)

FITZGERALD, Francis Scott Key (1896–1940), born in St Paul, Minnesota. His family was of Irish descent and his parents' prosperity enabled Fitzgerald to be educated at good schools and at Princeton, where he wrote an operetta but failed to graduate. He left university to join the Army in 1917 and served as an infantry lieutenant until 1919. He saw no action but was able to draft most of his first novel and begin work on some short stories which were later published in the *Smart Set*. Publication of *This Side of Paradise* (1920) brought him immediate fame as the leading spokesman of 'Jazz Age' youth, and sufficient money to marry Zelda Sayre. For the next ten years the Fitzgeralds stayed at the centre of a fast-moving, hard-living international set of American and European socialites, spending most of their time in New York, Rome, and the Riviera. Fitzgerald continued to work hard, though, and produced three volumes of short stories, *Flappers and Philosophers* (1920), *Tales of the Jazz Age* (1922), and *All the Sad Young Men* (1926), as well as *The Beautiful and Damned* (1922) and his masterpiece, *The Great Gatsby* (1925). In the 1930s Zelda's deteriorating health, and his own, curtailed Fitzgerald's activities, though he did produce *Tender is the Night* (1934) as well as another volume of stories, *Taps at Reveille* (1935). He spent his last years in Hollywood and at his death left an unfinished novel about the movie industry, *The Last Tycoon* (1941).

Mizener, A., *The Far Side of Paradise* (Boston, Mass., 1951; rev. edn 1965). (First of many critical biographies, but still useful.)

Turnbull, A., ed., *The Letters of F. Scott Fitzgerald* (1963; Harmondsworth, 1968).

Bruccoli, M. J., *Scott and Ernest: The Authority of Failure and the Authority of Success* (London, 1978). (Interesting account of the friendship and rivalry between Fitzgerald and Hemingway.)

Le Vot, A., *F. Scott Fitzgerald: A Biography*, trans. by William Byron (Harmondsworth, 1985).

See: Lehan, R. D., *F. Scott Fitzgerald and the Craft of Fiction* (Carbondale, Ill., 1966). (Relates Fitzgerald's work to the literature of the English Romantic tradition.)

Stern, M. R., *The Golden Moment – The Novels of F. Scott Fitzgerald* (Urbana, Ill., 1970). (Explores Fitzgerald's imaginative use of the American past.)

Callahan, J. F., *The Illusions of a Nation: Myth and History in the Novels of F. Scott Fitzgerald* (Urbana, Ill., 1972).

Stavola, T. J., *Scott Fitzgerald: Crisis in American Identity* (London, 1979). (Uses Erikson's ideas about the human life cycle to relate Fitzgerald's inner struggles to their contexts.)

Way, B., *F. Scott Fitzgerald and the Art of Social Fiction* (London, 1980). (Maintains that it is misleading to see Fitzgerald's main theme as the failure of the American Dream.)

FREDERIC, Harold (1856–1898), born in Utica, New York, where he spent his early years as a local journalist. In 1884 he became the permanent London correspondant of the *New York Times* and began to produce fiction, the best of which is set in the Mohawk Valley in upper New York State. This includes *Seth's Brother's Wife* (1887) and the work for which he is remembered, *The Damnation of Theron Ware* (1896), published in England as *Illumination*.

O'Donnel, T. F. and Franchare, H. C., *Harold Frederic* (1961).

See: Briggs, A., jun., *The novels of Harold Frederic* (Ithaca, NY, 1969). (Emphasizes the comic elements in Frederic's fiction.)

FULLER, Henry Blake (1857–1929), born in Chicago, the son of a bank cashier who was related to the Transcendentalist, Margaret Fuller. After graduating from high school and working for short periods in banking, he undertook his first European tour which led to the publication of his first novel, *The Chevalier of Pensieri-Vani* (1890). This was a successful witty romance set in Italy, and he followed it with *The Chatelaine de la Trinité* (1892). Back in Chicago, however, he was influenced by Mid-western realism and there wrote his best-known works, *The Cliff Dwellers* (1892) and *With the Procession* (1895). He worked as a book critic for various Chicago newspapers and was an active member of the Little Room, a group of artists who helped found Harriet Monroe's *Poetry: A Magazine of Verse* in 1912.

See: Ziff, L. *The American 1890s: Life and Times of a Lost Generation* (1966). (Chapter on Garland and Fuller, pp. 106–19.)

GARLAND, Hamlin (1860–1940), born in a pioneer log cabin at West Salem, Wisconsin, he spent his childhood on a 'Middle Border' farm in Iowa. By selling a nursery claim in North Dakota he raised enough money to move to Boston where he wrote *Main Travelled Roads* (1891) and his first novel, *A Spoil of Office* (1892). After his marriage to Zalima Taft he made his home in Chicago and produced *Rose of Dutcher's Coolly* (1895), *The Captain of the Gray-Horse Troop* (1902), *Hesper* (1903), *The Long Trail* (1907), and *The Forester's Daughter* (1914). Moving to New York in 1915 he then wrote the partly autobiographical work *A Son of the Middle Border* (1917) and its sequel *A Daughter of the Middle Border* (1921) which was awarded the Pulitzer Prize. In his later years in California, he wrote a book of reminiscences of the literary figures he had known, *Roadside Meetings* (1930)

Holloway, Jean, *Hamlin Garland, a Biography* (Austin, Tex., 1960).

See: Pizer, D., *Hamlin Garland's Early Work and Career* (Berkeley and Los Angeles, 1960).
Davidson, L. A., *Hamlin Garland: Centennial Tributes* (Los Angeles, 1962).

GLASGOW, Ellen Anderson Gholson (1874–1945), born in Richmond, Virginia, the eighth of ten children in an aristocratic family. Delicate health prevented her from receiving much formal education, but even as a young girl she was determined to be a writer and she had destroyed earlier work before publishing *The Descendant* anonymously in 1897. Even in her earlier fiction she reacted against the Southern sentimental tradition and her first novel was taken to be the work of Harold Frederic. In 1900, with the publication of *The Voice of the People*, she began the long series of novels exploring the social history of Virginia from the middle of the nineteenth century up to her own day. These included *The Battle-ground* (1902), *The Deliverance* (1904), *The Wheel of Life* (1906), *The Ancient Law* (1908), *The Romance of a Plain Man* (1909), and *The Miller of Old Church* (1911). She also wrote novels about the position of Southern women such as *Virginia* (1913) and *Gabriella* (1916). Of her later work, the best-known examples are *Barren Ground* (1925) and *Vein of Iron* (1935). In the 1920s she began a series of satirical novels of manners comprising *The Romantic Comedians* (1926), *They Stooped to Folly* (1929), and *Sheltered Life* (1932).

> Rouse, B., *The Letters of Ellen Glasgow* (1958).
> Godbold, E. S. jun., *Ellen Glasgow and the Woman Within* (Baton Rouge, La., 1972). (Explores the tensions in Glasgow's life between Southern traditionalism and modernist thought.)

See: Rubin, L. D. jun., *No Place on Earth: Ellen Glasgow, James Branch Cabell, and Richmond-in-Virginia* (Austin, Tex., 1959).
Raper, J. R., *From the Sunken Garden: The Fiction of Ellen Glasgow, 1916–1945* (Baton Rouge, La., 1981). (Concentrates on Glasgow's interest in phantasy.)

HEMINGWAY, Ernest Miller (1899–1961), born in Oak Park, Illinois. His father was a doctor who failed to persuade the son to follow the same profession, but who did succeed in passing on his own passion for sport. After a short spell as a journalist Hemingway joined a volunteer ambulance unit before America joined the First World War and was severely wounded in 1918. These experiences provided the material for part of *A Farewell to Arms* (1929). After the war he was sent to Paris as a correspondent for Hearst newspapers and there came under the influence of Gertrude Stein. In 1925 he published his first volume of short stories, *In Our Time*, and this was quickly followed by his comic burlesque of Sherwood Anderson, *Torrents of Spring* (1926), and the novel which established him as one of the leaders of the 'lost generation', *The Sun Also Rises* (1926). In the next year he published another collection of stories, *Men Without Women* and returned to the United States where he settled first in Florida before moving to Cuba. Throughout the 1930s Hemingway reworked his earlier themes in such novels as *To Have and Have Not* (1937), and *For Whom the Bell Tolls* (1940), and in other books about bullfighting, *Death in the Afternoon* (1932), and big-game hunting, *Green Hills of Africa* (1935). He also continued to write short stories, some of them, together with a play, based on his experiences in the Spanish Civil War. These are contained in *The Fifth Column* and *The First Forty-Nine Stories* (1938). He returned to Europe as a correspondent in the Second World War and wrote about this in *Across the River and Into the Trees* (1950). In 1954 he was awarded the Nobel Prize shortly after the appearance of his popular fable *The Old Man and the Sea* (1952). In 1961 he took his own life as his father had before him. His reminiscences of Paris, *A Moveable Feast*, was published in 1964, and in 1970 an unrevised work was issued, *Islands in the Stream*.

Ross, L., *Portrait of Hemingway* (Harmondsworth, 1962). (Brief account, originally published in the *New Yorker*, of two days spent with the novelist in 1950.)

Baker, C., *Ernest Hemingway: A Life Story* (New York and London, 1969). (Hemingway had praised Baker's earlier study of his life and works, *Hemingway: The Writer as Artist* (Princeton, 1952), and for this biography the critic was given access to all the unpublished material.)

Baker, C., ed., *Ernest Hemingway: Selected Letters 1917–1961* (London, 1981).

See: Tanner, T., *The Reign of Wonder: Naivety and Reality in American Literature* (Cambridge, 1965). (Excellent chapter on Hemingway's vision and style.)

Young, P., *Ernest Hemingway: A Reconsideration* (Philadelphia, 1966). (A revised and expanded version of an earlier book which Hemingway is said to have disliked. Nevertheless a penetrating psychological study of the fiction.)

Grebstein, N., *Hemingway's Craft* (Carbondale, Ill., 1973).

Donaldson, S., *By Force of Will: The Life and Art of Ernest Hemingway* (1977). (A 'mosaic' of Hemingway's ideas arranged thematically; includes chapters on war, sex, politics, sport, etc.)

A. Robert Lee, ed., *Ernest Hemingway: New Critical Essays* (London, 1983).

Brenner, G., *Concealments in Hemingway's Works* (Columbus, Ohio, 1983). (Argues the case for Hemingway as an experimental writer.)

HOWE, Edgar Watson, (1853–1937), born at Treaty, Indiana, he remained primarily a journalist and small-town editor, best known locally for his aphoristic editorials in the Atchison *Daily Globe* and *E. W. Howe's Monthly*. He was dubbed 'the sage of Potato Hill' and celebrated for his cynical iconoclasm. These qualities also characterize his best novel, *The Story of a Country Town* (1883), as well as *The Confession of John Whitlock* (1891) and *Country Town Settings* (1911)

Weber, B., *Introduction: The Story of a County Town* (1964).

Martin, J., *Harvests of Change: American Literature 1865–1914* (Englewood Cliffs, NJ, 1967), pp. 116–20.

HOWELLS, William Dean (1837–1920), born in Martin's Ferry, Ohio. His father was a newspaper-man and printer, unsuccessful in everything he tried according to his son who wrote about his early life in *A Boy's Town* (1890) and *Years of My Youth* (1916). Despite his irregular education Howells was encouraged by his father to read widely, and by 1860 had published two books and was contributing to the *Atlantic Monthly*. He spent the Civil War as American Consul in Venice and as a result produced *Venetian Life* (1866). On his return he worked for *The Nation* and the *Atlantic*, becoming editor of the latter in 1871. During the next ten years he wielded considerable influence which he used to promote the cause of realism in American fiction and began work on the first of his thirty-five novels, *Their Wedding Journey* (1872). Before he resigned his editorship to concentrate more on writing he had already produced a sizeable body of work including *A Chance Acquaintance* (1873), *The Lady of the Aroostook* (1879), and *The Undiscovered Country* (1880). Howells's best work was produced in the 1880s and early 1890s and included *A Modern Instance* (1882), *The Rise of Silas Lapham* (1885), *A Hazard of New Fortunes* (1890) and *A Traveller From Altruria* (1894). During part of this time (1886–92) he also contributed the 'Editor's Study' to *Harper's Monthly* in which he maintained his championship of Critical Realism. Howells's literary output continued to expand to include more than seventy volumes of novels, plays, criticism, and miscellaneous writing. His reputation kept pace with his work and he was elected President of the American Academy of Arts and Letters in 1910.

> Cady, E., *The Road to Realism: The Early Years, 1837–1885, of William Dean Howells* (Syracuse, NY, 1958).
> Cady, E., *The Realist at War: The Mature Years, 1885–1920, of William Dean Howells* (Syracuse, NY, 1958).
> Smith, H. N. and W. Gibson, eds., *Mark Twain–Howells Letters: The Correspondence of Samuel L. Clemens and William Dean Howells,. 1872–1910* (Cambridge, Mass., 1960).
> Howells, M., *Life in Letters of William Dean Howells*, 2 vols (1928).

> See: Carter, E., *Howells and the Age of Realism* (Philadelphia and New York, 1954). (Relates Howells's work to that of prominent intellectuals such as Taine and William James.)
> Kirk, C., *W. D. Howells, Traveler From Altruria* (New Brunswick, NY, 1962). (Deals with his social thought.)
> McMurray, W., *The Literary Realism of William Dean Howells* (Carbondale and Edwardsville, Ill. 1967). (A reading of twelve major novels.)
> Alexander, W., *William Dean Howells: The Realist as Humanist* (1979). (Concentrates on the years 1880–95.)

JAMES, Henry (1843–1916), was born in New York City, the son of Henry James sen., a mildly eccentric theologian, and brother of William, the distinguished philosopher and psychologist. He received an irregular formal education in America and Europe but was always subjected to the profound influences of his father's intellectual circle. He spent a short period in the Harvard Law School but by the late 1860s had already embarked on his career as a writer. In 1871 he published his first novel, *Watch and Ward*, and in 1875 his first volume of short stories. In the same year he moved to Europe, eventually settling in England in 1876. In his early European phase he developed the themes of the International Novel in such works as *Roderick Hudson* (1875), *The American* (1877), *Daisy Miller* (1879), and *The Portrait of a Lady* (1881). In 1886 he produced two novels *The Bostonians* and *The Princess Casamassima* in which he sought to gain greater popularity by consciously employing realistic techniques. He also made an unsuccessful attempt to write for the theatre and his later novels show the influence of his experiments in drama. These include *The Spoils of Poynton* (1897), *What Maisie Knew* (1897), *The Awkward Age* (1899), and *The Sacred Fount* (1901). During this time he also produced a large number of short stories including such masterpieces as 'The Figure in the Carpet', 'In the Cage', and 'The Turn of the Screw'. In his last phase James returned to the international theme which he explored exhaustively in *The Wings of the Dove* (1902), *The Ambassadors* (1903), and *The Golden Bowl*

(1904). As a sign of allegiance to the Allied cause in the First World War he became a British subject in 1915. Shortly before his death he was awarded the Order of Merit. In addition to his fiction James produced outstanding contributions in other areas such as literary criticism where his collected prefaces (*The Art of the Novel*) remain the most incisive analysis of fictional technique in English, and in travel writing with such books as *Portraits of Places* (1883) and *The American Scene* (1907).

Lubbock, P., *The Letters of Henry James*, 2 vols (1920).
Matthiessen, F. O., *The James Family* (1947).
Matthiessen, F. O., and K. Murdock, *The Notebooks of Henry James* (1947). (Cover a period of more than twenty years and offer a fascinating insight into the ways in which the novels were conceived and written.)
Edel, L., *Henry James: The Untried Years, 1843–1870* (Philadelphia and New York, 1953); *Henry James: The Conquest of London, 1870–1883* (1962); *Henry James: The Middle Years, 1884–1895* (1963); *Henry James: The Treacherous Years, 1895–1901* (1969); *Henry James: The Master, 1901–1916* (1972). (The definitive biography.)

See: Matthiessen F. O., *Henry James: The Major Phase* (1946). (Lucid, concise account of the late novels.)
Poirier, R., *The Comic Sense of Henry James* (1960). (An intelligent and sensitive criticism of aspects of James ignored by most critics.)
Cargill, O., *The Novels of Henry James* (1961). (Analyses all the major novels thoroughly and provides a useful synthesis of the extant criticism.)
Buitenhuis, P., *The Grasping Imagination: The American Writings of Henry James* (Toronto, 1970). (Demonstrates the importance of American elements in James's work.)
Chatman, S., *The Later Style of Henry James* (Oxford, 1972). (Good example of a linguistic approach to literary criticism.)
Lee, B., *The Novels of Henry James: A Study of Culture and Consciousness* (London, 1978).
Kappeler, S., *Writing and Reading in Henry James* (1980) (Attempts to apply Roland Barthe's assertion that 'the reader is properly the writer of the text' to some of James's more problematic works.)
Hutchinson, S., *Henry James: An American as Modernist* (London, 1982). (James's failure to create realistic novels led him towards a modernist aesthetic.)
Allen, E., *A Woman's Place in the Novels of Henry James* (London, 1984).
Rowe, J. C., *The Theoretical Dimensions of Henry James* (London, 1985).

JEWETT, Sarah Orne (1849–1909), born at South Berwick, Maine, where she spent most of her life. In 1869 she had a story published in the *Atlantic Monthly*, and later W. D. Howells persuaded her to publish a collection of local-colour sketches, *Deephaven* (1877). This was followed by over a dozen books including her masterpiece *The Country of the Pointed Firs* (1885) and a historical novel based on the life of John Paul Jones, *A Tory Lover* (1901).

Matthessen, F. O., *Sarah Orne Jewett* (Boston, 1929).

See: Cary, R., *Sarah Orne Jewett* (1962).
        Chase, M. E., 'Sarah Orne Jewett as a Social Historian', *Prairie
        Schooner* 36 (1962), 231–37
        Eakin, P. J., 'Sarah Orne Jewett and the Meaning of Country Life',
        American Literature, 38 (1967), 508–31.

KIRKLAND, Joseph (1830–1894), born in Geneva, New York, but spent his
    childhood in the backwoods of Michigan. He was admitted to the Bar in
    1880 and while practising as an attorney wrote several novels, including
    Zury: The Meanest Man in Spring County (1887) and *The Captain of
    Company K* (1891), a story of the Civil War.

        Henson, C. E., *Joseph Kirkland* (1962).

LEWIS, Sinclair (1885–1951), born in Sauk Center, Minnesota. His father was a
    country doctor of Welsh descent whose life provided some of the details
    for Lewis's later fiction. Lewis graduated from Yale in 1908 and held a
    variety of jobs during the following eight years. These were mostly
    connected with publishing, though he was also janitor of Upton Sinclair's
    socialist colony, Helicon Hall, for a short time. In 1916, having written
    two novels and several short stories, he became a free-lance writer, though
    it was not until 1920 with the publication of *Main Street* that he gained an
    international reputation. Most of Lewis's best novels were written during
    the next ten years. They include *Babbitt* (1922), *Arrowsmith* (1925), *Elmer
    Gantry* (1927), and *Dodsworth* (1929). He continued to write prolifically in
    the 1930s, but apart from *It Can't Happen Here* (1935), the later work lacks
    his earlier satiric power and intensity. Lewis was married twice, to Grace
    Hegger and to the columnist Dorothy Thomson. He refused the Pulitzer
    Prize in 1926, but was the first American to be awarded the Nobel Prize
    for Literature in 1930.

        Smith, H., ed., *From Main Street to Stockholm: The Letters of Sinclair
        Lewis, 1915–1930* (1952).
        Schorer, M., *Sinclair Lewis: An American Life* (1961).

See: Grebstein, S. N., *Sinclair Lewis* (1962). (Argues that Lewis's
        immaturity enabled him to become, not a great artist, but an
        excellent satirist and propagandist.)
        Dooley, D. J., *The Art of Sinclair Lewis* (Lincoln, Neb., 1967).
        (Attempts to restore the reputation destroyed by Schorer's
        biography.)
        Light, M., *The Quixotic Vision of Sinclair Lewis* (West Lafayette,
        Ind., 1975). (Conflict of romance and realism in the fiction.)

LONDON, Jack (John Griffith) (1876–1916), born in San Francisco, the
    illegitimate son of an Irish vagabond and astrologer and an American girl
    who later married John London, a grocer. He was brought up in poverty
    and worked at many different odd jobs to help support his family and
    obtain some formal education at Oakland High School and the University
    of California. His passion for travel and adventure led him to take part in
    the Klondike Gold Rush of 1897, to engage in dangerous ocean voyages,
    and to experience the Russo-Japanese War as a correspondent. He was also
    involved in socialist political activity, marching with Coxey's Army and
    running for Mayor of Oakland in 1905. These experiences, together with
    his omnivorous reading, all supplied the materials for the books which

made him the best-known and best-paid novelist in America. These include: *The Call of the Wild* (1903), *The Sea-Wolf* (1904), *White Fang* (1906), *The Iron Heel* (1907), *Martin Eden* (1909), and *John Barleycorn* (1913). Eventually his life of extravagant excess led to exhaustion and despair, and he died, probably by his own hand, at Wolf House, his ranch in California.

> O'Connor, R., *Jack London: A Biography* (Boston, Mass and Toronto, 1964).

See: Foner, P. S., *Jack London: American Rebel* (rev. edn, 1964).
> Feied, F., *No Pie in the Sky: The Hobo as Cultural Hero in the Works of Jack London, John Dos Passos, and Jack Kerouac* (1964).
> Martin, S., *The California Writers: Jack London, John Steinbeck, the Tough Guys* (London, 1983).
> Watson, C. N., jun., *The Novels of Jack London: A Reappraisal* (Madison, Wis., 1983). (Sees London as a serious artist attempting to reconcile Realism and Romanticism by creating a double vision of the world.)

MILLER, Henry, (1891–1980), born in New York City to German-speaking parents, he spent a few months at City College but soon left to travel around the country supporting himself with a variety of odd jobs. Miller says that he lived 'recklessly and rebelliously' up to his thirtieth year before settling down to become employment manager of the Western Union Telegraph Co. of New York. He gave up this post to become a full-time writer, moving to Paris in 1930 where he lived for nine years. During this time he wrote *Tropic of Cancer* (1934), *Black Spring* (1936), and *Tropic of Capricorn* (1939). He visited Greece in 1939 and wrote *The Colossus of Maroussi* (1941) before returning to the United States. After touring the country Miller produced a book about America, *The Air-Conditioned Nightmare* (1945), but his major creative achievement of the post-war period is the trilogy, *The Rosy Crucifixion*, comprising *Sexus* (1945), *Plexus* (1949), and *Nexus* (1960). For the last thirty-five years of his life he lived at Big Sur and Pacific Palisades on the California coast where he wielded an important influence on younger generations of writers in the 1950s and 1960s.

> Perles, A., *My Friend Henry Miller* (1956). (Miller's companion in Paris gives a revealing account of the writer's daily life.)
> Martin, J., *Always Merry and Bright: The Life of Henry Miller* (Santa Barbara, Calif., 1978; London, 1979). (An unauthorized but very thorough biography.)

See: Gordon, W. A., *The Mind and Art of Henry Miller* (Baton Rouge, La., 1967). (The first serious full-length study.)
> Hassan, I., *The Literature of Silence: Henry Miller and Samuel Beckett* (1967).

NORRIS, Benjamin Franklin jun. (1870–1902), born in Chicago where his father's business premises were destroyed in the Great Fire of 1871. His family moved to California in 1884 and Frank was educated at the San Francisco Boys' High School and the Art Association. He also studied art in Paris before entering the University of California at Berkeley. After his parents were divorced he studied creative writing at Harvard under Lewis

Gates in 1894 and began work on *McTeague* (1899) and *Vandover and the Brute* (1914). In 1895 he was involved in the Jameson Raid on Johannesburg, but was expelled from the Transvaal suffering from tropical fever. He moved to New York in 1898 and was sent to Cuba by *McClure's Magazine* to cover the Spanish–American War as a correspondent. After periods in California and Chicago collecting material for his 'Wheat' trilogy, he died suddenly in 1902. *The Octopus* was published in 1901, *The Pit* posthumously in 1903, but the final volume was never written.

> Walker, F., *Frank Norris: A Biography* (Garden City, NY, 1932). (Extremely detailed account partly based on interviews with Norris's family.)
> Walker, F., *The Letters of Frank Norris* (San Francisco, 1956).

> See: French, W., *Frank Norris* (1962).
> Pizer, D., *The Novels of Frank Norris* (London, 1966). (Rejects the view that Norris was a confused Naturalist.)

PHILLIPS, David Graham (1867–1911), born in Madison, Indiana, and educated at Princeton. After graduation in 1887 he became a journalist, first in Cincinnati, then in New York and in London as special correspondent for Pulitzer's *World*. In 1902 he became a free-lance journalist, having angered Pulitzer by depicting him in a newspaper novel, *The Great God Success* (1901). He then wrote a series of muck-raking articles for *McClures, Magazine* and the *Saturday Evening Post* as well as more than twenty novels on various social and political subjects. His best-known work dealing with political corruption and the life of a prostitute, is *Susan Lenox: Her Fall and Rise* (1917). This novel was published posthumously, Phillips having been shot dead by a lunatic.

> Filler, L., *Voice of the Democracy: A Critical Biography of David Graham Phillips* (Philadelphia, and London, 1978).

> See: Ravitz, A. C., *David Graham Phillips* (1966).

SINCLAIR, Upton Beall (1878–1968), born in Baltimore of prominent but impoverished family. He wrote novels in his youth in order to pay his way through the City College of New York and wrote six unsuccessful novels as a graduate student before he made his reputation and a fortune with *The Jungle* (1906). Most of his earnings were used to found a socialist colony, Helicon Hall, which later burned down, and to finance four unsuccessful campaigns for public office in California. Sinclair almost captured the governership of California in 1934 when he campaigned as leader of the EPIC League (End Poverty in California). He was a prolific writer, publishing more than a hundred works, of which the best known are *The Metropolis* (1968), *King Coal* (1917), *Oil* (1927), *Boston* (1928), and the Lanny Budd series dealing with various aspects of modern world history.

> See: Cantwell, R., 'Upton Sinclair', in *After the Genteel Tradition*, ed. by Malcolm Cowley (1936), pp. 37–51.
> Dell, F., *Upton Sinclair: A Study in Social Protest* (1972).

STEIN, Gertrude (1874–1946), born in Pennsylvania, she spent part of her early life in Europe and returned to live there permanently after graduating from

Radcliffe where she was strongly influenced by the theories of William James. Together with her brother, Leo, she entertained many famous painters and writers at her Paris salon, and began to publish her own fiction beginning with *Three Lives* (1902). She also wrote poetry which was as unconventional as her fiction (*Tender Buttons* (1914)), an autobiography which purports to be that of her companion (*The Autobiography of Alice B. Toklas* (1933)), an opera with music by Virgil Thompson (*Four Saints in Three Acts* (1934)), and works of criticism and literary theory such as *Lectures in America* (1935) and *The Geographical History of America* (1936). Her later fiction includes *The Making of Americans* (1925), *Lucy Church Amiably* (1930), and *A Long Gay Book* (1932).

> Brinnin, J. M., *The Third Rose: Gertrude Stein and her World* (Boston, Mass., 1959).
> Toklas, A. B., *What is Remembered* (1963).

> See: Hoffmann, M. J., *The Development of Abstractionism in the Writings of Gertrude Stein* (Philadelphia, 1965). (Good analysis of the early work.)
> Weinstein, N., *Gertrude Stein and the Literature of the Modern Consciousness* (1970). (Examines the fiction in the context of modern theories of language.)

STEINBECK, John, (1902–68), born at Salinas, California, of German and Irish stock. He studied marine biology at Stanford University but did not take a degree. After pursuing a variety of occupations and publishing three books, *Cup of Gold* (1929), *Pastures of Heaven* (1932), and *To a God Unknown* (1933), he eventually made his reputation with his fourth, *Tortilla Flat* (1935), set in Monterey where he had lived in poverty with his first wife, Carol Henning. This marked the beginning of Steinbeck's most productive period which lasted until the outbreak of the Second World War. During this time he wrote about various aspects of Californian society in the Great Depression and produced such works as *In Dubious Battle* (1936), *Of Mice and Men* (1937), *The Long Valley* (1938), and the novel which is widely regarded as his masterpiece, *The Grapes of Wrath* (1939). Steinbeck's work after the war is not so firmly rooted in any particular locality, and partly for this reason shows a falling-off in quality. It includes *The Wayward Bus* (1947), *The Pearl* (1947), *East of Eden* (1952), *Sweet Thursday* (1954), and *The Short Reign of Pippin IV* (1957). He also wrote several books of travel and commentary such as *Travels With Charley* (1962) and *Once There Was a War* (1958). The best statement of his social, moral, and philosophical beliefs is contained in the book he wrote with his friend and mentor, Ed Ricketts, *Sea of Cortez* (1941). In 1962 he won the Nobel Prize.

> Steinbeck, E., and R. Wallsten, eds, *Steinbeck: a Life in Letters* (London, 1975).
> Benson, J. J., *The True Adventures of John Steinbeck, Writer* (London, 1984).

> See: Lisca, P., *The Wide World of John Steinbeck* (New Brunswick, NJ, 1958). (Close reading of all the major novels.)
> French, W., *John Steinbeck* (1961, rev. edn, 1975).
> Fontenrose, J., *John Steinbeck: An Introduction and Interpretation* (1963). (An account of the myths underlying each of the novels.)

Levant, H., *The Novels of John Steinbeck* (Columbia, Miss., 1974).
(Analysis of Steinbeck's attempts to evade or overcome the
structural problems in his novels.)
McCarthy, P., *John Steinbeck* (1980).

TARKINGTON, Booth (1869–1946), born in Indianapolis, educated at Purdue
University and Princeton. After unsuccessful attempts to become a painter
or illustrator, he turned to fiction and had an early popular success with
his second novel, *Monsieur Beaucaire* (1900). Two of his novels, *The
Magnificent Ambersons* (1918) and *Alice Adams* (1921), won Pulitzer Prizes,
and his series of novels dealing with adolescence, beginning with *Penrod*
(1914), were also best sellers. Tarkington served briefly in the Indiana
House of Representatives and used the experience to write *In The Arena*
(1905). In addition to his many novels he also wrote twenty-five plays.

Woodress, J., *Booth Tarkington: Gentleman From Indiana*
(Philadelphia, 1955, New York, 1969).

TWAIN, Mark *see* CLEMENS, Samuel Langhorne

VAN VECHTEN, Carl (1880–1966), born in Cedar Rapids, Iowa, he was
educated at the University of Chicago, and after graduating in 1903 he
came to New York as assistant music critic of the *New York Times*. He
also wrote dramatic criticism for the New York *Press* before retiring at the
age of forty on account of 'hardening of the intellectual arteries'. He then
took up fiction and produced a number of witty, elegant novels about
New York society. These include *The Blind Bow-Boy* (1923), *Firecrackers*
(1925), and *Parties* (1930). His best-known works are *Peter Whiffle* (1922), a
pseudo-biographical novel, *The Tattered Countess* (1924), set in Iowa, *Spider
Boy* (1928), a satire of Hollywood, and *Nigger Heaven* (1926), which treats
Harlem life sympathetically and was an important influence in the Harlem
Renaissance. In 1932 he retired again and took up a third career in
photography.

Lueders, E., *Carl Van Vechten* (1965).

See: Kellner, B., *Carl Van Vechten and the Irreverent Decade* (Norman,
Okla., 1968).

WEST, Nathanael (Nathan Wallenstein Weinstein) (1904–40), born in New York
City, educated at Brown University where he also edited the *Americana
Magazine*. In the early 1930s West worked as the manager of a residential
hotel in New York where he befriended other artists and spent his nights
writing fiction. His first three novels, *The Dream Life of Balso Snell* (1931),
Miss Lonely hearts (1933), and *A Cool Million* (1934), all belong to this
period. In 1935 he went to Hollywood, adapted *Miss Lonelyhearts* for the
screen (*Advice to the Lovelorn*), and worked on a number of screenplays. He
also wrote a novel about Hollywood, *The Day of the Locust* (1939). West
and his wife, the former Eileen McKenney, died in an automobile accident
in California.

Martin, J., *Nathanael West: The Art of His Life* (1970). (Discusses
West's involvement with Dadaism and Surrealism using interviews
with writers, friends, and critics.)

See: Light, J. F., *Nathanael West: An Interpretative Study* (Evanston, Ill., 1961).
Comerchero, V., *Nathanael West: The Ironic Prophet* (Syracuse, NY, 1964). (Westian man seen as the dramatized victim of a declining Western culture.)
Reid, R., *The Fiction of Nathanael West: No Redeemer, No Promised Land* (Chicago, 1967). (Shows how West uses parody and techniques from popular art forms.)
Malin, I., *Nathanael West's Novels* (Carbondale, Ill., 1972). (Close reading of each novel.)

WHARTON, Edith Newbold (Jones) (1862–1937), born in New York City to a wealthy family and educated privately. She married Edward Wharton in 1885 and they travelled extensively, dividing their time between Newport, Rhode Island, and Europe, before finally settling in Paris in 1907. Her husband's mental illness gradually grew more severe and they were divorced in 1912. In the 1890s Wharton wrote a large number of short stories, but after 1900 turned her attention to longer works, producing *The Valley of Decision* in 1902 and *The House of Mirth* in 1905. In addition to writing about the upper stratum of New York society she was also concerned about the lives of rural New Englanders and wrote on this subject in *Ethan Frome* (1911). She was decorated for her voluntary work in France during the First World War and describes her experiences in *Fighting France, from Dunquerque to Belfort* (1915), and used the events of the war in two novels, *The Marne* (1918), and *A Son at the Front* (1923). Of her later work the best-known novels are *The Custom of the Country* (1913), *The Age of Innocence* (1920) which won a Pulitzer prize, and *Hudson River Bracketed* (1929).

Bell, M., *Edith Wharton and Henry James: The Story of Their Friendship* (1965).
Lewis, R. W. B., *Edith Wharton: A Biography* (1975).
See: Lindberg G. H., *Edith Wharton and the Novel of Manners* (Charlottesville, Va., 1975). (Wharton's novels explore the ways in which social conventions restrict the life of the spirit.)
Wolff, C. G., *A Feast of Words: The Triumph of Edith Wharton* (1977). (Psychological study of Wharton's treatment of sexual relationships.)
Ammons, E., *Edith Wharton's Argument With America* (Athens, Ga., 1980).
Walton, G., *Edith Wharton: A Critical Interpretation* (East Brunswick, NJ, 1982).

WOLFE, Thomas Clayton (1900–38), born in Asheville, educated at the University of North Carolina and Harvard where he studied play-writing in George Pierce Baker's course 'Workshop 47'. He taught for a few years at New York University but gave this up in 1930 to become a full-time writer. He travelled in Europe, especially Germany, but wrote most of his novels in Brooklyn. He developed pneumonia during a vacation trip to the West and died of a brain infection.

Nowell, E., *The Letters of Thomas Wolfe* (1956).
Nowell, E., *Thomas Wolfe: A Biography* (Garden City, NY, 1960). (The most detailed study of his life.)

See: Kennedy, R. S., *The Window of Memory: The Literary Career of Thomas Wolfe* (Chapel Hill, NC, 1962). (Analyses the literary manuscripts.)
Reeves, P., *Thomas Wolfe's Albatross: Race and Nationality in America* (Athens, Ga., 1968). (Examines the development of Wolfe's attitude to other races.)

WRIGHT, Richard (1908–60), born on a plantation near Natchez, Mississippi, he was brought up partly by relations after his father deserted the family, and partly in orphanages. In 1934 he moved to Chicago, joined the Communist Party, and began to write fiction. His first important work, a collection of four novellas *Uncle Tom's Children* (1938), won a literary prize, but it was *Native Son* (1940) that established him internationally. From Chicago he moved to New York, published an autobiographical work, *Black Boy* (1945), before leaving the United States to live the remainder of his life in Paris. His later work, such as *The Outsider* (1953), is strongly influenced by Existentialist ideas.

Webb, C., *Richard Wright* (1968). (First full-scale biography written by a close family friend who had access to unpublished materials.)
Fabre, M., *The Unfinished Quest of Richard Wright* (1973).

See: Margolies, E., *The Art of Richard Wright* (Carbondale & Edwardsville, Ill., 1969) (Traces development of Wright's principal themes through his twelve major works.)
McCall, D., *The Example of Richard Wright* (1969). (Discusses Wright in the context of Black literature, left-wing politics and civil rights.)
Brignano, R. C., *Richard Wright: An Introduction to the Man and his Works* (Pittsburg, 1970).

Index

Note: Bracketed page-numbers refer to bibliographical entries.

Cahn, Abraham
  The Rise of David Levinsky, 131–32
Caldwell, Erskine, 155–58, 159, 226, (273–74)
  God's Little Acre, 156; *Say! Is This the U.S.A.?*, 156; *Tobacco Road*, 156–58; *You Have Seen Their Faces*, 156
Cantwell, Robert
  The Land of Plenty, 125
Carlyle, Thomas, 9
Carnegie, Andrew, 5
Carruth, Hayden, 69
Cather, Willa, 114, 115–49, (271)
  Alexander's Bridge, 146; *Death Comes for the Archbishop*, 149; *My Antonia*, 145, 146, 148–49; 'The Novel Demeuble', 145; *O Pioneers*, 146–48; *The Professor's House*, 149; *Shadows on the Rock*, 149; *The Troll Garden*, 146
Céline, Louis-Ferdinand
  Voyage, au bout de la Nuit, 205
Chametzsky, Jules, 160
Chaplin, Charles, 127, 193
  Modern Times, 127
Chartists, 9
Chase, Richard, 106
Chekhov, Anton, 209
Chicago, 4, 5, 48, 49, 120, 125, 127–28, 133, 136
Chomsky, Noam, 12
Chopin, Kate, 65–67, (274–75)
  The Awakening, 65–67; *Bayou Folks*, 65
Churchill, Winston, 81
Civil War, 6, 63, 64, 154–55, 240–41
Clemens, Samuel Langhorne *see* Twain, Mark
Cobbett, William, 9
Columbian Exposition, 5, 49, 78
Communist Manifesto, 128
Conn, Peter
  The Divided Mind, 74
Conrad, Joseph, 38, 116, 215
Conroy, Jack
  The Disinherited, 125
Cooke, John Esten, 63
  Surry of Eagle's Nest, 64
Coolidge, Calvin, 211
Cooper, James Fenimore
  'The Leatherstocking Saga', 6
Cosmopolitan Magazine, 76
Cowley, Malcolm, 117, 118, 222, 227, 241

Exiles' Return, 118; *The Portable Faulkner*, 241
Crane, Stephen, 8, 28, 30, 38–43, 49, 118, 174, 176, 178, (276–77)
  'The Blue Hotel', 43; *George's Mother*, 43; *Maggie: A Girl of the Streets*, 5, 38–40, 43; *The Monster*, 43; 'The Open Boat', 42, 43; *O'Ruddy*, 43; *The Red Badge of Courage*, 40–43, 157–58, 178; *The Third Violet*, 43
Crashaw, Richard, 206
Crawford, F. Marion, 81
Cullen, Countee, 129
Cummings, E. E.
  The Enormous Room, 116

Dahlberg, Edward, 125
Darwin, Charles, 25
Daudet, Alphonse, 85
Davis, Richard Harding, 45
De Forest, John William, 32, 64, 121
  European Aquaintance, 32; *Miss Ravenel's Conversion from Secession to Loyalty*, 64, 121; *Oriental Aquaintance*, 32
Dell, Floyd, 141, 142, (277)
  Moon-Calf, 141
DeVoto, Bernard, 171
Dewey, John, 49
Dickens, Charles, 25
Dickinson, Emily, 11
Dixon, Thomas
  The Clansman, 46, 64
Donnelly, Ignatius
  Caesar's Column, 79
Dos Passos, John, 116, 117, 126, 129, 133, 167, 170, 174–87, 193, 200, (277–78)
  District of Columbia, 176; *Manhattan Transfer*, 175, 180–84; *One Man's Initiation, 1917*, 175; *Rosinante to to Road Again*, 179; *Streets of Night*, 179–80; *Three Soldiers*, 177–79; *U.S.A.*, 116, 174–75, 176, 178, 200
Dostoevsky, Fyodor, 32
Doughty, C. M., 213
Dreiser, Theodore, 8, 29, 30–31, 38, 49–55, 58, 72, 121, 126, 129–30, 170, 174, 176, 180, 216, (275)
  An American Tragedy, 53, 129–30, 170; *The Bulwark*, 54; *Dawn*, 50; *The Financier*, 53–55; *Jennie*